The Mission to Seafarers
A world mission agency of the Church of England

Earning a living at sea, bringing food to our tables and
resources for our industry, is one of the most dangerous
jobs in the world. On average 10 ships and 25 seafarers
are lost at sea every month. Pirate attacks on merchant
ships are on the increase with hundreds of assaults each
year – sometimes resulting in loss of life.

Through a network of chaplains, lay staff and volunteers,
the Mission has a presence in 300 ports around the
world, caring for the spiritual and practical welfare of
seafarers and their families.

If you would like to share in God's work among seafarers
by joining our worldwide team of chaplains or our
voluntary service scheme for young people, by
supporting us in prayer, or by inviting a preacher or
speaker to your parish, please contact us at:

The Mission to Seafarers
St Michael Paternoster Royal,
College Hill, London EC4R 2RL
Tel: 020 7248 5202
Fax: 020 7248 4761
Email: general@missiontoseafarers.org
Website: www.missiontoseafarers.org
Registered charity no: 212432

**Caring for seafarers
around the world**

THE
CHURCH PULPIT
YEAR BOOK
2004

*Sermons for Sundays, Holy Days,
Festivals and Special Occasions
Year C*

edited by Dr J. Critchlow

CANTERBURY
PRESS
Norwich

© Canterbury Press 2003

First published in 2003 by the Canterbury Press Norwich
(a publishing imprint of Hymns Ancient & Modern Limited,
a registered charity)
St Mary's Works, St Mary's Plain,
Norwich, Norfolk, NR3 3BH

www.scm-canterburypress.co.uk

British Library Cataloguing in Publication data

A catalogue record for this book is available
from the British Library

Scripture quotations are mainly drawn from the
New Revised Standard Version Bible © 1989
by the Division of Christian Education of the
National Council of Churches of Christ in the USA

ISBN 1-85311-544-4

Typeset by Rowland Phototypesetting Limited,
Bury St Edmunds, Suffolk
Printed in Great Britain by
St Edmundsbury Press Limited, Bury St Edmunds, Suffolk

Editor's Preface

'Do not fret or have any anxiety about anything' (Philippians 4:6, Ampl. Bible). The simplicity and directness of St Paul's command leave nothing to be desired, except the practical application.

A German doctor once remarked that if the lime-green flowering 'weed' of hedgerows and wastelands, Our Lady's Mantle (*Alchemilla vulgaris*), were to be taken as a regular preventive medicine by women, gynaecological operations could be reduced by two-thirds worldwide. Was the good doctor justified in his assessment? But just imagine if St Paul's words here were to be obeyed by those who hear them, the world would be startlingly, dramatically different from the state it's in today.

Necessarily early to comply with deadlines, I write this Preface as a quarter-century of tyrannical dictatorship crumbles, in a country known centuries ago as Mesopotamia, the traditional site of Eden, the Tower of Babel, Ur of the Chaldees, Nineveh, and the fabled Hanging Gardens of Babylon. This was where Belshazzar had his palace and where, in the time of Daniel's exile from Jerusalem, a hand mysteriously appeared and wrote on the wall: MENE, MENE, TEKEL, UPHARSIN:

> *For the kingdom now was finished*
> *Said the hand upon the wall.*
>
> Knowles Shaw

Once again, history's wheel has come full circle. But the fretting and anxieties continue. As nation after nation has discovered since the world began, it is easier to begin a problem than to end it.

We need to take St Paul's words to heart, with renewed commitment – for time is running fast, and our own point of no return comes closer every day.

Joyce Critchlow
Palm Sunday, 2003

CONTENTS

Unless otherwise stated, the readings are taken from *The Christian Year: Calendar, Lectionary and Collects* (London: Church House Publishing, 2000) and are for Year C.

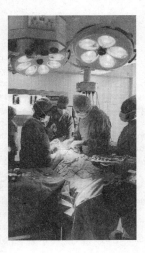

SERMONS FOR SAINTS' DAYS AND SPECIAL OCCASIONS

The readings in this section are taken from Brother Tristam SSF, *Exciting Holiness* (Canterbury Press, 1997); Robert Atwell, *Celebrating the Saints* (Canterbury Press, 1998).

First Sunday of Advent   30 November 2003
Principal Service   **Signs to Come**   Jer. 33:14–16;
Ps. 25:1–10; 1 Thess. 3:9–13; Luke 21:25–36

'There will be signs in the sun, the moon and the stars, and on the earth distress among nations, confused by the roaring of the sea and the waves.'
Luke 21:25

Another beginning
What signs are we looking for, as another year begins? Or haven't we worked up sufficient enthusiasm to start looking? Or do we think we shouldn't look for signs? In the days of Isaiah, Ahaz was asked to look for a sign from the Lord, but he refused (Isaiah 7:11, 12), on the grounds that it was tempting God. Yet God had told him to look. God knew what it would take, to turn around the spirituality of his chosen people, but he wanted those people to do their bit: he wanted them to want the salvation that he had in mind. After all, it was their destiny. But, no, Ahaz ducked the challenge. Then, said God through Isaiah: 'The Lord will give you a sign *in any case*' (Isaiah 7:14, NJB). God was not going to allow a cowardly king to get in the way of Emmanuel being born of a virgin. If his chosen people were not looking out for him, it would be their fault.

The sign that came
Centuries later, when the sign came, it fell to a group of shepherds to hear the great good news, and to respond: men who were quietly minding their own business, and for whom Emmanuel was probably nowhere near the top of their priority-list. Thirty or so years after that, the Jews around Jesus were not forty-second cousin to Ahaz. They looked God's sign eyeball to eyeball, and said: 'We wish to see a sign' (Matthew 12:38). And the Branch, foretold by Jeremiah, was pretty sharp in his reply.

So what do we do?
Does this mean that, with the coming of Jesus, we are never to ask God for any other sign? Does God never come to us with a challenge like he gave to Ahaz? Does he never say, 'Prove me, and see if I don't keep my promises?' Surely not – because God did not create automatons. He is forever challenging us to show

1

interest in him – in what he has done, is doing and may be going to do in our lives.

A too-familiar challenge?
At Christmas, it's easy to see the sign that God is showing. After all, we can all understand a baby. But the challenge comes in being challenged by such a well-known Baby. Meister Eckhardt once said: 'If the only prayer you say in your whole life is "Thank you", that would suffice.' Would it? Does God want no more? Are we not dealing with a sign who says, 'Ask, and you will receive'?

A right, and a wrong, way
Some folk who came to Jesus asking for a sign were looking for a sign which was already there – or a day which God has reserved for his absolute timing. They were not asking aright. The Lord who invites us to 'argue it out' (Isaiah 1:18), to ask that we might receive (Matthew 7:7), is not wanting us to dialogue, to tangle, with him over something we already have, or something that is not ours to know, but over how we can 'grow in the grace and knowledge of our Lord and Saviour' (2 Peter 3:18). Who gave us these muscular, articulate minds? God. Who says he can't abide lukewarmness (cf. Revelation 3:16)? God.

New-year resoluteness
So, what do we do about all that? Leave well alone? Leave it to someone else to wonder about? Or, with new-year resoluteness, do we go in spirit to the throne of grace and ask the Lord ourselves? We may be able to make a three-volume novel out of how-very-busy-we-are-just-now – but would God find that convincing? The Lord who asks of us is a dynamic God. Dostoyevsky once said: 'Every time you pray, if your prayer is sincere, there will be new feeling and a new meaning in it, which will give you fresh courage.' God has brought us to Advent Sunday to give us a sign. Dare we ask him to make our understanding of this ever clearer?

Family Service input
As the first candle on the Advent wreath is lit, ask the young people present to say, write, illustrate or mime the various ways in which they can bring the light of Christ to others in the coming days. The whole congregation may be included, in a parish outreach.

Come and see the shining hope; Hark, what a sound, and too divine for hearing; O come, O come, Emmanuel; Show me thy ways, O Lord.

First Sunday of Advent *Second Service*
The Valley of Decision Ps. 9; Joel 3:9–21;
Rev. 14:13—15:4 or John 3:1–17

'Put in the sickle, for the harvest is ripe.' Joel 3:13
'Use your sharp sickle and gather the clusters of the vine of the earth, for its grapes are ripe.' Revelation 14:18

The daily challenge
But *only* when the visible harvest is ripe? No – our 'valley of decision' (Joel 3:14) comes to meet us with each new day – and whether we make of it a boulder-strewn obstacle course or a sheltered path of refreshment and regrowth lies to a great extent with ourselves. If we can keep before us the encouraging truth that God never does anything to hinder us from growing in 'the grace and knowledge of our Lord and Saviour Jesus Christ' (2 Peter 3:18), we shall be in a better position to apportion praise and blame for any circumstances that meet us: Satan's 'valley of decision' is light years away from God's.

The present harvest
'Do you not say, "Four months more, then comes the harvest"?' asked Jesus on one occasion, of his friends. 'But I tell you, look around you, and see how the fields are ripe for harvesting' (John 4:35). There is never a time when we may not, if we will, make progress in God's service; and the start of a new church year is a particularly appropriate time.

> *One more day's work for Jesus,*
> *One less of earth for me.*
>
> A. Warner

Where we stand

An old gentleman who was stone-deaf never missed church on a Sunday. One day he was asked why he went when he could hear nothing of the service. 'I come because I want folk to know whose side I'm on,' he said, simply. If we manoeuvre, ever so skilfully, through our valley of decision, taking the line of least resistance, or choosing to go another way, we run the risk not only of disappointing God, but also of sending the wrong message to anyone else who is watching. Today's world may excel in misinformation, but Christians should not subscribe to it as well. Our valley of decision is where God can show us more of his will, where we can advance spiritually – maybe in company with others, maybe on a one-to-one basis with our Maker: the parameters are his.

When routine may be second-best

'Lord, make me an uncommon Christian!' was the prayer of a saint-in-training. Is it one which we can echo? Or do we love one comfortable, steady rut too much? We can, if we wish, stand back and look at the Church from outside – and Satan will not take a deal of interest in us; in fact, we may so relish the relative calm that we don't even realize the hassle has reduced. Or we can stay in the thick of things and show the world whose side we are on; it's uncommon enough to be a full-time Christian, for the world and the Devil to notice.

Making hay while it's sunny

Many years ago, while walking in the high fields, a woman had a vision. She seemed to see her own funeral, at her little village church, with the coffin bearing her name being lowered six feet under, and people standing round. But there was something wrong. 'Lord,' she heard herself saying, 'I don't know anyone here!' And a voice came: 'No. These are the people whom you *could* have told about me – but didn't!' So, why were they there, at her funeral? Because God was giving her time to spread his gospel, before she actually stepped from this chapter into the next. Jesus is still saying: the time for decisions is *now*; the harvest is always here, not months away in the future. May we get serious with God today, and catch up with his plans for our spiritual advancement, before we miss the vital lessons and experiences of our valley of decision.

Suggested hymns
Be thou my guardian and my guide; Lead, kindly light, amid the
encircling gloom; Lead us, heavenly Father, lead us; Take my life,
and let it be.

Second Sunday of Advent 7 December 2003
Principal Service **Check It Out!** Baruch 5:1–9
or Mal. 3:1–4; Canticle: Benedictus; Phil. 1:3–11;
Luke 3:1–6

*'In the fifteenth year of the reign of Emperor Tiberius, when Pontius
Pilate was governor of Judaea . . .' Luke 3:1*

Prove me!
Luke, the careful, cautious Greek doctor, goes on to 'ground' the
appearance of John the Baptist, to the precise time when Herod
(Antipas) was Tetrarch of Galilee, Philip of Ituraea and Trachonitis,
Lysanias ruler of Abilene, and Annas and Caiaphas high priests
in Jerusalem. Do you have any problem with John the Baptist? asks
Luke, implicitly. Then check him out against these contemporaries!
Who, with such a confident author, would dare to challenge his
authenticity? There will be some, Luke implies. Check me out!
Remember, Luke is writing to a fellow-scholar, Theophilus (Luke
1:3), who in all probability would rise to the challenge. We do not
need to: our Bible notes and commentaries bear witness to the
efficacy of Luke's homework and preparation in the compilation
of his Gospel. We can accept that his verifiable history is accurate,
and this surely gives us every reason to suppose that the rest of
his Gospel is likewise.

God's attention to detail
Malachi's prophecy, as with so much more, was coming to pass.
God was preparing to show his people what he had prepared for
them with great attention to detail. He knew that the vast majority
would not take on board what he was offering; but it did not
persuade him that the salvation of the world was not worth pursuing. Today, God's plans continue – with, or without, our participation. Yet it is still the case that 'there will be more joy in heaven

over one sinner who repents than over ninety-nine righteous people who need no repentance' (Luke 15:7).

A baptism of repentance
John's 'baptism of repentance' (Luke 3:3) invited men and women to make public what they believed privately – that God, through a symbolic act by a prophet, could effect their forgiveness and accept their intention to live a new life: it was, in essence, a washing away of accumulated sin and guilt, so that life could start over again with God. As simple as that? Yes! And therein lay its challenge, for the sophisticated, worldly wise who looked askance at the rough man from the desert. We have come a long way in two thousand years; and our challenge today, in the sanitized ceremonial of the baptistery, is to preserve the original, undiluted, unadulterated impact of John's message.

All flesh shall see
The world's salvation, once initiated, is unstoppable. Let no one ever believe that he, or she, can reverse God's designs. Satan can't – and human beings outside of God have nowhere near the power of Satan. Today, churches are growing around the world, led by the phenomenally rapid expansion of the Church in China. No less than when John preached at the Jordan, the world's salvation is on God's agenda. Who would choose not to be on the winning side?

On the home front
As Christmas draws closer, and many secular matters close to home claim our attention, can we not also reflect on the spiritual needs of those around us? If they themselves are unaware of their need, then it is greater. Can we celebrate a Christmas that excludes our near neighbours? If they have taken Christ out of Christmas, what have they got left? Can we not reach out and fill the spiritual vacuum? Can we not meet their need by sharing the reason for the season? Can we not share these verses of St Luke's Gospel with them, meeting any doubts of accuracy and historicity by the references Luke himself has given? Can we not appeal to their standards of consistency, that what God says is absolutely true? It is a fleece, such as Gideon used (Judges 6:36–40) – a convincing proof, such as Thomas was given (John 20:27). The Lord's gospel *can* be believed by sheer naked faith – yet God in his generous

mercy has given us so much additional, undeserved help along the way: just as he gave Joseph Scriven, in the writing of the hymn, What a Friend we have in Jesus.

Family Service input
Share the story behind Scriven's hymn (see below). The young people can be encouraged (1) to illustrate Scriven's story and (2) to compose a hymn of their own.

Suggested hymns
On Jordan's bank the Baptist's cry; Put your hand in the hand of the man; The great forerunner now is here; What a Friend we have in Jesus.

Hymn stories

What a Friend we have in Jesus
Joseph Medlicott Scriven (1819–1886) was born into a wealthy home in Banbridge, County Down. He studied, and then lectured, at Dublin's Trinity College, and fell head over heels in love with a beautiful Irish colleen. Tragically, on the evening before their wedding day, Joseph received the news that his fiancée had been drowned in an accident. Broken-hearted, he emigrated to Canada, joining the Plymouth Brethren and devoting all his energies to serving the poor in the community. He met another young woman, whom he married; but this marriage lasted only a short while before she died of a serious illness.

One day, he received news from Ireland, that his mother was ill. It bothered Joseph that he could not return to her, but he decided that the next-best thing would be to send her some words of comfort. With a letter, he enclosed the words of this hymn which he had composed specially for her without a thought that one day it might be published.

A little time later, Joseph himself fell ill, and when a friend came to visit him he noticed a rather dog-eared piece of paper on the table beside Joseph's bed. Picking it up, he read this hymn, and asked Joseph if he had written it.

With a quiet smile, Joseph replied: 'Well, not completely. The Lord and I did it between us.'

Surely he must be delighted to know what a favourite his hymn has become.

Second Sunday of Advent   *Second Service*
Not Always As It Seems   Ps. 75 [76]; Isa. 40:1–11;
Luke 1:1–25

'Both of them were righteous before God, living blamelessly according to all the commandments and regulations of the Lord.' Luke 1:6

God's unseen favour

To all intents and purposes, Zechariah and Elizabeth were the perfect God-fearing couple. Yet they carried the world's perceived stigma of sterility! But God had not abandoned them, nor was he unmindful of their longings for a child. 'Even before his birth' John was 'filled with the Holy Spirit' (Luke 1:15). When did that spiritual filling begin, if not in the obedience and uprightness of the Baptist's parents? We may not know for a long time the harvest our present-day seed-sowing is preparing – but, in God's timing, we shall know. Tell Jerusalem 'she has served her term', God ordered Isaiah to declare (Isaiah 40:2). And, where we pick up the story of Zechariah and Elizabeth, it is to learn that they have served their own spiritual apprenticeship; they are at last ready for what God has had in store for them.

The wider view

But was the world also ready? Was it prepared for its Saviour? Surely, the so-called religious were looking for him – in a way. They would not recognize him; but God had Mary and Joseph in his sights, and the shepherds, the Magi . . . and, later, the disciples. Jesus' coming had been arranged – because of, or despite, the world. In a similar way – for God is the same yesterday, today and for ever (cf. Hebrews 13:8), God's plans roll into action at times which may seem to us to be too late, or too soon – for all the world as if we believe our schedules are superior to the Lord's! The Master of time is mercifully patient; we are not the first, nor shall we be the last, to attempt limitation policies with the Almighty.

Our readiness – God's preparedness

So, are we ready for Christmas? Have we settled in our minds what we are ready to do? Are we going to welcome the Christ-Child into our hearts, and nurture him there? Or how are we going to share the blessings he brings? Are we going to put Christ into the Christmas of someone who as yet does not know him? With an open heart and mind, are we planning to leave the brandy butter on the shelf, and to spread *Jesus* around as generously as we can, this Christmas? Our neighbours' needs are not always what they seem – and neither are our own. We may believe we – or they – are in good standing with God, and not in desperate need of a rich helping of Jesus. If so, let us follow the advice in Isaiah 1:18, and argue it out with God. We need to remember that he is a God of surprises – as seen not only in his dealings with Zechariah and Elizabeth, but with virtually everyone whose life has counted for him. If we are willing to be surprised by him this Christmas, it may yet be the best that we have known.

Surprised by miracles
So often the divinely implanted baby of which Mary was to be delivered takes such a central point (and rightly so) on the Christmas stage that the lesser miracle of the aged Elizabeth's conception is overlooked. God's miracles are as many and varied as the folk to whom and in whom they happen. At times we may try to tell the Lord what we'd like him to do – or what we think may be necessary to get us out of a problem – but usually the answer he gives is something different, something much better. Perhaps this is because God knows our need before we ask – and sees our long-term requirements into the bargain! He views our problems from all sides, all dimensions, in the past, present and future.

> *Our God and our Brother, divine and yet human,*
> *Of infinite power, yet gentle as dawn;*
> *Great King Everlasting, yet Crucified Saviour:*
> *Our Advocate, Guide and Redeemer we own.*

Suggested hymns
Come, thou long-expected Jesus; Fill thou my life, O Lord my God; In full and glad surrender; Sleepers, wake! the watchcry peeleth.

Third Sunday of Advent   14 December 2003
Principal Service   **Be Glad!**   Zeph. 3:14–20;
Canticle: Isa. 12:2–6; Phil. 4:4–7; Luke 3:7–18

'So, with many other exhortations, [John] proclaimed the good news to the people.' Luke 3:18
'Rejoice in the Lord always . . .' Philippians 4:4

Looking on the bright side
Well, it's a familiar expression, even though it's less often put into practice; and it's better than looking on the dark side. But when the 'bright side' is the 'light of the world' (no less), such optimism can move mountains and turn the world inside out and upside down for God. Christmas is a good time for good news – but God has given us 365 days in the year (366 in 2004) when we can, if we wish, be a blessing to others by homing in on his good news and rejoicing. In the world today, if we have an open mind and open heart for it, there is a wonderful amount of good news. 'Sing aloud!' cries Zephaniah. 'Rejoice and exult!' (Zephaniah 3:14) – and then he declares: 'The Lord . . . [also] will rejoice and . . . exult' (v. 17). If we are not to assume that heaven is a gloomy place, God does a lot of rejoicing. Can we not resolve to give him cause for even more gladness? Surely it's a waste of time to practise being miserable here: there is no reason to hone such a negative achievement for the next life.

A praising heart
There is no room in a praising heart for gloom. If you doubt the truth of that, just put it to the test. Yet even at Christmas, when schedules go for a burton, or the unexpected happens, our spiritual fuses can become dangerously short. And this, while we're celebrating 'Joy to the world!' 'A cheerful heart is a good medicine,' says Proverbs 17:22. Why don't we take a dose of this more often, instead of wearing out the surgery mat in search of pills whose analysis we rarely read and even more rarely comprehend?

The best news on earth
The Love that came down, on the first Christmas, was God's parcel of joy – understood by a few, a very few: feared by more, and ignored by many. Did God cry, in exasperation and sadness? He may have done, but many since have given him cause to believe

that his saving act has been worth the effort. As Advent rolls on nearer to the happy event, can we not give God a free rein to take over our hearts with his joy? *Dare* we give him such freedom? Shall we not make ourselves vulnerable, in a world where too often sheer joy is poorly understood and at times deliberately misinterpreted? Let us take the risk – it is small, compared to that which God took in the giving of his Son.

Looking for the best
Looking for the best – in people and situations – as life increases in pace and 'hype' in the run-up to Christmas, can be difficult; yet to buck the challenge can mean our being sucked into the vortex of frenetic activity and tension. It is not a question of side-lining ourselves away from the joyful anticipation and planning: true joy, however quiet, is its own attraction, and we shall find others take notice. A world starved of genuine joy is nevertheless quick to identify it when it comes knocking at the door.

Keeping it up
'Rejoice in the Lord *always*!', St Paul urged the Philippians – and they, like ourselves, probably thought he was urging the impossible. But the 'impossible ideal' has always been at the centre of the Christian life: 'Be perfect . . . as your heavenly Father is perfect,' said Jesus (Matthew 5:48). Only perfect Love can teach us perfect joy – and that Love is waiting now to greet us in the joy of Christmas.

> *O perfect Love, all human thought transcending . . .*
> Dorothy Frances Gurney (1858–1932)

Family Service input
The story behind the hymn 'Great is thy faithfulness' (see p. 12). The young people could also be encouraged to write a hymn on the subject of 'joy', or a prayer(s).

Suggested hymns
Christ is the King, O friends, rejoice; Hark! the glad sound, the Saviour comes; Rejoice in the Lord always; The kingdom of God is justice and joy.

Hymn stories

Great is thy faithfulness
Thomas Obadiah Chisholm (1866–1960) lived to see the success of his hymn, which was introduced to Britain by George Beverley Shea, the Canadian gospel singer who accompanied Dr Billy Graham when he conducted his first London Crusade at Haringay Arena in 1954.

An American minister, the Revd Chisholm was born on 29 July 1866, in a little log cabin in Franklin, Kentucky. He had a fairly scanty elementary schooling, yet became a teacher in his school at the tender age of 16. Later, he became aware of a vocation to the ordained ministry.

He wrote over twelve hundred hymns in his long life, although beset by illness from his mid-forties until his death at the age of 94. It was in 1923 that Chisholm sent the words of this hymn to the editor of the American Hope Publishing Company, William Runyon, who was also a Methodist minister. The lines, based on two verses in the third chapter of Lamentations, so impressed Runyon that he prayed God for a tune worthy of them; and the words and music have been inseparable ever since.

In a world that is so fast-paced, and a society where so much is 'throw-away', this hymn, which seeks to redress the balance and speaks of the constancy and consistency of God, is needed now as never before.

Third Sunday of Advent *Second Service*
Double Joy Ps. 50:1–6[62]; Isa. 35;
Luke 1:57–66[67–80]
'[Elizabeth's] neighbours and relatives heard that the Lord had shown his great mercy to her, and they rejoiced with her.' Luke 1:58

Sharing good news
Elizabeth's joy would be doubled, in the joy of those who came to wish her well. This is one of the loveliest verses in the Bible, and it gives us a beautiful picture of the close-knit family and friendship circle into which John the Baptist had been born. We may look back with nostalgia to the days when neighbours knew

each other – but those bonds, if frayed or fractured, can surely be re-formed, and Christmas is a good time to begin the process.

The blossoming desert
Isaiah tells of the desert blossoming abundantly like the crocus (Isaiah 35:1, 2) – the frail little flower that thrusts up through the snow and cheers us when the days are still cold and short. A morning, an afternoon – and then the little golden, purple or white goblets wilt – but with the next rising of the sun others come to take their place. Shared joy can be just as ephemeral, but lovely while it lasts. Elizabeth may not have lived to see the beheading of John on the orders of Herod, but no one could take away the joy she shared at his birth. Joy, happiness, gladness – call it what you will – is not to be measured and calculated by worldly standards. One cannot complete a form for it, like insurance, with all possible risks taken into account. Joy is to be seized when it comes, for however long it comes, and by whoever it comes, in the proportion that it comes. Make the most of it, give it all away – and bless God for it. Joy kept to oneself shrivels; shared, it expands with a grace that comes from the Source of joy himself. Wherever we live, and whatever circumstances surround us, it's pretty certain that our particular 'desert' is not blossoming to capacity, so can we not help it towards that state?

Looking forward
Advent is not only a time for counting the blessings that we have been given, but also of anticipating the blessings to come, of cheering the present darkness (physical and spiritual) with the prospect of light (physical and spiritual) to come; of looking forward to the commemoration of the first coming of Jesus, as we prepare for his even greater second coming. The way we have travelled is behind us, written indelibly on the landscape of our lives. We may look back at it with pride or thankfulness or regret – or even with anger – but it is now unalterable. It has brought us to a place where we have not been before, and to which we shall not return. There will be questions we are asking today, which we have not asked before: questions of faith, sharing, life and death. Yet Advent leads us into a time when joy brings people together – when families converge, cards and presents are exchanged; there are parties, celebrations, extra services – all defying the world situation, the cold weather, long nights and short days. The Hang Seng, the Footsie

and the Dow-Jones all take a break – and much of the rest of the world doesn't even realize it's managing without them.

Just a Child
What does it take to persuade men and women in their millions to cast away the works of darkness and put on the armour of light (Collect for Advent, BCP)? Just a Child: a Child with enough love to embrace also all the millions who don't as yet accept his light. The Christmas challenge comes, in this so-familiar Child.

Suggested hymns
Hark, a thrilling voice is sounding; Like a mighty river flowing; Rejoice! the Lord is King; To God be the glory.

Fourth Sunday of Advent   21 December 2003
Principal Service   **By God's Will**   Mic. 5:2–5a;
Canticle: Magnificat, or Ps. 80:1–7; Heb. 10:5–10;
Luke 1:39–45[46–55]
'It is by God's will that we have been sanctified through the offering of the body of Jesus Christ once for all.' Hebrews 10:10
'Blessed is she who believed that there would be a fulfilment of what was spoken to her by the Lord.' Luke 1:45

In God's will
Beautiful things happened to Elizabeth and Mary, because they were living *in* the will of God. *By* that same will, the life implanted in Mary's womb by God went on to be the bridge for all believers between this chapter of life and the next. In the most wonderful, powerful overriding of natural laws, human inventions and the most devilish of schemes, God would have his way. Let us never persuade ourselves, whatever comes against us, that the power in us is not stronger than the power attacking us (cf. 2 Kings 6:16; 1 John 4:4).

Starving our doubts
'Feed your faith, and starve your doubts', is a good slogan to use at any time – but especially at Christmas, when more than the

usual amount of food is consumed. A faithful heart, kept in the will of God, has no room for doubts. Instead, it is 'fixed' (cf. Psalm 57:7 – 'My heart is fixed, O God, my heart is fixed; I will sing and give praise'; and Psalm 108:1 – 'O God, my heart is fixed . . .' (KJV), trusting in God's word, God's love and God's timing. If we feed on these positives, starving what does not come of God into negativity, we shall not live an unchallenged life, but we shall have that inner peace that passes understanding. God will give us beauty for ashes, colour for drabness, life for inertia, richness for barrenness.

As God intends

This is how God intends us to live: in utter trust and devotion to him. From first to last, our Lord's gospel was to show folk how to live in God's will. How are we doing? We may say: 'Shine, Jesus, shine – shine through us – let us be your light to the world . . .' But do we know what we are asking? Are we sure we want *all* of Jesus to shine through us? Or do we settle for lighting up some-one's darkness just a little, with a tiny fraction of the good news? Hasn't God told us to share his gifts freely, not calculating or measuring them (cf. Matthew 10:8)? We are dealing – yes, even when we meet the Christ-Child in the manger – with a thorough-going, dynamic, practical, encouraging and *exciting* Lord. He is inviting us right now to get to know *all* of him, not just a bit (the most comfortable, undemanding bit) but his whole self. His invitation lies before us, this Advent. We are faced with the RSVP. And what happens after that? That is God's business. It's not what *we* are going to do: it's that our willingness and openness gives *God* the freedom to do what he is going to do, in us. Our availability – God's ability. Are we getting right with his programme? We are partners in his great enterprise of evangelizing the world, no less. All of it – not just a bit.

The time starts now

Yes, now – with our Christmas schedules hotting up, and time at more of a premium than usual. Let's get out our Bibles and dig into them – meditating, memorizing, *praying* the precious parables and promises into our hearts; taking hold of the guidance and the sheer good news of God, as though our lives depend on it – for they do. And if someone notices, and asks why you're all lit up, will you be able to tell them? Will you be able to point them to

Jesus – to say, 'It's not me, but Christ!'? Maybe *you* won't, but give the Holy Spirit in you a free rein, and the power that effected the birth of Jesus will have no problem in sharing your good news.

Family Service input

To provide a special bookmark for the lectern Bible(s), with local Christian interest, encourage the young folk to make markers showing their church, on coloured card, laminating these with self-adhesive transparent film; extra markers can be made for worshippers to take home and/or for selling on the church bookstall (examples, p. 17).

Suggested hymns

A great and mighty wonder; Behold, the mountain of the Lord; Once, only once, and once for all; Tell out, my soul, the greatness of the Lord.

Fourth Sunday of Advent *Second Service*
Let Justice Flow   Ps. 123[131]; Isa. 10:33—11:10; Matthew 1:18–25

'Have mercy upon us, O Lord, have mercy upon us; for we have had more than enough of contempt.' Psalm 123:3

When right prevails

Jesus came as a child into a very imperfect world, where (as now) so often might was right, and justice observed when convenient. Humankind could accept the Lord, or reject him: but when he comes the second time, justice will come into its own. We are all geared up now to welcome Jesus as a child – yet we may also find time this Christmas to ask: How long? 'How long before your second coming, Lord, as Judge?' How far have we progressed along the road of justice, since the earliest times when unlimited retribution was the norm; through Deuteronomic days when the fairer 'eye for eye, tooth for tooth' law was introduced; to the present day, when practically every nation boasts a judicial system, and practically every society finds loopholes in it?

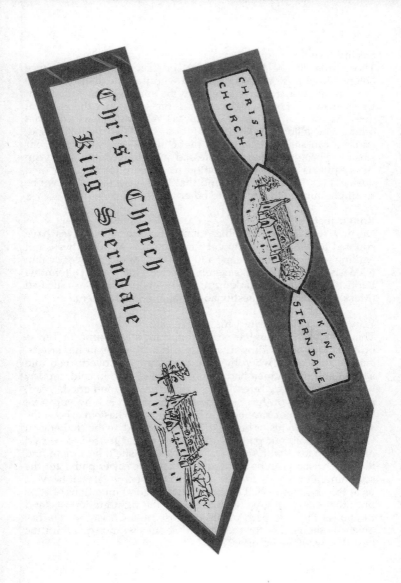

Saving face

Those who choose to forget that God has declared vengeance belongs to him (Romans 12:19), and who trample justice into the mud in an effort to 'save face', may be surprised on Judgement Day, when the Lord weighs souls in his scales, not theirs. What does it matter, if we justify ourselves? Why should we care that others have a good opinion of us? If our hearts are one with God, and we can sleep contented at night in the realization that our sins have been repented of, confessed and forgiven, the world can surely put its own construction on us. We are to mind our own business (cf. John 21:21, 22), and that is to serve God. Can we be so single-minded? Dare we be otherwise?

Rough justice?

On any reading of the Bible, many of those whose lives have counted for God seemed to get rough justice. Abraham was kept waiting for a son for 25 years, and was then asked to sacrifice him (Genesis 22:1ff.). Job was severely afflicted (Job 1 and 2). John the Baptist lost his head (Mark 6:27); and even our Lord was crucified (Mark 15:37), after a questionable trial and arraignment.

Why doesn't God protect his own?

This is a question that has been around for a long time. St Teresa of Avila was once riding in a pony cart with some of her sisters, between convents, when the axle broke, the cart overturned into a ditch and the women had an unscheduled bath in cold, muddy water. Exasperated, Teresa looked up to heaven, and cried: 'Lord, it's no wonder you have so few friends, if this is how you treat them!' We may not have been so blunt, but who has not echoed the saint's protest in his or her heart? Where would be the challenge if God strewed all our paths with fragrant roses? It used to be said of one old lady that if there was a hard way, she'd be sure to find it. The Christian can be assured that there are easier paths, for the searching. But where do they lead? To the pearly gates of heaven, or to the shackles of hell beyond all those good intentions? Let us pray that God will give us grace to see the right guideposts, and to choose the true path of his purpose, this Christmas. He has given us the reason for the season. Should we not give him the best that we have on offer?

Earth has many a noble city; Jesus, hope of every nation; Lord, the clouds are gathering (Let justice flow); Thy way, not mine, O Lord.

Christmas Eve   24 December 2003
Morning Eucharist   **New Knowledge**   2 Sam. 7:1–5, 8–11, 16; Ps. 89:2, 21–27; Acts 13:16–26; Luke 1:67–79

'And you, Child, will . . . give knowledge of salvation to [God's] people.' Luke 1:76–77

The right kind of knowledge
The first Adam's wife had sinned by coveting knowledge (Genesis 3:5). The second Adam's forerunner would give people *true* knowledge, *saving* knowledge, whereby they would be able to accept life in the next world as well as in this. One type of knowledge brought death – the other, life eternal. Praise God, it's the true knowledge that will be ours this Christmas. Fyodor Dostoyevsky once said: 'Prayer is an exploration into the heart of God, a journey into knowledge. And it is made easier at Christmas, because God comes to us as a Child.'

The importance of John
John the Baptist was careful to point people away from himself to Jesus, denigrating his own standing and emphasizing the greater role of the Saviour. But the office and person of the forerunner had a significance which we have done well to consider in these past weeks of Advent. Jesus did not move suddenly on to an empty, unprepared stage; John, very convincingly, had paved the way, linking the old prophecies with which people were familiar, to the coming Saviour with whom they were not familiar: that is still a sound teaching method. The fact that many failed to make the prophetic connection – still less to recognize Jesus – was neither John's fault nor God's. The people had been given generous help and every opportunity to accept Jesus.

The Christmas-Child

And we, with that wonderful gift of hindsight – what do we make of the Christmas-Child? Do we confine him to the manger, or can we identify him as our daily Companion, Redeemer, Saviour and Brother? He is so much more than what he seems. As we hear again the Christmas story, paraphrased for the children among us, we can become like children and imbibe once more the wonder of it all. Yet, though the crib may be part of our church 'decorations', the *cross* is still on the altar. We, who have known the Christ of Calvary and resurrection, surely see more than the Child of Bethlehem. Has he not taken our sin and dropped it in the deepest ocean of God's love, and put up a sign: 'No Fishing'?

Finding Jesus

As the shepherds looked at each other, half-dazzled by the light, they heard music in the air, and suddenly one angel had become many, all singing: 'Glory to God in highest heaven – and on earth peace and joy to everyone!' And then the music faded, and the sky grew dark again, except for the stars. The shepherds rubbed their eyes, and wondered what the vision had meant. 'He said, "In Bethlehem, this very night!"', said one. 'Let us go and find this Saviour!' said another. May this be our mission also, this Christmas. To seek him, is an acknowledgement of our need; and to need him is our very reason for being born.

> *May the humility of the shepherds,*
> *the perseverance of the wise men,*
> *the joy of the angels,*
> *and the peace of the Christ-Child,*
> *be God's gifts to us this Christmas time*
> *and always. Amen.*

Suggested hymns

All my heart this night rejoices; O little town of Bethlehem; The Lord at first did Adam make; Silent night.

Christmas Day   25 December 2003
Midnight or early Eucharist   **This Little Child**
Isa. 52:7–10; Ps. 98; Heb. 1:1–4[5–12]; John 1:1–14

'a son ... through whom he also created the worlds', Hebrews 1:2
'All things came into being through him ... the world came into being through him.' John 1:3, 10

All through him
This triple affirmation of the part that Jesus played in the creation of the worlds is surely too much for us to take on board on Christmas Day. We can cope with a baby – but how much more can we take? Is this not the greatest miracle in history – the reducing of the world's creator, into a tiny child? Well, miraculous it may be. It is God at work in person, in the saving of the world. This little child that meets us today, looks out with eyes that are older than creation, and challenges us to make him and his mission known.

Bringing in – taking out
Joy brings us together for worship at Christmas, and another miracle occurs as the Lord charges us with even greater joy to take and share with others when we leave the church today. How they in turn use it, once we have shared it with them, is a matter between themselves and God. We shall have played our part in the process. There are those too jaded by the months of commercial Christmas 'hype' to greet this festival with the freshness and joy it deserves. Do we accept this as inevitable, given the modern world? No! Here, again, God can work a miracle. If you doubt it, look into the eyes of those leaving church today. Let us realize that this is *his* day, and he is the Master. And the blessed assurance should boost our joy even more.

Angels at work
A young postgraduate student was being interviewed on the radio. She was collecting information for a thesis, from men and women in many walks of life, who claimed to have seen angels. At the outset, she confessed to being sceptical about the whole thing; but the testimonies of over a hundred and fifty people had convinced her that, yes, there *are* visitations from other-worldly beings – and, yes, they act like, and often resemble, the angels of biblical days; they defy logical, reasonable or common-sensible explanations.

21

Yet for many people angels in the Bible are accepted, while their twenty-first-century counterparts are often questioned. At the heart of the Christmas story, we find angels at work: announcing the coming of Jesus to Mary and to Joseph; proclaiming his birth to the shepherds; warning the wise men to return to their own country by a different route; and telling Joseph to flee with Mary and Jesus to Egypt, away from the dangerous paranoia of Herod.

Believable

It is important to notice that the people at the centre of the Christmas story *believed* what the angels told them: whether Jew or Gentile, simple or educated, they took notice, however strange the message may have seemed. May we also today have open hearts and minds for God's messages this Christmas. He is still the Master of the unexpected, the incredible, the impossible. Let us wrap our hearts around this tremendous truth, as we meet the little Child who later will stand as a man before Pilate and receive the unbeliever's question: 'What is truth?' (John 18:38).

> *This is the Truth sent from above,*
> *The truth of God, the God of love,*
> *Therefore don't turn me from your door,*
> *But hearken all both rich and poor.*

Traditional, Oxford Book of Carols, 68

Suggested hymns

All my heart this night rejoices; Away in a manger; Hark! the herald-angels sing; How lovely on the mountains.

Christmas Day   *In the day: Principal Service*
Given for Us   Isa. 9:2–7; Ps. 96; Titus 2:11–14; Luke 2:1–14[15–20]

'[Jesus Christ] it is who gave himself for us that he might redeem us from all iniquity and purify for himself a people of his own who are zealous for good deeds.' Titus 2:14

A personal gift
Surely nothing can be more personal than the giving of oneself. Freely, unreservedly and undeservedly, Jesus left glory to redeem us from the mess we had got ourselves into. Christmas morning is a time for celebration rather than self-flagellation; but let us wrap our hearts around the sheer love that prompted God to do what he did. What will it take for the whole world to join us? A lot more prayer, a lot more trust and a lot more evangelizing. Today is a holiday – but prayer, trust and evangelism are integral parts of a Christian's make-up. Christ still comes to a world that to a great extent is concerned with other matters.

The challenge of Christmas
The challenge of Christmas is: How much do we care? Are we content to let folk take Christ out of Christmas, and to see this time as virtually a secular vacation? Or has Christ taken such a hold of our hearts that we are constrained to do something about it? 'The love of Christ urges us on', says St Paul, 'because we are convinced that one has died for all, therefore all have died' (2 Corinthians 5:14). Because one made the effort, can we sit back and do nothing? Christ comes today as a baby needing all the love and attention a normal child needs – but so much more, because his reason for coming to us is so much greater. *That* is the challenge of Christmas. We can smother its impact under tinsel and parties – but he will still remind us: 'I came, I gave myself for you . . . to purify you . . .' For what? To be zealous in good deeds. We hear again, in our reading from Isaiah, of 'the zeal of the Lord of hosts' (Isaiah 9:7); but God seeks to operate along a two-way process, and he is looking out for our zeal.

Energy for God
At Christmas many people find an energy they did not suspect they had: much more than usual is accomplished, even though the days are at their shortest, darkest and often coldest. And, in the case of Christians, much of this zeal is directed towards the things of God. As the thirteenth-century scholar-theologian, St Thomas Aquinas, said: 'God is the Unmoved Mover' (*Summa Theologiae*): always active, yet constant; always dynamic, yet consistent; always encouraging, yet at peace with himself – just, for all the world, like the Baby who has called us to worship this morning. It is the best example of all – and the little Child is urging

us to follow it. Our zeal may call forth ridicule, disparagement or downright antipathy from those who have not taken up the challenge, but at least they will be paying us the compliment of noticing that our lives are making an impact.

Love grows
For true love, motivated by the love that gave Jesus, is never passive, never inert, but dynamic, positive, for ever growing and reaching out. We may not embrace the world with our love – but we can try. We may not knowingly bring thousands of souls to Christ – but we can try. We may not even strike a positive note with the folk next door – but unless we try, will they ever know whose side we are on? Fear of failure had no place in God's heart, when he gave Jesus to us for a season: the more we accept the joy that Christmas brings, the less inclined we shall be to admit fear into our worship, our witness, our way of living.

As we draw ever closer to the Unmoved Mover, in the exhilaration, encouragement and power of the Christmas Jesus, let us be ready for God to open up doors of opportunity for service that he knows we can walk through.

Joy to the world! Let Christ's light shine among us, to his glory! Amen.

Suggested hymns
Christians, awake; O come, all ye faithful; Once in royal David's city; While shepherds watched.

Christmas Day   *Second Service*
God's Is the Glory   Ps. 8; Isa. 65:17–25; Phil. 2:5–11
'Be glad and rejoice for ever in what I am creating . . .' Isaiah 65:18
'Let the same mind be in you that was in Christ Jesus . . .' Philippians 2:5

God is working out his purpose
The world is an exciting place to live! Every day, every hour, God is creating new people, new situations, new beauty, new opportunities. If we step on board, he will involve us more and more in these works; if we choose to go our own way, his creativity

will carry on. His activity did not stop 'in the beginning', in the first white days of Genesis. We do not know how many other worlds he is keeping in motion; but his powerful interest in this particular one is constantly evident.

Be glad!
It is a great comfort to know that God is in control – that he is in his heaven (even though all may not yet be right with the world) – but can we not show our delight a bit more? Can we not spend quality time giving God the credit for all the good he is doing? John the Baptist's mission was successful, because he concentrated not on himself and his virtues, but on pointing people's attention to Jesus. Christ's own mission was successful, because at every opportunity he gave God the glory. Those who have made the most impact for God are the ones who have pointed others away from themselves, and in the direction of the Lord. It is still the best way of being a Christian and *enjoying the enterprise*.

No recalcitrants!
God is not looking for lukewarm or unwilling helpers, whose daily duties are done under duress, and whose occasional appearance at worship is in the nature of 'part payment' towards eternity. For the sheer joy set before him, Jesus could even face the cross (Hebrews 12:2); any obstacle in our path is surely less traumatic. It may be easy to be joyful on Christmas Day, but God is also Lord of the cold, dark days of January, and the times when illness or tragedy come to test our Christian mettle. Can we sing under all circumstances? Well, the higher we rise above our circumstances, the sweeter will be our melodies.

'Rejoice for ever in what I am creating' – present imperative, and ongoing activity. What is God creating in our lives today? Encouragement? Stickability? Or a dissatisfaction with where we are, and a desire to be a better Christian? Well, he might be doing all of these, but the example of the Child in the manger surely tells us more emphatically than anything: 'Forget yourself, and look at me – look, until you see yourself in me.'

And let us be prepared to see a different person, in Jesus, from the person we may think we are; because this little Christmas Child is so much more than we think or see; and he can work miracles as great as only he knows how. Yes, even in you, and even in me.

Antithesis to boredom
Of all callings, the Christian life is the greatest antithesis to boredom. Pope Paul VI once said:

> Man is assailed by limitless aspirations, but defeated by his own limitations. He has walked on the moon, but limps on the earth. He is divided in his heart, having put God out on the fringe of his life, and set his treasure on vain things. Having lost his sense of wonder, he is bored with work, bored with life, tired even of God.

Please God, let us never give way to such unadulterated pessimism; and if anyone subscribing to this attitude crosses our path, may God give us grace to do something about it. If the world had really sunk so low, would God not have given up on us by now?

As the Child of Christmas shows so beautifully and powerfully today, God has certainly not given up on his created beings.

> *This will be a sign for YOU.*
> *YOU will find a child . . .*
> *Lying in a manger.*
>
> Luke 2:12

Suggested hymns
A great and mighty wonder; Come and join the celebration; It came upon the midnight clear; Unto us a Child is born.

First Sunday of Christmas   28 December 2003
Principal Service   A Child's Understanding
1 Sam. 2:18–20, 26; Ps. 148; Col. 3:12–17; Luke 2:41–52

'After three days [Mary and Joseph] found him in the temple, sitting among the teachers, listening to them and asking them questions. And all who heard him were amazed at his understanding and his answers.'
Luke 2:46–47

The divine mind
Jesus had indeed left glory, humbling himself to an earthly existence, being confined in a human body – but he was still conscious

of his true identity, and though he had emptied himself of so much (Philippians 2:7), yet the divine knowledge of God and the things of God remained indissolubly part of him. Thus, though he looked like a normal 12-year-old, he seems to have sounded like one of the theological doctors. The dons were 'amazed' – and with justification, for a carpenter and his young wife were not likely to have instilled such learning in the lad. That God has seen fit to open this little window for us, into 'the hidden childhood' of Jesus, is infinitely precious, and there are lessons to be learned.

It is healthy to question
Questions have their part to play in the Christian's life, as in any other. If we have no questions, we have no interest in learning more. The doctors in the temple questioned Jesus, but he gave as good as he got. We can never out-question God – nor can we harm our minds by stretching them out in the pursuit of God-given knowledge. When we have stopped asking, we shall have stopped living.

Ever learning
Though the young Jesus was God incarnate, with a knowledge of everything that has been, is and will be, he sought out the teachers of his day, to question them and to receive with quiet composure their answers. Let us never be too fearful, or too self-confident, to approach those with great learning, and to discuss with them the things that really matter. Everyone has something to give – and among the erudite are those who seem to believe it is better to give than to receive!

Questions can bear much fruit
Perhaps, that day in the temple, one of the doctors was called Nicodemus; perhaps the seed sown by the young Jesus found a place in his mind, and quietly grew until one night, twenty or so years later, he came to Jesus for more knowledge (John 3:1f.). We do not know – but, doctors of the law being the perceptive people they are, the group in the temple would not forget the lad of twelve. The questions we may ask, or be asked, may have far-reaching effects, and may involve many people over a wide area. Let us not 'play' with words, for on a day long ago the Master warned: 'You will have to give an account for every careless word you utter; for by your words you will be justified, and by your

words you will be condemned' (Matthew 12:36–37). On the positive side, words can bring the difference between despair and
hope, death and life: 'Your words have supported those who were
stumbling,' said Eliphaz to Job (Job 4:4) – and Eliphaz is not
usually remembered for his optimism.

The words spoken by Jesus that day in the temple were not
wasted; and by the same token, every word that we speak is heard
by God. At Christmas, we give voice to much joy, a lot of singing
and probably more enthusiasm than at many other times of the
year. If a little Child can call forth such zeal, how much more is
the living, growing Spirit of the Lord capable of energizing our
hearts and minds!

Well, we could make one of our New Year resolutions, the
testing of this possibility!

Family Service input

During the sermon, invite the young people to cut out and paste
on cards/order of service sheets items from the current Christian
press. Incorporate these into the intercessions.

Suggested hymns

I cannot tell why he whom angels worship; Jesus, hope of every
nation; The heavenly Child in stature grows; Thou didst leave thy
throne and thy kingly crown.

First Sunday of Christmas *Second Service*
True Identity   Ps. 132; Isa. 61; Gal. 3:27–4:7
or Luke 2:15–21

*'So you are no longer a slave but a child, and if a child then also an
heir, through God.' Galatians 4:7*
*'. . . and he was called Jesus, the name given by the angel before he was
conceived in the womb.' Luke 2:21*

The importance of names

The writing of John the Baptist's name restored Zechariah's speech
(Luke 1:64); Jesus' own name had been declared by the angel at
the annunciation of his conception (Matthew 1:21; Luke 1:31); Jesus
gave some of his closest friends special names: Peter, the Rock

(Mark 3:16); James and John, Sons of Thunder (Mark 3:17); and after conversion Saul became Paul (Acts 13:9). Centuries earlier, the practice seems to have begun, with Abram and Sarai becoming Abraham and Sarah (Genesis 17:5, 15). This is God at his most loving, intimate and generous, telling those he loves just how much they matter to him.

The importance of titles
These are not the grandiose titles beloved by high society, but titles which explain the standing of the person involved. Take yourselves, God is saying, in Galatians 4:7 – I'm not calling you slaves any longer, because I don't want to have a master–slave relationship. I'm calling you my children – and by virtue of that, you are my heirs. What a privilege! What an inheritance! And what a responsibility, because this is a question of grace – God's wholly undeserved gift and unmerited favour: sons and daughters of the Power that holds the universe in place; brothers and sisters of the Love that came down at Christmas! Can we take it in? No, we are not asked to; simply to believe, and to be thankful.

> *I am now a child of God,*
> *For I'm washed in Jesus' blood;*
> *I am watching and I'm longing while I wait,*
> *Soon on wings of love to fly*
> *To my home beyond the sky,*
> *To my welcome, as I'm sweeping through the gate.*
>
> J. Parker

Let us never grow too grand to echo the lovely old gospel song. Surely we are not ashamed of our pedigree in Christ? Through a trauma we cannot imagine, he has claimed us for eternity. We may have the dearest friend on earth, but there are times when we need to be alone. Yet Christ has 'taken us on' for ever! What a great heart of love he must have, for many a time we give him little enough reason to love us.

Living up to our name
It still matters what we are called. Some of us take exception to our names given in childhood and alter them when we become of age. In an indefinable way, we take on board the character we

believe best illustrates that name. It is not so very different with
the name Christ gives us. We are CHRIST–IANS. We belong to
Christ, and thereby are children of the same heavenly Father. We
go around in his name, on his business, with his light, power, joy
and mission – whether or not we share this precious realization
of identity, or keep it under wraps. If we keep it secret, little by
little its efficacy is watered down, until we're in danger of forgetting who we are.

Changed by a name
Abraham, Sarah, Paul, the apostles – all were changed by their
names into men and women who could be used mightily by God.
What difference has becoming a Christian made to us? What difference are we making to others, because we are who we are? These
are good questions to ponder on the last Sunday of 2003. We may
even progress to a third: How is our identity in Christ going to
influence others in 2004?

Suggested hymns
In full and glad surrender; Lord, for the years; Love came down
at Christmas; Stand up, stand up for Jesus.

Second Sunday of Christmas 4 January
Principal Service **Spiritual Blessings** Jer. 31:7–14;
Ps. 147:12–20; Eph. 1:3–14; John 1: [1–9]10–18
or Ecclus. 24:1–12; Canticle: Wis. of Sol. 10:15–21;
Eph. 1:3–14; John 1:[1–9] 10–18

*'Blessed be the God and Father of our Lord Jesus Christ, who has blessed
us in Christ with every spiritual blessing in the heavenly places.'*
Ephesians 1:3

God's goodness
God has *blessed* us, in Christ (v. 3); he has *chosen* us, in Christ (v.
4); he has *destined* us, through Christ (v. 5); he has *freely bestowed
grace* on us, in Christ (v. 6); he has *lavished grace* on us, in Christ
(vv. 7–8); and he has made known *wisdom* and *insight* to us, in
Christ (v. 9). Isn't he *good*? And what is he looking for in return?

In verse 14, Paul tells us: we have received all this, so that we can live 'to the praise of his glory'. Or, as a later theologian put it: 'Man's chief aim is to glorify God.' We are not here to make money, to work for more leisure, to carve our name with pride on the pages of history, or to have a good time. We are here to live out our identity as sons and daughters of God, to his glory.

Prioritizing

Let us not worry about whether Ephesians was actually addressed to the church in Ephesus, or was a sort of general letter for all the churches in Asia Minor: as beloved, chosen, destined and grace-lavished Christians, it's for US.

And let us keep well away from debates as to whether St Paul or someone else wrote it. God in his wisdom meant it to be part of the New Testament; and as blessed, chosen, destined and grace-lavished Christians, it's for US.

When God made us, he designed us for eternity. And he did a good job. If we thought of a figure, and tacked on to it as many noughts as we had time and strength to do, we should come nowhere near the cost of Calvary: that was the price God paid to keep US in his plan; that is how much we matter – our participation matters – to him.

We are blessed – so, how do we show it? Doesn't God's blessing give us love and compassion for others? Doesn't it make us care for them, and long to show them Christ – to share Jesus with as many as God brings into our lives?

We are chosen. 'You did not choose me, but I chose you,' Jesus told his friends (John 15:16). We must not get complacent, in believing we've done God a great favour by 'choosing Christ'. That is getting our faith back to front. God did the choosing, at Calvary, for we were on his mind.

We are destined – for glory, for eternity. Here on the proving ground God has his eye on 'for ever'. Can we show enthusiasm about this? Let us show him that we care. We are bound for glory; why do we at times give the impression that eternity doesn't concern us?

We've been given grace – lavishly, in abundance. God's unmerited favour has been showered on us. Perhaps, if we had earned it, we would value grace more. But God is saying: 'Accept it as my free gift to you. My Son went to Calvary, and bought it for you.' We are not to get uppity about our grace – but we can broadcast it, as freely and as frequently as we like; we can share it, as lavishly as it has been given: in fact, it is not a lot of use unless we do share it.

God's contract

God's contract with us is munificent, but it takes two to tango, and we must keep our end up. The Bible gathering dust on the shelf will not bring a single soul to Christ, unless we attend to it: open it, read, mark, learn and inwardly digest it (Collect for Advent 2, BCP), and then go and share it with someone. We needn't get hung up about who we can share it with; there is a massive mission field out there, which will stay that way unless someone makes a start, somewhere.

Family Service input

Using texts from the day's lections, illuminate or illustrate them on white or coloured card; laminate, and use for Bible/prayer book markers, New Year/birthday cards, or notelets.

Suggested hymns

Angel-voices, ever singing; Go, tell it on the mountain; God is working his purpose out; Lord, who left the highest heaven.

Second Sunday of Christmas   *Second Service*
Abiding in Us   Ps. 135; 1 Sam. 1:20–28; 1 John 4:7–16
or Matthew 2:13–23

'God abides in those who confess that Jesus is the Son of God, and they abide in God.' 1 John 4:15

A combined operation

Literally, the Christian never walks alone. The Almighty has not only looked down from glory, he has come down in the form (in a manner of speaking) of his Holy Spirit, and has taken up residence with us and in us. We could not have reached the stage we are at now were it not for his guidance and protection. God knows that, left to our own devices, we should make a pretty poor fist of life. We need the Spirit's abiding, for help in prayer, in perseverance and penitence. Recently, a research scientist declared: 'Answered prayer is the most convincing experiment I have ever undertaken.' Prayer is only possible because the Spirit in us links up with the Almighty.

One condition
There is one condition governing the abiding of the Spirit: that we boldly stand up for Jesus, and tell out the truth loud and convincingly, that he is the Son of God. When did we last do that? Or do we take it for granted that people know what we believe? They may well know, but St Paul has underlined the importance of straight talking. 'If you confess with your lips that Jesus is Lord, and believe in your heart that God raised him from the dead, you will be saved' (Romans 10:19). We shall probably spend some time in praising when we get to heaven; our notes there will be all the sweeter the more we practise the theme in this present life.

Best friends
Best friends are always in contact – by proximity, conversation or simply thought. So it should be with Christians and their God, until the bond becomes so strong that nothing on earth can break it. Best friends know a lot about each other – not to the detriment but to the cementing of their friendship. God already knows everything there is to know about us, but we need constantly to be pressing into his word and to be dialoguing with him in prayer, to learn more about him. God will never let us down, but he is the best of friends when we do something stupid, showing a love and patience that tells us better than words ever could, that he doesn't believe we have made a permanent blunder.

God's faith
Walking with God's faith in us means that we can trust God to do in us what we could not do ourselves; through us, he loves those with whom we may have problems; he can lead us where ordinarily we would not want to go. Most important of all, in us he is working to make us what we would never think we could become. Have you ever looked back and been amazed with something you have achieved, a problem you have solved, a quarrel you have healed, a testimony you have given? Dwell no longer on your virtue, but give your Best Friend the credit! Best friends also tell each other secrets; in prayer, we can rest assured that God is always listening; but how often do we listen out for what he

wants to tell us? In our stillness and silence, the world does its best to crash in with distractions and noise; we need to learn to refocus on God, time after time after time. Giving attention to God is one of the greatest challenges facing a Christian in today's fast-paced world. But it can be done. We are dealing with someone who, as ever, is the Master of time:

> Not a brief glance, I beg, a passing word,
> But as thou dwell'st with thy disciples, Lord:
> Familiar, condescending, patient, free;
> Come not to sojourn, but abide with me.
>
> Come not in terrors, as the King of kings,
> But kind and good, with healing in thy wings,
> Tears for all woes, a heart for every plea;
> Come, Friend of sinners, thus abide with me.

H. F. Lyte

Suggested hymns
Abide with me; Be thou my vision; Master, speak, thy servant heareth; Spirit of the living God.

Baptism of Christ (First Sunday of Epiphany)
11 January   *Principal Service*   Fire and Spirit
Isa. 43:1–7; Ps. 29; Acts 8:14–17; Luke 3:15–17, 21–22

'[John said], "I baptize you with water, but one who is more powerful than I is coming . . . He will baptize you with the Holy Spirit and fire."' Luke 3:6

'. . . You are precious in my sight, and honoured, and I love you.' Isaiah 43:4

The God of contrasts
Fire and Spirit-filled baptism can sound alarming – and in a way so it is; plenty of those assembled at Pentecost were amazed (Acts 2:12). This type of baptism marks a spiritual watershed in a person's life, and is not to be underestimated. Yet it has been

instigated by a gentle, caring God – the God of the precious compassion of Isaiah 43.

> *Just as I am, thou wilt receive,*
> *Wilt welcome, pardon, cleanse, relieve;*
> *Because thy promise I believe,*
> *O, Lamb of God, I come.*

> *Charlotte Elliott*

If we are not prepared to be stimulated, energized, even shocked by God, have we set our hand to the wrong plough? If we cannot bring ourselves to rest in the loving, gentle, everlasting arms, are we relying on our own strength, our own virtues, our own merits? Our walk with the Almighty is with a Lord who gives us the freedom of expression, combined with paternal authority and protection. Have we recognized both in our God? If not, today is the time to straighten out our faith.

Our thrilling Lord

We are all candidates for a miracle, capable of being thrilled by God into greater service, deeper love and stronger faith. Wow! (And just reflect, when was the last time you said 'Wow!'?) At baptism, God meets us one-to-one, in a special way, a different way from anyone else's baptism experience. Someone has rightly said:

> *Don't underestimate your worth*
> *by comparing yourself with others.*
> *It is because we are different*
> *that each of us is special.*

> *Anon*

So, what are we special folk to make of the year 2004? In the course of this year we may find ourselves in the depths of loneliness, horror, weakness, pain, or under assault of one form or another. But Jesus has been to those depths before. Or we may be right in the thick of things, with the Lord opening one door of opportunity after another, and cramming every day with service, sacrifice and challenge. Jesus has been there before, as well. The time to get really serious with God is when we find ourselves in the grey area in-between – when problems don't keep us on edge, and life is pretty good. Danger! We may not be hassled by the Devil – but what are we doing for God?

After baptism
After baptism we are, in a sense, not our own. God has laid claim to us, and we literally owe him our lives. At any time he can step in and call us home. That shouldn't worry us, but it should spur us on regularly to review our ministry and mission. We have a life to live, a soul to feed, a gospel to share, a commission to honour. And we have the gentlest, most caring and loving of fathers, to see us through to the stage of 'mission accomplished'.

On fire for God
Once God has lit us up with the fire of Spirit-baptism, we may not be conscious of it but others will notice. Baptism is an irrevocable step: once carried out, it cannot be reversed; once the fire has been given, it cannot be taken away; once God has touched us, claimed us, called us, chosen us and inspired us, we are different. Just how different may never be put into words.

But God, in his infinite variety of operations, is not confined to dealing in words. In baptism, we are one with Christ – and that's the best company of all to be in.

Family Service input
Invite the young people to design a parish 'Baptism' card, for presentation to children/parents at christenings.

Suggested hymns
Amazing grace; Christ, when for us you were baptized; How firm a foundation; When Jesus came to Jordan.

Baptism of Christ   *Second Service*   Dead to Sin and Alive to God   Pss. 46, 47; Isa. 55:1–11; Rom. 6:1–11 or Mark 1:4–11
'So you must consider yourselves dead to sin and alive to God in Christ Jesus.' Romans 6:11

The empty cross
The empty cross of Calvary is a constant reminder that on a certain Friday afternoon at 3 o'clock, the sin of the world was crucified: not whipped, not stripped of its power, but crucified. More than this, every person from that time forward who was to take up his or her own cross and follow Christ, died to sin and took on the life that Christ had won: the life of eternity.

Earthly language can go no higher – yet these words encapsulate also the most basic truths of Christianity: truths that we need to translate into the day-to-day running of our lives. The world's sin may have been crucified, but the Devil, a master in the art of deception, still tempts us whenever he can with a parody of sin which looks so genuine that we are sometimes deceived. Perhaps, if we could recall Sergei Bulgakov's warning more often, we should be deceived far less:

> *As long as there is evil in the world,*
> *the Lamb is still being slain.*

Could we but visualize the bleeding wounds of Jesus, would we make compromise with sin? It does not have to be a dramatic murder or theft – conveniently 'forgetting' an overpayment in change at the supermarket, or reusing a stamp that has escaped the franking machine in the morning's mail, can start the Saviour's blood flowing again.

The positive side
For we are 'alive to God in Christ Jesus'! Calvary has given us our open door to new life, and we should be singing all the way to eternity. We have a hope that exceeds all others, a chance of a life so complete as to make this life a mere overture. This is the training ground for an experience that is beyond time, beyond earthly limitations – and far, far beyond sin. We must make the most of our overcoming of Satan in the here and now, for we shall likely not see even a painting of him in the life to come.

Contradiction in terms
Using the most convincing negative – the shameful cross – our Lord gave the most convincing positive – the resurrection – to show the world that the Master had come into his own: not for personal advancement or aggrandisement, but simply to save all

37

who would believe. Accepting this contradiction in terms, and believing the impossible, the followers of Jesus were – and are – to follow in his footsteps. We are not to compose wonderful eulogies, for ourselves or others, but simply to plant our feet where Christ has already stepped. How? By believing that if we step out in faith, he will do with us what as yet we cannot do; he will say with us what as yet we do not know how to say; he will go with us where as yet we fear to go; and he will make of us what he knows we can become. What's more, he'll work his miracle on us so gently, so sensitively, that we may be tempted to believe we've done it ourselves!

Alive in Jesus

We are alive in Jesus now – and in the next chapter of life we shall be even more alive in him. He will see to that, and we can have the utmost confidence in the Lord who never breaks a promise.

If we are Christians in the world today, we are empowered by Jesus, and the surroundings, the trappings, the circumstances, are, in a sense, irrelevant. Christ is empowering us, and his power is greater than any situation or circumstance. It is what is in us, of Jesus, that counts. In plain English, it constitutes the difference between making it to eternity – or not.

Suggested hymns

Crown him with many crowns; In the cross of Christ I glory; Name of all majesty; To the name of our salvation.

Second Sunday of Epiphany 18 January
Principal Service **A God Who Gives** Isa. 62:1–5; Ps. 36:5–10; 1 Cor. 12:1–11; John 2:1–11

'To each is given the manifestation of the Spirit for the common good ... All these [gifts] are activated by one and the same Spirit, who allots to each one individually just as the Spirit chooses.' 1 Corinthians 12:7, 11

Specially chosen

God's spiritual gifts are specially chosen for his specially chosen people. With unparalleled love and care, our Father matches up individuals and gifts, so that no two people are alike or have the same gifts. If we covet another person's gifts, we need to realize that our Father has decided that we are best suited to those he has given us, and vice versa. It should give us a great uplift to recognize that no one but ourselves can make the most of our gifts – at the same time remembering that every gift is to be used 'for the common good'.

For life
The gifts of the Spirit are not given as 'a lump sum' at our birth; a newborn child is very limited in its use of available resources. In God's perfect timing, the gifts are manifested, from the cradle to the grave. The Almighty knows exactly when the need for such gifts is greatest, and when the opportunities for their use are most apposite. We can exercise our extra gift of free will, and pass up such opportunities – but the chance may not be given again.

A shared resonsibility
Our church fellowship, family, work environment and wider circle of friends all share a responsibility of encouragement and affirmation in God's utilization to bring out the best in us. How are we fulfilling this mission? Remember how Barnabas, as one of the greatest encouragers in the New Testament, stood by the converted Paul and defended his integrity and the veracity of his intentions, when the other disciples showed understandable scepticism (Acts 9:26f.). The world today is in need of many more Barnabases – folk who will recognize the best in others, who will support rather than condemn, who will offer the steady hand of friendship when others fall back on suspicion and mistrust. It is often so much easier to find an excuse to exclude strangers, rather than to welcome them. God has not majored on exclusivity in his distribution of spiritual gifts, but of individuality; and the two are very different.

Gifts for God's work
Surely the giver should have first call on the exercise of his or her gifts! Primarily, they are to be used in the service of God. This will inevitably involve others, for the 'common good' is virtually a prerequisite. Oftentimes they will not know whose are the gifts, unless we tell them; if we try to take the credit for ourselves, the efficacy of the gift will be watered down. Giving God the praise opens the door wider for him to do greater things through us.

Saints' Crossword

Clues Across

1. 'Hail, Mary, . . . of grace.' (4)
3. Example of the saints for us. (4)
5. The Almighty. (3)
6. Two Gospel writers. (4, 3, 4)
9. Mother of the Blessed Virgin. (4)
10. Hidden from earthly sight by this? (4)
13. Nathanael. (11)
15. 1 Nov. is . . . Saints. (3)
16. Jesus' Mother. (4)
17. Author of NT book. (4)

Clues Down

1. Border of a saint's picture. (5)
2. Author of Revelation. (4)
4. . . ., the Rock. (5)
7. Welsh town's saint. (5)
8. St Michael fought him. (5)
11. Abraham's early name. (5)
12. 'Christians, . . ., salute the happy morn.' (5)
14. Saints are often painted in these. (4)

Following great examples
The saints through history have been fine examples: Francis, of humility; John Chrysostom, of preaching; Bernard of Clairvaux, of kindness; Thérèse of Lisieux, of bravery and patience; Patrick, of missionary zeal. We can read any book of the saints, and see how God's spiritual gifts were used in the service of others, for his glory and for the furtherance of his kingdom. And we can surely not fail to point up the difference between the generosity of God, who gives all, and the Devil, who gives nothing. Yet there are those who will still go running after nothing, under the impression that they, not Satan, control their destiny.

Family Service input
The Saints' Crossword (opposite) for the young people can also be duplicated for the not-so-young.

Suggested hymns
Christ from whom all blessings flow; Great is thy faithfulness; Of all the Spirit's gifts to me; Thy way, not mine, O Lord.

Second Sunday of Epiphany   *Second Service*
United in Love   Ps. 96; 1 Sam. 3:1–20; Eph. 4:1–16
or John 1:29–42
'[Christ], from whom the whole body, joined and knitted together by every ligament with which it is equipped, as each part is working properly, promotes the body's growth in building itself up in love.' Ephesians 4:16

Looking out
'Looking out' for each other is the hallmark of a Christian: recognizing others' gifts, and encouraging them in the using of these gifts, strengthens the body of Christ on earth. We may think we

Solution
Across: 1. Full. 3. Help. 5. God. 6. Mark and Luke. 9. Anna. 10. Veil. 13. Bartholomew. 15. All. 16. Mary. 17. Jude.
Down: 1. Frame. 2. John. 4. Peter. 7. Asaph. 8. Devil. 11. Abram. 12. Awake. 14. Oils.

have no aptitude for such mission. Then recall St John: 'Those who do not love a brother or sister whom they have seen, cannot love God whom they have not seen' (1 John 4:20). In today's Old Testament reading, it was not until Samuel had found God that he was enabled to be of godly use to others. If we are open to what God is doing in our lives, we shall be used by him in others' lives – probably for a significant time before we have cottoned on to what he is doing.

A listening ear

God may give us the patience and compassion to be a good listener, in which case, we shall find we are being used as others share a burden of sorrow or worry – or, yes, a time of joy, though it has been truly said that we find less of a problem in sharing our woes than our pleasures. Today, the complaint, 'He/she has never time to talk!' is increasingly common, and more often than not really means 'no time to listen'. Time for others is one of God's most precious gifts, and priceless in its exercise.

Teaching Christ

The gift of teaching Christ to others is many-faceted; we can show Christ without saying a word, by our love and concern, our thoughtfulness and gentleness, our way of life and example; or we can preach and teach on the Bible, explaining, drawing out the precious texts and bridging the two-thousand-year span by means of Christian history – always being mindful of pointing our listeners to Christ and not to ourselves. We can minister to people at times of birth, marriage and death, and at the many stages in-between – so long as we show Christ and not ourselves. Satan is forever on the prowl, trying to provoke us into turning God's spiritual gifts into aids for our own advancement.

Strength in integration

As the body of Christ becomes more integrated, so it becomes stronger. Then, perhaps with little or no warning, fraction, disagreement or disappointment occurs, and so disintegration. What has happened? Satan has not given up. Years ago, he managed to persuade one of the inner circle of disciples to betray Jesus – a disciple who had spent three years in the mission team, and who had seen at first hand the wonderful miracles worked by his Master; a disciple to whom Jesus had shown nothing but love and patience, even to including him at the Last Supper. Christians likewise are not immune from Satan's attacks, though – like Judas – we have the choice of compromising or standing firm.

Just as Satan quoted scripture to Jesus in the desert (Matthew 4:6), he can attack us through our spiritual gifts; through personal pride in their use, or in their misuse; and we need to pray for guidance against such dangers.

Joy in our gifts
But God, the giver, encourages us to take delight in what he has given us. Nowhere in the Bible do we read of God wanting long-faced, gloomy, lukewarm, recalcitrant followers. Take stock of your gifts: there may be so many, you cannot count them all; but those you do identify, take time to thank God for, and ask for grace abounding to use them with joy. It is a prayer we cannot make too fervently, or too often.

Suggested hymns
Come down, O love divine; Give thanks with a grateful heart; Holy Spirit, come, confirm us; Now thank we all our God.

Third Sunday of Epiphany 25 January
Principal Service **Daily Miracles** Neh. 8:1–3, 5–6, 8–10; Ps. 19; 1 Cor. 12:12–31a; Luke 4:14–21
'. . . This day is holy to our Lord; and do not be grieved, for the joy of the Lord is your strength.' Nehemiah 8:10
'Then [Jesus] began to say to them, "Today this scripture has been fulfilled in your hearing . . ."' Luke 4:21

Expectation
Every day, if we expect to be surprised by God, he will not disappoint us. As Christians, we may become proficient in prayer, study, service and ministry, but how high is our joyful expectation that God is here, God is loving us, God is prepared to do great things among us? The workers who had toiled against severe odds to get Jerusalem's walls and gates repaired were not only physically but spiritually whacked at the end of the enterprise; and it needed Nehemiah's confidence-building words to persuade

them that their efforts were worth celebrating. The congregation at Nazareth needed to be shocked out of the complacency that often accompanies a liturgical service, by Jesus telling them that history had come alive for them that very day in the person of their preacher.

God is still working miracles, still giving us a loving shake, as if to say: 'Wake up and take a joyful part in what I am doing!' Are we missing out on his nudges? 'I will signal for them and gather them in, for I have redeemed them,' said God (Zechariah 10:8). (For 'signal', read 'hiss', KJV.) Literally, to get our attention, God will say, in so many words, 'Pssst!' Perhaps it will be a silent reminder, of the heart, or perhaps a clarion call, like thunder. But provided we are spiritually alert, we shall get the message.

Faith v fear

Fear and foreboding take up our time, for the most part unnecessarily, as well as being contrary to God's laws. Most if not all our fears end in nothing, and are thus an awful waste of time and spiritual (as well as physical) resources. Faith – looking for good in every circumstance (and expecting to find it) – keeps us in the frame of mind where God can best work in our lives. Faith also begets faith: the one-time England cricketer and pioneer missionary, C. T. Studd, used to say that faith was like smallpox – highly infectious and capable of spreading to all in its vicinity. 'Let's spread some godly infection!' he would say, and spent a lifetime himself putting his words into action.

Adverse reaction

Nor should we allow adverse reaction to dampen our faithful expectations. At first, the Nazareth congregation gave Jesus a good hearing, but then doubts and criticism crept in; they turned on the 'local man' and even threatened his life. Their change of heart left Jesus unmoved: he had given his message. If the local recipients rejected it, he would go to the next towns. By the same token, if our faith and witness receive the cold shoulder, do we move to other pastures? Do we give up on the carpers and criticizers? It may seem hard to do, but it is biblical: 'Whenever you enter a town and they do not welcome you, go out into its streets and say, "Even the dust of your town that clings to our feet, we wipe off in protest against you"' (Luke 10:10–11). The fire and hope and joy of God's message – and our joyful expectation of daily

44

miracles – is not to be quenched by unbelief and rejection. God is not willing that any should perish for lack of hearing his word – but the choice of acting on it lies with them; the joy of living it, praise God, is yours and mine.

Family Service input
Encourage the young people to design parish notelets, cards, etc., featuring a view of their church, or the diocesan arms.

Suggested hymns
Christ is the King, O friends, rejoice; Forth in the peace of Christ we go; God's Spirit is deep in my heart; I come with joy to meet my Lord.

Third Sunday of Epiphany   *Second Service*
The Tenth Command   Ps. 33; Num. 9:15–23;
1 Cor. 7:17–24 or Mark 1:21–28
'Let each of you lead the life that the Lord has assigned, to which God called you.' 1 Corinthians 7:17

Be content
The life to which God has called us is that for which he has specifically designed us. We may look at others, who may seem to be living 'in clover', where the grass is so much greener than it is with us, the assets seem to be so much greater, the hassle virtually non-existent – and we may feel a bit (or a lot) covetous, in contravention of the tenth commandment (which increasingly appears not to bother too many people these days).

But God has chosen our way, our family, our friends. He engineers our situations; and the opportunities he gives us are tailor-made for us alone. We could respect a God who set us all on the same course and left us to muddle along as best we could; but surely we can also *love* a God who deals with us on such a personal, caring level. God has not called us to a life that anyone else is living. Any mistakes we make can, by his grace, be turned around to give us advancement within the parameters he has set specifically and uniquely for us. It doesn't necessarily make for an easier life, but for a more varied, interesting and exciting one.

Past, present and future

It's a case of learning from the past, living in the present and trusting for the future, with a God to whom past, present and future coalesce into one life, one purpose, one walk of salvation.

> *The life I have is all I have,*
> *And the life I have is yours,*
> *But the love I have for the life I have*
> *Is yours and yours and yours.*
>
> *Anon.*

The Giver of our life deserves no less than our full enthusiasm for living out his will for us. Take a look at the stars on a clear night: their order, yet variety; their combined pinpricks of light chasing out the darkness that would otherwise envelop the world. Can the Power that made the stars be anything but dynamically exciting? Step out on a clear, sunny morning: see the snowdrops telling of spring to come, the grass greening in sheltered places, the birds getting their new notes. Can the Love that made Nature be anything but caring and innovative?

This is the powerful Love that has created us for each new day, for special people, special events, special gifts as part of our very own special work for him. Doesn't it thrill you? If not, ask him why – and be prepared for him to tell you. We disappoint God not by dialoguing with him, but by ignoring him.

One life

We only travel once through the world. In the next, our journeying may be much more extensive. But presently we need to do all we can, for as many as we can, while we can. If we bend our mental, physical and spiritual energies to God's will, we shall not have time to covet anything anyone else has, or seems to have.

'What is that to you? Follow me!' Jesus roundly told Peter, who couldn't resist poking his nose into another disciple's business (John 21:20). God is more than able to fill our lives with our mission. We are to care for others, to show compassion and concern and to help where we can – but not to muscle in where God wants to be God in their lives.

How do we get the balance right? By asking God daily to show us – simply because he and he alone knows all the answers all the time.

Suggested hymns
God's Spirit is in my heart; Guide me, O thou great Redeemer; Jesus, Lord, we look to thee; Thy way, not mine, O Lord.

Fourth Sunday of Epiphany   1 February
Principal Service   **Love Is the Greatest**
Ezek. 43:27—44:4; Ps. 48; 1 Cor. 13:1–13; Luke 2:22–40
'And now faith, hope and love abide, these three: and the greatest of these is love.' 1 Corinthians 13:13

Love makes the difference
The love at the heart of Christianity (cf. John 3:16) marks it out from all other religions. A love greater than human comprehension at a definable point in history stepped into the normal life of this earth and, in the best and most positive way, began to turn it upside down (cf. Acts 17:6).

> *Far beyond all human comprehension,*
> *Measured by an infinite dimension,*
> *Wonderfully broad in its intention,*
> *Is the boundless love of God.*
>
> *Haldor Lillenas*

This love, applied to any situation, makes a difference for God. It makes the impossible possible, the uncertain certain, the loss a gain, the trivial important, and the invisible visible. It's the stuff of which miracles are made – and it goes on for ever, getting stronger with the spreading. When Jesus walked the earth, Love incarnate entered the temple and local synagogues, infusing love into the religious observances and their participants, who had to a great extent lost sight of love in an overzealous desire for circumspection in the minutiae of the law.

47

What is this love?
In 1 Corinthians 13, St Paul gives us the best-ever definition of the out-working of our divinely implanted love. The language and cadences may vary with the Bible versions, but, in whatever form we hear or read this chapter, surely some part of it makes a special impact.

> [Love] is always ready to make allowances,
> to trust, to hope and to endure whatever comes.
>
> 1 Corinthians 13:7, NJB

> [Love] is not touchy or fretful or resentful;
> it takes no account of the evil done to it.
>
> 1 Corinthians 13:6, Ampl. Bible

Love is forgiveness in action, seventy times seven, and for ever. Love is the difference between humanity and divinity. And love is the only weapon that can defeat the Devil. Satan had increasingly been having his way with men and women, until Love incarnate looked him in the eye and said, 'Away with you, Satan!' (Matthew 4:10). With God's Spirit in our hearts, we are equipped to give the Devil a similar come-uppance. But are we bold enough?

Love in the temple
It was sheer love that brought Simeon and Anna to Jesus in the temple that day when Mary had come for her purification rite and to make the formal presentation of her Child. And is it not love that brings us to worship each week? But the Church is in the world and of the world: God's love must extend from it, to everyone. Jesus came for all, not just for saints, or even for sinners who may be saints one day.

If 'the time has come for judgement to begin with the household of God', according to St Peter (1 Peter 4:17), surely with the household of God begins also love. Christians are the front-line troops, and as such don't follow others' initiations, but should start the spiritual ball rolling – whether of 'love, joy, peace, patience, kindness, generosity, faithfulness, gentleness or self-control' (Galatians 5:22–23). Love is limitless – and the river of God's love with its source in heaven, its appearing in Bethlehem and its growth into a mighty ocean from Calvary onwards, is unstoppable. One day, it will cover the earth – but somewhere in that mighty flood of love, will be the love that we have shown and shared.

God gives such a generous interest on the love we share, it's a wonder we don't share more of it more often. What will it be like, in eternity, to be living completely in love? Well, the more we practise it here, the less traumatic will be the transition.

> *Greater than my sin and condemnation,*
> *Great enough to give me full salvation,*
> *And to fill my soul with jubilation,*
> *Is the matchless love of God.*
>
> *Haldor Lillenas*

Family Service input
According to age, encourage the young people to draw or make a plan or copy of the Tabernacle, Solomon's or Herod's temple (see pp. 50–53).

Suggested hymns
A new commandment I give unto you; Gracious Spirit, Holy Ghost; Love divine, all loves excelling; O perfect love.

Fourth Sunday of Epiphany   *Second Service*
Tent and Temple   Ps. 34; 1 Chr. 29:6–19;
Acts 7:44–50 or John 4:19–29a

'Our ancestors had the tent of testimony in the wilderness ... And it was there until the time of David, who found favour with God ... But it was Solomon who built a house for [God].' Acts 7:44–47

God with us
When the Israelites operated a nomadic lifestyle, the tent of testimony rested where they rested, and moved when they moved. When they came to the promised land, and won or built towns and cities, they wanted also a more permanent house of prayer. The Christian Church has inherited the custom of having a 'fixed abode' for the worship of God. Is it a question of limiting or confining the Almighty on a local basis, or do we actually worship

Solomon's Temple

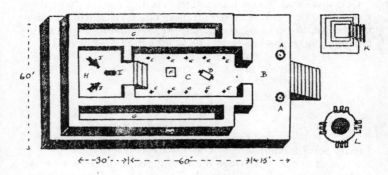

Ground Plan

A Freestanding pillars of Jachin and Boaz
B Vestibule (porch)
C Holy place (sanctuary)
D Table for loaves of proposition
E Ten candlesticks
F Altar of incense
G Three-storey side chambers
H Holy of Holies
I Ark of the covenant
J Cherubim
K Bronze altar
L Bronze sea

Front View

G Side Chambers (treasury)
A Pillars of Jachin and Boaz
K Bronze altar
L Bronze sea
M Flat roof

The Tabernacle

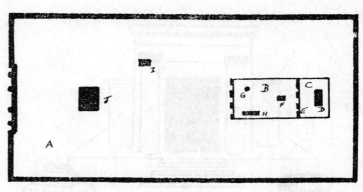

A Court of the worshippers
B Holy place
C Holy of holies
D Ark of the covenant
E Veil
F Altar of incense
G Menorah (candlestick)
H Table of shewbread
I Laver
J Altar of burnt-offering

Plan of the Second (Herod's) Temple on Zerubbabel's Foundations

(Zerubbabel's erected *c.* 520 BC) – Herod's begun 20 or 19 BC

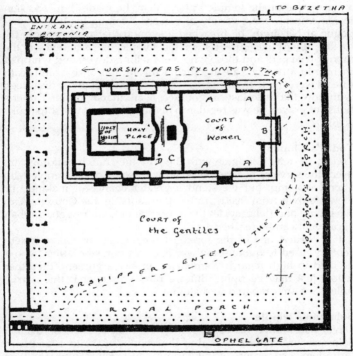

A Money chests
B Beautiful Gate

C Court of priests
D Bronze laver

him better in a recognized, consecrated and often elaborately decorated and apportioned building than, say, in a forest clearing, or
on the slopes or the summit of a mountain?

The example of Jesus

According to the Gospels, on the occasions when Jesus went into
a synagogue or the temple at Jerusalem, he made it an occasion
to remember – for a variety of reasons. Visiting his home synagogue at Nazareth, he preached a sermon that made people try
to kill him (Luke 4:16–30). In the temple, he rounded on the
money-changers and those who were selling doves, and whipped
them into a frenzy, causing such a furore that once again death
threats were made (Mark 11:15–18). Yet even though he disagreed
with how the ecclesiastical grandees were managing his Father's
house of prayer, he was regular in his attendance at worship (Luke
4:16).

Today's Church

Today, we may not agree with the way the church buildings are
used, the services ordered, or even with some of the people who
attend worship; but we stand a greater chance of making our
views known from inside, rather than outside, the Church. With
sensitivity and delicacy, let the matter be talked through, until an
agreement can be reached.

F. F. Bruce, one of the foremost theologians of the twentieth
century, used to quote some words of his minister father, whom
he held in high regard: 'Remember, in any argument, the other
fellow just may be right!' But we rarely discover if this is true
unless we are prepared to dialogue.

Solomon's temple

David had blotted his copybook on the marital front, so his son
Solomon was chosen by God as the builder of the first temple in
Jerusalem. The writers of the various construction accounts were
keen to give a pen-portrait of the building's magnificence and its
significance, to a nation who had come a long way since the
nomadic days of Abram. But reading between the lines, there must
have been those in Israel who were not so happy with the foreign
– alien – building style. Convincingly Phoenician, for example,
were the two pillars, Jachin and Boaz, flanking the pylon (porch).
The carved pomegranates and interior decoration were likewise

non-Jewish. Hiram of Tyre supplied the craftsmen, at Solomon's request, and they obviously took pride in illustrating their native traditions. There would be many Jews who would wrestle with their consciences over the overt compromise with the second commandment (Exodus 20:4)!

Today the Church is still largely 'established' in bricks and mortar, with an intricate system of traditions and government. More laity than ever before are playing key roles in decisions which are reflected in the daily ordering of services and outreach. Each and every Christian can make his or her voice and views known. On this Sunday when we reflect on the early tent of testimony and the later temple(s), can we also ponder today's Church and our participation in it?

Suggested hymns
How firm a foundation; Lord, her watch thy Church is keeping; The Church of God a kingdom is; The Church's one foundation.

Third Sunday before Lent (Proper 1) (Septuagesima) 8 February *Principal Service*
Life-Changing Decisions Isa. 6:1–8[9–13]; Ps. 138; 1 Cor. 15:1–11; Luke 5:1–11

'Then I heard the voice of the Lord saying, "Whom shall I send, and who will go for us?" And I said, "Here am I; send me!"' Isaiah 6:8
'When they had brought their boats to shore, they left everything, and followed him.' Luke 5:11

Strange conditions?
No visible security or tenure of office, no elaborately worked-out insurance and remuneration, no stated hours or provision for holiday entitlement . . . What strange conditions! Yet Isaiah, and later the disciples, set their hand to the plough and accepted the Lord's invitation.

Do we, as Christians, count the hours we give to the Lord? Do we take on more secular work, to the detriment of our work for God? Do we ever look at those outside the Church, and (even a tiny bit) envy their apparent freedom and/or affluence? If so, surely we could use God's time in better ways! For, at the rate of 60 seconds every minute, we are heading for an eternity where time will be no more. We may presently seem to have an abundance of time – and we have enough for what God wants us to do – but time is not for ever.

Beyond the point of no return
Are we looking to mere involvement or total commitment to Christ? And what (some may ask) is the difference? Take, for example, a plate of eggs and bacon: the eggs, we could say, are involved – but the pig is committed. Commitment is 'going wholeheartedly beyond the point of no return', giving oneself so completely to God that there is no going back. Among the 12 disciples, Judas was involved, while 11 were committed. Constrained, compelled by love for Christ, the Christian may not even be aware of the depth of his or her commitment – but others will recognize it. No committed believer in the Bible ever declared he or she was filled with the Holy Spirit – but others noticed, and remarked on it (see, e.g., Luke 1:80; 4:14; Acts 7:55).

The threshhold of Lent
Today we stand on the threshhold of Lent, on the first of the three '-gesima' Sundays leading up to Ash Wednesday: a very appropriate time to take stock of our own commitment. We cannot always 'see ourselves as others see us', and most of us are too shy to ask others how they think we are doing; so it's probably a case of self-assessment and review. Let us not gloss over our weak points, nor bask for too long on those with which we are best pleased. God is a God of mercy, justice and understanding: in all likelihood he will view us in a better light than we see ourselves – and, as St Paul says, we see now as 'in a mirror dimly' (1 Cor. 13:12).

Strength for service
God is not looking for physical Primo Carneras, simply committed souls who, like Isaiah and the disiples, will volunteer for whatever God has in mind. We can rest assured that the opportunities that come knocking at our door have not come to the wrong address. God is not in the business of making mistakes. If we decline these opportunities, it is tantamount to throwing a present from our earthly parents back in their face.

No conditions
We may try to bargain with God, to lay down conditions of service, to establish some sort of security or verification: 'Lord, if you will guarantee such and such, then I'll go forward . . .' After all, Gideon set out his fleece.

But in Gideon's day Christ had not died and risen again, nor had the Holy Spirit been given. We are to trust – in a God who does not let folk down. We are to rely on a Saviour who can break out of death's clutches. We are to speak as the Holy Spirit directs (Matthew 10:20; par. Luke 12:12).

A dependence that gives us so much freedom is a vocation that is unique and everlasting, as high as the heavens and as broad as the earth; it could only come from God. And it's on offer to you – and to me!

Family Service input
Write a hymn for Septuagesima.

Suggested hymns
And can it be that I should gain; Forth in thy name, O Lord, I go; I, the Lord of sea and sky; We sing the praise of him who died.

Third Sunday before Lent (Septuagesima)
Second Service   **All for Jesus**   Ps. [1]2; Wis. 6:1–21
or Hos. 1; Col. 3:1–22 or Matthew 5:13–20

'And whatever you do, in word or deed, do everything in the name of the Lord Jesus, giving thanks to God the Father through him.' Colossians 3:17

Recipe for life
In a few words, this verse is a recipe for life. Show thankfulness and gratitude to God in all you say and in all you do. In his word he has already said all we need to know; in his creativity, sacrifice and resurrection, he has already done more than we shall ever be called upon to do. The greatest truths have been said, the hardest acts have been accomplished; we have no cause to complain about our lesser Calvaries.

'Thank you'

From our childhood, the policy of saying 'Thank you' for every-thing from a toffee to a compliment is endorsed. At times we may forget, or give thanks unwillingly, but we tend to accept that exercising gratitude is the 'correct thing'. Thankfulness – even as a token gesture – does not feature as large in the Bible, the few instances in the Gospels being when Jesus gave thanks for the loaves and fishes before multiplying them among thousands (John 6:11); his thanks over the bread and wine in the cenacle (Matthew 26:26–27); and the day when he healed ten lepers, only one of whom returned to say 'Thank you' (Luke 17:15); the NRSV, unlike the KJV, equates 'thanks' in this latter instance with 'praise'. Per-haps, were we to make the same connection, our lives would have more praises and less pleas, more thanks and less negative thinking.

Doing everything in Jesus' name, no matter how menial the task, elevates it from the mundane to the sublime. It invokes the Lord in its execution, and shares the ownership, the expertise, the outcome and the impact. It turns the trivial into something important for God, and gives a new dimension to our life and our reason for living.

In the Second World War, the Catholic sisters in Belgium and other occupied continental countries, who were forced to admit more and more of the enemy forces into their hospitals, were often torn between their natural aversion, their faith, and their professional training. 'All for Jesus!' they would tell themselves and their co-workers, as they fetched and carried for those whose bullets had shattered their families' lives. And the three simple little words made the impossible possible.

'All for Jesus!' Can we say this about every facet of our lives, or are we holding anything back? Are our motives divided between Jesus and someone or something else? If so, let us come to God about it – for the Lord will keep reminding us of it until we have had the matter out with him.

'All for Jesus!' If we take it seriously, it means working for his honour, not our own; the advancement of his kingdom, not our own sphere of influence; the sharing of his gospel, not our own philosophy: himself, not ourselves. Every reader of the Gospels knows about John the Baptist – yet we do not *know* John, simply because everything he did and said was not for himself, but all for Jesus. We all know about Stephen, the first martyr, but we do not know him, because he pointed those who heard him preach away from himself and to Jesus.

In today's world, self-effacement is not popular; the world loves the 'rags-to-riches' story, the struggle and achievement of the 'self-made man'. How it must grieve the Creator, to hear of anyone thinking themselves, or being called, 'self-made'! Yet in a sense, it is true: what such a person has 'made' is the 'self' – the antithesis to the Christian way of life: 'Then Jesus told his disciples, "If any want to become my followers, let them *deny themselves* and take up their cross and follow me"' (Matthew 16:24; cf. Mark 8:34; Luke 9:23).

Suggested hymns
All for Jesus; God, we praise you, God we bless you; Now thank we all our God; Take up thy cross, the Saviour said.

Second Sunday before Lent (Sexagesima)
15 February   *Principal Service*   Divine Planning
Gen. 2:4b–9, 15–25; Ps. 65; Rev. 4; Luke 8:22–25
'After this I looked, and there in heaven a door stood open! And the first voice, which I had heard speaking to me like a trumpet, said, "Come up here, and I will show you what must take place after this."' Revelation 4:1

Supreme headquarters
G. B. Caird has seen, in this verse of Revelation 4:1, John being

summoned to the control-room at Supreme Headquarters ... a room lined with maps, in which someone has placed clusters of little flags ... It is war-time, and the flags represent units of a military command. The movement of flags may mean one of two things: either that changes have taken place on the battlefield, with which the map must be made to agree, or that an order is being issued for troop movements, and the flags are being moved to the new positions the units are expected to occupy ... The strange and complex symbols of John's vision are, like the flags in this parable, the pictorial counterpart of earthly realities; and these symbols too may be either determinative (what is to happen) or descriptive (what has happened). (G. B. Caird, *The Revelation of St John the Divine* (A. & C. Black, 1966), pp. 60, 61)

Certainly the Divine Court is in session, and something is about to happen (if you can't wait, read about it in chapter 5!). The *trumpet* recalls God's presence on Sinai, signalled by the penetrating blast of a horn (Exodus 19:18–20). Through the open door, John in his vision enters and sees God, as a serene, scintillating beauty, glowing with the lustre of gemstones (cf. James 1:17; 1 John 1:5).

The emerald rainbow
What is this rainbow? The Greek word *iris* suggests a complete circle, perhaps suggesting to John the need for a peaceful, complete relationship with God.

From the throne came lightnings, voices and thunderings (cf. Exodus 19:16–19). Flashes of lightning can illuminate, but they can also prove fatal; these lightnings from God's throne speak of revelation (illumination) and his fiery judgement. The voices (cf. Romans 10:18) could signify the growing number of Christian preachers and teachers on earth.

The sea of glass
Doesn't this represent the pure, cleansing word of God? (Cf. Ephesians 5:26 and John 15:3: 'You have already been cleansed by the word that I have spoken to you.'). Whoever is admitted into the presence of God, must have been thoroughly cleansed by his purifying, life-giving word. This continues to cleanse, as it grows, in the heart of a Christian – as plants and herbs grow in a garden, each one in its unique way helping to purify the atmosphere and spread its beneficial influence.

The four living creatures
The prophet Ezekiel had seen God enthroned on a celestial chariot, accompanied by living creatures (Ezekiel 1:5–11, 22–28). In a later vision, Ezekiel again saw this chariot, but this time he described the living creatures as 'cherubs' (Ezekiel 10:9–15). The four living creatures seen by John must surely represent the many cherubs of God, high-ranking creatures in his divine organization. John would see nothing strange in cherubs being so close to God himself, for in early days, when the tabernacle was the place of wor-

ship, there were two golden cherubs on the ark of the covenant; and from between these cherubs God's voice gave commands to the nation (Exodus 25:22; Psalm 80:1).

This wonderful fourth chapter of the Apocalypse gives us a vision we need to return to time and again. It speaks of the life that has been, to the life that is, of the life that will be. It has been given to us for a multifaceted purpose – to stretch our minds; to encourage us and thrill us; to link cause and effect; to stimulate anticipation of eternity; and to give us renewed awe, wonder and respect for God. Is this all? By no means! Let each of us seek our own revelations from God, in prayer.

Family Service input
Plan a Bible Garden (see suggestions below) in a portion of the churchyard/vicarage garden, etc., or even in pots on a sunny windowsill.

A Bible Garden

Herbs – Culinary and Biblical

Old Testament

Garlic Egyptian onion Leek Melon Cucumber	Herbs of Egypt
Coriander	Wilderness wanderings
Horehound Lettuce Chicory Endive Sorrel Horseradish	Bitter herbs of the Passion

New Testament
Lilies of the field (anemone?)   (Matthew 6:28–29)

Mint
Rue
Cumin
Dill
} (Matthew 23:23)

Grapevine (Matthew 7:16)
Fig tree (Luke 6:44)
Mustard (Matthew 13:31, 32)
Mulberry (Luke 17:6)
Olive (Luke 10:34)
Aloes (John 19:39)

Suggested hymns
All creatures of our God and King; Angel-voices, ever singing;
Jerusalem the golden; Ye choirs of new Jerusalem.

Second Sunday before Lent   *Second Service*
How Many Times?   Ps. 147; Gen. 1:1–2:3;
Matthew 6:25–34
*'[Jesus said] "Therefore I tell you, do not worry ... Can any of you by
worrying add a single hour to your span of life? ... Why do you
worry ... ? ... Therefore do not worry ... Do not worry ..."' Matthew
6:25ff.*

Getting the message across
How many times does Jesus have to tell us not to worry? Whenever
we wake in the morning, and whatever the weather is doing, most
of us (it's virtually guaranteed) will be worrying over something
before we've got out of bed. How did we pick up the habit? Even
more important, how can we kick it? Only by catching ourselves
as quickly as possible, asking (yet again) for divine help, and
offloading the worry on to God: time after time after time, for
we've become such proficient worriers, the habit will not be beaten
in a hurry.

The doubting disciple
We may home in on doubting Thomas and decide that, since his
doubts were convincingly demolished after one short week (John

20:26), a bit of worrying is not too serious. But worry – any worry – begins as doubt: doubt that God is in control, that he loves us, that good is stronger than evil, that our Creator leads us to no challenge we are not equipped by his grace to meet. Worry is doubt that is out of control. It's bad news, and Jesus simply says, Don't do it! Worry is not only a lack of faith in ourselves (on its own, that would not matter), but a lack of faith that God *is*, that he is who he is, and that he is *good*.

The impossible ideal?
Is it possible to have a life without worry? No. Is it possible to *live* without worry? Yes. Jesus tells us plainly that in this world we shall have problems (John 16:33); but our faith can make the difference between allowing ourselves to worry over these problems, or meeting them in the strength of Christ, with confidence that he will see us through.

Worrying at its worst, is sinful, because it runs contrary to the will of Jesus; at its best, it is anti-social. The people we meet have enough problems of their own, without hearing about our fears and phobias. It has been said that only our best friends are privileged to hear our good news: we are less discriminatory when it comes to moaning and groaning. Why can we not start enlarging the number of 'best friends'?

Take a leaf out of God's book
In the earliest days of the world, God kept on creating things that he saw as 'good'; at every stage of the enterprise, he ran the early equivalent of a 'time-and-motion' study on his work to date – and the verdict was invariably 'good' (Genesis 1:10, 12, 18, 21, 25, 31). And each day, as the sun infuses the sky and the earth with new light and new warmth, Nature (who has not fallen into the habit of worrying) turns her face to the light and prepares to give the new day her best.

> *No, the heart that has truly loved never forgets,*
> *But as truly loves on to the close –*
> *As the sunflower turns on her god when he sets*
> *The same look that she turned when he rose.*
>
> Thomas Moore (1779–1852)

63

We are not sun-worshippers: rather than heliotropism we need to cultivate theotropism; for with our sights set on God, there is every possibility that we shall praise, trust and step out in faith – instead of giving way to worrying. Next time you feel worry stealing a march on you, turn to look at God: how would Jesus cope with your problem? What does God's word have to say on the subject? Or, if the worry is forgettable, do just that and get involved in helping other people cope with their troubles. It does work!

Suggested hymns
Happy are they, they that love God; Help us to help each other, Lord; How firm a foundation; Praise, O praise our God and King.

Sunday next before Lent (Quinquagesima)
22 February   *Principal Service*   Revealed in Christ
Ex. 34:29–35; Ps. 99; 2 Cor. 3:12–4:2;
Luke 9:28–36[37–43a]

'When one turns to the Lord, the veil is removed.' 2 Corinthians 3:16
'And while [Jesus] was praying, the appearance of his face changed, and his clothes became dazzling white.' Luke 9:29

Without a veil
Moses had veiled the reflected glory of God in his face, when he returned from meeting the Lord (Exodus 34:35); but he removed the veil when drawing aside to commune with God. Jesus, on the other hand, allowed the disciples to see the full glory of his transfiguration.

One can drive into the country on a morning when the thick mist cuts visibility to a few yards, yet travel over the same route a few hours later, and the sunshine lights up the view for miles. The beauty had been there before, but hidden by a blanket of fog.

The overshadowing cloud
Fog, mist, cloud. Perhaps some will tell us these are three names for the same thing, which has been with us since the world began. But the disciples on Tabor experienced a very special sort of cloud – so special, it has always been spoken of in the singular (Luke

9:34, 35). It was no ordinary cloud, but the glory, the brightness, the majesty, the beauty, which surrounds God himself, hiding him from the eyes of most ordinary folk – because most ordinary folk can't cope with the brilliance of God's glory. This *Shekinah*-glory shone in the face of Moses, and shone even brighter around Jesus on the mount. It ushered in the laws, or commandments, of the Old Covenant – and it was there again around the Lamb who had come with the New Covenant: the promise to us, through the sacrifice of Calvary, of eternal life.

A new dimension

We are taken, with today's lessons, however briefly, into a new dimension – a dimension where the living and so-called 'departed' meet and mingle across the centuries; where bodies materialize and then dematerialize back into the ether; where suddenly the chasm between the physical world and the spiritual world seems to be no chasm at all. For a brief, shining, glory-filled moment, we transcend time and space, life and death, logic, reason and common sense.

Back to earth

And then, the readings over, we are brought back to the present reality: we are once again confined, it seems, to these physical bodies – bodies which each have an average of 20 square feet of skin, with up to 5 million hairs, 650 muscles, 206 bones, 100 joints, 60,000 miles of arteries, veins and capillaries, 13,000 million nerve cells . . . We are, as the psalmist says, 'wonderfully made' (Psalm 139:13). Yet God, in the transfiguration experience, did even *more* wonderful things with the human body. If nothing else, today's readings should open up for us new possibilities, new ways in which the Lord's *Shekinah*-glory can influence and enlighten our lives, and others' lives; new ways in which God, in these precious verses, may be leading us into a deeper knowledge of himself, a greater awareness of faith, a re-evaluation of our worth and uniqueness in his sight.

The disciples on the mount were given their vision to encourage them to listen to Jesus. Today, God gives us spiritual insights, spiritual light – *Shekinah*-light – for exactly the same reason. If, in the words of St Peter, we are not growing 'in grace and knowledge of our Lord and Saviour Jesus Christ' (1 Peter 3:18), we are not shining with sufficient *Shekinah*-glory to be noticed.

Let us pray that in the coming season of Lent, God will shine his glory even brighter on our prayers and praises, our worship and witnessing, our meditation and melody-making – and to him be all the glory.

Family Service input
Compile a prayer collection for use at services, in Bible groups and for private devotions at home or in hospital.

Suggested hymns
Christ, whose glory fills the skies; In days of old on Sinai; Jesus, these eyes have never seen; 'Tis good, Lord, to be here.

Sunday next before Lent *Second Service*
The Time Has Come Ps. 89:1–18; Ex. 3:1–6;
John 12:27–36a

'Jesus answered, "This voice has come for your sake, not for mine. Now is the judgement of this world; now the ruler of this world will be driven out."' John 12:30–31

Success in sight
We can sense the anticipation, even relief, in these words of Jesus. He had said, a little while before, 'I have a baptism with which to be baptized, and what stress I am under until it is completed!' (Luke 12:50). Now, completion is in sight; but he is thinking not of himself (though he is fully aware of the pain it will cost him to reach completion), but of those for whom he has come and for whom he will suffer. This is selflessness on the grandest scale of all time.

We can safely believe that at no point in his ministry Jesus ever considered the possible failure of his mission. It was God's will, and would therefore be fulfilled – as surely as after Jesus had said to his friends, 'Let us go across to the other side', the wildest storm possible could not have stood in his way (Mark 4:35ff.). But the anguish that tore at his heart as his mission progressed was the unbelief and animosity he experienced, and the hold that Satan had strengthened among people of different levels in society, varying creeds and none. He knew also that even with his sacrifice completed, the ongoing life of the Church would be the responsibility of 11 frail disciples; but the realization that his Holy Spirit could turn fragility into strength would even out the equation. There was every reason to be positive!

Positive thinking

Can we, with our lesser problems, be as positive? The Holy Spirit is not on record as ever having been recalled. He is still here, empowering frail folk to turn the world around for God. Satan, too, is still around, attempting as ever to even out the equation from a negative angle.

The challenge in this reading from St John's Gospel faces us as representatives and ambassadors for Christ today: how are we making a difference for Christ?

High-profile disciples?

It can be very fulfilling to live and work quietly, efficiently, diligently and faithfully; but are we sure that this is the mission and ministry that God has in mind for us? Have we from time to time felt a calling to something else, a wider field of witness, a change to our ordered existence? If the 11 disciples had stayed in Jerusalem (as, for a time, they decided to do, until increased persecution forced them out), would the rest of the world still be waiting for the gospel? Let's not forget that, two thousand years on, far too many people are still waiting for the gospel.

Satan loses less sleep over *quiet* Christians, than those who stick their spiritual heads above the parapet and give the old Devil a fair run for his money. When communism was at its peak, it was often heard: 'If the Christians were as fervent in proclaiming their beliefs, the Church would grow.' It had an effect, though not the effect the communists wanted to see.

What do we need, as the match to light the fuse of Christian boldness? Surely it is being lit this very day, with these verses from St John's Gospel. There is a time and a place for living quietly – but also one for standing up and being heard. Let us pray that God will show each of us which time is for us. His answers may surprise us, as he reveals more of his Spirit in us.

We are destined for glory: our realization of identity in Christ can involve millions more besides ourselves.

A charge to keep I have; Father, I place into your hands; Father, we love you (Glorify your name); Just as I am.

Ash Wednesday   25 February   *Principal Service*
Lenten Expectations   Joel 2:1–2, 12–17 or Isa. 58:1–12; Ps. 51:1–17; 2 Cor. 5:20b—6:10; Matthew 6:1–6, 16–21 or John 8:1–11

'*[So we are ambassadors for Christ] since God is making his appeal through us; we entreat you on behalf of Christ, be reconciled to God. For our sake he made him to be sin who knew no sin, so that in him we might become the righteousness of God.' 2 Corinthians 5:20–21*

What do we expect?
A young man was accepted for training as a Trappist monk. Silence was, of course, the rule of the monastery, outside service times – apart from two words which could be addressed to the abbot once a year. At the end of his first year, the young man told the abbot: 'I'm cold.' 'Go away and reflect on it,' was the reply. Another year went by. 'I'm hungry,' said the young man. 'Go and reflect on it,' he was told again. At the end of the third year, 'I'm off,' he told the abbot, who said, sadly: 'I'm not surprised – you've done nothing but complain ever since you arrived.'

Apocryphal, perhaps! Yet how often reality is a long way from our expectations of life and situations. And today many people have preconceptions of what it means to be a Christian and a member of the Church. And some, when they join the Church, find it very different from what they had expected. If one were to ask a thousand people to say what they thought the Church stood for, and how it operates (or should operate), and why it does what it does, one would get a thousand different answers.

At the Jordan
What expectations had the people gathered at the Jordan, when Jesus was baptized? Probably most of them had not clarified in their minds what was happening. Then the Spirit took Jesus into the wilderness, to get his mission straight with God . . . while life in the rest of the world went on as normal.

Christ was to come up against the religious hierarchy of the time, throughout his mission. He was to object to their methods, their mismanagement of his Father's house – but all of this would not stop his regular attendance at worship.

What has changed
We still find plenty to puzzle over in our Christian life; but the Church is primarily the place where we can hear and read the word of God in the context of corporate worship. Christ suffered the desolation and solitude of the desert, so that we should not need to. As members of his body, we need him, but we also need each other, and the strength that corporate worship, corporate witness, corporate work for God gives. And we need it especially in Lent, as Satan remembers that it was after this time that Jesus emerged as Victor, and he, Satan, was forced to eat humble pie.

God's precious word
It was the word of God that Jesus used every time in the wilderness temptations to defeat Satan – even though Satan grew so daring that he was quoting scripture to Jesus. But Satan was not only tangling with a scripture-filled opponent, but with the word of God himself – the word made flesh, the word incarnate. It is this word on which we need to go to work, in Lent, if we also are to meet and overcome Satan's advances. St Paul underlined its importance in his letter to the Romans:

> *How are they to call on one in whom they have not believed? And how are they to believe in one of whom they have never heard? And how are they to hear without someone to proclaim him? ... Faith comes from what is heard, and what is heard comes through the word of Christ.*
>
> *Romans 10:14, 17*

The ancient Jews used to bind around their heads little leather pouches, or phylacteries, in which were folded texts of the law. They then had a visible reminder of God's word – in much the same way that today we wear our ashy cross, to remind us of the sacrifice Jesus made for us. But there is no real substitute for having the word of God in our hearts, as Jesus had it.

Our expectations of Lent may vary – may even, like the young

69

Trappist novice, be very different from reality. But can we make time to consider what God's expectations of us may be?

Suggested hymns
Be thou my vision; Christian, seek not yet repose; Father of heaven, whose love profound; Forty days and forty nights.

Ash Wednesday *Second Service (and Litany for Lent)* **Drawing Near to God** Ps. 102; Isa. 1:10–18; Luke 15:11–32

'Come, now, let us argue it out, says the Lord: though your sins are like scarlet, they shall be like snow; though they are red like crimson, they shall become like wool.' Isaiah 1:18

Litany for Lent: Attende, Domine

> *To thee, Redeemer, King of highest heaven,*
> *Lift we our eyes in grief and deep abasement;*
> *Listen, O Saviour, to our supplication.*
> **Hearken, O Lord, have mercy upon us,**
> **For we have sinned against thee.**
>
> Head of the Corner, right hand of the Father,
> Way of salvation, gate of life eternal,
> Wash thou away the stain of our offences.
> **Hearken, O Lord, have mercy upon us,**
> **For we have sinned against thee.**
>
> Lord, we beseech thee, from thy throne of glory,
> Bow down thine ear to hear our cry of sorrow;
> Look down in mercy on our sore transgressions.
> **Hearken, O Lord, have mercy upon us,**
> **For we have sinned against thee.**
>
> All our misdoings now we lay before thee,
> Unveil with contrite heart each guilty secret;
> Saviour, in pity grant us thy forgiveness.
> **Hearken, O Lord, have mercy upon us,**
> **For we have sinned against thee.**

Guiltless, a captive taken unresisting,
By false accusers brought to condemnation;
Save, Lord, and help the souls thou hast redeem-ed.
Hearken, O Lord, have mercy upon us,
For we have sinned against thee.

The God of the impossible

By the grace of God, our sins of scarlet can become as pure white wool; by the grace of God, our purple past can be changed to glorious purity; our expectations of death have, by the same divine grace, become already the hope of eternal life. Our God is the God of the impossible: the God of the miraculous, the wonderful, the eternally dependable. When the Devil comes against us – as he will this Lent – let us wrap the armour of these divine truths around our hearts.

But there is one condition to be met before these truths can become reality in our lives: our ongoing dialogue with God. 'Come now, let us argue it out,' God is still demanding – and that is not too strong a word. Let us, therefore, order our case with the Almighty, setting out the reason why he should pardon us.

God already knows

God already knows the reason. It hung on a cross at Calvary. This is our only plea, the only argument that carries weight with the Almighty.

> *Jesus, the Name high over all,*
> *In hell, or earth, or sky;*
> *Angels and men before it fall,*
> *And devils fear and fly . . .*
>
> *We have no other argument,*
> *We want no other plea;*
> *It is enough that Jesus died,*
> *And that he died for me.*
>
> *Charles Wesley*

'Pleading the blood of Jesus' isn't a phrase heard as much today as a century or so ago; but in Lent – as at any time – it is our insurance against attack from ulterior forces. It stands between us and the enemy. Paradoxically, it washes away the accusing scarlet of our sins, into a whiteness that is Christ's alone. A negation of this precious, cleansing blood is, in effect, to say 'Thanks, but no thanks' to life in Christ. 'Come now, let us argue it out' – surely we know whose side we want to be on?

Getting real over sin
In past times, the religious in monasteries and convents were accused of being overscrupulous with regard to sin. God does not want us to navel-gaze to the point where our daily ministry suffers. He simply wants us to remember that the 'blood of Jesus cleanses us from *all* sin' (1 John 1:7) – big sin, little sin, remembered or forgotten. May we accept this, and go forward in the joy of the new start that God gives us.

Suggested hymns
Dear Lord and Father of mankind; Jesus, lover of my soul; Lord Jesus, think on me; O Jesus, I have promised.

First Sunday of Lent   29 February
Principal Service   **Making the Right Time**
Deut. 26:1–11; Ps. 91:1–2, 9–16; Rom. 10:8b–13;
Luke 4:1–13
'When the devil had finished every test, he departed from [Jesus] until an opportune time.' Luke 4:13

The Devil's accommodation
This text points up an important difference between God and the Devil (you will no doubt be able to find many more): while God's work is to go on constantly ('Proclaim the message; be persistent whether the time is favourable or unfavourable', 2 Timothy 4:2), the Devil picks and chooses his times – for his strength is second-best, and thus he cannot afford to use time with the freedom that God employs. Can we not take great encouragement from this!

There are those who suggest that Jesus was *alone* in the desert – that the temptations came to him as bad thoughts. Do you believe that? Satan may come at us with bad thoughts – among all the rest of his weaponry. But is it possible to believe that the Son of God, without spot of sin, ever did (or ever could) admit Satan into his mind or body? Is it not preferable to suggest that, *in some form*, Satan came against Jesus – from outside him – in that desert? Later, Jesus told his friends, 'Whoever has seen me, has seen the Father' (John 14:9), 'The Father and I are one' (John 10:30). Surely there is no way God the Father could ever think an unworthy thought.

Jesus supports us!

Nothing helps us more than the knowledge that someone has faith in us. Primarily, that someone is Jesus – who has called us, chosen us and empowered us. He is wanting us, willing us, to make it. His victory in the wilderness gives us hope to carry on. As one of our modern hymns puts it:

> *Past put behind us, for the future take us,*
> *Lord of our lives, to live for Christ alone.*
>
> Timothy Dudley-Smith

He is saying to us now, while the imposition of last Wednesday's ashes is fresh in our minds: 'What are you going to *do* for me, this Lent?'

Well, what is to be our answer? He doesn't ask, 'What are you *not* going to do?' Frankly, Satan is not going to worry if we give up chocolate – and sugar as well – for Lent. But what are we going to do, positively, for Jesus? We have six weeks before the triumph of Easter: six weeks to build on the victory Jesus won for us in the desert. In six weeks' time, the spring will have come, the days will be longer, the clocks will have been altered and the sun will be warmer. But, what will we have done?

Making Lent matter more than a few uneaten chocolates, and a couple of pounds of sugar still taking up space on the shelf, is surely an acknowledgement of the work Jesus has done for us. He didn't stop at giving things up – although he did give up a lot: glory, freedom, heaven itself, for thirty-odd years. But can we reflect on all he *did*, as we start another Lent: the preaching, teaching, healing, loving, caring, sharing. There is so much scope here for us to do something this Lent which will not only make a difference in our lives, but in the lives of others.

Let us start with our household of God, which St Peter tells us is the place to start (1 Peter 4:17), but let us not stop here: there is a lot of room, and millions of people, out there, in what is also God's world and God's workplace.

Family Service input
Ask the young people to draw, model or describe the various parts of the church, and how they complement each other in worship and at the other times when the church is being used.

Suggested hymns
Awake our souls, away our fears; I'm not ashamed to own my Lord; Seek ye first the kingdom of God; What a Friend we have in Jesus.

First Sunday of Lent *Second Service*
I . . . I . . . I   Ps. 119:73–88; Jonah 3; Luke 18:9–14
'God, I thank you that I am not like other people . . . I fast twice a week; I give a tenth of all my income.' Luke 18:11–12

Top of the list
It comes top of the list of favourite subjects – ourselves: that wonderful person whom we believe we know so well, who comes through all crises, who has most (if not all) of the complaints known to science, yet who still manages to do and say great things and to influence a lot of people; who knows most things about most folk, yet who has somehow been lumbered with the worst neighbours and fortune anyone could possibly have. There is something of the Pharisee in the best of us!

Anyway, who would want to identify with the tax-collector? Even his profession is a massive turn-off, and he's not eloquent in prayer: how close can you get to God, in seven little words? Well, much closer than the Pharisee managed, for all his high-sounding rhetoric. Let's be honest, there is something also of the tax-collector in the worst of us!

Teaching with humour

When Jesus told this parable, surely he did it with a twinkle in his eye and a smile hovering on his lips, for it encourages more than it discourages. It is a model of *how*, as well as of *how not* to pray, live, worship and interact with God and our fellow human beings. The two men are Everyman, and thus speak to us all. While we hope we don't emulate the Pharisee, most of us don't go as far in the direction of humility as the tax-collector: we fall somewhere in between.

Directional prayer

While the Pharisee was ostensibly directing his prayer to God, in essence it was a self-extolling, self-explanatory eulogy: 'Look what a fine, upstanding, religious man am I!' The tax-collector's restrained but heartfelt seven words were aimed right at the merciful heart of God, homing in on the Lord's goodness, and his own unworthiness.

No, we are seldom so self-effacing. We may ask for mercy, but only rarely do we simply call ourselves sinners. We may confess, but in the same prayer usually manage to include some wants.

True prayer

What, then, is true prayer? What is God looking for in our dealings with him?

Worship? Yes, let us spend some time in every prayer praising God simply because he is God.

Confession? Of course, for none of us is perfect, so there will always be something to confess.

Gratitude? Without doubt – and if we will never come to the end of thanking God for his goodness, it doesn't mean we must never begin our thanksgivings.

Intercession? Again, yes – our prayers for others can have wide-reaching effects. They also give balance to our lives and reduce the times 'I' and 'me' and 'mine' and 'my' form part of our prayers.

We are not to worry about how to pray what we are encouraged to pray. God has the advantage of knowing our innermost thoughts and he can meld these with our spoken prayers to achieve the message we intend him to receive.

Prayer is the soul's sincere desire,
Uttered or unexpressed;
The motion of a hidden fire
That trembles in the breast.

Prayer is the simplest form of speech
That infant lips can try;
Prayer the sublimest strains that reach
The Majesty on high.

O thou by whom we come to God,
The Life, the Truth, the Way,
The path of prayer thyself hast trod,
Lord, teach us how to pray.

James Montgomery

Suggested hymns
Lord, speak to me, that I may speak; Lord, teach us how to pray
aright; Lord of the Church, we pray for our renewing; Pray when
the morn is breaking.

Second Sunday of Lent   7 March
Principal Service   **Expecting Jesus**   Gen. 15:1–12,
17–18; Ps. 27; Phil. 3:17–4:1; Luke 13:31–35
*'Our citizenship is in heaven, and it is from there that we are expecting
a Saviour, the Lord Jesus Christ.' Philippians 3:20*

Jesus will come
St Paul had not read Acts; how could he? It was being written by
him (and, to a lesser extent, by others) each day of his missionary
life; but Peter and the disciples – or, more likely, Luke, his travelling companion – would have told him of the angel's words at
Christ's ascension: 'This Jesus, who has been taken up from you
into heaven, will come in the same way as you saw him go into
heaven' (Acts 1:11). Without going into the arguments of either
metaphysics or astrophysics, if Jesus ascended we can surely
believe that he can return.

'Our citizenship is in heaven.' The language is simple and matter-of-fact. We are on the electoral roll of heaven, fully integrated members awaiting our final transfer. The fare is paid, the accommodation is prepared. We have just a little time left here, to improve our talents for the great day, and then we shall be off.

> *I know not when my Lord will come,*
> *At night or mid-day fair,*
> *Nor if I'll walk the vale with him,*
> *Or meet him in the air.*
> *But I know whom I have believed,*
> *And am persuaded*
> *That he is able*
> *To keep that which I've committed*
> *Unto him against that day.*
>
> Daniel W. Whittle (1840–1901)

In this greatest of all contract situations, if anyone backs out it will not be Christ.

Looking out for Jesus

'Hark! the glad sound, the Saviour comes!' we cheerfully sing at Christmas, and come to church to greet a Child in the manger. But how often do we look out for Christ's second coming? Are we ready for it, or would he disturb our long-range plans and cherished ambitions? Are we concentrating on sharing the gospel with as many people as we can, who may otherwise meet their Lord unprepared? 'To expect' means 'to await with eagerness'. Is the second coming – the Parousia – at the forefront of our expectations? Probably not, for it has delayed for nearly two millennia: why should it occur in our brief time here?

Only God knows

Only God knows the day and hour: it is so precise (Mark 13:32). He has it planned with the same attention to detail that he has shown in the creation and all subsequent history. Shall we – if we have already died and gone to glory – shall we come with Jesus? Or, if we are still here, will we recognize him when he comes? Yes – by the print of the nails, and the wound in his side. And what will he ask? Or will he need to ask at all? Isn't God writing up the record day by day? The twenty-ninth chapter of Acts must be the longest ever written – and it is still not complete.

Daily blessings

When we wake in the morning, can we not pray that God will help us to be a blessing to someone – anyone – that day? In heaven, everything will be blessed by God, and the more we have shared his blessings here, the more 'at home' we shall be when we have made the transition. For earth is not unconnected with heaven: the same God is Lord of both; the earth, in an indefinable way, is the road that leads us to the Eternal City – 'For here we have no lasting city, but we are looking for the city that is to come' (Hebrews 13:14), whose builder and maker is God. If for no other reason than this, we can expect it to outshine anything we have either known on earth, or can imagine.

Family Service input

Share with the young people the story behind 'In heavenly love abiding', and either encourage them to write a complementary verse, or to illustrate Anna Waring's lines (see below).

Suggested hymns

All my hope on God is founded; In heavenly love abiding; Jerusalem the golden; Light's abode, celestial Salem.

Hymn Stories

In heavenly love abiding

Anna Laetitia Waring (1823–1910) wrote these words when still quite young. It is a hymn of hope, well grounded in faith, and has in recent years been taken from its Free Church background into mainstream Protestant hymnals. It has given courage and hope to many mourners at countless funerals, but is by no means confined to times of sorrow. Anna was not yet 30 when she composed it, and she was to live for another 60 years before going to her own 'green pastures' ahead.

She remained unmarried, giving herself to learning Hebrew in order to get to the heart of the Old Testament scriptures, especially the poetry of the Psalms. She was also active in many good works, in particular supporting the Discharged Prisoners' Aid Society, visiting prisoners in Bristol and helping to get ex-prisoners on their feet.

The hymn is capable of being sung with either this life or the next – or both – in mind. In the mercy of God, we do not know the future – whether beyond the grave, or even within the next minute. So Anna's words form a hymn for all occasions, all circumstances, all situations and all time.

Second Sunday of Lent *Second Service*
Stern, but Glorious Ps. 135; Jer. 22:1–9, 13–17;
Luke 14:27–33

'[Jesus said], "So therefore, none of you can become my disciples if you do not give up all your possessions."' Luke 14:33

A calculated risk?
The conditions are stern, but they are glorious. Jesus does not hold out 'pie in the sky', or the prospect of material advancement (at least, in the way that the world understands advancement). So he is looking for people as serious and determined to make a success of their Christian life as the man who calculates the cost of building a house or going to war. Life with Christ will be as tough, but the rewards will be longer-lasting, than any secular endeavour.

'None of you . . . if you do not give up *all* . . .' This is no-compromise, all-or-nothing language. Can we meet Jesus' conditions? Not in our own strength, but in his plus ours. But what does 'give up' mean? Actually parting with everything, or trusting in God more than in possessions? (And do these two actually mean the same thing?) This is the challenge of the Christian call, and we duck it at our peril. If we place our trust in God, it may be that he will ask for everything else. Or it may be that he will show us how to use everything else in his service, according to our situation. Are the talents he has given us – whether of teaching, preaching, languages, medical or other skills – dependent on our having material back-up? We live in a world where personal worth is reckoned by one's bank balance. While we live, the question is: 'How much has he got?' And when we are gone, 'How much did she leave?' Surely life – and death – are worth more than this!

A genuine commitment

It may be easy to say, 'I'm a Christian', but Jesus is looking for a genuine commitment, which is anything but easy. Words without dedication are empty; true dedication doesn't shout about what it is, it simply gets on with the job – and the job is its own advertisement.

God's investment

God has saved us from eternal oblivion; he has given us life and everything we have. He asks, in return, for all we can give (which is not ours but his, anyway). Don't we get the better of the bargain? And let us not be overhard on ourselves: as Christians, we are using the talents God has given us – if not to capacity, then at least pursuing that goal. In showing Christ and his light to others, we are going some way towards saying 'Thank you' for his redemptive act on Calvary; we can never repay that sacrifice, or come anywhere near matching it, but may God help us to do all we can.

God is claiming our attention

It is our attention – pure and undivided – that God is after. Once we have focused on to him, the rest will follow. Are we worried? Look to Jesus. Are we sick? Look to Jesus. Are we joyful? Look to Jesus (if we're not looking to him already, as the source of our joy). There is no magical 'abracadabra' in looking to Jesus: no quick fix or dramatic turnaround of our troubles – but an assurance that he is there, and he will take the load and bear it for us, showing us in his good time a way beyond the problem.

No single operation

When we have joined forces with Jesus, we do not operate a single canoe. God does not leave us to navigate either the rapids or the calm water on our own. Our freedom of choice may run athwart his will, but we shall soon learn the difference between going our way and his. The realization will be more difficult, however, if we have insisted on taking our goods and chattels with us. Today, God is inviting us to check just how much this excess baggage may be impeding our Christian progress.

Be thou my guardian and my guide; O, the love of my Lord is the essence; Take up thy cross, the Saviour said; Will you come and follow me.

Third Sunday of Lent   14 March
Principal Service   **Fair Dealing**   Isa. 55:1–9; Ps. 63:1–8; 1 Cor. 10:1–13; Luke 13:1–9

'Let the wicked forsake their way, and the unrighteous their thoughts; let them return to the Lord, that he may have mercy upon them, and to our God, for he will abundantly pardon.' Isaiah 55:7
'He replied, "Sir, let it alone for one more year . . ."' Luke 13:8

Another chance
God is magnificently fair in his dealing – fair to the point of magnificent unfairness. His thoughts, his *modus operandi*, are not of this world. Though in his anger he can annihilate, obliterate and eliminate, he is also long-suffering, generous and forgiving. The vine-dresser giving his fig tree another chance, is a down-to-earth example of the Lord's patient dealing with his people. If the Christian life and eternity hung on every 'make-or-break' word, act or decision, none of us would make any significant progress along the way to God. But our Creator gave us (and allowed us to keep) free will, which he knows will get us into all sorts of problems. And it's the extrication from trouble, the overcoming of Satan, the constant falling and getting up again, which builds our Christian character, determination and stickability.

God's move
Yet we are not to court trouble for trouble's sake, nor to provoke God by tangling with trouble unnecessarily, nor to test the Lord by being slow to forgive, or intolerant with others' failings – for there is a 'cut-off point' for each of us, when God in his wisdom calls this life to a close, and our spiritual progress or backsliding, success or failure, growth or retardation, is assessed once for all by the Almighty. We need to take every chance he gives *today*, for there may be no tomorrow. By the same token, those who have let us down in any way may need the chance we give them *today*,

forgiveness, tolerance, generosity should never be put off till tomorrow.

Different ways

God's ways of working are not the world's ways – and let's thank him that this is so. The world careens along on its self-made roller-coaster of intolerance, censure and impatience, and often Christians who go in the opposite direction are classed as 'spineless', 'helpless' or 'weak-kneed'. Do we mind the verdict of the world? One day we shall need to mind the verdict of God.

Christ's great chance

In a month's time, we shall be caught up in the joy of Easter; our young folk are even now designing Easter cards which will be distributed throughout the parish. Easter was the day when Christ gave the world the greatest chance of all time: to think and work beyond death – for eternity; to be able to escape from the long-established stain and stigma of sin, into the purity and light of God's forgiveness. Yet look how many people, in two millennia, have chosen to stay with sin and decline eternal life! Jesus was so right, when he said: 'If they do not listen to Moses and the prophets, neither will they be convinced even if someone rises from the dead' (Luke 16:31). Has God, therefore, given us, his disciples, an impossible task? No – for some will listen, some will take on board the great truth of Easter, and some of the rest will continue to make life difficult. But the world today has more Christians than at any time in history. Time is going on, and the Day of Reckoning is nearer than it has ever been. This should not be seen as an impending threat, but as a great encouragement to do all the good for the Lord that we can, while we can. As Jesus himself once said, 'We must work the works of him who sent me, while it is day' (John 9:4).

Family Service input

Involve the young people in designing a parish Easter card or series of cards.

Suggested hymns

Dear Lord and Father of mankind; Gracious Spirit, Holy Ghost; Love Divine, all loves excelling; Where is love and loving kindness.

Third Sunday of Lent   *Second Service*
This Is the Time   Pss. 12, 13; Gen. 28:10–19a;
John 1:35–51

'[Jesus] said to them, "Come and see." They came and saw where he was staying, and they remained with him that day. It was about four o' clock in the afternoon.' John 1:39

'[God said], "I will not leave you until I have done what I have promised you."' Genesis 28:15

Our times are in God's hands
The following once appeared, unsigned, in a parish magazine:

Precious Time
Imagine there is a bank that credits your account each morning with £86,400. It carries over no balance from day to day. Every evening the bank deletes whatever part of the balance you failed to use during the day. What would you do? Draw out every penny, of course!

Each of us has such a bank. Its name is TIME. Every morning it credits you with 86,400 seconds. Every night it writes off, as lost, whatever of this you have failed to invest to good purpose. It carries over no balance. It allows no overdraft. Each day it opens a new account for you. Each night it burns the remains of the day. If you fail to use the day's deposits, the loss is yours. There is no going back. There is no drawing against the 'tomorrow'. You must live in the present on today's deposits. Invest it so as to get from it the utmost in health, happiness and success! The clock is running. Make the most of today.

To realize the value of ONE YEAR, ask a student who failed his exams. To realize the value of ONE MONTH, ask a mother who gave birth to a premature baby. To realize the value of ONE WEEK, ask the editor of a weekly newspaper. To realize the value of ONE HOUR, ask the lovers who are waiting to meet. To realize the value of ONE MINUTE, ask a person who missed the train. To realize the value of ONE SECOND, ask a person who just avoided an accident. To realize the value of ONE MILLI-SECOND, ask the person who won a silver medal in the Olympics.

Treasure every moment that you have, and remember that

time waits for no one. Yesterday is history. Tomorrow is a mystery. *Today* is a gift – that's why it's called the Present.

Man-made timetables
The monastic life was structured, around work, worship and prayer, to make the best possible use of every minute. We are often just as conscious of time, and tell ourselves (and others) how busy we are. But is God at the receiving end of our time – or someone else? God has given us time, so that we can live to a pattern of waking and sleeping – a little more of one, a little less of another, according to the seasons, but basically as an aid, not a hindrance, to our Christian living. We heard that, when the first disciples met up with Jesus, it was 'about 4 p.m.'. When Jesus died on the cross, it was 'about three o'clock' (Matthew 27:46); and every history book we pick up will tell us, more or less as precisely, when the greatest happenings took place. In this life, we are 'timed' from the cradle to the grave. After that, eternity will tell how proficient we become in managing without time.

The constancy of time
Our work for God is allowed the same amount of time as was allowed for the work of St Paul, St Ignatius, St Francis, Mother Teresa and the rest. If we have 'no' time, or 'insufficient' time, it's not God who has lost the minutes and seconds. Jesus never complained over a lack of time: instead, he calmly, unhurriedly bent all his energies into utilizing time and making time work for him. He could rest in the knowledge that he would have sufficient time to fulfil his work. We, too, can have such assurance, for our God is still the Master of time.

Suggested hymns
A few more years shall roll; Days and moments quickly flying; O God, our help in ages past; O for a closer walk with God.

Fourth Sunday of Lent (Mothering Sunday)

21 March   *Principal Service*   **God's Chosen Ones**

Readings for Mothering Sunday: Ex. 2:1–10 or
1 Sam. 1:20–28; Ps. 34:11–20 or Ps. 127:1–4; 2 Cor. 1:3–7
or Col. 3:12–17; Luke 2:33–35 or John 19:25–27

'As God's chosen ones, holy and beloved, clothe yourselves with compassion, kindness, humility, meekness and patience.' Colossians 3:12

That's what mothers are!

That's what mothers are – and a lot more besides. God valued motherhood so highly that he caused Jesus to have a mother for his 33 years on earth. Mary's conception was special; but then, so was she – favoured above all women (Luke 1:28). She nurtured her Son, bringing him up to observe the recognized religious customs as well as regular worship on the sabbath (Luke 4:16). She was loyal to him throughout his mission (cf. Luke 8:19), and even went all the way with him to Calvary (John 19:25f.), and continued to help in the earliest days of the Church (Acts 1:14): a truly remarkable woman and mother. And her Son loved her dearly, even planning for her well-being after he had gone (John 19:26–27).

Mother Church

Do we also look to Mother Church for these qualities? If we do, but do not find them in the Church, then we need to question why. For if the Church does not nurture her own children, how can she reach out with compassion, kindness, and the rest, to others? And how will those outside be encouraged to join us if they are not made to feel loved and cherished? It is of little use to say we live in troubled times, when there is internal denominationalism and time wasted on fruitless questions, with apathy and intolerance outside: it has always been so. One can search for sustained periods in history when the Church was at peace with herself and the world – and find none. It will probably be so until the end of time. But she is still 'Mother Church' – imperfect, but nevertheless aiming for perfection.

We, the chosen
We, the chosen, know who we have believed – the one Lord who can make perfect what is as yet imperfect. What do we expect from Mother Church? More than we can give in return? There was a terrible time in history when the pope served an interdict on England and excommunicated John, the king. No marriages were solemnized, no children baptized, no funerals conducted. All the churches stood locked and deserted. Priests were forbidden to say Mass. 'Mother' was not fulfilling her mission! Do we take her for granted, in these days of relative calm? Still she waits, with open doors and regular worship, for those who may return when they have eaten their fill of pigs' feed (cf. Luke 15:16); that is what, in essence, the world has to offer.

Memories
Whether our mothers are here, or hereafter, we have memories of their compassion, kindness and selfless care. It is usually our mother who teaches us to pray; our mother who sits us on her knee and introduces us to the stories of the Bible; our mother who first brings us to church. A woman who had brought up six children in the faith confessed on her death-bed to a friend: 'It's been a struggle, but I feel now that I've only just learned how to rear a Christian child!' Bless her, perhaps God is using her talents even now, in some far-off universe. With all their special gifts, the Lord surely will not see mothers 'out of work' in the hereafter! Let us bring our memories, our gratitude, our love – for our mothers, for Mary and for Mother Church – to God today. He is our Father, truly – but somewhere in the great Father-heart of God beats a mother's love: it must be so, for God made mothers.

Family Service input
Encourage the young people to make up little posies (from flowers already to hand) for their mothers, and/or design text-cards to present to their mothers.

Suggested hymns
For the beauty of the earth; Jesus, good above all other; Jesus' hands were kind hands; Shall we not love thee, Mother dear.

Fourth Sunday of Lent *Second Service*
No Longer in that Way

Principal Service readings: Josh. 5:9–12; Ps. 32;
2 Cor. 5:16–21 or Luke 15:1–3, 11b–32

*'From now on, therefore, we regard no one from a human point of view,
even though we once knew Christ from a human point of view, we know
him no longer in that way.'* 2 Corinthians 5:16

The power within

'The Lord does not see as mortals see; they look on the outward
appearance, but the Lord looks on the heart' (1 Samuel 16:7). This
is simpler to understand than the progressive theology of St Paul.
Regarding a person 'from a human point of view' is not only
looking on the outward appearance, but – with the watershed of
Jesus Christ and the turnaround of life and eternity that he brought
– it also means recognizing (or not) Christ in a person. If that
person is a Christian, it will show – in the light in their eyes, their
general bearing and outlook, as well as the messages coming from
their heart.

The Spirit actor

This recognition is the meeting of spirits:

> *Speak to him, thou, for he hears;*
> *Spirit with spirit can meet;*
> *Closer is he than breathing,*
> *Nearer than hands and feet.*

Tennyson, The Higher Pantheon

The Holy Spirit, having been given to all believers ever since the
coming of Christ, means that fellow Christians are linked – invis-
ibly but strongly – by the interaction of the Spirit within each. So
the coming and the ascension of Jesus has (as St Paul has realized)
advanced the recognition of our fellow human beings significantly.
By the same token, the Spirit working inside us recognizes and
alerts us to evil in others. We do not identify the individual per se
as evil, but rather Satan working through that person. We all have
free will; we could all, if we so wished, compromise with Satan.
As Christians, we have declined his evil offer (except when he

takes us off guard) – but there are many who have fallen for his snare. Yet our ability, in the Spirit, to recognize the source, rather than the manifestation, as the evil, means that we are already on the way to being able to reach out in love and compassion to the sinner, while still hating the sin.

A new look

Making a 'snap' decision merely on the basis of what we see or hear, is relatively easy, very common and often wrong. Seeing and deciding with the spiritual eye of faith takes more practice and more time, but is more likely to be right. Jesus was interested in everyone, not in their outward appearance – their clothes, height, colour of hair – but in their physical, spiritual and mental well-being. If we have the 'mind of Christ' (1 Corinthians 2:16), we shall likewise see people not merely as people, but as fellow creations, our sisters and brothers, with (like ourselves) a soul to be saved, eternity to live for, a Lord to know and love, and a mission to fulfil – and we shall go to work on them, in love, in the name of Jesus. When we meet our Maker, he'll probably not be overly concerned with our Christian denomination, but on how many souls we've told about Christ. The Dutch evangelist Corrie ten Boom would minister to anyone, anywhere, at any time, be they airport officials, taxi-drivers or hotel porters. Many of those who had cause to thank her for leading them to the Lord, will by now probably have done just that. May we, too, bend our efforts in the present mission field, so that in glory we can be united again with friends.

Suggested hymns

Forgive our sins, as we forgive; I cannot tell why he whom angels worship; Tell out, my soul, the greatness of the Lord; The Church's one foundation.

Fifth Sunday of Lent (Passion Sunday)
28 March   *Principal Service*   **Becoming Like Christ**
Isa. 43:16–21; Ps. 126; Phil. 3:4b–14; John 12:1–8
'I want to know Christ and the power of his resurrection and the sharing of his sufferings by becoming like him in his death.' Philippians 3:10

Intimate knowledge
To know *of* Christ is possible for everyone who can hear or read
the Bible; but to *know Christ* is a far deeper, greater blessing: to
know him as Brother, Friend, Guide and Lord is a deep joy; to
know him as Saviour is the greatest joy, and yet the most searing
pain, of all. For as Saviour he suffered before being raised; he bled
before defeating death for ever. St Paul in today's reading has had
to come to terms with the realization that knowing Christ involves
a double sharing – a twofold operation that must not be divided:
we cannot experience with our Saviour the joy of resurrection if
we have not also first walked the way of the cross with him.

Preparation
Passion Sunday – which seems, at first sight, to come about 12
days too soon – gives us an opportunity to prepare ourselves for
Holy Week and what is ahead. In a special way, we can begin this
traumatic fortnight which culminates in the triumph of Easter, as
our Lord began it, knowing what lies ahead: the experience of
Palm Sunday, and then the acceleration of suspicion, treachery,
love, fellowship, cruelty, sacrifice and the quietness of the tomb.
Jesus could foresee all this, yet he guided his friends through each
day as it came, trying to prepare them for events which he knew
would show them their weaknesses as well as their strengths.

The inevitable
The betrayal of Judas, the machinations of the chief priests, the
volatility of the crowds, the misunderstandings of the Roman authorities – it seemed to be all coming together in the foreknowledge
of God with a dreadful inevitability. And yet God could have
called a halt to the Passion at any time! Legions of angels were
waiting to intervene at a moment's notice, and to bear Jesus away
from danger. God alone knows how he could have effected the
'rescue', in a billion different ways.

But the saving of Jesus would have left the rest of the world
without hope, and the Father-heart of God would not do it. Passion
Sunday brings us to a place where, in gratitude for all he went
through for our sakes, we can come alongside Jesus in his agony
of love and allow that love to cleanse our hearts of unworthy
thoughts and feelings, before we step out with him into the coming
days.

Put your hand in the hand of the Man who stilled the water;
Put your hand in the hand of the Man who calmed the sea;
Take a look at yourself, and you can look at others differently;

> By putting your hand in the hand of the
> Man of Calvary.

> Gene MacLellan (alt.)

The cost involved
To walk the way of the cross with our Saviour is not an easy
option: the experience can show us parts of ourselves we did not
know and do not wish to know. But the hand in which we have
trusted our own is pure Love. And we can have confidence that
Jesus will also show us more of himself: the deep, deep love that
led him to go through the Passion. Are we brave enough to take
the risk? Yes – because we, like Jesus, know what happened after
Calvary.

Family Service input
Ask the young people to colour the Passion cross (opposite), or
to design one of their own.

Suggested hymns
Beneath the cross of Jesus; Jesus, the Name high over all; We sing
the praise of him who died; When I survey the wondrous cross.

Fifth Sunday of Lent   *Second Service*
Opening the Wrong Door   Ps. 35; 2 Chr. 35:1–6,
10–16; Luke 22:1–13

'The chief priests and the scribes were looking for a way to put Jesus to
death, for they were afraid of the people. Then Satan entered into Judas
called Iscariot, who was one of the twelve.' Luke 22:2–3

The wrong invitation
By their evil thoughts and intentions, the chief priests and the
scribes had given the wrong spiritual invitation – had opened the
wrong spiritual door – and Satan, ever an opportunist, answered

90

God so loved the world, that He gave His only Son.

the invitation, and pushed open the door wider. We need not inveigh against the plotters till kingdom come: there, but for the grace of God, go we. The fact that, so far, we have not invited Satan into our hearts is cause only for continued vigilance: he doesn't wait for any second invitations.

It is tragic that, although the people's acceptance of Jesus put something of a brake on the plotting of the priests, in the end it was one of the disciples closest to Jesus who proved to be the compromiser with Satan. It is hard – don't we know – to keep saying: 'Away with you, Satan!' (Matthew 4:10). Judas (perhaps after several 'rounds') let down his guard, and took the easy way of compromise. Sometimes Satan still seems to have success with those who appear outwardly to be the least likely to succumb to his advances.

Chain reaction

Yes, Judas was already on the way to disaster. John tells us he was the mission team's treasurer, but helped himself to the funds he held (John 12:6) – and, yes, he may have latched on to the priests' declared animosity to Jesus, to go one step too far. But the priests, those invested with sacred authority and by virtue of their office supposedly upholders of the spiritual state of the nation, in their own compromise with evil, met up with the Satan in Judas, and an evil flashpoint had been reached. It is the 'down side' of the beneficial meeting of Holy Spirit with Holy Spirit among Christians. So often it needs two to tango – for good or evil. That is why we need spiritual vigilance in all the circumstances to which we are brought. Who knows how long the priests may have hesitated – or Judas continue with his embezzling on the quiet? It was the fate of both the priests and the betrayer that the saving purposes of God were to come to a head at a certain Passover at a certain time in history. If the betrayal had not been by Judas, it would have been by someone else; if the priesthood had not included Annas and Caiaphas, it would have included someone else. Satan would have worked through anyone who was sufficiently weak to say, even just once: 'I will betray ... Crucify him!'

Lack of patience

Very often, when Satan gets to a person, it is because he or she has run out of patience – with themselves or others or God. We tell ourselves (in so many words) that we can write history better than God. It may be only the briefest of thoughts, or we may have psyched ourselves to this point over a period of time; but the moment when we let go our hold of patience is the moment that Satan has been waiting for.

Time for a check
Passion Sunday gives us time to check ourselves on the Lenten road. Are we prepared for Palm Sunday and the start of Holy Week? Are we prayed-up for guidance to stay with Jesus through the Passion? We must not forget that Satan moved in on the priests and Judas when their thoughts were largely divided between other things: the Passover, the Jerusalem crowds, the Zealot uprisings, the Roman army of occupation . . . The Devil has most success not when our thoughts are concentrated, but when a variety of details, worries and threats are vying for our attention – *or* when life is running smoothly on well-oiled wheels and our guard has been let down. Satan's *modus operandi* is as old as the . . . Garden of Eden.

Suggested hymns
Be thou my Guardian and my Guide; Guide me, O thou great Redeemer; Lead us, heavenly Father, lead us; O sacred head, sore wounded.

Palm Sunday   4 April   *Principal Service*
Standing By   Isa. 50:4–9a; Ps. 31:9–16; Phil. 2:5–11; Luke 22:14—23:56 or Luke 23:1–49
'[Jesus said], "You are these who have stood by me in my trials, and I confer on you, just as my Father has conferred on me, a kingdom."' Luke 22:28

Our greatest Friend
How could Jesus speak such words of friendship and trust when he knew with divine foresight that Peter would soon deny him, and the rest would run away – not to mention the betrayer? 'You have stood by me . . .' As the weekend wore on, Peter and the others would remember those loving words, which denial and

desertion had turned to swords that pierced each heart. We have all been to the same place, and have known the anguish that longs for our friend to return so that we can tell him how much we love him, and ask for forgiveness.

A royal gift
Only a monarch can give a kingdom. But where is his robe, his crown, his throne? 'My kingdom is not from this world,' Jesus was soon to tell Pilate (John 18:36). And yet he was – and is – more surely a king, more surely regal, than any earthly monarch. And shall we be 'a kingdom, priests serving God' (Revelation 1:6; 5:10)? Yes – as 'saints from every tribe and language and people and nation' (Revelation 5:9). And we, like the disciples, are not perfect; no one can ever say they have attained eternal life and honour therein by their own efforts, through their own ability. It is all through grace, God's unmerited favour, shown in the love that gave Jesus to die.

> *Oh, how great was the love that was shown*
> *To us! – we can never tell why –*
> *Not to angels, but men; let us praise him again*
> *For the love that gave Jesus to die!*

> *El Nathan*

Eternal friendship
If there was ever any doubt that friendships made on earth continue in heaven, these words of Jesus surely clinch the matter. God is faithful, and the earthly manifestation of faithfulness that grows into friendship is set to withstand the lesser bond of death. We can have the greatest confidence that we shall meet our loved ones and continue our friendships as though death had never intervened – though the *how* and the *when* and the *why* are still to be made known.

All that is true . . .
God never wastes time, and he does not ask us to do what he would not. When he tells us to 'think about these things', he is serious (Philippians 4:8); things like truth, honour, justice, purity, joy and worthiness; anything that falls into these categories, he

says: You concentrate on them. Do we believe that death will cancel these out? No way!

Today, as we meditate on this Holy Week to come, with its joys as well as its sorrows, can we, like Jesus, focus on the joy that was to see him through (cf. Hebrews 12:2)? As he spoke with his disciples, he thought of their loyalty and friendship – for he knew that, apart from Judas, these positive qualities were to prove in the end stronger than denial and desertion.

As our Saviour once again accompanies us through Holy Week, what would we like him to focus on? Our loyalty and friendship, certainly – and is there anything else? Can we make a little nosegay of our spiritual gifts for him, to give him joy this Holy Week? Remember the times of sharing that helped him, at the first Passion: the ride into Jerusalem; going out to Bethany of an evening with his friends; the shared meal in the cenacle; the foot-washing, the long talks . . .

What spiritual *companionship* can we offer to him in these busy, crowded days? – we, who have no reason to deny or desert him? – we, who know, as Peter and the rest did not, that Easter will follow Good Friday?

Family Service input
Make palm crosses (see p. 96) for congregational/parochial distribution.

Suggested hymns
All glory, laud and honour; I will sing the wondrous story; Lord Jesus, think on me; Ride on, ride on in majesty.

Palm Sunday   *Second Service*
New Owners of the Vineyard   Ps. 69:1–18; Isa. 5:1–7; Luke 20:9–19

'[Jesus said], "What then will the owner of the vineyard do to them? He will come and destroy those tenants and give the vineyard to others."'
Luke 20:15–16

Folding a Palm Cross

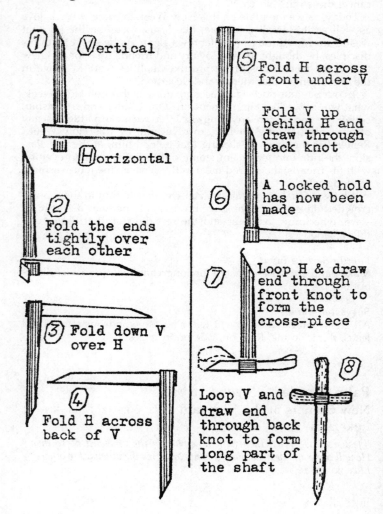

① Vertical

Horizontal

② Fold the ends tightly over each other

③ Fold down V over H

④ Fold H across back of V

⑤ Fold H across front under V

Fold V up behind H and draw through back knot

⑥ A locked hold has now been made

⑦ Loop H & draw end through front knot to form the cross-piece

⑧ Loop V and draw end through back knot to form long part of the shaft

96

God's work goes on

Note that the vineyard is not taken away from its first tenants by destruction; the tenants themselves are destroyed – and all the work they have put into the vineyard is taken over by new tenants! All the work that God has invested in this earth will similarly go on, whether we make a success or a hash of our lives. Were it to be otherwise, we should end up in chaos. This is not to say that we can 'throw in the towel', and declare that nothing we may do can affect our 'vineyard'.

The Jerusalem vineyard

As Jesus rode down the Mount of Olives, he had an excellent view of the city of Jerusalem – the vineyard mismanaged by God's chosen tenants, which would be given to others. Even today, Jerusalem knows little peace, after two thousand years which have seen Jew, Muslim and Christian fighting and clamouring over stones and mortar, boundaries and borders, and shedding blood on the very places where Christ once walked.

Ars longa, vita brevis

'Art is long, and time is fleeting', and enough of Jerusalem survives to make it a vital place of pilgrimage. But what of the Lord's vineyard? The whole of planet earth is his mission field. Jerusalem has spawned disciples to many countries on every continent. Some parts of the vineyard are being well tended and are producing a good harvest; other parts are being mismanaged or have been temporarily appropriated by those actively working against the kingdom of God.

> *Go, work in my vineyard, I claim thee as mine,*
> *With blood did I buy thee, and all that is thine –*
> *Thy time and thy talents, thy loftiest powers,*
> *Thy warmest affections, thy sunniest hours.*
> *I willingly yielded my kingdom for thee –*
> *The song of archangels – to hang on the tree,*
> *In pain and temptation, in anguish and shame,*
> *I paid thy full ransom, my purchase I claim.*

> *Anon.*

The work in God's vineyard may be long and (in the short term) unrewarding; but we have a vineyard-owner who sees and records with appreciation every smallest part of our labours. We have inherited the work of former tenants. Others coming after us should have cause to thank God for our efforts. Just to do each day all we can is our allotted work – and the greatest privilege anyone can ever enjoy. We are not asked to die in agony on a cross, but to spread the gospel. Who can compare with our God for such magnificent unfairness!

A gift – for life

The new tenants of the vineyard, in Jesus' parable, had the privilege of work given to them: if they worked well, then it was, literally, a life assurance; if they fell down on their obligations, then history's wheel, ever turning, would see them removed from office and their employment given to others. Today, each of us owes something – perhaps many things – in our lives, to those who have gone before. We, in turn, will be making someone else's life a little easier, somehow, for the future. It is all part of the integration of the members of Christ's body. This truth should keep us from individual pride and self-sufficiency. If we cannot give individuals specific acknowledgement (for we do not know how many have contributed to our present position), then let us at least give God the glory for working in all our lives.

The natural vines may respond to good treatment, without knowing who it is who is tending them. Similarly, in our work for Christ, it is Christ who is important: we are merely instruments in his hands.

Suggested hymns

Father God, I wonder how; Father, I place into your hands; Father, let me dedicate; Take my hands.

Monday of Holy Week 5 April
Declaration of Intent Isa. 42:1–9; Ps. 36:5–11;
Heb. 9:11–15; John 12:1–11

'Six days before the Passover Jesus came to Bethany, the home of Lazarus, whom he had raised from the dead.' John 12:1

Renewing the friendship

It was a renewing of the friendship with this little family, after Lazarus had been resurrected. It was also a brave declaration of intent. By openly visiting Lazarus and his sisters (surely, since the raising, in what would be the most famous house for miles around), Jesus was saying, in effect: 'If you want to arrest me, here I am.' Well, his unspoken offer would be taken up, five days later. Rather more obliquely, it was also an underlining of his power: an emphasizing of the efficacy of Lazarus' restoration to life. Jesus had not merely revived an invalid: Lazarus was as well as he had ever been. Who, in their right mind, would want to arrest a man who could restore and raise the dead? When people allow Satan to take them over as completely as Judas and the chief priests, the inference is that they are not then of a sound mind.

On this Monday in Holy Week, before the more tragic events of Thursday and Friday occupy us, can we reflect on what friendship meant to our Lord? The inner circle of disciples, with whom he had so closely lived and interrelated for the past three years, had been a precious part of his mission. Then this little home at Bethany had given him a welcome and hospitality (we know that Martha was at home in the kitchen!), and at this critical time afforded him also shelter for the night. We are not told how the friendship with Lazarus and his sisters began, but it had grown into an intimacy that obviously meant much to Jesus. We may reflect on our own friends, and all that they mean to us. Do we cherish them as we should? Do we simply tell (or show) our friends how much we love them? (Perhaps they, too, take us somewhat for granted!) Let's remember that a telephone call, a letter, a hug, a kiss or a bunch of flowers brings more joy both to giver and receiver, than a funeral wreath.

What folk may think

There were death threats taken out against Lazarus (John 12:10), but Lazarus and his sisters did not allow these to interrupt their friendship with Jesus. Perhaps they felt that, as Jesus had proved himself Master of life and death, they had nothing to fear from the chief priests. In any case, they were continuing to support and welcome the Lord who had so convincingly gone to work on a four-day-old corpse (John 11:39f.). If we stop to wonder what others may think, at every turn, our progress through life will be severely curtailed. Do you believe a course of action is right? Have you prayed about it? Are you still happy with it? Then, *go for it*, and hesitate no longer! The world is not so full of shining lights for God that it can't benefit from a few more!

As the sun sinks this evening on Bethany, and the little house where friendship is giving Jesus a respite before the trauma to come, let us hear again the soft hoof-beats of yesterday's donkey, and the excitement of the crowds who had little idea of who and what they were cheering:

> *Along the steep road, where the crowds throng to meet him,*
> *His donkey steps out on the palms that are strown;*
> *But where is the robe, and the crown, and the carriage?*
> *No earthly king here, but a Lord riding home.*
> *The Palm Sunday crowds on the roadside that morning*
> *Knew little by knowledge, yet hailed you in faith;*
> *Their shouts now we echo, as knowing you better –*
> *Our King, yet the carpenter's Son of the lathe.*

Suggested hymns
For the beauty of the earth; I heard the voice of Jesus say; Lord, through this Holy Week of our salvation; The duteous day now closeth.

Tuesday of Holy Week   6 April
Walking in the Light   Isa. 49:1–7; Ps. 71:1–14;
1 Cor. 1:18–31; John 12:20–36

'Jesus said to them, "The light is with you for a little longer. Walk while you have the light, so that the darkness may not overtake you . . . While you have the light, believe in the light, so that you may become children of light."' John 12:35–36

Keeping Jesus in sight
The disciples could naturally see Jesus; we see him by faith, through the Holy Spirit. There need be no difference, for his light is the same yesterday, today and for ever; and it's the most powerful weapon against Satan that God has provided or will ever need to provide. But keeping Jesus in sight is not always easy: the Devil has become proficient in the art of deflection. We can memorize

large chunks of the Bible, keep our prayer lines open to God, be diligent in church attendance, and energetic in study-groups, sick visiting, bereavement counselling and the rest – and still Satan will muscle in when least expected.

Thought-training

A defence that is always capable of being strengthened is thought-training: not merely the 'power of positive thinking', but training: our minds to the things of Christ – the fruits of the Spirit (Galatians 5:22–23), lovely, pure and beautiful thoughts (Philippians 4:8). The more our minds are lightened in these ways, the harder Satan will find it to dim them with any dark ideas of his own. How far we take 'walking in the light' is between us and God. We may decide to wear brighter colours, drive a light-coloured car, give our curtains at home a face-lift, grow vivid flowers this summer in the garden – there are many practical ways in which our spiritual decision to walk in the light of Christ can be complemented and accentuated. It highlights the message that we are sending to the world in general: 'I'm walking in the light!'

> *I'm unafraid as on I go, for Jesus walks with me,*
> *He led me from my darkness, from my sins he set me free,*
> *Walking in the light, walking in the light,*
> *Walking on to glory, where there is no night,*
> *I'm singing 'Hallelujah!' as I travel on my way,*
> *Walking in the Saviour's light.*

> *John W. Paterson*

The 'hot' line

An old gospel hymn used to start 'I just telephone upstairs when there is trouble.' All the walking tall and stepping out in the light of Jesus will not give us immunity from trouble; but the closer we are walking with God, the quicker our divine connection will be, on the 'hot line to heaven'. If only we would focus on God's help being a mere breath away, perhaps we should not allow trouble to catch us off balance, or get us screwed up in anguish and fear. But we are human – and it is desperately human to fear what we see before trusting what is invisible.

The light we can see
But take a look at the countries, the cities, the communities, families and individuals you know, where the light of Christ has made a difference. Can we say we do not *see* this light? Slowly but surely, from the first glimmer in Bethlehem, Nazareth and Jerusalem, it has spread and continues to grow. In the beginning, darkness covered the deep (Genesis 1:2), then God brought physical light. But as the years went on, the spiritual light of sinlessness at creation became darker and darker, as humankind built on Eve's sin. A return to pure inner light began with the coming of Christ, and is still gaining in strength – until, at his second coming, his bright *Shekinah*-glory will once again hold sway.

We can surely look forward to this as, day by day, step by step, we draw closer to it, walking in the Saviour's light.

Suggested hymns
Light's abode, celestial Salem; Lord, the light of your love (Shine, Jesus, shine); Lord, through this Holy Week of our salvation; The light of the morning is breaking.

Wednesday of Holy Week   7 April
The Butt of Hostility   Isa. 50:4–9a; Ps. 70;
Heb. 12:1–3; John 13:21–32
'Consider him [Jesus] who endured such hostility against himself from sinners, so that you may not grow weary or lose heart.' Hebnews 12:3

The sin of Judas
Jesus had shown to Judas the same love and friendship he had extended to the other disciples – yet from within the innermost circle of those men, one made compromise with Satan (John 13:21f.). The message here is surely not to conduct a 'witch-hunt' in our local community of believers, but to examine our own hearts and to springclean our motives and intentions before any imperfections grow into something worse.

Why did Jesus attract hostility? Because he was pure goodness. Nothing stirs Satan into action more than that. The Devil will take as much notice of out-and-out sinners as the chief priests took of Judas once he had served their purpose: 'What is that to us? See to it yourself' (Matthew 27:4). But practising Christians annoy the Devil by being 'Christ' in the modern world: Christian light turns Satan 'on' in a way nothing else does.

In the world

'In the world you face persecution,' Jesus has promised us (John 16:33); yet many Christians grumble at trouble, even as much as non-believers. Somehow, they think that a 'Christian' tag should be an insurance against hassle.

Well, so it is, in a way – an insurance of the Christian's means of overcoming trouble, in the strength and power of Christ, which is worth a million times more than dodging it or being somehow immune from it in the first place. Antibiotics are a wonderful advance in medicine: they take over the body's immunization arsenal and fight infection for us. But when the prescription has run its course, not only do we need an input of yoghurt or kindred foods to replace the beneficial bacteria which the antibiotics have indiscriminately knocked out with the 'bad 'uns'; but the body has as a whole to reorganize itself back to fighting infection as God originally intended. The world is increasing its short-term 'fixes' – but God works with eternity in view. We cannot start a week's course of new tablets every time hassle comes along. We need the constant, ever-powerful, continually effective Spirit of Christ working, growing, energizing and strengthening within us.

A certainty

Ever as certainly as when he promised 'I am with you always' (Matthew 28:20), the forecast of trouble can be taken as inevitable. Would we have it otherwise? How could we meet Christ face to face in glory – he who has suffered so much for us – if we had had an easy ride? Where would be the challenge, the thrill of victory, the reliance on our Lord to win through for us and with us and in us? Christ's work did not finish at Calvary; it will continue until the last believer has been safely brought home to God. Not by our efforts, but by his strength; not by our merits, but by his virtue; not by compromise with darkness, but in Christ's clear light, shall we make it through to eternity.

Holy Wednesday

As we reach the middle of Holy Week, the mounting tension is set tomorrow to move into first communion, then crisis, with

Gethsemane, the arrest and the trial before the Sanhedrin to-morrow night. From the acclamations of last Sunday, feelings will harden into outright hostility. Before we share in the Passion with Jesus, perhaps we can bring our present troubles to him, lifting in prayer those who may be giving us a hard time. The Lord of the Passion will hear, and will help – because he has been where we are now.

Suggested hymns
Fight the good fight; Lord, her watch thy Church is keeping; Lord, through this Holy Week of our salvation; Oft in danger, oft in woe.

Maundy Thursday 8 April
Proclamation of Death Ex. 12:1–4[5–10]11–14;
Ps. 116:1–2, 12–19; 1 Cor. 11:23–26;
John 13:1–17, 31b–35
'For as often as you eat this bread and drink this cup, you proclaim the Lord's death until he comes.' 1 Corinthians 11:26

By death came victory
It is no morbid proclamation, for by Christ's death came victory. He killed death for us, taking away not the inevitability but the permanence of death. His reason for making the meal in the cenacle such an unforgettable and unique experience was to remind the disciples of his death before it had happened, and Christians in general for all time to come. The commemoration (as institution) took place before the event, and has continued ever since.

The greatest event
Yet this meal, commemorating and celebrating the greatest sacrifice ever made, is only rarely the subject of sermons. Many churches tonight will have a more or less informal meal, followed by an all-night vigil of Bible reading and private prayer. Although the Eucharist is celebrated in most churches every Sunday as the main service of the day, its accompanying address rarely focuses on the actual ritual; and it is fair to say that many Christ-

ians would struggle to put into words their understanding of the liturgy.

Variations in meaning

The Eucharist means different things to different people – within the same denomination, and even more so between the Churches. Do we see it as a memorial, or a re-enactment of sacrifice? Do we understand the bread and wine as symbols, or as transubstantiated into the very body and blood of Christ? Do we use wafers or pieces of real bread (brown or white)? Do we use fermented or unfermented wine? Do we drink from a common chalice or from individual cups? And, does it matter?

St Paul tells us his understanding of the right way – which is low on practicalities and high on spirituality: 'Examine yourselves, and only then eat of the bread and drink of the cup' (1 Corinthians 11:28). We can become so engrossed in the technicalities that the true meaning of the ritual is lost. What began as a relatively simple meal between close friends in an upper room in Jerusalem has at times become so overlaid with ceremonial as to become a rite to be worshipped rather than a sacrifice to be honoured. Perhaps, if we were to prune away some of the ritual, the central part of the service would impact more strongly.

A personal request

The request of Jesus, that the disciples reconstruct the cenacle meal as a remembrance of the event it foreshadowed, was a personal way of telling the world it must not forget the saving act which bought eternal life. To the Greeks, it would seem foolishness, that a man could die the most shameful of deaths and that that death should be remembered again and again. To the Jews, it was a real stumbling block – for, as a Jew, Jesus had died in a Roman way, sentence having been passed at a Roman trial (in which nevertheless their chief priests had played a large part). At a distance from Judaea, and two thousand years on, to some extent we have become anaesthetized to the cross per se, and focus on Jesus' act of dying rather than the means by which he died. Because his Passion took place where it did, and at that point in history, it must needs be a crucifixion. God was saving the world through the death and resurrection of his Son: he would accomplish his purpose by whatever means.

So, as we 'eat the bread and drink the cup', can we pray that our

Lord will clarify in our minds *his* understanding of our presence at the communion rail, and that he will give us the right words to say when others ask us why?

Suggested hymns:
And now, O Father, mindful of the love; Author of life divine; Once, only once, and once for all; We hail thy Presence glorious.

Good Friday   9 April   *Principal Service*
No Case Against Him   Isa. 52:13—53:12; Ps. 22; Heb. 10:16–25 or Heb. 4:14–16; 5:7–9; John 18:1—19:42

'[Pilate] went out to the Jews again and told them, "I find no case against him."' John 18:38
'Pilate went out again, and said, to them, "Look, I am bringing him out to you to let you know that I find no case against him."' John 19:4
'Pilate said to them, "Take him yourselves and crucify him. I find no case against him."' John 19:6

Legal and moral?
It has been said by some that while the crucifixion was immoral, it was nevertheless legal. Yet this threefold assertion by the Roman procurator Pilate surely wipes away any vestiges of legality surrounding the 'conviction' of Jesus. But the chief priests were so far down the line of irrationality after their overnight, overwrought 'trial' that they found it impossible to retrench. 'Crucify him (anyway)!' There is a dreadful inevitability in what Pilate was unsuccessfully trying to maintain as an impartial hearing. Legality as well as immorality had all but vanished.

Tension that tightens
It can seem awful, on Good Friday, to compare our smaller tensions with the anguish of our Lord; yet in his calm dignity and acquiescence to the will of God, surely we can gain strength for the immoral injustices that come our way. Sometimes our antagonists tell themselves (and us) that they, too, like the Jerusalem priests, are doing God's service by giving us a hard time. How do we counter such an argument? By prayer. By recalling that 'in quietness and in trust shall be [our] strength' (Isaiah 30:15). It is

all too often true that 'there is no justice in this world'. Therefore, unless we turn our problem over to God, we shall tear our nerves to shreds, whiten our hair and sooner rather than later stop our hearts – to no avail.

The only way in which Jesus could go through each terrible hour of Good Friday, was to keep his prayer line open to God, keep anger and retribution at bay, and consider others in mitigation of his own sufferings. It is the supreme example of overcoming Satan. We, even with our lesser troubles, don't attain that degree of quietness and trust – but let us not get weary of trying.

'I find no case'

'I find no case against him.' Pilate had asked: 'What is truth?' (John 18:38), and at least he spoke truly here – for there was no case against the Son of God. No one in their right mind could have found a case. But the chief priests were not operating in their right minds that morning: Satan had taken them a long way from rationality.

It is the same at times today. There are fanatics inside the Church as well as outside: those who perhaps genuinely believe that they are acting in the best interests of themselves or others. Goodness can draw many to its side – yet some come for the wrong reasons. That is part of the risk of following Jesus. If we so wish, we can play safe and keep our distance. On Good Friday, there would be more people standing 'afar off', merely watching the proceedings and not wanting to become involved – *many* more, than the relative few on the steps of Pilate's hall who were making all the noise. Staying on the sidelines has always been popular: the periphery of any trouble is not likely to lack attenders. But is that where we want to be? In no-man's land? On the spiritual fence?

Well, we may have an easier life on earth from that perspective: but it will be shorter – much shorter – than the eternal life which Jesus went to so much anguish to win for us.

Suggested hymns

Forgive them, O my Father; His are the thousand sparkling rills; O come and mourn with me awhile; When I survey the wondrous cross.

Good Friday *Second Service*
Primus inter Pares Pss. 130, 143; Gen. 22:1–18;
John 19:38–42 or Col. 1:18–23

'[Christ] is the head of the body, the church; he is the beginning, the firstborn from the dead, so that he might come to have first place in everything.' Colossians 1:18

Shared resurrection

Just think what an encouraging verse this is! The 'beginning' means the start of an experience which is ongoing; the 'firstborn' means that more will follow; and 'first place in everything' means that Jesus is Lord of all. Yet he is truly 'first among equals', for he has called us, who will experience the resurrection he accomplished, his brothers and sisters (Matthew 12:50; Mark 3:35). The cruelty of Good Friday led to the inauguration of a never-ending process which one day will see God's purposes for this earth fully worked out. We are not to ask how, why or when – simply to follow the example of Jesus, taking one day at a time and doing our best to stay in the will of God.

Living for ever

Living for ever, with our sights on eternity and our energies on the present minute, helps us to keep God's business in perspective. To the casual onlooker, everything Jesus had taught may seem to have come to a shattering end on Good Friday: even his closest disciples thought so. Our own prospect can never look so dark, whatever the trouble. Yet, had Peter and the others put as much faith in our Lord's promise of resurrection as in his healing miracles, they would not have lost hope for the best part of three days.

Are we selective?

Are we as selective in our acceptance of Jesus? Do we focus on the words and deeds we can relate to our own situation, and put his *un*comfortable teachings, or the miracles we find hard to understand, into cold storage until (we tell ourselves) we are further advanced in the faith – or which we think may be more applicable to someone else?

In their original context, Jesus' teachings were structured in (at least) three layers: (1) simple but memorable stories as an introduction for the mildly interested (e.g. Luke 8:4–8, the parable of the sower); (2) an explanation, for his seriously enquiring disciples (e.g. Luke 8:9–15); and (3) teaching, by experience, for his closest friends (as in the Transfiguration, Mark 9:2f.).

By contrast, the 'teaching through experience' of Good Friday was available to all who drew close enough to Calvary. So much was crowded into those few hours that inevitably we shall all be selective to a degree in the amount with which we can cope – though our hymns, readings and prayers today can do much to focus our minds. No matter how few or how many Good Friday services we have ever attended, today, if we pray him to give us new insight, new awareness, God will answer. Even better than we ourselves, he knows what we can most profitably take in.

First and foremost
Someone was needed to go the whole way to hell and back. The complete route had never been experienced by anyone – still less anyone who was powering through hell with the weight of the world's sin, and out the other end with all of eternity. The very volume that Jesus carried, spiritually speaking, was enough to knock the daylights out of hell. May we reflect on the *power* that Jesus took to the cross, the *force* that sent him beyond death and out of the tomb, as tonight we thank him – inadequately, but sincerely – for the prize his effort won.

Suggested hymns
Beneath the cross of Jesus; Glory be to Jesus; My song is love unknown; Sing, my tongue, the glorious battle.

Easter Eve 10 April *(not the Easter Vigil)*
The Christian's Reply Job 14:1–11 or Lam. 3:1–9, 19–24; Ps. 31:1–4, 15–16; 1 Pet. 4:1–8; Matthew 27:57–66 or John 19:38–42

'Above all, maintain constant love for one another, for love covers a multitude of sins.' 1 Peter 4:8

Antidote to evil

This is the Christian's reply, the arch-antidote to the evil that was abroad on Good Friday – LOVE. Jesus showed it to the women of Jerusalem when he acknowledged their sympathy (Luke 23:28); to the soldiers in their rough cruelty (Luke 23:34); to Mary and John (John 19:26–27); and to the penitent thief (Luke 23:43). It had been love that brought him to the cross, and love was going to see him through death and out into eternity. The more of God's love that we can show and share, the greater difficulty Satan will have in piercing our spiritual armour.

Is there someone who has a grievance of any kind against us (or vice versa)? We may not physically *like* that person – but God loves him; can we let God's love flow through us? The more we can pray in love for someone, it becomes easier to see him as a brother – yes, even though it may take a lot of praying!

Change of heart

We know that a change of heart began in at least one observer at Calvary. 'He praised God and said, "Certainly this man was innocent"' (Luke 23:47). We may reverently wonder what this centurion went on to believe. Would he ever be the same again? Have we touched someone's life with the love of Jesus and seen the beginnings of spiritual transformation? If so, we have an inkling of the loving power that drove Jesus on to see the fulfilling of his mission.

A lot of sins

Love is strong. St Peter tells us that it is powerful enough to hide a lot of sins – and anything which can do that is surely worth cultivating. The sins we remember, we can confess; but even in one short day are there not some we conveniently or actually forget? Suppose we never recall these? Are we to be for ever damned? No, St Peter teaches, God is kinder than that; if we show and share his love, even those forgotten sins can be obliterated from the record. Hallelujah!

The love-walk

Walking in God's love means taking no note of imaginary or real insults, calumnies or similar weapons of Satan. Refusing to bear a grudge, for instance, robs it *by love* of its power to injure us.

Overcoming fear *by love* takes away the strength of fear to incapacitate us for God's work.

When shall we realize that God *would not allow* evil, if at the same time he did not provide the means to overcome it? The realization will come with practice: a lot of practice. The long-established tendency to fear will take perhaps a lifetime to eradicate.

So close to joy
We are so close to the joy of Easter Day. How are we going to share its joy? its love? its triumph? Can we shed our worries, our hang-ups, our grudges, our phobias – just for one day, as a new beginning? And then, the next day, for just one day – and so on? Or will Easter come and go, and leave us, spiritually speaking, prisoners of our fears?

Like Mary, we have shared the grief of Friday.

Like Mary, can we embrace the joy of Resurrection Day?

Time is rushing us into Easter. Can we make this quality decision – now?

Suggested hymns
Be thou my vision; Forth in thy name, O Lord, I go; Low in the grave he lay; Resting from his work today.

Easter Vigil 10–11 April **He Told You!**
Ex. 14:10–31; 15:20–21; Ps. 114; Rom. 6:3–11;
Luke 24:1–12, and a minimum of two further OT
readings from: Gen 1:1—2:4a; Gen. 7:1–5, 11–18;
8:16–18; 9:8–15; Gen. 22:1–18; Isa. 55:1–11; Canticle:
Isa. 12:2–6; Ps. 136:1–9, 23–26; Ps. 46; Ps. 16;
Baruch 3:9–15, 32–44 or Prov. 8:1–8, 19–21; 9:46–6;
Ps. 19; Pss. 42, 43; Ps. 143; Ps. 98; Ezek. 36:24–28;
Ezek. 37:1–14; Zeph. 3:14–20

'Remember how he told you when he was still in Galilee, that the Son of Man must be handed over to sinners, and be crucified, and on the third day rise again.' Luke 24:6–7

111

How could anyone forget?

How could such close friends forget a promise like this? Did they reject it as being far-fetched? Yet Jesus had given them ample justification to believe him over his three-year ministry. Had the fear of Good Friday so paralysed their minds that they could not believe death for Jesus was not the end? No one can step convincingly into another's shoes – and who is to say that we should have been any more credulous than these women?

The angels

The two men in dazzling clothes, at an inexplicably empty tomb, may have reminded Peter and his friends of the Transfiguration experience (Mark 9:3); but the women had presumably not been told of this (Mark 9:9 – 'As they were coming down from the mountain, [Jesus] ordered them to tell no one about what they had seen, until after the Son of man had risen from the dead'). Be this as it may, sudden realization jerks the women into memory-recall mode, and they leave the tomb in a flurry of excitement that, yes, the unbelievable can be believed! In these earliest minutes of another Easter Day, we can dispense with the uncertainty and can surely go straight into full and utter joy. Christ *is* risen!

An obligation to suffer

Christ had to suffer. The writing had been on the wall. He must be handed over . . . crucified, and on the third day rise again (v. 7). There could be no other way, no other saviour, no other salvation. The whole world, and people till kingdom come, was waiting for Christ to complete his mission. It had to be.

That the Romans were in power, and crucifixion their recognized form of torture, also had to be. Christ had to die on the tree, in a much more shameful manner than the Jewish form of despatch either by stoning or by a spear. In the end, we know his body was speared – but this was *post mortuum* (John 19:33–34). It did not matter then how much blood and water left the body of Jesus: his Spirit was already in his Father's hands (Luke 23:46; John 19:30).

How long in hell?

'Thou shalt not leave my soul in hell, neither shalt thou suffer thy Holy One to see corruption' (Psalm 16:11, BCP), sang the psalmist, centuries before the prophecy came to pass. As we ponder on the actual moment of dying, we can only reverently accept that for

Jesus *time* was no more: the triumphing over principalities and powers (cf. Colossians 2:15) may have taken a millisecond or most of the weekend. Who knows, and does it matter? By the time the tomb opened, the mission had been accomplished. We make our Easter gardens, roll the stone away, gaze at the tiny shreds of folded material, and say, 'How beautiful!', as we look at the spring flowers brightening the moss and stones.

We can understand the primroses and hyacinths, the tiny daffodils and hazel catkins. But we still cannot comprehend the power that moved the stone, or the care that folded the abandoned graveclothes. And why need we understand? Easter and its joy is not about logic, but simple, genuine faith.

Let's share the grand message: 'Christ is risen! He is risen indeed!'

Suggested hymns
Alleluia, alleluia, hearts to heaven and voices raise; Jesus Christ is risen today; The day of resurrection; Ye choirs of new Jerusalem.

Easter Day   11 April   *Principal Service*
Eternal Brotherhood   Acts 10:34–43 or Isa. 65:17–25; Ps. 118:1–2, 14–24; 1 Cor. 15:19–26 or Acts 10:34–43; John 20:1–18 or Luke 24:1–12

'Jesus said to [Mary], "Do not hold on to me, because I have not yet ascended to the Father. But go to my brothers and say to them, 'I am ascending to my Father, and your Father, to my God, and your God.'"'
John 20:17

Still in the family
The relationships forged prior to the resurrection were to continue in essence unchanged: Mary could relate to Jesus (almost) as before, though he told her not to cling to him. Why was this? Because, in his resurrection body, though it *felt* like a normal body (and though he was able to eat as normal, Luke 24:39, 42), it could appear and disappear at will (John 20:19), and to do this while Mary was holding on to him would surely have given her a shock which Jesus would not inflict.

Easter is primarily a time of joy, but it also brings a challenge: to see the divide between this life and the next, not as a yawning chasm, but as a very thin line – a line that can, in spirit, be crossed at will. The Easter message is one of continuity. Much, inevitably, changes on the physical perspective, when death intervenes; but the risen Jesus brings the challenging message: Look! life and love go on; life in a grander, freer mode. Relationships known in this life continue unchanged in the next – and I am with you, wherever you are, whatever you are doing.

Sometimes we may sense the proximity of our loved ones: an indefinable awareness – comforting, yet fleeting. Most of us are in fact shy about sharing such experiences. Mary, after all, was not believed when she ran to the disciples with her Easter news (John 20:18; cf. Luke 24:11). But if we can take the risk of not being believed, our sharing may encourage others to do likewise. God's glimpses of life's next chapter did not stop with Revelation: when he decides that we need the spiritual 'lift' that such a glimpse can give, he provides one. And who does not benefit from a bit of encouragement?

The best of all days
Easter itself – the best of days – gives us great encouragement, and faith to believe that God is very much in control. Jesus may have had to work hard for most of that day to persuade his nearest and dearest that his resurrection had taken place; even today, there are many otherwise orthodox Christians who have reservations about Easter. Can we share our joy with some of these? Can we pray the Lord to give us the right words at the right time?

> *He was born, like you and I,*
> *In a body that must die,*
> *Yet his death was not for ever,*
> *   He lives on.*
> *Who is this, who, when we've met,*
> *Is right here with us, and yet*
> *   He's with God –*
> *What makes us think that's somewhere else?*
>
> *Hubert Richards*

The Easter Christ knows no bounds. He is here, with us, as really as he was with Mary in the garden. Yet he is really with God – and it's only our limited language that gets in the way of explaining it better. Our loved ones in glory know him no less truly. Yet he is still mindful of the earth where once he left the linen grave-clothes. One day he'll even more truly return, in glory, from glory – but he will never again need those trappings of death.

> *One day the grave could contain him no longer,*
> *One day the stone rolled away from the tomb;*
> *Jesus arose! over death he had conquered,*
> *Now he is risen, my Lord evermore!*
> *. . . One day he's coming, oh, glorious day!*
>
> *J. Wilbur Chapman*

Family Service input
Have ready sufficient moss, stones, three crosses, linen, small containers for water, flowers or potted plants, and involve the young people in creating an Easter garden.

Suggested hymns
Jesus Christ is risen today; Jesus lives! thy terrors now; Now the green blade rises; The strife is o'er.

Easter Day *Second Service* **Even to Me**
Pss. 66, 114, 117; Isa. 43:1–21; 1 Cor. 15:1–11 or John 20:19–23

'Last of all, as to someone untimely born [Jesus] appeared also to me. For I am the least of the apostles, unfit to be called an apostle, because I persecuted the Church of God.' 1 Corinthians 15:8–9

Lowest in the ranks
Although, in all honesty, Paul knows he has worked harder for the gospel than any of the other apostles (v. 10), albeit in Christ's strength rather than his own, he is humble enough to see himself as below them in ranking. Why? Because the memory of his history of persecuting the Church prior to his conversion is always with him. God has forgiven him, and has dropped that sin deep down out of sight in the sea of the divine forgetfulness – and for that Paul is eternally grateful. But Paul is human, and it is very human

115

to remember our failings, even when God has forgotten them. If *we* don't, it's likely that others will jog our memories. Paul's persecution had been so energetic and convincing, there would still be plenty of people around with long memories. He could not hide his past, so he makes his thankfulness for God's forgiveness a part of his preaching and teaching. 'Look! God has done this for me – picked me out of the depths of anti-Christian awfulness, and has shown his faith and trust in me as a missionary for Christ! And what he has done for me, he can do for anyone!' This is the gist of his message.

The 'resurrection chapter'

And Paul's joy erupts in what has come to be known as the 'resurrection chapter' of 1 Corinthians. It is a simple but hard-hitting defence of the resurrection, couched largely in conventional legal terms: 'This has happened . . . these are the witnesses . . . these are the repercussions and the ongoing reasons for it . . . you can and must believe it, because it affects all of us for eternity.'

It is meant to appeal to Jews seeking the truth about Jesus; to Greeks still caught up in the worship of a pantheon of deities; and to everyone else who wonders if such a turnaround of the normal death-interment-corruption pattern could be possible.

The plain case

It is a 'case for the defence', set out as plainly and directly as Paul knew how. Behind it is nevertheless an unspoken regret that he was not a witness, with Peter and the others, of the Passion and that first Easter Day. But, he consoles himself, he has been given revelation-experiences of his own (e.g. v. 8), and for these he is so thankful.

It surely means that we can have a particular empathy with Paul, as we share his 'resurrection chapter' – for we, too, have shared in the Passion and the first Easter *at secondhand*, though the scenes are so familiar to us as to be a part and parcel of our spiritual experience. Wouldn't we have longed, though, to have been there, standing, wondering, fearing, then finally joyfully believing, with Peter and the others! We can understand something of Paul's longing to have been a part of it all.

What Paul has done . . .

Peter, James, John and the others went on to fulfil their missions in varying ways; but Paul went further, travelled more, preached

116

more, wrote more – and suffered more. At a time when travel was possible throughout the Roman empire, but often dangerous, and pagan religions as well as animosity and apathy towards the Church was rife, he pressed on.

The Easter story challenges us in the same way today. We have it, in our Bibles and in our hearts. What are we going to do with it?

Suggested hymns
Christ the Lord is risen again! Come, ye faithful, raise the strain; Thine be the glory; This is the day, this is the day.

Second Sunday of Easter   18 April
Principal Service   **Bearers of News**   Acts 5:27–32; Ps. 118:14–29 or Ps. 150; Rev. 1:4–8; John 20:19–31

'But Thomas (who was called the Twin), one of the twelve, was not with them when Jesus came. So the other disciples told him, "We have seen the Lord." But he said to them, "Unless I see the mark of the nails in his hands, and put my finger in the mark of the nails and my hand in his side, I will not believe."' John 20:24–25

Standing with Thomas
In a way, we stand alongside Thomas, in that we usually hear about the gospel from someone else – whether it is in childhood on our mother's knee, or from teachers in Sunday school or day school, or later in life from friends, neighbours, the media or who-ever. Thomas could not take it, even from people whom he knew and loved and had worked with for years. And, as we know, Jesus still loved him enough to keep him waiting only one short week before he gave his doubting friend all the proof he had asked for, and more. But, how do we cope? Do we demand proof from God every time? Do we put out a fleece, like Gideon? Do we hedge the gospel around with conditions and caveats? If we are asked, point-blank, 'Do you believe in the resurrection?' how confident are we in our reply? Would a questioner seeking Jesus find him in the answers we give? Are we being true ambassadors for Christ – or would our enquirer go away unsatisfied, unconvinced? These questions are part of the challenge of the risen Christ. Four months

117

or so ago, we were challenged by the Child in the manger – but now the risen Christ asks of us so much more, for all eternity is at stake.

A joyful challenge
It is a challenge that should not dilute our Easter joy, but rather accentuate it. God has not given us belief for doubt, life for death, hope for despair, for us to enjoy our Easter eggs today and to resume the worries of the world tomorrow. If Easter is to mean anything at all, then it must mean everything. The Christ whom the tomb could hold no longer is waiting for what we are going to make of the joy he has given us. We can delay, we can give way to the 'holy bargaining' in which Thomas indulged – and, yes, God may consider that we are lost unless he does something as convincing as Jesus did. But, dare we take that risk? Have we not more belief under our belts than had Thomas? We have the whole of the New Testament; we have two thousand years of Christian growth and witness, to say nothing of Christ's personal dealings with us. Yes, we are surely more spiritually mature than Thomas – but that gives us surely more spiritual responsibility.

Beyond the point of no return
We are 'into' Christ, beyond the point of no return. Can we not grasp with all our spiritual strength the sheer freedom this implies? God has signed our contract in the blood of Calvary, which nothing on earth (or in heaven) can obliterate. For all eternity, we are committed. With our future so assured, can we not give Jesus everything we have? It is his, anyway, for him to claim convincingly at any time, in any place, as we navigate the sea of life.

Keep on growing
'Grow in grace and knowledge of our Lord and Saviour Jesus Christ,' St Peter continues to urge us, even command us (2 Peter 3:18). We can grow through communion with Christ – but, as members of his body the Church, he intends also for us to grow through and by others. Thomas disbelieved what his friends were telling him of Christ. May we not make the same mistake. Ministry is not a one-man operation, but a sharing in the gospel which knows no inclusivity: 'God so loved the world, that he gave his only Son, so that *everyone* who believes in him . . . may have eternal life' (John 3:16).

Family Service input
Share the story beind 'Eternal Father, strong to save (see below)
with the young people; encourage them to illustrate it and/or to
write a hymn for sailors and the sea themselves.

Suggested hymns
Christ the Lord is risen today; The first day of the week; Eternal
Father, strong to save; The Lord is risen indeed.

Hymn stories

Eternal Father, strong to save
Whenever we remember those who put to sea, leaving family and
friends to harvest the fruits of the sea for us – to ferry merchandise
to and from other countries for our benefit, and those on warships
and naval patrols who do so much to keep our country safe – we
sing this sailors' hymn.

Its author, William Whiting, was born in 1825 in Kensington,
West London, where his father was a grocer. When William was
four years old, the family moved to Clapham, which then was a
village on the south side of the capital, in the Winchester Diocese.

William applied his energies to studying, and became a Master
at the Quiristers (Choristers) School, where he taught for 36 years.
He wrote this hymn in 1860, and it was quickly adopted by sailors
throughout the British empire, then the Commonwealth, and even
by the French Navy.

When Sir Winston Churchill met President Franklin D. Roose-
velt aboard the warship *Prince of Wales*, in the North Atlantic
during the Second World War, this was the hymn Churchill chose
to be sung at the service.

Originally written for one of Whiting's pupils who was about
to sail to America, he titled it 'For those at sea', and added the
text: 'They that go down to the sea in ships, that do business in
great waters; these see the works of the Lord, and His wonders
in the deep' (Psalm 107:24). Whiting died in 1878.

Second Sunday of Easter *Second Service*
Don't You Know? Ps. 16; Isa. 52:13—53:12 or
53:1–6, 9–12; Luke 24:13–35

'Then one of them, whose name was Cleopas, answered him, "Are you the only stranger in Jerusalem who does not know the things that have taken place there in these days?"' Luke 24:18

A city in ferment

This spontaneous reaction of Cleopas to the apparent ignorance of Jesus gives us a precious hint as to the state of Jerusalem behind the accounts in the Gospels: a city not carrying on as normal, not even observing the protracted ceremonies and celebrations attendant to the Passover season as normal; a Jerusalem in ferment, as believers asserted the testimony of the empty tomb and abandoned grave-clothes; the Jewish religious hierarchy claiming that the body of Jesus had been stolen (Matthew 28:13); the Romans perpetuating the policy of Pilate in washing their hands of the whole affair; and everyone else discussing the question and probably offering their own theories as to what exactly had happened.

The relative silence on all this by the other evangelists is natural enough; they were basically interested in affirming the reality of the resurrection, rather than what the Jerusalem public in general had to say about it. But Luke's reportage of Cleopas' remark heightens the courage of the disciples in remaining in Jerusalem at such a time. True, there is something in the human psyche that draws us to the place where our loved ones have shared their last hours with us – but Jerusalem on the resurrection day could have been anything but a health resort for known followers of Jesus. We can reverently surmise that, as the hours passed, such high-profile persecutors as Annas and Caiaphas would have their revengeful ardour curbed by the suspicion that, yes, the 'King of the Jews' *had* actually risen from the dead. As the hours extended into days and weeks, and Pentecost confirmed the turnaround from fearful ex-fishermen and tax-collectors into unstoppable ambassadors for Christ, the high priest and high priest emeritus would have even more cause for concern.

Giving way to worry

Yet Jesus, very convincingly, chided Cleopas and his friend for giving way to worry and doubts, and allowing the general unrest and excitement to deflect them from the one thing necessary for their salvation. Christ had risen! We, too, can be 'infected' by the prevailing local conditions (of the weather, the news, our friends' preoccupations), to the detriment of our ongoing mission. Not many years ago, a Roman Catholic priest returned home to Britain, having been tortured and imprisoned in the Asian country where he had been ministering. After a short furlough, he went back *to the same country*, with several crates of Bibles and teaching material for men studying for the ministry. On the quayside, officials forced him to open every one of the crates for inspection, with his bare hands. As the ship turned away from the harbour, a passenger with whom the priest had struck up a friendship on the outward voyage, called from the rail: 'How goes it with you?' The priest looked up from the crate he was opening, and pointed aloft: 'I'm keeping my eyes on the cross!' he shouted, with a smile of triumph. May we do the same, no matter what distractions the Devil tries to bring our way. Cleopas and his friend had taken their eyes off Jesus and were focusing on the problem of the empty tomb, not on the solution of the resurrection truth. Jesus redirected their hearts with a joy that gave them courage to return immediately to Jerusalem.

Our eyes on Jesus?
Have we got our eyes on Jesus today, or on some extraneous part of the Easter celebrations? Or on something else entirely? If we pray him, God will redirect us. If we can manage the manoeuvre ourselves, it will show him that we are even more committed. And then he will lead us on.

> *I do not know what lies ahead, the way I cannot see,*
> *Yet one stands near to be my Guide,*
> *He'll show the way to me.*
> *I know who holds the future,*
> *And I know he holds my hand.*
> *With God things don't just happen,*
> *Everything by him is planned.*

> *Eugene Clark and Alfred B. Smith*

121

Alleluia, alleluia, hearts to heaven and voices raise; Jesus calls us, o'er the tumult; Now the green blade rises; The strife is o'er, the battle done.

Third Sunday of Easter   25 April
Principal Service   **Amen to This!**
Acts 9:1–6[7–20]; Ps. 30; Rev. 5:11–14; John 21:1–19

'Then I heard every creature in heaven and on earth and under the earth and in the sea and all that is in them, singing, "To the one seated on the throne and to the Lamb be blessing and honour and glory and might for ever and ever!" And the four living creatures said, "Amen!" And the elders fell down and worshipped.' Revelation 5:13–14

So let it be
In many churches, the affirmatory 'Amen' is usually a *sotto voce*, even desultory, acknowledgement by the congregation that the minister has come to the end of a prayer or the Gloria. Far from being a resounding agreement, the next prayer is often under way before many worshippers have even framed the word. Why are we so chary in our response?

> For ever with the Lord,
> Amen, so let it be;
> Life from the dead is in that word,
> 'Tis immortality.

> James Montgomery

In a loud voice
Had the four living creatures merely whispered their affirmation, conceivably the aged John may not have heard it – so we can believe that it was given in pretty good volume. 'Amen' goes beyond a nod of the head, or even a simple 'Yes'. It is meant to be a heartfelt acknowledgement that the truths which undergird our lives here, and those that comprise eternity – the majesty of God, the sacrifice of Christ, the multifaceted power of the Spirit – have reached our inner being. Well, they have, haven't they? *Amen*!

It is as though we are saying: I believe – committing ourselves, as often as we say it, to the things of Christ. It is, in effect, a triple affirmation of the past, present and future; the 'yesterday, today and for ever' of Christ. With this simple, single word, handed down from the religion of our Lord's own day, we declare our debt to the Old Covenant, our allegiance to the New, and through Christ our eternal hope.

One word

One word – echoing through the courts of the Almighty in heaven! As we catch the echo, let us return it with a good rate of interest, conscious not only of the solemnity of our affirmation, but also of the joy our enthusiasm will bring to God. Heaven is full of corporate worship; Jesus made it his business (Luke 4:16). Let us participate in it fully; for it to reach the throne of heaven in perfect harmony, it needs all of us to play our part.

How often do we thank God for the precious glimpses of heaven and eternity, given us hither and yon in Holy Writ? And nowhere more generously and beautifully than in the Apocalypse. He needn't have done it: he could have kept us a hundred per cent in ignorance. But he is God. He is good. And on any study of these peeps beyond the veil, we can find no justification for the assumption that heaven is a place of solemn mien and whispers. It's noisy, exciting and even alarming at times, with the worship so fervent, the doorposts shake in their sockets (Isaiah 6:4)! How often do we raise the roof with 'Amen!' here on earth? and surely the most stoutly constructed of our buildings is flimsy compared to the architecture of heaven!

High-profile worship

Is there a case for lifting the profile of our worship? Shall we come and argue it out with the Lord (Isaiah 1:18)? The more energy and life we give to God, the more he will give us in return. The Bank of the Holy and Undivided Trinity has never yet failed to give any of its clients an abundant rate of interest on investment. We can draw on it with confidence, for neither is it ever in danger of being stripped of its assets, filing for bankruptcy or going into liquidation.

As we stack up the 'assets', can we resolve to thank God that, with St Paul, we can truly affirm that in Christ 'every one of God's promises is a "Yes". For this reason it is through him that we say the "Amen", to the glory of God' (2 Corinthians 1:20).

Family Service input
Encourage the young people to write or illustrate a hymn on 'The Easter Jesus'.

Suggested hymns
Alleluia, alleluia, give thanks to the risen Lord; Christ the Lord is risen today; I know that my Redeemer lives, what joy; Through all the changing scenes of life.

Third Sunday of Easter   *Second Service*
If Only   Ps. 86; Isa. 38:9–20; John 11:[17–26] 27–44

'Martha said to Jesus, "Lord, if you had been here, my brother would not have died." ' . . . '[Mary] said to him, "Lord, if you had been here, my brother would not have died." ' John 11:21, 32

How much trust?
Are we trusting Jesus for less than we know he can give? There was nothing wrong with the faith of Martha and Mary, as far as it went. They trusted Jesus the Healer one hundred per cent; had he been there when Lazarus was ill, he would have healed him, for sure! But the sisters were trusting Jesus for less than he knew he could give; and so he deliberately delayed his arrival in Bethany until he could give them a far greater blessing.

Can we ever ask God for too much? No: he may deny us what we request, but for our good – not because we ask beyond his means to provide.

> *Trust him, when your wants are many;*
> *Trust him, when your wants are few;*
> *Trust him, when to trust him only*
> *Seems the hardest thing to do.*
>
> *Anon.*

God's timing is not always synchronized with our expectations, and waiting for an outcome to our prayers can indeed be the hardest thing to do. We can reverently imagine the feelings of Martha and Mary, as they sent the message for help to Jesus and waited for him to come – getting more and more anxious as Lazarus' condition worsened. Then came the 'end', as they saw it, and still no sign of Jesus and no word of explanation for the delay. God does not need to explain himself or his actions. The sisters were learning that the hard way.

In the East, death and burial would take place the same day. And still no Jesus, even for the funeral! *Four days* of anguish later, and he comes. And, 'Lord, if you had been here . . . !' is the nearest they come to a rebuke. Their friendship softened the words into 'my brother would not have died', and they ran to greet their friend.

And Jesus definitely had not come 'too late'.

God's perfect timing

Likewise, the resurrection of Jesus was at the perfect time, according to God's will. It didn't matter that Jerusalem was busy with other things: the Zealot uprisings, the ongoing problems in Galilee and the Decapolis, the Roman army of occupation and the many tensions that brought. Jerusalem being the seething, volatile city it was, would have busied itself with other things, at whatever time in history God had chosen for the greatest happening the world had ever known. If we are waiting for *our* understanding of 'the perfect time', for any of our plans or someone else's, chances are we are in for a long wait – and, like as not, God will surprise us in some way while we are waiting for something else.

Keeping faith

But however long it takes, let us take a leaf out of Martha's and Mary's book, and keep faith. Although they believed Jesus had come too late, they nevertheless ran to welcome him. Although the words of pent-up anxiety came tumbling out, they were still glad to see him. Although, even at the tomb, Martha ventured a last protest of practicality versus spirituality, she still did as Jesus commanded and had the tomb opened.

And then, after all the tension, the waiting, the weeping – the miracle, greater than the sisters had expected, yet fulfilling the deep longing of their hearts: to have Lazarus restored to them, as whole as if he had not been ill, never mind had died!

> *Never be sad or desponding,*
> *If thou hast faith to believe;*
> *Grace, for the duties before thee,*
> *Ask of thy God and receive.*

> Fanny J. Crosby

Suggested hymns
Alleluia, alleluia, hearts to heaven; Come, let us join our cheerful songs; Low in the grave he lay; The day of resurrection.

Fourth Sunday of Easter   2 May
Principal Service   **Look at What I Am Doing**
Acts 9:36–43; Ps. 23; Rev. 7:9–17; John 10:22–30

'Jesus answered, "I have told you, and you do not believe. The works that I do in my Father's name testify to me; but you do not believe, because you do not belong to my sheep."' John 10:25–26

Black is white?
There is a saying, of the attitude of people who do not want to believe what is staring them in the face: 'Black is white, and blue is no colour at all!' It is a version of Jesus' words: 'Do you have eyes, and fail to see? Do you have ears, and fail to hear?' (Mark 8:18). He was healing the sick, raising the dead, curing the blind, preaching the gospel to (i.e., enriching the lives of) the poor. What better testimony could he give as to who he was?

> *Convince a man against his will,*
> *And he'll be of the same opinion still.*

Those who criticized Jesus were not to be converted, no matter what he did. He would rise from the dead, and they still would not believe (cf. Luke 16:31). What gets into a person, at some point between their eyes and their heart, and turns white into black, good into evil, positive into negative, belief into disbelief, truth into falsehood? Satan: twisting, lying, distorting, destroying and killing.

126

The only solution

So what can we do? Leave these obstinate souls to get deeper into the pit that the Devil is persuading them to dig? When Jesus sent out the first mission teams, his orders fell within pretty tight parameters: 'Go nowhere among the Gentiles, and enter no town of the Samaritans . . . If anyone will not welcome you or listen to your words, shake off the dust from your feet as you leave that house or town' (Matthew 10:5, 24). Are *we* to leave the unwelcoming to their own devices? Well, it may be so; but only after we have given them the gospel news; only when they have been given a chance of believing for eternal life; only when, in Jesus' name, we have tried; only when, however briefly, they have had an opportunity to see Christ's love in action. If they pass up that opportunity, the seed has been sown, and we have done our duty.

Remember the millions of poppy seeds, laid dormant for months in Flanders fields, and brought to glorious, colourful beauty by the churned-up mud of the Great War's carnage. Think of the hope kindled in so many hurting hearts which, ever since, these red poppies have brought.

Remember building sites in many cities, where masonry has been razed and earth – dry and seemingly inert – brought to the light of day: on every site, within a few short weeks or even days, seeds invisible to the naked eye have sprung to life and colour. Who knows when a seed we have sown in an apparently cold heart will be warmed in God's good time into something beautiful for Christ?

Gospel seed

A Chinese student at a British university became friends with a group of Christians who shared the gospel with her – but, her course completed, she returned home seemingly unaffected by their ministry. Years later, her sister enrolled at another British university, and in turn struck up a friendship with local Christians. Why? Because her elder sister had told her that Christians were friendly and to be trusted: really good people to know. It was not long before this younger sister became a Christian. Had the earlier ministry to her sister been wasted?

Family Service input

Encourage the young people to sow a collection of flowers, for planting as a 'Garden of Hope' in the churchyard/for growing as pot-plants indoors/ for local nursing homes, rest homes, etc.

Suggested hymns
For the beauty of the earth; Living Lord; Loving Shepherd of thy
sheep; Who are these like stars appearing?

Fourth Sunday of Easter   *Second Service*
Clothed with Power   Pss. 113, 114; Isa. 63:7–14;
Luke 24:36–49

*'You are witnesses of these things. And see, I am sending upon you what
my Father promised; so stay here in the city until you have been clothed
with power from on high.' Luke 24:48–49*

Stay here
Stay in Jerusalem, ablaze with venom towards Jesus and his known
followers? Stay, when prudence dictated a diplomatic retreat to
Galilee? Sometimes today God tells us to stay in the hot spot,
where, even though we may not be active in mission or anything
else, it is nevertheless the place he wants us to be until a new part
of his plan for us is made known. The one thing that kept the
disciples in the seething hot-bed of Jerusalem was this command
of Jesus to 'stay'.

The reason why
Jesus was thoughtful enough to give them the reason for staying.
As he had promised, God would give them power for the next
stage of their ministry. For 40 days from the resurrection to the
ascension, they had wondered; very soon now, they would know
what form that power would take; in ten short days, it would be
made clear to them at Pentecost, in the descent of the Holy Spirit.
With divine forethought and understanding, they were to be
equipped with all the languages and courage they needed to go
out from Jerusalem to as many lands as they could reach. God
keeps his promises – always, and with a degree of generosity that
can leave us wondering why we ever doubted that he was able.

Eye-witnesses
The disciples had been eye-witnesses to the events of the past
three years leading up to the ascension of Jesus and the giving
of the Holy Spirit. They could therefore speak from first-hand

experience. Jesus had done great things for them. For us, he does no less, and we have his same Holy Spirit. We may not have a physical bond of ministry to equal that enjoyed by Peter and the others (and envied to some degree by St Paul); but we have his abiding word: the New Testament, which is like no other book, but is an inspired, composite record of the life of Jesus and the earliest days of the Church. Is it our number one, most-read book? Is it our constant companion, and the source of all our conversation, strength and witness? We *are* witnesses, in an even fuller way than the disciples – for our Lord, in word *and* Spirit, never leaves us.

Full-time or part-time?
No one but ourselves can determine whether we use God's resources to the full, or selectively: whether we are full-time or part-time Christians. Probably we have all known what it is to visit a home and to refer to the Bible, only to be told: 'Oh, we have one somewhere – in the loft, I think.' Or to welcome a stranger to a flower festival, and to be asked: 'Where does this text come from? Who wrote this book called Revelation? Is it in print?'

In 2004, with so many people still ignoring, or still ignorant of the world's bestseller, what can we do – we, who, like the disciples, 'have been clothed with power from on high'? Will it need the second coming of Jesus to bring the world to an awareness of God? The answer is surely 'Yes'. But will even this convert those who do not want to believe? No: they will go, as God has foretold, to the 'second death', because their names are not written in the Lamb's Book of Life (Revelation 20:14–15). We are not their saviour or their judge. God is both, and will exercise all the power at his command.

Meanwhile, may we use all the power he has given us, to spread and share his word. We shall not convince the world – but we shall make a difference.

Suggested hymns
And can it be?; Father of mercies, in thy word; I come with joy to meet my Lord; Let saints on earth in concert sing.

Fifth Sunday of Easter   9 May
Principal Service   **Even to the Gentiles**
Acts 11:1–18; Ps. 148; Rev. 21:1–6; John 13:31–35

'When they had heard this they were silenced. And they praised God, saying, "Then God has given even to the Gentiles the repentance that leads to life."' Acts 11:18

Taken by surprise

When we have stopped being surprised by God, we have stopped growing in faith. He delights in surprising us – just as an earthly father plans beautiful surprises for his children. The inclusion of non-Jews in the salvation brought about by Calvary was not new (see, e.g., Genesis 12:3; 28:14; Isaiah 2:2; Haggai 2:7; Zechariah 14:2); but the ultra-conservative Jews had chosen to see the Messiah's role as exclusively for the Jews. Peter himself had hesitated to break with what he had always understood as 'tradition' (Acts 11:18), but the vision and the subsequent meeting with Cornelius had convinced him of the wider application of Christ's sacrifice.

On the face of it, the subject was fraught with danger: if the Gentiles were to be treated equally with Jews in the Christian order of things (e.g. Galatians 3:28), wasn't this likely to dissuade *any* Jews from accepting the gospel? The apostles, had they lived nineteen centuries or so later, would surely have said 'Amen' to the declaration of C. T. Studd (cricketer, pioneer and missionary): 'No craze so great as that of the gambler, and no gambler for Jesus was ever cured, thank God!'

Is our own journey of faith leading us through danger and excitement just now? If not, why not? None of the risks we can take come close to that taken by God when he sent his Son to be the Saviour of the world: scratch accommodation on the night of his birth; a long trek into Egypt out of reach of a puppet-king with paranoia; a wilderness experience with Satan; continued animosity, suspicion and intrigue during his ministry – and then Calvary. And, as the final insult, lies that the disciples had stolen his body while the guards at the tomb were sleeping on duty. Can our experiences ever come near to these? So why don't we do, and dare, more for God? Why don't we take him at his word, that he will see us through?

130

> *Set free from present sorrow,*
> *We cheerfully can say:*
> *'E'en let the unknown morrow*
> *Bring with it what it may.*
> *It can bring with it nothing*
> *But he will see us through;*
> *Who gives the lilies clothing*
> *Will clothe his people too.'*

William Cowper

Seeing Christ in others

It is a big thing to know Christ in our lives: an even greater thing to be able to see him in others. Those Jews who accepted with grace that God could save Gentiles, would experience a new freedom and openness in their own lives. If we look for Jesus in others, we shall find him – and in finding him there, experience more of him in our own. How this works, no logician or psychoanalyst can fully explain: it is divine alchemy beautifully and majestically at work. Can we find our Lord in those with whom we are less comfortable? Those who, like Jew and Gentile, have not been traditionally of our creed, culture or colour? Can we find largeness of spirit to accept that they can break with centuries-old beliefs, to accept Christ? As we work through these questions, the enormity of the Jews' acceptance of Gentiles to God's salvation will surely impact more strongly.

Family Service input

Have to hand copies of the current religious periodicals/newspapers for the young people to extract topics for inclusion in the intercessions, or to make an intercessions book of their own.

Suggested hymns

From Greenland's icy mountains; Hills of the north, rejoice; In Christ there is no east or west; O, what their joy and their glory must be.

Fifth Sunday of Easter *Second Service*
At the Tomb Ps. 98; Dan. 6:[1–5]6–23;
Mark 15:46—16:8

'As they entered the tomb, they saw a young man, dressed in a white robe, sitting on the right side, and they were alarmed. But he said to them, "Do not be alarmed. You are looking for Jesus of Nazareth, who was crucified. He has been raised. He is not here. Look, there is the place they laid him."' Mark 16:5–6

Master of the situation
When we rush into an experience that turns out to be very different from what we have expected, it can be very disturbing. And if someone who is on top of the situation says, 'Don't worry!' we probably don't take their advice. The three women were no exceptions: even after the short conversation with the calm young man, they ran from the tomb in stark terror. Wouldn't we have done the same? And don't we, on occasion, seek for Jesus – in an unfamiliar situation, perhaps – and instead of a prayerful, comforting word, we are met by a stranger who is difficult to believe? Is it really God speaking? But we are not receiving the message for which we were looking!

A natural errand
The women's errand that morning was understandable: they had been prevented by the lateness of the hour from caring for the body of Jesus on the Friday. They had been forced to stay at home on the sabbath. What more natural than to come to the tomb with their spices at the earliest opportunity? In fact, they had been so intent on their mission, they had not even allowed the problem of the stone to deflect them. With a disregard that comes at such a traumatic time, they had probably tacitly assumed that someone would be around. And they were proved right – if not in a way they could comprehend.

But love had brought them. The one-time friends of Jesus had not beaten a path to the tomb. These women were made brave by love. Yet bravery has its limits – and an angel in an empty tomb proved too much to cope with.

Better than our neighbours?

At times we may believe we are making a better fist of being a Christian than our neighbours. But before long we are faced with our 'angel in the tomb', which throws us out of spiritual kilter. And while we are recovering our equilibrium, someone else goes on ahead. Have we been on the wrong tack? The young man knew the women were looking for Jesus: there was nothing amiss with the object of their journey; but they were looking for the 'wrong' Jesus in the wrong place. They had in mind a corpse in a tomb: well, that is where one would expect to find a corpse. But Jesus was alive – very, very much alive: Jesus of *Nazareth* was to be found back in *Galilee*. You do not look for the living in a tomb.

But after three days – as Martha and Mary had in their minds 'locked' Lazarus into the tomb, after four days (John 11:39) – the women could not think of Jesus as being anything but a body in a tomb. The shock of his disappearance, combined with the angel and the stone that had been moved, was too much. 'Do not be alarmed'? They were terrified, and quickly put some distance between themselves and the unknown.

But the mystery of Easter morning was in their minds, and would not allow them to forget until belief and acceptance chased away terror.

We, who *know*, do not associate terror with Eastertide – but how close does our joy bring us to the risen Jesus?

Suggested hymns

All in an Easter garden; Good Christian men, rejoice and sing; Jesus lives! thy terrors now; We sing the praise of him who died.

Sixth Sunday of Easter (Rogation Sunday)
16 May   *Principal Service*   Answered Prayer
Acts 16:9–15; Ps. 67; Rev. 21:10, 22—22:5;
John 14:23–29 or John 5:1–9

'During the night Paul had a vision: there stood a man of Macedonia pleading with him and saying, "Come over to Macedonia and help us."
... The Lord opened [Lydia's] heart to listen eagerly to what was said by Paul.' Acts 16:9, 14

The request – and the response

Paul 'was convinced that God had called' (v. 10), and he answered the call, to find a mission field ripe for harvest in Macedonia, with, among others, Lydia, the seller of Thyatira's famous purple cloth decidedly eager to hear the gospel. It would have been easy for Paul to disregard the dream, or to make excuses that Macedonia was not on his agenda, or the weather was bad, or there was enough to do at Troas to make further travel unnecessary. Instead, he took heed of the call and promptly responded. We can spend so much time thinking about a course of action that we never get around to taking it. Paul was made of sterner stuff.

Going to the source

Rogation Sunday (from the Latin *rogare*, 'to ask'), encourages us to look again at our prayer life: how we pray, how much we pray, and if our prayers are fairly evenly divided between the four 'ACTS':

Adoration
Confession
Thanksgiving
Supplication

– or weighted more heavily to some of these than to others.

Traditionally, when less of the population lived in (sub)urban areas, Rogation Sunday saw congregations asking God to bless the seed and livestock for the coming year. Many rural churches still hold 'Rogation walks', when the priest and people process round the parish, holding a short service of prayer and blessing at each farm. More urban congregations sometimes bring bowls of seed to their services for blessing, and so feel part of the traditional Rogation custom. But the wider understanding of this day is a reflection of the part that prayer plays in our lives. We ask God for many things, even in the course of a single day: but prayer is a two-way operation. When God makes a demand on us, do we respond with the alacrity St Paul showed in the request to go to Macedonia?

Fellowship

Prayer at its most sincere is fellowship with God – surely, yet imperceptibly, growing into God, as Paul had been doing ever since his conversion. How often do we simply rest in God, worshipping, adoring, even revelling in his glory, his majesty, his wonderful goodness and care for us? However much we do this already, we should try it more often! From this comes an awareness of our own shortcomings: we need to get these confessed, repented of and forgiven, before they grow out of proportion or become so well established in our lives that we take them for granted. As we thank God for his forgiveness, and widen our gratitude for his other mercies, we can come at last to intercessory prayer – asking for others as well as (perhaps even more than) ourselves: and at least at Rogationtide we need not worry if this part of our praying is more than the rest.

'Ask, and it will be given to you' (Matthew 7:7). But even at Rogationtide, can we not turn this round, into a prayer of commitment, that – as Paul – whatever God asks of us, we undertake to give him?

Family Service input
Let the young people construct a 'prayer tree' (from either a silver-covered branch, or a natural young tree in leaf, growing in a pot). Write prayers on local/national/international themes: the sick, the bereaved etc., and tie each prayer to the tree. Keep it updated and topical.

Suggested hymns
Dear Lord and Father of mankind; Jesus calls us, o'er the tumult; Lord, in thy name thy servants plead; O for a thousand tongues to sing.

Sixth Sunday of Easter *Second Service*
Go – and Make Pss. 126, 127; Zeph. 3:14–26;
Matthew 28:1–10, 16–20

'[Jesus said], "All authority in heaven and on earth has been given to me. Go therefore and make disciples of all nations, baptizing them in the name of the Father and of the Son and of the Holy Spirit."' Matthew 28:18–19

Urgent and dynamic
There's an urgency, as well as a dynamism, in this charge of Jesus. If we pause to consider the logistics, the sheer scope of his commission will overwhelm us. So let us not linger too long on the imponderables, but spiritually get moving. Statisticians could no doubt tell us how many non-believers have died even while we have been worshipping in church today: dying before someone has reached them with the gospel. Despite the wonderful advances in telecommunications and technology over the past century, millions in today's world remain unreached. There is ever as much urgency to fulfil Christ's commission as two millennia ago. Pray God that millions more Christians will be set on fire for Jesus, and that *mission* will become the Church's top priority, as in the earliest days of the apostolic Church.

A wider mission field
The need truly is for millions, rather than just a few – for, while the world is the same size, the population has grown out of recognition. Yet God, the Great Statistician, will never allow the harvest to be beyond the ingathering of his labourers: *pro rata*, we can accomplish today whatever Paul, Peter and the others could do in the first century. They used the resources to hand, and moved mountains. We, with so many more helps, can surely manage to turn the world upside down for God.

Great moves
Great moves are being made, as more and more land is covered for Christ, more translations of the Bible are being undertaken, and the print-runs of existing translations and versions increase every year. But it is not only the initial impact that the gospel makes on a new believer that is important: the follow-up ministry is crucial. It was said of the early Billy Graham Crusades of the 1950s that thousands of people who had 'made a decision' for Christ at the great services were subsequently lost due to a lack of follow-up. That the commitment of some may have dropped away in any case is surely a poor reason for the mature Christians in the many parishes involved falling down on their nurturing. We may have forgotten how long it took for acceptance to grow into full commitment – the time varies with each Christian – but while we are praying for and helping to support the missions in far-flung areas, let us also pray for grace to help those struggling

or enquiring Christians on the home front, perhaps as close as the house next door, or those sitting in the next row at worship. Even mature Christians need fellowship, shared experiences, Bible reading – or simply someone 'coming alongside'. Everyone has inner struggles which only rarely surface in company, but which can often be better coped with for the knowledge that someone cares.

Baptism
Baptism in the Church takes many forms – from the recognized formal baptism by water (total immersion or otherwise; in childhood or later), to the step of commitment, recognition of what is involved, ministry, witness, sharing ... The list goes on. When Jesus said, 'I have a baptism with which to be baptized, and what stress I am under until it is completed!' (Luke 12:50), he was not referring exclusively to the time when John poured some Jordan water over him. Can we reflect on all that 'baptism' – with water, with Spirit, with fire – means to us?

Suggested hymns
Be thou my vision, O Lord of my heart; Have faith in God, my heart; Peace, perfect peace, is the gift; Tell out, my soul, the greatness of the Lord.

Ascension Day   20 May   Baptism with Power
Acts 1:1–11 or Dan. 7:9–14; Ps. 47 or Ps. 93;
Eph. 1:15–23 or Acts 1:1–11; Luke 24:44–53

'[Jesus said], "You will be baptized with the Holy Spirit not many days from now ... you will receive power when the Holy Spirit has come upon you ..."' Acts 11:5, 8

Famous last words?
These, literally, are famous last words of Jesus, spoken (if as is likely we can accept Luke's chronology) immediately before he ascended to his Father. Baptism had played an important role at the beginning of his earthly ministry. Now (as we saw in our consideration of Matthew 28 last Sunday) at its end it is also of great importance. The two baptisms are linked, yet different. One – baptism by water – was delivered from the outside, to the body;

the second, spiritual baptism, saw the divine implantation of the Holy Spirit, who was to work from the inside outwards. The two are complementary, for – this side of glory – we are body and soul. With water, the body is symbolically cleansed and prepared for its Christian life; with Spirit, it is equipped for a ministry and commitment which will continue into eternity. Once given, baptism cannot be 'un-done'. In simple terms, it 'earmarks' a person for life. The misuse of free will may lead that person a long way in the opposite direction – may, in fact, lead him or her beyond the point of no return; but even after death he or she will be a baptized soul – and, we may reverently hope, with a 'last chance' at the final hurdle (see, e.g., Revelation 20).

No sad farewells

Although their best friend was leaving them, Jesus did not allow any sad farewells at the parting. He inspired them with a joyful anticipation of the powerful baptism of the Spirit, and an expectation of ongoing ministry: 'I am sending upon you what my Father promised' (Luke 24:49). It was sufficient to send his friends back to Jerusalem to wait for the promised gifts, 'with great joy' (Luke 24:52). The turning of potential devastation into great joy (in men who until recently had been martyrs to fearfulness) was the last miracle of Jesus before his return to glory.

When we part from our friends – whether for a few short hours, or when one of us is returning to our Maker – may we make the parting sweet. We may not be able to infuse it with the joy that Jesus managed; but 'last words', of whatever duration, are important. If we can recall them with pleasure rather than regret, they will carry a blessing.

The 'how' of Christ's ascension

We may never know exactly how Jesus ascended – though one day, please God, we shall experience where he went. The learned Greek physician does not try to be clever about the technicalities: Luke says, simply, that he 'was carried up into heaven' (Luke 24:51), and that 'he was lifted up, and a cloud took him out of their sight' (Acts 1:9). Do we want any more details? Well, yes, being human we should love to have them; but God has decided that we have what we need to know. The Lord's personal ministry on earth was over; from Pentecost, it would continue through his followers – and, because it is of God, its success is assured. On a bad day, when Satan seems to have us in a tight corner, and bad news is all that appears to be around, may we remember this. God has not been to so much trouble, to give up now.

> *Though you may be going*
> *through a dark and anxious time,*
> *Smile, and keep your courage,*
> *for surrender is a crime.*

Anon.

The Devil doesn't like us to smile. It reminds him too much of Easter Day. But Christians can never be reminded too much – can we?

Suggested hymns
All hail the power of Jesus' name; Christ triumphant, ever reigning; Crown him with many crowns; Hail the day that sees him rise.

Seventh Sunday of Easter (Sunday after Ascension Day)   23 May   *Principal Service*
Ministry under Pressure   Acts 16:16–34; Ps. 97; Rev. 22:12–14, 16–17, 20–21; John 17:20–26

'At the same hour of the night [the jailer] took them and washed their wounds; then he and his entire family were baptized without delay. He brought them up into the house and set food before them, and he and his entire household rejoiced that he had become a believer in God.' Acts 16:33–34

Getting God's work done
After a 'severe flogging' (Acts 16:23), Paul and Silas could have been forgiven for taking things easy once they had been thrown into jail. But not a bit of it: they kept up a prayer meeting with such vociferous hymn-singing that none of the other prisoners could get to sleep (v. 25)! Then they underwent an earthquake with its attendant excitement – and ended up converting and baptizing the jailer and his whole family. Not a bad night's work!

If we look for one, we can always find an excuse for postponing serious work for God. Why do we waste time in looking? God has lined up enough work to keep us fully occupied, if only we'll buckle to and attend to it. But what about our clothing, our food, our subsistence? 'Strive first for the kingom of God, and his righteousness, and all these things will be given to you as well,' promises Jesus (Matthew 6:33). It's a question of working hard and trusting hard; but we are often more proficient in the former than the latter. God intends that both should go together. (Yes, Lord, Amen – but don't take me 'to the wire'!)

Ministry is always possible

There is never a wrong time for ministry: 'proclaim the message; be persistent whether the time is favourable or unfavourable,' Paul wrote to Timothy (2 Timothy 4:2) – and the writer knew what he was talking about. Anywhere, anytime, in any company – God's word can make an impact, even when the odds seem stacked against success.

God's window

We are God's windows to the world, through which his light can shine and his truth be made known. In earlier centuries, when only the priests with a Latin education knew what the services were about, the congregations could study the stained-glass windows and learn from them not only the beauty of God's light coming through the coloured glass, but more importantly the Bible stories depicted in the craftsmanship. As the sun moved through each day, or rain and cloud altered the light, so the glass would take on new shades and highlights, and different facets of the subjects would be seen. Similarly, in our ministry, different people will pick up varying revelations and insights. And just as a window shows only what is shone through it, so Christians to be true to their vocations need to show and share only what God is directing, through his indwelling Spirit. A power stronger than themselves moved Paul and Silas to pray and sing in the prison, despite the agonizing pain of their wounds and bruises. Can we so rise above physical concerns, and above something that often proves even more of a distraction: fear, worry, anxiety?

If we pause to consider that the jailer and his family may otherwise have died without knowledge of Jesus . . . yes, surely then we get a divine input of courage that will make our Holy Spirit jump for joy – and ensure that we too don't stand still.

Family Service input
Design a stained-glass window – which perhaps could be incorporated somewhere in the church or church hall. Have to hand coloured transparent film, black tape, etc.

Suggested hymns
Alleluia, sing to Jesus; Come, let us join our cheerful songs; O for a heart to praise my God; The head that once was crowned with thorns.

Seventh Sunday of Easter *Second Service*
The Gifts He Gave Ps. 68; Isa. 44:1–8; Eph. 4:7–16 or Luke 24:44–53
'The gifts he gave were that some would be apostles, some prophets, some evangelists, some pastors and teachers, to equip the saints for the work of ministry, for building up the body of Christ, until all of us come to the unity of the faith and of the knowledge of the Son of God.' Ephesians 4:11–13

Until we come
This is a long text, but so full of encouragement that all of us need it – all and often. When God comes and calls us for ministry, he fully equips us for the task. If we try to tell him we cannot manage any of the work, it is tantamount to accusing him of failing to provide the necessary equipment (virtually calling him a liar) – or pretending that we don't know how to use it, or have mislaid it. One thing we cannot do is to give our equipment, our talents, to someone else. Read again both the parable of the pounds (Luke 19:11–27) and the talents (Matthew 25:14–30): did any of the servants – even the lazy ones – manage to *give away* what their master had entrusted to them? We can let our talents lie unused, but, once given by God, they are ours till the end of time. Used in the service of others, they appreciate in value; but nothing can destroy them or change their ownership. Time spent in reflecting on what

God has given us, and how we can use it, is precious. Time spent in using each talent is even more precious.

Unity of the faith

Our talents, as we have seen, interact and interrelate in a complementary way with those of other believers; and their combined operation works towards a unity of the faith. How do we see such unity? In a joining together of denominations, as is seen all too briefly in one week each year, when we focus on praying for 'Christian Unity'? Or in a low-key, neighbourly reaching out to each other, which can usually involve non-churchgoers? Or in mega-movements, where a parish may actually close one church and have two congregations subsequently meeting for worship (at the same time, perhaps) in the remaining building? We may even live in a parish where unity is proceeding along all these lines. 'That they may become completely one', was the prayer of Jesus to his Father that has echoed through Christianity for all of its history (John 17:23).

Are we directing our talents to unity, or to building up our own denomination and our own way of worshipping?

Some pastors, some . . .

All the time we are learning not only to use our talents, but to recognize and value those of other people – remembering the labourers in the vineyard, and being content with (and grateful for) what has been given to us. When we see someone exercising a particular form of ministry (perhaps teaching or pastoring), let us rejoice in their gift and affirm their ministry. Rest assured, we shall have a talent which they have not been given. Each adult Christian also has an important role to play in helping younger believers to recognize and utilize their particular gifts. Can we not recall someone – perhaps many years ago – recognizing a talent which we didn't know we had, and thus setting us on the road to a fruitful ministry? May we never be slack in thus helping others.

One day a man walking by the lake recognized in a few fishermen the talents of preaching, healing and evangelism. Peter, Andrew, James and John may not even have been churchgoers at that stage – and they were to experience several 'blips' along the way to full-time ministry; but each of them, with God's grace, proved faithful to the call.

Who will be the Peters, Johns and Andrews of this generation? Or the next? Perhaps someone who is, as yet, unaware of the talent within them. Could that be because any of us has not yet seen it, either?

Suggested hymns
For the beauty of the earth; Lord, enthroned in heavenly splendour; Make me a channel of your peace; We are one in the Spirit.

Day of Pentecost (Whit Sunday)   30 May
Principal Service   **The Spirit Is Here!**   Acts 2:1–21
or Gen. 11:1–9; Ps. 104:24–34, 35b; Rom. 8:14–17 or
Acts 2:1–21; John 14:8–17[25–27]

'Divided tongues, as of fire, rested on each of them. All of them were filled with the Holy Spirit, and began to speak in other languages, as the Spirit gave them ability.' (Acts 2:3–4)

Glossolalia?
If by *glossolalia* we mean 'Spirit-language' – words of ecstasy (and often great beauty and resonance) but not of any known earthly language – then the languages given at Pentecost were not *glossolalia*, for the various native languages of the assembled congregation were quickly recognized (Acts 2:6f.). The language gifts of the Spirit were designed not only to impact on the assembly, but also to equip the disciples for evangelizing in the world beyond Jerusalem. Greek and Latin would be among them, for those who were not already familiar with these; but God was looking more closely at the various races who were sprinkled throughout Asia Minor and south-eastern Europe (vv. 9ff.). The fact that most, if not all, of the disciples were unlettered men would heighten the crowd's amazement.

Spread the news fast!
Is there not an underlying sense of urgency here, too? God was not prepared to wait for the Judaean disciples to evangelize and train pastors locally: he wanted the gospel spread quickly into the known world. We may believe that if we are to do any serious

work for God, we need to spend a long time in preparation. Some ministries truly require a period of training – yet many have gone straight out in faith and have had rich spiritual rewards. If we wait until we think we have prepared ourselves for God, we may find that the work we could have done has been accomplished by someone else. When God calls, he is challenging us to answer. Our work is here and now. We can safely leave the long-term planning to him.

All were filled
The Holy Spirit was given with consummate generosity and inclusivity. No one was left out, envying the gifts of someone else. If we ever catch ourselves coveting another's talents or fortune, let us remember Pentecost. If God is the same yesterday, today and for ever, he is not operating an exclusive policy in his distribution of gifts today. We have a precious talent (at least one), if we'd only look for it. If we look, and still don't find it, then let us have the humility to pray God for revelation. And we can be sure our talent is uniquely suited to us.

Voices of caution
Human nature being what it is, we can be pretty sure there would be plenty of cautious advice freely given to the disciples after Pentecost: 'Stay where you are known! How will you manage, launching out into the unknown without experience of foreign travel? How will your families cope? A man's job is to provide for his wife and children . . .'

But Jesus had told them to go (Matthew 28:19), and now the time had come. Yet some of the disciples did hesitate, and it took an upsurge in persecution eventually to persuade them to move out first to Pella, and from there further and further afield. Once started, the gospel ball just went on rolling.

Our mission
How is our gospel ball moving? At a rate of knots, or is it gathering moss? Sometimes our ministry seems to be static, with little or nothing to show for quite a lot of effort. Then suddenly there comes a breakthrough, a revelation, an encouragement that, yes, we are on the right track; we are where God wants us to be. While at other times God seems to be moving us so fast we can hardly catch breath; worry not, the Lord knows precisely what we can stand.

Whitsuntide comes, as the days are near their longest and everywhere new growth is well on the way to fruitful and eventual harvest: a time of sunshine, warmth and rejoicing; a time also to take spiritual stock, and to remember that even among the countries represented at the first Christian Pentecost, there are many people who still have not heard the gospel. The Spirit of that Pentecost brought new work for every Christian there. What is the Spirit of Pentecost 2004 asking of us?

Family Service input
Teach the young people the Lord's Prayer in at least one foreign language.

Suggested hymns
Come down, O Love Divine; Come, Holy Ghost, our souls inspire; Gracious Spirit, Holy Ghost; When God of old came down from heaven.

Day of Pentecost *Second Service*
The Lord Is the Spirit Pss. 36:5–10; 150; Ex. 33:7–20; 2 Cor. 3:4–18 or John 16:4b–15

'Now the Lord is the Spirit, and where the Spirit of the Lord is, there is freedom. And all of us, with unveiled faces, seeing the glory of the Lord as though reflected in a mirror, are being transformed into the same image from one degree of glory to another; for this comes from the Lord, the Spirit.' 2 Corinthians 3:17–18

The more we look to Jesus
Simply put, the more we look to Jesus, the more we shall become like him. Moses' face shone with reflected glory when he had been with God on the mount at the giving of the Decalogue; how much more (says St Paul), with the rending of the veil by Christ, will his glory shine in us! And has he not told us, 'You are the light of the world' (Matthew 5:14)?

But it is his light, his glory: it all comes from 'the Lord the Spirit', and to him be all the credit. He brings also a freedom: the freedom not to sin. Can we take it? Can the Lord trust us not to misuse such a gift? Being human, we shall make the wrong decisions at times – yet God trusts us to allow the Holy Spirit to tell us where we've gone awry; we need to become well versed in listening for that still, small voice within.

Glory by degrees

We understand degrees: the more one has, usually the more learning one has collected – and usually the higher one's standing in the world. Glory-degrees are not quite the same: as we go on in the will of God, the more we become like Jesus; we may not realize the growing likeness, but others will, even though they probably won't give it a name. By degrees, we take on increasingly the glory of Jesus. Such degrees put the learned honours of the sophisticated world to shame. Age cannot weary these, nor will the years condemn – they are designed for all eternity.

What is Jesus like?

And so what is Jesus like? For what are we aiming? He has said that whoever has seen him has seen the Father (John 14:9). But what does the Father look like? St John tells us that the 'Word became flesh and lived among us . . . full of grace and truth' (John 1:14). Does that help? Perhaps St Paul comes closest, when he analyses God's Spirit, comprising 'love, joy, peace, patience, kindness, generosity, faithfulness, gentleness and self-control' (Galatians 5:22–23). If we cultivate these attributes, by degrees we shall take on the aspect of Jesus, shall we not? It will not come about by our own efforts, but by the growing of these fruits of the Spirit, *by the Spirit* in us.

The hardest thing to do

Showing the fruits of the Spirit, in a world seemingly hell-bent on disturbing our spiritual equilibrium, is never easy. The inner peace we need has to be gained on a spiritual battlefield. If God never sleeps, neither does Satan; and the Devil is not generous enough to allow us a spiritual amnesty, even for a day, while we luxuriate in acquiring an inner calm. All spiritual degrees need to be fought for and won during the heat of battle. When the strife is over, and we are in glory, there will probably be no further degrees to be gained. The time for action is now, and there will be no truce until Satan has got his deserts at the Judgement Day.

Glory hardly gained

But glory hardly gained is precious. We are in the fight of our lives, and in the best of company; 'the one who is in you is greater than the one who is in the world,' says St John, encouragingly (1 John 4:4).

Since others will see any glory we have more clearly than we do ourselves, let us look for it in others. The more we find, the more it will lighten up our life, and so reflect more in turn – growing by degrees!

Suggested hymns

Born by the Holy Spirit's breath; From glory to glory advancing; Holy Spirit, come, confirm us; Spirit of God, unseen as the wind.

Trinity Sunday 6 June *Principal Service*
Jesus' Own Spirit Prov. 8:1–4, 22–31; Ps. 8; Rom. 5:1–5; John 16:12–15

'[Jesus said], "I still have many things to say to you, but you cannot bear them now. When the Spirit of truth comes, he will guide you into all the truth, for he will not speak on his own, but will speak whatever he hears; and he will declare to you the things that are to come."' John 16:12–13

The Undivided Trinity

This is a beautiful passage of confirmation of the closeness of the Trinity. John has already told us that Jesus and the Father are one (John 14:9); now we learn that Jesus and the Spirit are not divided: when one speaks, it is as the other. Whatever Jesus has left unsaid when he goes back to glory will be spoken by the Spirit when he comes. The continuity is awe-inspiring: it is the Company of the Holy and Undivided Trinity at work – and how!

Things to come

Surely Jesus is not referring here to things outside our experiences, such as the day and time of his second coming – for this is known only to God (Matthew 24:36; Mark 13:32). Rather, the Spirit will act now as our Guide, leading us 'into all the truth', making known God's will to us as he brings us into each new situation. We have no excuse for echoing Pilate's question, 'What is truth?' (John 18:38). Pilate did not have the advantage of the indwelling Holy Spirit, though he was looking Truth incarnate in the face.

Ongoing divine assistance

The patience and perseverance of God with humankind is phenomenal. From creation itself, the Trinity has overseen this earth, and continues to do so. It would have been understandable had Jesus ascended to the Father, leaving the early Church to sink or swim. But God's love is stronger than the evil he knew would surface and attack the young Christians. So the Holy Spirit came, to carry on, not the saving work of Jesus – that had been convincingly accomplished – but the guiding power that the Church has always needed, and still needs, to get it to the threshold of eternity. The Spirit comes, not confined to a human body, not ministering over a small area in the Near East, but powerfully, completely and dynamically in each believer. Never has the Undivided Trinity worked on so many fronts, to ensure that eternity is not a many-mansioned city waiting empty for inhabitants who without divine help failed to make it beyond the grave!

Help, Lord!

One of the shortest of 'arrow' prayers, yet one we need to make every day. God has provided all the assistance we need; it is there for the asking. Shall we not use it to the full? No, we cannot – because God's love and help is always greater than our need! Hallelujah!

> *When we have exhausted our store of endurance,*
> *When faith seems to fail ere the day is half done;*
> *When we come to the end of our hoarded resources,*
> *Our Father's full giving is only begun.*
>
> *His love has no limits, his grace has no measure,*
> *His power has no boundary known unto men,*
> *For out of his infinite riches in Jesus,*
> *He giveth and giveth and giveth again.*
>
> *Annie Flint*

148

Many things to say

This is such a precious, 'human' touch – of a friend having to say farewell, yet longing to say so much more! And yet it is also a measure of his concern for his friends, not to overload them with more teaching than they could take in. It is a lesson in sensitivity which we also need.

Family Service input

Using traditional symbols of the Trinity, encourage the young people to make designs of their own, for incorporation in the parish magazine/newsletter.

Suggested hymns

Father of heaven, whose love profound; Holy, holy, holy, Lord God Almighty; Meekness and majesty; Three in One and One in Three.

Trinity Sunday *Second Service*
What Do We Know? Ps. 73:1–3, 16–28; Ex. 3:1–15; John 3:1–17

'Now there was a Pharisee named Nicodemus, a leader of the Jews. He came to Jesus by night and said to him, "Rabbi, we know that you are a teacher who has come from God, for no one can do these signs that you do apart from the presence of God."' John 3:1–2

A teacher of the law

One of the finest theological minds in Jerusalem had sought out Jesus, not to criticize him but to engage him in scholarly debate. Or so he thought. Jesus' theology sounded too simple for the erudite Nicodemus – yet proved in the end too difficult for him to understand. He knew a lot of things: he had spent his life learning more and more; he knew Jesus was a teacher from God. That was a wonderful beginning; reading between the gospel lines, few of his fellow Pharisees would have admitted as much, even if they privately considered it possible. And Nicodemus explained, openly, candidly, that Jesus' provenance was borne out specifically by the 'signs' (miracles, healings, etc.) which he did.

This was good theological stuff. But it was 'head-knowledge'.

Nicodemus had weighed up the evidence like the ecclesiastical lawyer that he was, and had come to a considered conclusion. It was correct, as far as it went – but how far was that? Not far enough for Jesus. Nicodemus knew *about* him, but he did not know *him*. He was certainly some way from accepting him as Son of God. Yet he was heading in more or less the right direction – and his visit (albeit clandestine) showed that he wanted to learn more.

Book-knowledge

We can pass degrees in book-knowledge about Jesus. We can even apply ourselves to learning all four Gospels from memory. Quite a number of scholars have been very proud of attaining such a feat of memory. We can do all that, without getting any further than Nicodemus was at the outset of his visit. That he knew quite a lot more by its conclusion was largely because he was willing to stay and have not only his mind but his heart brought to a deeper spirituality by Jesus.

And yet there are many who have reached such spiritual knowledge without a fraction of Nicodemus' learning – many for whom 'book-knowledge' would be difficult to comprehend, yet who have accepted and come to know Jesus by simple, loving faith. 'Except you become as a little child . . .' (cf. Mark 10:15; Luke 18:17). The kingdom of heaven does not demand a PhD as its 'Open sesame'.

The Trinity

On Trinity Sunday, when the enigma of 'Three in One, and One in Three' comes once more to the fore, many of us feel like Nicodemus – floundering in high theology; knowing what we *know* about the Trinity, yet having difficulty with a language that is earth-based. Through the Christian centuries, theologians of the first rank – Nicodemuses of their day – have struggled in the same way; but arguably still the most beautiful explanation is in the *Quicunque Vult*, or Athanasian Creed, an affirmation of belief, compiled if not by Athanasius himself then by his followers.

> . . .
> *The Father is made of none:*
> *neither created nor begotten.*
> *The Son is of the Father alone:*
> *not made, nor created, but begotten.*

The Holy Ghost is of the Father and of the Son:
neither made, nor created, nor begotten, but proceeding.
So there is one Father, not three Fathers;
one Son, not three Sons:
one Holy Ghost, not three Holy Ghosts.
And in this Trinity none is afore, or after another:
none is greater, or less than another;
But the whole Three Persons are co-eternal together,

and co-equal.

Suggested hymns
Bright the vision that delighted; Father most holy, merciful and loving; Father, we adore you; Most ancient of all mysteries.

First Sunday after Trinity (Proper 6)
13 June   *Principal Service*   **She's a Sinner!**
1 Ki. 21:1–10[11–14] 15–21a; Ps. 5:1–8; Gal. 2:15–21;
Luke 7:36—8:3

'Now when the Pharisee who had invited [Jesus] saw it, he said to himself, "If this man were a prophet, he would have known who and what kind of woman this is who is touching him – that she is a sinner."'
Luke 7:39

Two women
The Old Testament reading dealt with a woman who is remembered for her wickedness: Queen Jezebel, who manipulated her husband Ahab, and engineered the shameful stoning of Naboth. But the Gospel reading has Simon the Pharisee classifying 'Mary' as a sinner, when she had redeemed her past by showing so convincingly her love for Jesus. She had pointed up Simon's lack of courtesy and kindness, by anointing Jesus with the beautiful perfume. Presumably Simon considered that an invitation to a Pharisee's house, and a meal, was sufficient hospitality for a guest who was not a recognized Pharisee.

Is there any justice in this world? One treacherous woman seems to get away with murder, while another's purple past is held against her as she carries out a kindly act! But Jezebel came to a gruesome end, while 'Mary' was honoured by Christ. Yes, there is justice – in God's good time.

Not counting the cost
Simon the Pharisee had counted the cost of inviting Jesus to dinner: the invitation itself was an honour; the meal commensurate with Simon's (not Jesus') status – therefore niceties like foot-washing and oil for the guest's hair could be dispensed with. Mary, on the other hand, had been extremely generous with the provision of her unguent – and she had complemented this by daring to enter the room and to attend to Jesus. Simon's had been a cool official-dom, Mary's an act of selfless love. Jesus very publicly showed which found favour with him. Do we measure our love for God, or calculate deliberately how much we can give him, or how much time we can spare for him? That is not love: it is a grudging duty.

> Teach us, good Lord, to serve thee as thou deservest;
> To give, and not to count the cost;
> To fight, and not to heed the wounds;
> To toil, and not to seek for rest;
> To labour, and not to ask for any reward,
> Save that of knowing that we do thy will.
>
> St Ignatius Loyola

Applying labels
Jezebel had earned her label of wickedness and conniving; but 'Mary', with her act of generous love, had blotted out her sinful past. Yet Simon would probably not be alone in perpetuating her old lifestyle. We seem to have much better memories for others' sins than their deeds of goodness; and a bad reputation can be extended by those who love to criticize for many years after the reason for it has gone.

> The evil that men do lives after them;
> The good is oft interred with their bones.
>
> Shakespeare, Julius Caesar

How often, for instance, is the man on the cross next to Christ remembered as 'the penitent *thief*' rather than, say, 'the reformed character'? And had it not been for this man, would we have

152

known the wonderfully encouraging words of Jesus: 'Today you will be with me in Paradise' (Luke 23:43)?

Let us resolve to cultivate a good 'forgettery' for others' failings, and to thank God for their good deeds.

Family Service input
Encourage the young people to extract from copies of the current Christian press items for inclusion in the intercessions, or as part of a parish project.

Suggested hymns
And can it be; Forgive our sins, as we forgive; Help us to help each other, Lord; Ye that know the Lord is gracious.

First Sunday after Trinity   *Second Service*
The Kingdom's Growth   Ps. 52 [53]; Gen. 13;
Mark 4:21–41

'[Jesus] also said, "The kingdom of God is as if someone would scatter seed on the ground, and would sleep and rise night and day, and the seed would sprout and grow, he does not know how."' Mark 4:26–27

How come?
We sow seeds in the earth, in faith – but we cannot make them grow, although we may increase the probabilities by waiting until the soil has warmed up after the winter, watering the ground in dry weather, rendering the earth to the phrase beloved of old gardening manuals, 'a fine tilth' – but the seeds' eventual growth or otherwise is in the hands of God. So is the growth of the kingdom of heaven. We may share the gospel with someone, may even plead with tears as we tell of what Jesus means to us, may press a Bible into their hands and pray fervently with them – but it is God who then deals with the seed we have sown. At times, when nothing seems to happen as a result of our sowing, we may feel discouraged, as a farmer who sees no return from a crop he has sown. Has the labour been in vain? Work for God is never in vain: the earth in that field has been cultivated, and will yield a return in due season – perhaps for the sower, perhaps for someone else. The soul whom we have nurtured may come to God, or may

in some way help someone else to come. We have done what we could (cf. Mark 14:8).

God is on duty

The farmer who sows seed does not need to stand on guard duty over it; he has done his work, and God will carry on. There will be times when, even under adverse conditions, the seed will grow and produce a good harvest – as well as times when, given optimum conditions, little or no growth will take place. So it is with the kingdom of God: it can extend in places which seem least likely to promote its growth, while in affluent areas little troubled by poverty or physical disasters, it grows slowly or not at all. The pattern of growth defies known understanding – and at times its rapidity takes our breath away.

Sowing for ever

Our efforts at seed-sowing may seem very ineffectual, as a tiny mustard seed held on the palm of a hand. Can you see it? Just about. Measure it in mathematical terms, and it is a tiny part of a tiny part of an inch: in fact, a lot of mustard seeds laid in a line would be needed to make an inch. Remember that smile we gave someone the other day? It was a seed. The time we share at Bible Group? The outing we cancelled, to help a neighbour in the garden? The night we waited up with someone for news from the hospital? The grit we spread, to get a friend's car up the icy hill? The shopping we collected for the housebound soul in the next street? All seeds – all helping the advance of the kingdom of God: all noted by God, though often forgotten by us. Can we sow more seed, more often? If we ask God to show us how, we must be careful not to miss the opportunities he gives.

When the sowing seems to go wrong

But Satan doesn't take a vacation and allow us to get on calmly with our sowing; he will grab the seed for himself, if he can. If not, he'll do his best to see it doesn't grow. Our hope lies in his best being worse than God's. At times, our well-intentioned sowing may be misinterpreted, misunderstood. If we have done our best, we can leave the outcome with God; he may show us a way in which the situation can be redeemed – or he may choose someone else for that work. Or he may seemingly do nothing, and then it can be hard for the seed-sower, who feels let down and aggrieved. Remember – the Lord knows what he is about!

How is our garden for God's kingdom coming along? While ever we are still here, there will be space to sow more seed. For encouragement, we can reflect on that vast 'cloud of witnesses' – seed-sowers who have been before us.

Suggested hymns
For the beauty of the earth; I come to the garden alone; Sow in the morn thy seed; The earth, O Lord, is one wide field.

Second Sunday after Trinity (Proper 7)
20 June *Principal Service* Demon-Possession
1 Ki. 19:1–4[5–7]8–15a; Pss. 42, 43; Gal. 3:23–29;
Luke 8:26–39

'Those who had seen it told them how the one who had been possessed by demons had been healed. Then all the people of the surrounding country of the Gerasenes asked Jesus to leave them; for they were seized with great fear.' Luke 8:36–37

Physical v. spiritual
When the physical comes up against the spiritual, there is so much that it cannot account for – cannot write in a report, or study tissue in a petrie dish, or fasten a nice understandable label to it – that fear sets in. We see it throughout the Gospels, and we see Jesus having to repeat his command: 'Fear not!' Though he came with a gospel of love and compassion, some people feared him because they did not understand, and fear stopped them from taking the first step of faith. The fear is even more pronounced when the physical comes up against the power of evil. Do we understand demon-possession any more today than in Jesus' time? In many ways, no. We try to explain it away under various tags which don't really get us any further: 'mental illness', 'obsession', 'paranoia', 'schizophrenia'. We seem to think it's 'old-fashioned' to say 'possessed' or 'lunatic'. And since more than a few scientists have admitted that they don't yet know a millionth part of how the mind/brain/spirit (even soul) works, it's not surprising that

demon-possession today still induces fear in others, akin to that produced in Gerasa.

Afraid of good works?

Paradoxically, those people seemed to have been more concerned over the man's cure, and the loss of their pigs, than they had been over the patient's previous condition. Demon-possession, after all, was a fact of life: one merely ostracized the sufferer, driving him beyond the fringes of society. If he died, so be it. If he managed to scrape a subsistence, he should do it away from the view of normal folk. It was a policy that suited the Devil: by possession of one man, he was causing others to show bad feeling.

But then Jesus came, healing all sickness, all disease, including demon-possession. No one had operated such 'pan-medication' before: even a man born with blindness was healed. But the demons writhed and squealed under such authoritative treatment. So-called 'normal' folk were shocked out of the complacency that had grown accustomed to the lunatic beating himself into semi-oblivion on the gravestones. And – their pigs had gone, too! Fear and economic hardship combined, it made them beg Jesus to go. The irony was so sad: God was prepared to do such great work among them, but they had insufficient spiritual stamina to cope with it.

Today's problem

We should not be quick to assign this incident exclusively to first-century Palestine. Its circumstances are replicated today across the world, ranging from lethargic or dangerous 'mental illness', to outright witchcraft and Satanism. Now and then the existence of such possession surfaces in the criminal courts: headlines are made one day and forgotten the next, as a few – a very few – practitioners are 'sent down' and lost for a while to society.

Our dilemma is precisely that of the Gerasenes. Do we shut our eyes to the problem, putting a fair distance between ourselves and any of the 'possessed' who come close? Do we distinguish between 'harmless' and 'wicked' possession? Or do we pray that God will show us how, in the power of his Spirit, we can help those people to get rid of the demons? 'Oh, there is no cure!' we are told. Does God say that? One man, 2,000 years ago, calmly said of his followers: 'These signs will accompany those who believe: by using my name they will cast out demons . . .' (Mark 16:17; cf. Luke 9:1). Lord, give us holy boldness!

Share with the young people the story behind the hymn, 'All things bring and beautiful', and encourage them to illustrate it.

Suggested hymns
Christian, dost thou see them?; For the healing of the nations; Jesus, the name high over all; Thine arm, O Lord, in days of old.

Hymn stories

All things bright and beautiful
Cecil Frances Humphreys (1818–1895) composed this hymn, and many others, primarily for children, but it has always been a favourite with older Christians too. She wrote it, with more verses than we normally sing, in 1843, at the age of 25. She was then living at Markree Castle, at Colloney, County Sligo, overlooking the often stormy waters of the Atlantic. In 1845, she married an earnest young curate, William Alexander, who later became the Archbishop of Armagh.

Quiet, with a nice sense of humour, and a dignity which endeared her to young people yet conveyed an air of gentle authority, Mrs Alexander led a busy life helping her husband in his parishes, attending to the sick, comforting the anxious and bereaved – and writing more than a hundred hymns.

In this lovely hymn, she portrays God as rejoicing in all the good things he has created, including humankind. If we become worried and think we are not important enough to make a difference in the world, it is good to read or sing these verses, and to see ourselves as God intended us to be – his own, his chosen, with a special vocation to fulfil in life.

Mrs Alexander seems to have had several passages of scripture in mind (e.g. Ecclesiastes 3:11; John 1:3), as she portrays God as the Creator of all that is good in the world. He made it all. We, too, are his – and he also did a good work when he made us.

Second Sunday after Trinity   *Second Service*
Testing for Health   Ps. [50] 57; Gen. 24:1–27;
Mark 5:21–43

'Then one of the leaders of the synagogue named Jairus came and, when he saw [Jesus], fell at his feet and begged him repeatedly, "My little daughter is at the point of death. Come and lay your hands upon her, so that she may be made well, and live." . . . [The woman] had heard about Jesus, and came up behind him in the crowd and touched his cloak . . . Immediately her haemorrhage stopped, and she felt in her body that she was healed of her disease.' Mark 5:22–23, 27, 29

Unfair treatment?
It is easy to read this account of two healings and to feel a sense of unfairness. Jairus, desperate with anguish for his little girl, was tested right 'to the wire'. The woman, on the other hand, only had to elbow her way through the crowd, and – to all intents and purposes anonymously – touch the fringe of Jesus' cloak, and her healing was instantaneous.

Poor Jairus! He asked and asked Jesus for help, then he had to wait while the Master stopped to identify the woman and make public what she had intended to be private; then he was pole-axed by the news that his girl had died, and had to suffer agony until, back at the house, Jesus increased a healing miracle into a resur-rection.

Why are some of us still tested (apparently) more than others? Oh God, why?

Because we are friends?
Some will tell us that God tests his friends more than others: the closest and most faithful friends most of all. Such an explanation may be cold comfort if we are currently undergoing a rigorous testing. How much more, Lord? Are you taking us all the distance? And well he might. We have little say as to the amount or the severity of the testing that God decides. Was Jairus a close friend of Jesus? Presumably not; the synagogue rulers are not noted in the Gospels as having welcomed the new preacher in their midst. Remember Lazarus and his sisters at Bethany: these *were* close friends of the Lord – yet he tested Martha and Mary greatly, before, as with Jairus's girl, performing a much more wonderful miracle than the one for which they had been looking. This would seem to

bear out the theory that those close to Jesus receive more stringent training, pruning and moulding.

Individual cases
God surely tests each of us to the degree that he knows we can stand. Is this not replicated in our tending of the plants in our gardens? We fuss around over a choice specimen, giving it tender loving care, making life as easy as possible – and often it dies, because its system is not being stimulated by normal conditions to produce strong growth. God knows that 'suffering produces endurance, and endurance produces character, and character produces hope . . .' (Romans 5:3–4). Would we really settle for less? Would we follow Christ for second best?

'Will there be a cure?'
'Will there one day be a cure for every sickness and disease?' The question is constantly being asked – and it is being answered, as new herbs and plants with exciting new properties are being discovered. These plants often end up in laboratories, where synthetic forms are produced, and the scientists rather than God receive the credit. And so has grown up the difference between medicine and faith healing. Are the two opposed or complementary? We can look at the Church in many parts of the so-called 'Third World', where healing in the name of Jesus is believed and practised, and ask: 'Are we in the West missing out on God's will to heal?'

Suggested hymns
Great is thy faithfulness; Lord, as I wake, I turn to you; Rock of ages; Ye that know the Lord is gracious.

Third Sunday after Trinity (Proper 8)
27 June   *Principal Service*   **'Wherever You Go'**
2 Ki. 2:1–2, 6–14; Ps. 77:1–2, 11–20; Gal. 5:1, 13–25;
Luke 9:51–62
'As they were going along the road, someone said to [Jesus], "I will follow you wherever you go." And Jesus said to him, "Foxes have holes,

and birds of the air have nests; but the Son of Man has no where to lay his head."' Luke 9:57–58

Good intentions

The road to hell is paved with them: literally, we sometimes let them carry us away. One may wonder how many people had similar good intentions, as Jesus ministered in Judaea and Galilee. But few stood the course – and even some of those denied or deserted their Master. We know we should not offer what we have not got, nor promise what we cannot fulfil; yet in the euphoria of the moment we speak in haste, not weighing our words, and get ourselves into all sorts of predicaments later on. 'I tell you,' warns Jesus, 'on the day of judgement you will have to give an account of every careless word you utter; for by your words you will be justified, and by your words you will be condemned' (Matthew 12:36–37). This should make our appreciation of the sacrifice of Jesus all the greater; for, *knowing in advance* the pain and torture involved, he calmly went through with it. By contrast, the man who was so ready to say he would follow had no real commitment, even though he could see no danger ahead: the thought of sleeping in scratch accommodation (or none) was in itself too much for him to take.

When Jesus calls

When Jesus calls us to any work (for we are, presumably, some distance further than our initial commitment), do we delay, and weigh up the pros and cons? Or do we look instead for what we hope is an easier way? Or do we pretend we haven't heard – perhaps because there's something else we'd rather do? The man in our text was like the second brother in Jesus' parable of the two sons (Matthew 21:28–32): full of initial enthusiasm, but quickly cooling off. God knows we cannot keep 'on the boil' all the time, but he is looking for followers whose enthusiasm keeps at a good working temperature.

Light to the world

Can we sit as light to the world as Jesus sat – not necessarily without a fixed abode, but unencumbered with the trappings that many would declare are essential: a paid-off mortgage, life insurance, a pension, etc.?

This world is not my home,
I'm just a-passing through,
My treasures are laid up
Somewhere beyond the blue.
The Saviour beckons me
From heaven's open door,
And I can't feel at home
In this world any more.

Traditional, arr.
G. R. Timms

Jesus calls us to do nothing, dare nothing, that he has not already done and dared. We are, literally, his 'ministers without portfolio' – writing our own portfolio in the Lamb's Book of Life, as we journey on. Shall we be able one day to read our life's story? Perhaps. In an interview with Dr Billy Graham, to mark the evangelist's eightieth birthday, Sir David Frost asked Billy what he'd like God to do for him on his arrival in glory. 'I'd like for him to have a sort of film of my life,' replied Billy, 'so I could see the parts where I went right, and also those where I could have done better. But I'd also like for the Lord to edit it here and there, 'cos there are parts of my life I'd rather nobody else saw!' We can surely empathize with Billy on that point.

We may never know, yet perhaps we can reverently hope, that some recalcitrants like the man in our text were so spiritually stirred by the resurrection of Christ, and the descent of the Spirit at Pentecost, that they gained new zeal and made a full commitment before it was too late.

Family Service input
Encourage the young people to compose a hymn based on today's theme of commitment.

Suggested hymns
I heard the voice of Jesus say; Take up thy cross, the Saviour said; Thou didst leave thy throne and thy kingly crown; Will you come and follow me?

Third Sunday after Trinity   *Second Service*
Home-Grown Antipathy   Ps. [59:1–5, 16–17] 60;
Gen. 27:1–40; Mark 6:1–6

'Then Jesus said to them, "Prophets are not without honour except in their home town, and among their own kin, and in their own house." And he could do no deed of power there, except that he laid his hands on a few sick people and cured them. And he was amazed at their unbelief.'
Mark 6:4–6.

Proximity can breed contempt
Relationship has been described as 'the worst ship that ever sailed'. Antipathy and animosity are unwelcome enough from any source, but when they come from those we would expect to be our friends and neighbours, the cross is especially hard to bear. The problem is such a long-standing one that we are probably not going to effect a worldwide change in it now; but that Jesus suffered rebukes and rudeness from the home-town folk with whom he had grown up surely gives us courage and fortitude if we have to weather a similar storm. The infighting and gossip that are too often found in fairly small communities can metaphorically produce more undercurrents than would sink the QE II. 'I've been here, too; I know just how you are suffering,' Jesus continues to say.

To go – or not to go?
So do we need to pull up stumps and go to a place where we are not known, for our mission to bear fruit? Perhaps. Yet Jesus, knowing all things, must have foreseen the reaction of his one-time neighbours. Still he returned, but would/could not do any great work there – though a few healing miracles (at least for the patients involved) would be memorable. Later, maybe, after his resurrection, it would dawn on these narrow-minded Nazarenes that the 'local boy' had indeed made good. But their chance to make good, too, had come – and gone. Their future ministry, which could have started in the company of Jesus, would (if at all) be undertaken after his return to the Father.

Doing what is nearest
Doing what is nearest, faithfully and well, even without recognition, is never wasted – so long as we do not ignore God's nudging if in fact he is urging us to go further afield. We can be satisfied

with our milieu, but the question is: Is the Lord satisfied? Are we doing as much as is possible now, or is he pointing us in another direction? Is the Lord 'working with' us (Mark 16:20), or can he only lay his hand here and there on our ministry? If we are so content that there is nothing left to wish for – danger! It's probably time to go out to fresh fields and pastures new!

Jesus was amazed
He would have foreseen home-town hostility, yet he was still amazed that folk could be so pig-headed as to reject all that he was offering. He was going to endure Calvary for people such as these. Would the cross make a difference to them? The same question faces the Church today: Why can so many turn their backs on Christianity? Yes, it offers a challenge – but in innumerable walks of life challenges are met with enthusiasm, whether it's climbing Everest or sailing round the world. And the challenge of Christ leads to eternal life. Is it not simply *amazing* that people don't want eternal life? The answer must surely stem from a lack of love: love for God, love for the Christ who sacrificed all to gain all, love for friend and neighbour – love with its heart set not merely on earth, but on eternity. This is a special sort of love, not motivated by prudence, economy, safety or insurance, but faith: peace, joy, patience, kindness, generosity, faithfulness, gentleness and self-control (Galatians 5:22–23).

Suggested hymns
Forth in thy name, O Lord, I go; Lord, for the years; Tell out, my soul, the greatness of the Lord; When I needed a neighbour.

Fourth Sunday after Trinity (Proper 9)
4 July *Principal Service* The Heavenly Record
2 Ki. 5:1–14; Ps. 30; Gal. 6:[1–6] 7–16;
Luke 10:1–11, 16–20

'The seventy returned with joy, saying, "Lord, in your name even the demons submit to us!" . . . [Jesus said], "Nevertheless, do not rejoice at this, that the spirits submit to you, but rejoice that your names are written in heaven."' Luke 10:17, 20

Advance party

The 70 extra troops had been sent out in pairs to the places on Jesus' forthcoming itinerary (v. 1), with power specifically to 'cure the sick' (v. 9). Their ministry had been so blessed that Jesus told them, 'I watched Satan fall from heaven like a flash of lightning' (v. 18): an intriguing glimpse into the dynamics of the spiritual domain which as yet we don't see in full, only the outworkings of both good and evil in the lives of men and women. But it is an indication that Jesus blamed Satan for demon-possession and that the power of Jesus' name is the means to overcome it – in the language of the time, to topple Satan from his throne.

Time for joy

Being human, the disciples could not restrain their joy as they reported to Jesus the success of their mission. No less pleased for them he nevertheless redirected their elation to the fact that God was keeping a record of their names in his heavenly archives. They had been *instrumental* in the healing ministry; but the power that had been working through them had been divine. Yet still today it is much easier to take the credit when God works through us than to accept blame when we've bungled things.

The 'extras'

These 70 'extras' had obviously a vital role to play, advancing ahead of Jesus and the Twelve, paving the way for his ministry. Perhaps some of them had been drawn from those who had followed John the Baptist. Although we hear relatively little of them, they would probably be in the assembly at Pentecost when the Holy Spirit descended – and from there would go on to further mission. Their presence here is an indication of how the mission of Jesus was growing, and of how Satan was being increasingly put under pressure.

Outreach today

The Church in the West today practises outreach not so much in foot-slogging between communities, as in prayer, giving and telecommunications. There is not so much of the 'hands-on' approach, at least beyond the immediate parish; but as long as we keep Satan on the defensive, we are surely extending Christ's kingdom.

Confidence in ministry
Whatever form our ministry takes, let us 'go for it' with the confidence that took those 70 disciples into unknown territory with the power of Jesus' name. The actual area may have been familiar (some of them may even have been sent out to minister to people in their home towns), but the work they were doing had not been done before. Are we breaking new ground for Christ, or simply treading water? Have we the confidence *in him*, to launch out into the deep, in his name, if we believe he is calling us to do just that?

> *Sitting still and wishing never made a person great;*
> *The good Lord sends the fishing, but we've to dig the bait.*
>
> *Anon.*

How are we shaping, as fishers of men and women?

Family Service input
Start (or extend) a church library. Ask for donations of/and for books, and sort into subjects. Draw up an issuing system, for the young people to operate; extend to nursing homes, hospitals etc.

Suggested hymns
Go forth and tell; How firm a foundation; Jesus, Lord, we look to thee; The kingdom of God is justice and joy.

Fourth Sunday after Trinity *Second Service*
Who Is This? Ps. 65 [70]; Gen. 29:1–20; Mark 6:7–29
'King Herod heard of it, for Jesus' name had become known. Some were saying, "John the Baptizer has been raised from the dead; and for this reason these powers are at work in him."' Mark 6:14.

A strange conclusion?
Surely resurrections were not as common as all that! Why should Herod decide that the revival of John was the most likely reason for the new preacher whom everyone was talking about? Would we suggest something similar, were an unknown evangelist to visit our parish? But Herod had not wanted to take the major step of killing John. Herodias and Salome had tricked him into the

awful deed, and he must have been a prey to doubts and misgivings ever since. If John *had* come back to life, Herod would feel somewhat relieved!

But no one was to be as helpful as that, to a weak-willed puppet-ruler who let his illegitimate wife manipulate him.

The work was growing

These verses tell us that the mission of Jesus was advancing. Time was important, for he knew that his was not to be an extended ministry, though it would probably be longer than the one John had known. Even in today's world of long-range schedules, we should not calmly assume that our particular ministry will continue on present lines, or in the same place ad infinitum. From the outset, Jesus required a flexibility in his chosen followers which may seem to sit uneasily in modern times. To a greater extent, we can make technology move for us; but the gospel of a loving Christ still needs the personal touch: loving hands, eyes lit up with the Spirit, and a compassion that is seen very specially in a smile that no machine could ever give.

There are so many places today where Christ's followers – as these early disciples found – are still not welcome. Yet the people within these places still need to be given the chance of learning about Christ, for God is not willing for even one person whom he has made, to die for ever (cf. 2 Peter 3:9). If Christ is rejected, it may be disheartening for us; who, after all, can be a Christian and not care about those who turn away from all he is and all he is offering? But we have spread the news, and there are plenty more acres to harvest.

When Jesus comes

When Jesus comes, and the final accounts are made up, the record will be clear. God does not make mistakes. What we have done – all we have done – will be seen; and the names of those to whom we have ministered will be there before the Almighty. But by that time we shall have learned not to rejoice that we have been responsible for the good work: we shall have given the glory and the credit to whom it belongs. We are worthless slaves: we have done only what we ought to have done (Luke 17:10)! Our life here and now is a working-out of our duty: it may be long or short, but God has allowed us time to do *all* we ought to do; may he give us also the willingness to accomplish all.

Despite opposition
It is tempting, when we have suffered opposition, to retrench –
to shrink back into our shell and call a halt to whatever mission we
had been engaged in. Jesus resisted such temptations: opposition
moved him to continue steadfastly with the job in hand. He learned
of the beheading of his cousin and took his disciples to a quiet
place to pray, then resumed his mission with unabated zeal. He
would not throw away the work that John had given his life to
do. And we should do well to reflect that opposition is very often
the prelude to success. A prospector had sunk several deep wells,
but had found nothing. Disheartened, he sold the land for less
than he had paid, and within days the new owner had struck
a rich bed of oil. With Jesus' example before us, we must never
give up.

Suggested hymns
Beneath the cross of Jesus; In full and glad surrender; When peace
like a river; Who can cheer the heart like Jesus?

Fifth Sunday after Trinity (Proper 10)
11 July   *Principal Service*   **Divine Transfer**
Amos 7:7–17; Ps. 82; Col. 1:1–14; Luke 10:25–37
*'[Jesus] has rescued us from the power of darkness and transferred us
into the kingdom of his beloved Son, in whom we have redemption, the
forgiveness of sins.' Colossians 1:13–14*

It's all God's work!
God has done all the work: the rescue, the transfer, the redemption
and the forgiving. It makes all the work we can ever do for him
small by comparison; yet we are in love bound to do all we can.
Our work has begun, when Christ forgave us. On Calvary, he
looked down through future history and initiated the work that
we are doing today. Are we busy for God? Are the days too short
for all we want to do? Are we bending our efforts towards helping
others out of the power of darkness where, but for the grace of
God, we would be still? St Paul is a wonderful example of the
new life and purpose that the transfer from the darkness of persecution gave to him: from being zealous in attacking the Church,

he became its hardest working preacher, teacher, missionary and evangelist. He, a Jew born and bred, learned to reach out to Greeks and Romans, and a fair sprinkling of other nations, of many creeds – at a time when pagan religions were rife, and physical esteem high (much as we have in today's world). No wonder that he told the Corinthian Christians, 'I have become all things to all people, so that I might by any means save some' (1 Corinthians 9:22)! Are we so full of Christ, that we can share his gospel with anyone we meet? The young, the old, the sophisticated, the unlettered, the people who know us well, the strangers we may meet only once? Can we paint so clear a picture of what Christ is, and what he means to us, that they see him and not ourselves? If we are not sure of how to do this, can we have faith to begin, trusting Jesus to give us the right words? 'It is not you who speak, but the Spirit of your Father speaking through you,' Jesus told his friends on one occasion (Matthew 10:19). We can trust him implicitly, for the Lord is never strapped for words.

Getting to the root of scripture

An invalid woman in her seventies decided to use the long evenings, when she could not leave the house unaided, to study the main languages underlying the Bible text. Several years later, she could read the Old Testament in Hebrew and the New Testament in Greek (not the classical Greek of Homer, nor the Greek of today, but koine, New Testament Greek – virtually the 'esperanto' of first-century Asia Minor). And then her evenings were even more occupied, as friends, neighbours and people from her local church called to share with her the rich insights she had gained from going to the roots of Holy Writ.

'The translator is a traitor', says an old proverb – not because translators set out deliberately to alter the meaning of a text, but simply because no two languages have exact parallels for every word; and each language over the years has built up its peculiar collection of sayings, proverbs and the like which are virtually untranslatable. Thank God the Bible, too, is unique – not only for its collection of various languages, but also because we believe that it is divinely inspired, which means that whatever language or version we use, God can give us new insights, new revelations, new courage, hope and joy, every time we read it: not only for our personal benefit, but also for all those times when someone asks us the reason for our faith.

The Hebrew and Greek Alphabets

Hebrew		*Greek*	
א	'Aleph	α	Alpha
ב	Beth	β	Beta
ג	Gimel	γ	Gamma
ד	Daleth	δ	Delta
ה	He	ε	Epsilon
ו	Waw	ζ	Zeta
ז	Zayin	η	Eta
ח	Heth	θ	Theta
ט	Teth	ι	Iota
י	Yodh	κ	Kappa
כ	Kaph	λ	Lambda
ל	Lamedh	μ	Mu
מ	Mem	ν	Nu
נ	Nun	ξ	Xi
ס	Samekh	ο	Omikron
ע	'Ayin	π	Pi
פ	Pe	ρ	Rho
צ	Cadhe	σ	Sigma
ק	Qoph	τ	Tau
ר	Res	υ	Upsilon
ש	Sin	φ	Phi
ת	Taw	χ	Chi
		ψ	Psi
		ω	Omega

Family Service input
Encourage the young people to (1) write out the Hebrew and
Greek alphabets and illustrate them, or (2) write the Decalogue in
Hebrew and the Lord's Prayer in Greek.

Suggested hymns
Come, ye faithful, raise the anthem; Hark, my soul, it is the Lord;
Lord, teach us how to pray aright; Thy kingdom come, O God.

Fifth Sunday after Trinity   *Second Service*
Interior Cleansing   Ps. 77; Gen. 32:9–30; Mark 7:1–23

*'Then [Jesus] called the crowd again and said to them, "Listen to me,
all of you, and understand: there is nothing outside a person that by
going in can defile, but the things that come out are what defile.'* Mark
7:14–15

Understand!
We are not told how many of the assembled crowd understood
these words of Jesus; certainly the disciples needed an explanation
when they were alone with him. There may have been many
occasions when our Lord sighed over the obtuseness of his
listeners: how, for instance, he must have welcomed the quiet
determination of Nicodemus, to stay and argue out what he *wanted*
to understand! But let us not do the crowd, or the disciples, an
injustice: they had inherited strict laws on food and ceremonial
cleanliness; and to have Jesus telling them, in so many words, that
no food could defile a person, no exterior stains or dirt could touch
the soul, was breaking new ground to say the least. Surely these
words of Jesus would return with special clarity to Peter, in the
vision when God was preparing him to take the gospel to non-
Jews, beginning with Cornelius (Acts 10:1ff., especially v. 15).

The hindrance of convention
Read the Bible any which way, and you will see that God can be
very unconventional! We hedge ourselves around with rules and
regulations, in an attempt to make life easier – but that is not
God's way. He works to a more simple, much freer, method: a
few – yet comprehensive – laws, with freedom of movement and

understanding, to make life not a regime but a delight. If we have reached a point where there is no delight in living, we need to look at how much we are really living. 'I delight to do your will, O my God,' sang the psalmist. Why? 'Your law is within my heart' (Ps. 40:8). Can we say 'Amen' to that?

The danger within

The more of God's law and word, love and vision that we can have inside us, the less room there will be for the dangers that Jesus has warned us can defile (Mark 7:21–23). If Satan can find a space in our heart that is not given to the things of God, he will sow a load of junk that will play havoc with our spiritual digestion. We shall go around spreading spiritual garbage that belies our Christian profession. Who, once chosen, called and commissioned by God would want to be doing that?

Yes, this language may be strong – but it is true. We compromise with Satan at our peril, instead of concentrating on 'whatever is true, whatever is honourable, whatever is just, whatever is pure, whatever is pleasing, whatever is commendable' (Phil. 4:8). Because, let's not fool ourselves; whatever is in our hearts, will be what comes out. The best deceivers in the world cannot keep a deception up for ever. Truth will out!

Are there human conventions restricting our lives and hindering our work and witness for God? Are they standing in the way of others seeing Jesus in us? Have we taken these conventions for granted, simply because they've been around for a long time? If they are not Bible-based, Christ-based, God-centred, then let us question whether our Christian walk would be improved by the jettisoning of this baggage.

It's not an exercise in restriction, but in enabling us better to fulfil our mission: Jesus was releasing his contemporaries from human restrictions which were hampering rather than helping their work for God. Let us remember that if love is the first of the Spirit's fruits, joy comes a close second. God is not looking for long-faced, solemn Christians anxious all the time about whether we are observing laws which the Almighty has not made.

Suggested hymns

Give me oil in my lamp; Happy are they, they that love God; Like a mighty river flowing; What a Friend we have in Jesus.

Sixth Sunday after Trinity (Proper 11)

18 July *Principal Service* **'Lord, Don't You Care?'**

Amos 8:1–12; Ps. 52; Col. 1:15–28; Luke 10:38–42

'But Martha was distracted by her many tasks, so she came to [Jesus] and asked, "Lord, do you not care that my sister has left me to do all the work by myself? Tell her then to help me!"' Luke 10:40

A lot for granted

Martha took it for granted that Jesus would support her case for justice. She is replicated today, in those who decide in their own minds that they are badly treated, and then tell God that he should be doing something about it. We're all guilty of that, in one way or another – and still the Lord deals with us as lovingly and gently as he dealt with Martha. Yet his message is clear: put the things of God first. Martha's kitchen-sinkery was important in an age where hospitality to guests had a high profile. But Mary's attention to Jesus was even more crucial. It is easy to allow everyday matters to distract us from our time for God. We live in an age where timetables and schedules, leisure and pleasure, vie for every minute of our time; yet there are still as many hours to a day as Jesus had for his ministry. How important, how essential, is our busyness? One day, it will all be history.

Rich diversity

Jesus loved the sisters in the house at Bethany: Mary, for her quiet gentleness and devotion, *and* Martha, with her impetuous, energetic nature. The time he spent with them is evidence that they were very dear friends. Martha would probably be engrossed in housework till she died; that was her bent. Though after Jesus' words she may have 'downed tools' and listened to him when he called, her mind may still have been racing with domestic questions. When we become Christians, we change in some way – perhaps in many ways, depending on what we have been and done before – but there are parts of us which we may find hard, even impossible, to change. And impatience is very difficult to cure! Tertullian, a fiery Christian preacher of the second century, used to sigh and long for 'that most excellent gift' of patience – but he is not on record as having obtained it! Three years of ministry with Jesus made a great preacher out of Peter, and a bold evangelist in place of a fearful disciple – but neither is he on record as having embraced patience. It is arguable that this is one of the most elusive gifts of the Spirit: if we believe it is unattainable, then we shall probably not have great success in accepting it; but if we pray God for grace to embrace it, then he may grant that grace – if patience is needed in our particular ministry. Patience is high on the list of the Spirit's fruits, hard after 'love, joy and peace' (Galatians 5:22). As Christians, with the indwelling Spirit, we have the *potential* for the exercise of patience, and even the most impatient among us may show patience in some things. Perhaps Martha was patient with her neighbours, or in prayer. We do not know, but we can take great encouragement from the way in which Jesus continued to love her.

As we reflect on the differences between these two precious friends of our Lord, can we pray about how we are delighting him in the use of his Spirit's fruits? How much are we showing and sharing of love, joy, peace, patience, kindness, generosity, faithfulness, gentleness and self-control? And how much does the exercise of these gifts by others, encourage us in our daily life? And how often do we simply take time to thank God for these gifts? They are things that 'will not be taken away', ever (Luke 10:42).

Family Service input
Have to hand copies of the current Christian periodicals/newspapers. Encourage the young people to cut out news items and make a collage for church/parish prayer.

Suggested hymns
How firm a foundation; I come with joy to meet my Lord; Jesu, our hope, our heart's desire; Peace, perfect peace, in this dark world of sin.

Sixth Sunday after Trinity *Second Service*
You – and Us! Ps. 81; Gen. 41:1–16, 25–37;
1 Cor. 4:8–13 or John 4:31–35

'Already you have all you want! Already you have become rich! . . . To the present hour, we are hungry and thirsty, we are poorly clothed and beaten and homeless . . .' 1 Corinthians 4:8, 11

Unappreciative
These Corinthian Christians don't know when they are well off!
They don't appreciate their luxury, says an impatient St Paul, who
is feeling the rigours of ministry. They have been given the gospel,
they've been put on the right road to God. Physically, life is good
for them, with a roof over their head, money in their pocket and
food on the table. What more do they want? Why can't they go
full steam ahead for Christ? Look at us! he says, with pardonable
heat. We have none of your comforts – but we have the gospel,
and we are living it to the full! His is a life of trust in God,
while they are relying on what this world can offer. The gospel
is permanent, but riches, warmth and beautiful houses can all take
flight. Paul values what he is handling – the Corinthians are taking
a lot for granted, and are coming 'unstuck' in their faith. Paul is
vehement – but only because he loves these new Christians and
wants them to grow in their faith.

They that are rich . . .
Luxuries per se are not evil, but we can let them get in the way
of spiritual progress. They are also dangerously cumulative: a little
leads on to more – and where do we stop? Can we not hear Paul
cautioning: 'Better not to start!' Think of Jesus turning the question
into a smile, but still determined to get the message across, with
a camel and the eye of a needle (Matthew 19:24; Mark 10:25; Luke
18:25). That three of the four evangelists chose to include it in their
accounts points to its efficacy: this is a question that affects most
of us, except for those already so poor that they have no luxuries
in prospect.

No gift-wrapping
The gospel of Jesus needs no gift-wrapping; it was born in
borrowed accommodation, ratified in blood and sealed in love.
Mind you, it cost Jesus more than all the luxuries of the world
put together. Within the constraints of our English language, it is
valueless and priceless. How can we work that out? Only if we
come in faith with the ingenuousness, the simplicity of the mind
of a child.

Did the Corinthian Christians consider they had grown out of
childhood?

St Paul had done more growing up than most: a strict legal
training, energetic persecuting, a traumatic conversion – and now,

leader in the mission field. But he knew where his priority lay: Jesus first, Jesus last and Jesus all the way in between. The gospel for him stood alone, unsupported by luxuries. He would flog himself ever onward, not caring about food, clothes or shelter, until he died; and then he would declare to anyone who asked that he was but an unprofitable servant doing only what it was his duty to do.

Who could expect the sophisticated Corinthians to take this on board, but a man who practised what he preached.

Today's world
We can look at the Corinthians' background of luxury and pagan religions, and see that there are many similarities between their world and ours. Would Paul get as hot under the collar if he visited (or wrote to) us today? Well, he may ask, where is our missionary outreach? Where are the visiting evangelists? His understanding of the gospel was one of mission, rather than the very elaborate parochial system which the Church of today has spent centuries in constructing and operating.

It may sound revolutionary, but could Paul say, 'Close your churches, and get on your bikes?' Would he? So long as we believe that God has ongoing work for our carefully bounded parishes, we can continue to enjoy them; but if he seems to be pointing us forward and outward to wider horizons – what then?

Suggested hymns
Blest are the pure in heart; For my sake and the gospel's, go; Go, tell it on the mountain; Let us with a gladsome mind.

Seventh Sunday after Trinity (Proper 12)
25 July   *Principal Service*   How Much More!
Hos. 1:2–10; Ps. 85; Col. 2:6–15[16–19]; Luke 11:1–13

'[Jesus said], "If you then who are evil, know how to give good gifts to your children, how much more will the heavenly Father give the Holy Spirit to those who ask him!"' Luke 11:13

The divine pattern

'How much more!' is a good description not only of the Father's giving of his Spirit, but of everything he is and does. His natural world is one of abundant beauty and munificence, and he deals with his children with even more generosity, despite our often cavalier attitude to much of his giving and his care.

And yet there is another side to the coin. Jesus gave us the 'pattern prayer', which covers all of our life and our needs; but often the Lord's Prayer forms only a small part of even our regular praying, as we talk on and on to God about anything and everything. With God nothing is trivial: he is interested in all that we do. Are we giving our Lord's own prayer the weight that he intended?

We have also moved a long way from the pattern of our Lord's own life, when he, the Son of God, could say to an enquirer: 'Foxes have holes, and birds of the air have nests; but the Son of Man has nowhere to lay his head' (Luke 9:58). After Christ's ascension, his followers gathered for worship in 'house churches' (much as many do in China, especially rural China, today); then the hermits' cells of the desert; then the great desert monasteries of Egypt and Syria, and later throughout Christendom; and so to the magnificent cathedrals, abbeys and parish churches. How much more! All built for the glory of God, with the finest craftsmanship available.

How much more have we to help us in our faith, on the purely physical front, than had the first disciples! How much more, also, have we to distract us from loving God with all our heart, all our mind and all our strength! This is, after all, the 'greatest and first commandment' (Matthew 22:38). If our long prayers and beautiful architecture help us to fulfil this, and its close runner-up, 'love your neighbour as yourself', then how much more will God be pleased. If we can use our advances in technology and communications to the same ends, again, how much more will God be pleased. But if any of these things – estimable though they may be in themselves – comes between us and our perceived vocation; if we hear the gospel and have an uneasy twinge that our faith today has been either watered-down or altered the teaching of our Lord, then we need to come to God and 'argue it out' reverently with him in prayer (cf. Isaiah 1:18). How much more is God wanting to help those who are deeply committed not only to 'working out' their own faith, but also to helping others realize theirs! How much? More than we dare to ask or think (Ephesians 3:20).

We come into God's presence to argue our case – not as servants, but as friends, sisters and brothers, of his dear Son. He is predisposed not only to giving us a good hearing, but to helping us above what we are asking. That is magnificent, divine unfairness in action! It is the stuff that has kept Christians on their feet when everything else is against them. On bad days, when we may even contemplate compromising with depression and doubt, despair and denigration, let us remember that with God on our side *we cannot lose*: victory is assured, and may in fact be just ahead; so often opposition of any kind is the sign of coming success. We are winning, we are progressing! How much more does our striving delight our Lord!

Family Service input
The feast day of St Bridget (Abbess of Vadstena) was on 23 July. In her honour, encourage the young people to plan/construct/describe a monastery: abbot's house, gatehouse, church, cloisters, infirmary, refectory, kitchens, dormitories, garden, graveyard, barns, orchard, etc.

Suggested hymns
At the name of Jesus; Lift high the cross; Lord, teach us how to pray aright; The Lord will come and not be slow.

Seventh Sunday after Trinity *Second Service*
Watch Out!   Ps. 88; Gen. 42:1–25; 1 Cor. 10:1–24 or Matthew 13:24–30[31–43]

'So if you think you are standing, watch out that you do not fall. No testing has overtaken you that is not common to everyone. God is faithful, and he will not let you be tested beyond your strength, but with the testing he will also provide the way out so that you may be able to endure it.' 1 Corinthians 10:12–13

Why?
One of the most frequently asked questions, among believers and non-believers alike, is surely: 'Why is there so much evil in the world?' If a Christian is asking it, he or she usually phrases it: 'Why does God allow so much evil?' It's all a part of the challenge

of life. This life, beautiful though it is (despite Satan's machinations), is but the prelude to eternity's concerto. The prize is so great, why should we not undergo the rigours of testing in order to reach it? Only those who die young are spared the testing: and in their case their parents and friends are the ones who suffer the testing.

Testing also provides a means of proving God's faithfulness. Brother Andrew, founder of the Open Doors Bible ministry to Christians in persecuted areas, used to call it 'Walking the Royal Way'. There were times in his life when he relied completely on God for finance and the necessities of life. When he was training for ministry, at a Bible college in Scotland, the students would be sent out on evangelistic missions for several days at a time, virtually as our Lord despatched his first missionaries. They were given £1 each, for the complete financing of the mission – booking the various halls, overnight accommodation and catering. And they were expected to return their £1 (with interest, if possible) on their return to the college! God never failed them – and his ingenuity in providing for the students, and those to whom they were ministering, on many occasions left them speechless with awe.

Testing God!

'Put *me* to the test,' says the Lord of hosts; 'see if I will not open the windows of heaven for you and pour down for you an overflowing blessing' (Malachi 3:10). If we give to the Lord his due, he will repay us with abundant, overflowing interest. Can we, dare we, take up this challenge from God? We are so geared to insurance policies for everything, from the car and the house to pensions and 'life': dare we stake all on the word of the Holy and Undivided Trinity Assurance Company? No forms to fill in, and our premium has already been paid – at Calvary.

Of course, testing God means that Satan takes more than a passing interest in us, too, doing his best to pick holes in our divine insurance policy: 'Are you sure God wants you to take such a radical step? Isn't it prudent to "put something by"? Doesn't God want you to earn a lot, so that you could give more away to help others . . . ?' The Devil's arguments are many and subtle: he's been at the game a long while.

In a tight corner
There will be those days when the testing seems to hem us in on
all sides. Surely God is trying us too much? No – it usually means
we have been underestimating our spiritual stamina: there's never
anything amiss with God's judgement. We can shout, or scream,
or cry – we don't usually go as far as fainting – and sometimes
we crack, and take the Devil's way out. For, while God always
provides a way out of trouble, so does Satan. God's way is the
hard one, and it may involve danger and social, economic, physical
or spiritual hurt. Satan's is the easier way, the 'dodgy' way, where
we can bend the rules (if not actually break them), and wangle a
solution, but lose our honour in the wangling. With God's way,
we can walk out of trouble with our head held high.

Not too much of a choice – is it?

Suggested hymns
Father of heaven, whose love profound; Forgive our sins, as we
forgive; Prayer is the soul's sincere desire; Thy kingdom come, O
God.

Eighth Sunday after Trinity (Proper 13)
1 August   *Principal Service*   **Don't Be Greedy!**
Hos. 11:1–11; Ps. 107:1–9, 43; Col. 3:1–11;
Luke 12:13–21

*'And [Jesus] said to them, "Take care! Be on your guard against all
kinds of greed; for one's life does not consist in the abundance of possessions." ' Luke 12:15*

Don't covet
Jesus' teaching is a version of the tenth commandment, 'You shall
not covet' (Exodus 20:17). Greed is a form of covetousness: we are
wanting something that may very well be able to be gained at no
one else's expense; but (like our neighbour's house) do we need
it? We can argue that if we can make a lot of money, we can give
a lot to the Church, or to 'good works' in general: isn't it then
doing a lot of folk a lot of good?

Maybe. But that was not how Jesus operated. His attitude to

the poor was to enrich them with the preaching of the gospel (Matthew 11:5) – not with pouring cash into their empty pockets or overdrawn bank accounts. This seems a strange attitude in today's world. Even James seems to be more in line with modern thinking: 'If a brother or sister is naked and lacks daily food, and one of you says to them, "Go in peace; keep warm and eat your fill", and yet you do not supply their bodily needs, what is the good of that? So faith by itself, if it has no works, is dead' (James 2:15–17).

'You always have the poor with you,' Jesus told his disciples (Matthew 26:11); and his comment made such an impact (as well it might) that both Mark (14:7) and John (12:8) record it also. We may wonder why Jesus, who spent so much time healing every sickness and every disease, is not on record as ever having (in material terms) made a poor person rich. Is our world too obsessed by wealth to – a daring thought! – value poverty as it ought?

> *The world wants the wealth to live in state,*
> *But you show us a new way to be great;*
> *Like a servant you came,*
> *And if we do the same,*
> *We'll be turning the world upsidedown.*
>
> Patrick Appleford

Good greed!

There is a greed that every Christian can cheerfully cultivate! A greed for souls, a greed for sharing God's word; for ministering to as many people as we can; a greed for spreading Christ's love in loveless hearts, Christ's light in darkened souls, Christ's compassion in angry or hurt lives. That's good greed, and it needs to be cultivated more. While we're getting this, we shall not have as much time to go running after the other sort of greed.

Getting our minds off the mindset of the world, and on to that of God, doesn't come overnight. It needs months, years – even a lifetime – of hard work, because the current of the world is always set to pull us in the opposite direction, always telling us where the grass is greener. The junk mail plopping daily into the letter-box is full of ideas for us to 'get rich quick', or to acquire more and more possessions to cut more and more of a dash with the neighbours. Are the neighbours bothered? No, they're either playing the same game, in which case the greed looks like spiralling out of control, or else they're hooked on the 'other' greed, God's zeal for souls, in which case they won't even notice our efforts to impress. It's easy to see who's wasting the effort!

We can surely pray today, with extra meaning and earnestness, the prayer that Jesus taught us: 'Lead us not into temptation' – temptation of Satan's kind of greed. Let us be givers, not getters – *giving* ourselves, our love and light and power of Christ, so that others may *get* the advantage of coming to know him and the abundant giving of himself.

Family Service input
'Prayers for the Nations' – encourage the young people to write on cards the Lord's Prayer in as many languages as possible, and display their results on a World Prayer table in the church. (Useful, too, for the weekly intercessions, and for mission/unity projects, etc.)

Suggested hymns
All my hope on God is founded; Be thou my vision; He that is down needs fear no fall; When all thy mercies, O my God.

Eighth Sunday after Trinity   *Second Service*
Aiming for Excellence   Ps. 107:1–32; Gen. 50:4–26; 1 Cor. 14:1–19 or Mark 6:45–52
'So with yourselves, since you are eager for spiritual gifts, strive to excel in them for building up the church.' 1 Corinthians 14:12

Giving to each other
The gifts of the Spirit are liberally given by a generous God, to be shared in a generous spirit. As a mother gives all she has to her children, not only for their good but for the growth and integration of the family, so God's gifts are for his Church, with individual members being the instruments of their application. We can take Christian pride (in the most positive sense) in their use, so long as we do not hog the credit for ourselves.

Sometimes sharing is difficult, whether it's sharing our faith, our joys or our troubles. How, then, can we break through this barrier of natural reticence? What is the point of God's gifts if we do not know how to share them? Paul tells us, in today's reading, that sharing 'revelation or knowledge or prophecy or teaching' is the most important spiritual gift (v. 6). 'How are they to hear without someone to proclaim [Jesus]?' this same Paul asked the Roman Christians (Romans 10:14). For centuries the Church saw practically all preaching (prophesying, revealing, teaching) done by the priests: only in the last few generations has the exercising of this gift been seriously explored by the wider body of Christ; but this expansion of understanding is now unstoppable, and its benefits are being seen in the (sometimes phenomenal) growth of the Church in parts of the world today. It is probably no exaggeration to see William Tyndale's work in giving English-speaking Christians the Bible (or at least the New Testament and parts of the Old, before he was martyred) in their mother-tongue, as the watershed that began opening up the scriptures to the laity. Yet change came slowly – far too slowly, with hindsight – until the last 150 years, when it moved into higher gear. Hallelujah!

How can this gift grow?
How can we, as individuals, increase this gift in our lives, so that we can use it to build up others in the faith? Bible reading and prayer are fine, and we need both in good measure; but we also need grace to go out and get hands-on experience. Once the hurdle of reticence has been cleared, the sharing can grow and grow. We all have questions – many questions – about our faith. Often we bring these to God in prayer, and either leave them with him for action or take them back and worry about them ourselves. Jesus told us not to do this – we still do, far too often. But have we ever thought how the sharing of these questions may help someone else, may in fact encourage them to reciprocate and to let us in on problems (or pleasures) of their own? There are matters discussed properly at PCC meetings, and those which regularly surface in Bible Groups – but the ones we keep for our personal consumption (or indigestion) are probably those which could benefit the Church for being shared. How often, for instance, do we meet to discuss matters arising from Sunday's readings and sermons? The best time is while they are in the forefront of our minds. But, over coffee and biscuits after the service, do we switch to other matters? Let's reflect that we are still in God's house.

Language fatigue?
It has been said of cats that the one thing from which they never
suffer is insomnia! We can also say of the tongue that it rarely if
ever suffers from lack of use. But how are we using our powers
of speech for God? Are these tremendously powerful vocal chords
in tune with the Holy Spirit, or singing another song? Paul values
the gift of tongues when he is speaking to God, but emphasizes
that our duty to our fellow members in Christ's body is to build
them up, in language they can understand. 'The tongue is a fire,'
warns St James (James 3:6). Let's make sure it burns brightly –
for God, and his glory, as we aim for excellence in speech.

Suggested hymns
All for Jesus, all for Jesus; Angel-voices, ever singing; Go, tell it
on the mountain; Tell out, my soul, the greatness of the Lord.

Ninth Sunday after Trinity (Proper 14)
8 August   *Principal Service*   **Reversal of Roles**
Isa. 1:1, 10–20; Ps. 50:1–8, 22–23; Heb. 11:1–3, 8–16;
Luke 12:32–40

*'[Jesus said], "Blessed are those slaves whom the master finds alert when
he comes; truly I tell you, he will fasten his belt and have them sit down
to eat, and he will come and serve them." ' Luke 12:37*

Divine condescension!
What a reversal of roles! Who else but a God so motivated by love
that he gave his only Son to die for us, could also offer us such
divine condescension on the great day of his coming? Yet we
become immersed in our long-range schemes, our short-term
schedules, until the first thought of our minds on waking each
morning is so often one of worry. When Jesus comes, will he find
us fretting over something that really doesn't matter? Oh, *no*, Lord,
I'll be ready!

> *'Are ye able,' said the Master,*
> *'To be crucified with me?'*
> *'Yes,' the sturdy dreamers answered,*
> *'To the death we follow thee.'*

'Are ye able?' still the Master
Whispers down eternity;
And heroic spirits answer,
Now, as then in Galilee:
'Lord, we are able,
Our spirits are thine,
Remould them, make us
Like thee, divine.
Thy guiding radiance
Above us shall be
A beacon to God,
To faith and loyalty.'

Earl Marlatt

Are we – shall we be – able to sit down on that great day, while the Lord treats us to a banquet? We shall have earned not even a morsel of that food by anything we have done, but by who we are: souls for whom Christ has died, souls whom he has loved so much he paid the highest price that has ever been paid. We are not our own – here, or in eternity; we are *his* – first, last and all down the line. He has called us to the banquet; our faithfulness here is all he asks. We need to be mindful of the time: God is allowing us all the time to do all that he wants us to do: no more, no less. We need not hurry or worry – just keep on keeping on sharing, giving, loving those whom God gives us, making the most of the opportunities he brings, simply in love for him and ever mindful of what he has done and is doing for us.

The struggle

The struggle comes now. By the time Jesus serves us at that banquet, we shall not be worrying ourselves into indigestion – spiritual or physical. We shall be beyond the valley of struggle. Shall we get to glory battered and bruised? Quite possibly: is not Christ himself still carrying the wounds of Calvary? If we have not picked up some 'scars for glory' on our pilgrimage here, how many risks will we have run? How many trials shall we have faced? How many brushes shall we have had with the Devil? For, if Satan has not been roused to put obstacles in our way, how hard have we been working for God?

Please God, when the struggle is over, we shall be primed and ready for the next stage of mission – *after* we have enjoyed that banquet of celebration!

> *Not to the strong is the battle,*
> *Not to the swift is the race,*
> *Yet to the true and the faithful*
> *Victory is promised through grace.*
>
> S. Martin, Conquering Now
> and Still to Conquer

Grace, let us remind ourselves, is God's free and full unmerited favour. We are front-line troops in the greatest army ever formed – but we passed no quota of IQ tests or physical fitness routines to get into uniform. We are brothers and sisters of our Leader, and destined for glory. No truce while the foe is still unconquered.

Family Service input
Encourage the young people to work with flowers, fruit and trees of the Bible (see below): illustrating; embroidering (for kneelers, etc.); growing, and making into posters/cards/artwork.

Suggested hymns
Jerusalem the golden; My soul, there is a country; The Lamb's high banquet called to share; Wake, O wake, for night is flying.

Flowers, fruits and trees of the Bible

Some of the plants mentioned in the Bible are found only in the Holy Land and neighbouring countries; some have died out; some remain to be identified precisely, and are to be found under different names in the various Bible versions. A selection of the most familiar are listed below.

Flowers and herbs
Aloes (John 19:39)
Anemone (lilies of the field) (Matthew 6:28–29)
Anise (Matthew 23:23)
Balm (Genesis 37:23)

185

Bulrush (Job 8:11)
Burning Bush (Dictamnus) (Exodus 3:2–4)
Coriander (Exodus 16:31)
Cumin (1 Samuel 28:25, 27)
Garlic (Numbers 11:5)
Hyssop (or marjoram) (Exodus 12:22)
Myrtle (Isaiah 55:13)
Ricinus (gourd) (Jonah 4:6–10)
Rose (2 Esdras 2:19)
Rose of Sharon (Song of Solomon 2:1)
Rue (Luke 11:42)
Saffron (Song of Solomon 4:14)
Wormwood (Deuteronomy 29:18)

Fruit and vegetables
Apple (or perhaps apricot) (Genesis 2:9)
Bean (2 Samuel 17:28)
Cucumber (Numbers 11:5)
Fig (Genesis 3:7)
Leeks (Numbers 11:5)
Lentils (Genesis 25:30)
Melon (Numbers 11:5)
Mustard (Matthew 13:31–32)
Onion (Numbers 11:5)
Pomegranate (Deuteronomy 8:8)
Vine (Genesis 9:20–21)

Trees
Ash (Isaiah 44:14)
Bay (Psalm 37:36)
Box (Isaiah 41:19)
Cedar (Psalm 29:5)
Date Palm (Exodus 15:27)
Fir (Isaiah 55:13)
Juniper (1 Kings 19:4–5)
Mulberry (2 Samuel 5:23)
Oak (Genesis 13:18)
Olive (Genesis 8:11)
Pine (Isaiah 41:19)
Poplar (Genesis 30:37)
Tamarisk (Genesis 21:33)

Walnut (Song of Soloman 6:11)
Willow (Psalm 137:1-2)

Ninth Sunday after Trinity   *Second Service*
Called to Console   Ps. 108 [116]; Isa. 11:10—12:6;
2 Cor. 1:1-22 or Mark 7:24-30

'Blessed be the God and Father of our Lord Jesus Christ, the Father of
mercies and the God of all consolation, who consoles us in all our afflic-
tion, so that we may be able to console those who are in any affliction
with the consolation with which we ourselves are consoled by God.'
2 Corinthians 1:3-4

Universal sadness
If there is one thing certain in this uncertain world, it is that
sooner or later we shall need to console someone or to be consoled
ourselves. The reason could be trouble, tragedy, sorrow of many
kinds, but inevitably bereavement will stand highest on the list.
What do we do when a person has lost a loved one? If we are
quite young, the cry for help may come before we ourselves have
been in that situation; or we may have learned the hard way, that
grief has as many forms as there are people to grieve. What we
should not do is to act as though (1) the bereaved person has an
infectious disease, and walk in the opposite direction, or (2) avoid
mentioning the departed, as though he or she has dropped out of
mind as well as out of sight.

Memories are precious
At a time of loss, memories are extra-precious; and, though they
may hurt, the bereaved usually want to be allowed to talk (often
at length) about the departed. If the person listening has known
the deceased, and can share memories, that is good; but in any case
having the love and patience to listen is the greatest consolation we
can give – no matter how often the memories are repeated, or
jumbled: it is a way of lessening grief in the shock of the parting.

The first week
Various happenings lead up to a bereavement: it can come at the
end of a long illness, or a time of gradual weakening; or it can be

tragically sudden, as in the case of an accident. The departed can be young, or full of years; they can have left young children, or have been recently married; they can have been a pillar of the church, or a non-believer. Whatever the reason, death seems to come 'too soon', and we are shocked into an awareness that God has intervened convincingly and has made a choice for us which we would not have made for ourselves. In the first week, between the death and the funeral, the bereaved are numb, as God seems to 'shut down' the vital parts of us that relate to others and to life in general, and to carry us through the days on virtual 'auto-pilot'. We work, however subconsciously, towards the funeral: the cars, the flowers, the service, the funeral tea. Friends come and go, and we don't care about the time: in fact, we probably forget to wind up the clocks. We wonder how we shall get through the funeral – but get through it we do, because most of us can cope with a crisis.

The second week, and further . . .
It is after the funeral that the real time for consolation comes – when the visits tail off, when probate and legal matters demand attention, and when the pieces of life have to be picked up again. God's precious gifts carry on, as strong and certain and comforting and *vital* today as when Jesus promised them – and the consoler is the purveyor of these gifts. Let us pray to God for the right words to say, the right time to listen – yes, and perhaps the right time to weep with the one we are consoling.

A new chapter
God intervenes at death, to end one chapter and to begin another. We who are left behind cannot yet turn the page and experience that new chapter with the departed in quite the way that we experienced the first. Our friend has gone on ahead, gone beyond time. He or she has crossed tomorrow's field of snow, leaving no footprints but a host of memories. And God is looking after our friend.

Suggested hymns
Abide with me; In heavenly love abiding; Jesus, lover of my soul; Let saints on earth in concert sing.

Tenth Sunday after Trinity (Proper 15)

15 August   *Principal Service*

Seeing with Our Spiritual Insight   Isa. 5:1–7;
Ps. 80:1–2, 8–19; Heb. 11:29—12:2; Luke 12:49–56

'[Jesus] said, "You hypocrites! You know how to interpret the appearance
of earth and sky, but why do you not know how to interpret the present
time?"' Luke 12:56

Various interpretations

It is a little like a person being able to interpret Russian fluently
but not having a clue about Mandarin Chinese; the analogy is not
perfect, but it illustrates how patchy is our interpretative equipment. A student can be a genius at mathematical interpretation
but a complete dunce when faced with a problem in music. Yet
Jesus is here criticizing the people for not recognizing something
which was far more predictable and understandable (not least
because their scriptures were full of prophecies relating to him)
than the weather – which, as we know, is difficult enough to
predict and understand today, despite the accumulation of technology and science. The 'present time' was the living example of
their old prophecies – but they could not see what they had been
looking for for centuries!

Priorities

We can gen up on the weather forecasts many times a day; we
can hold forth authoritatively on the GDP, the Footsie or a hundred and one other financial concerns, but, as our Lord told Martha
on one occasion, 'there is need of only one thing' (Luke 10:42):
God – his word, his work, his witness, his worship. We shall not
interpret all that fully until we close this chapter of life and move
on to the next; but the earlier we make a start, the better we shall
become at it.

Looking for God

Do we look for God in everything, or does an occasional realization
take us by surprise? If we look for him, we shall find him, because
God (as St Thomas Aquinas famously declared, in the *Summa*) is
everywhere, in everything. Have we got a joy? God is there. Have
we a problem? God is there, too – for he has promised to show

us how to solve it (1 Corinthians 10:13). Can we look at all the persons we can see, right now? God is in all of them, for he made them. He is in the air we breathe, the houses and trees we see. Only when we have this extended awareness of God can we begin fully to relate him to what we are experiencing, every moment of the day or night.

Recollection

The old monks used to call this awareness of God 'recollection'. They drew aside from the world into the monasteries to find it. St Paul, St Peter and countless others, including ourselves, have found – and continue to find – it, in the bustle of everyday life. So long as we get our priorities right, and don't confuse God and what he is doing with anything else. We can have some sympathy with those first-century folk who were weather-watchers: it is still possible to be so locked on to looking for some particular thing that our attention paradoxically switches off, and we end up missing the point: it's a bit like weeding a long garden border and failing to see the biggest dandelion of all.

Easy – but dangerous when what we are missing is Jesus himself. We need to remember that he called these first-century Jews 'hypocrites' – a hard word, meaning literally that they were living a lie: ostensibly expecting the Messiah, yet failing to see him when he met them eyeball to eyeball.

If Jesus comes back to earth before we die, we shall not make the same mistake – shall we?

Family Service input

Today being the Feast of the Assumption, discuss with the young people the symbols of Mary in the Church (see p. 191), and encourage them to illustrate/colour them.

Suggested hymns

Awake, my soul, and with the sun; For Mary, mother of our Lord; Lord, speak to me, that I may speak; My song is love unknown.

Symbols of Mary

The Lady Chapel
This is to be found in cathedrals and many of the larger churches, and is dedicated to Our Lady. Here the symbols relating to Mary are concentrated, though may also be seen in other parts of the church.

For example:

Mary's flowers:

> the LILY denotes her purity;
> the ROSE her beauty;
> the VIOLET her humility.

The rose is often seen in heraldic, stylized form, while the lily may be embroidered on altar-coverings, together with corn and grapes, thus symbolizing also our Lord's Eucharist.

Mary's colour
BLUE is the colour of Mary; look for this in banners, stained glass, kneelers, etc. It is often decorated with the FLEUR-DE-LYS, which is a stylized form of the IRIS and LILY, both Marian flowers.

Mary's Monogram
Encourage the young people to illustrate variations of the ancient monogram from which the letters MARIA may be read:

Tenth Sunday after Trinity   *Second Service*
Generosity – Divine and Human   Ps. 119:17–32;
Isa. 28:9–22; 2 Cor. 8:1–9 or Matthew 20:1–16

'Now as you excel in everything – in faith, in speech, in knowledge, in utmost eagerness, and in our love for you – so we want you to excel also in this generous undertaking . . . For you know the generous act of our Lord Jesus Christ, that though he was rich, yet for your sakes he became poor, so that by his poverty you might become rich.' 2 Corinthians 8:7, 9

The difference
Jesus gave all – all for us. Out of his abundance, he could have given a lot and made a difference. But he gave all he had. No one can ever match the price he paid, for our salvation. That is generosity on a divine scale. And how does it look on a human scale? We, in contrast, have relatively little, and more often than not our generosity is relatively little: those who give the 'widow's mite' and leave themselves with nothing are few and far between. 'Giving till it hurts' has dropped out of fashion. Yet we still expect God to honour his promise of eternal life.

Not just money
Generosity doesn't concern only money: in fact, many even in the 'affluent' parts of the world don't have any money, never mind money to spare. 'Cardboard city' (in whatever location) makes the headlines at Christmas, but exists all the time. We understood it, on the streets of Calcutta, when Mother Teresa was alive – but the poor of Calcutta didn't all go to glory when she died. And even among families with homes and furniture, there are many who are struggling to survive on inadequate wages and hand-outs.

Whether sick or poor, God is not asking us for what we have not, but to give to him what we *can*: no more, maybe – but no less. Yet money is not the only debt we can pay; he has also given us time and talents. How much time do we give him in a normal day? Spare minutes, or quality time? And how many of our talents (have we ever even counted them) are being used in God's service? A little girl cried to her mother, on returning home from Sunday Club: 'How can I share my gifts with God? I've only got Teddy!' Yet within the hour, she was letting the toddler next door play with her precious teddy bear. Do we rack our brains trying to think of some great thing we can do for God, while letting simple little opportunities pass us by? A wise person once said something like this: 'We may not all do many great works – but we can all do many little works well!'

God is smarter!
We may decide we can use our money, time or talents in a certain way – but if we let God in on the act, he can multiply their efficacy and influence beyond our dreams. 'Lord, please take over my finances; guide me in the use of all the time you give me; show me how to use my gifts in the service of others. And, dear Lord, make your will for me so plain that even I can't get it wrong.' That's a very daring, powerful prayer. Are we brave enough to make it, and mean it? Giving God such a free rein in our lives is risky: we know he will take us at our word; we know he will act; but we don't know in advance *how* he will act! We do know, however, that those who have taken this mighty step – St Paul, St Teresa of Avila, C. T. Studd, Albert Schweitzer, Mother Teresa – have not lived to regret it.

> *Some want to live*
> *within the sound*
> *of church or chapel-bell;*
> *I want to run a rescue-shop*
> *within a yard of hell!*
>
> C. T. Studd

So wrote the cricketer-turned-missionary who, when inheriting a fortune at age 25, sat down at his desk and calmly wrote cheques to various churches and charities until he had given everything away.

Lord, help *me* to be a blessing to someone today.

Suggested hymns
In full and glad surrender; Just as I am; Now thank we all our God; When peace like a river attendeth my way.

Eleventh Sunday after Trinity (Proper 16)

22 August *Principal Service* Free from Bondage

Jer. 1:4–10; Ps. 71:1–6, Heb. 12:18–29; Luke 13:10–17

'[Jesus said], "Ought not this woman . . . whom Satan bound for eighteen long years, be set free from this bondage on the sabbath day?" When he said this, all his opponents were put to shame, and the entire crowd was rejoicing at all the wonderful things that he was doing.' Luke 13:16–17

Satan is to blame!

It was Satan's fault that the poor woman was in such a pitiable condition. Jesus lays the blame squarely on the Devil's shoulders. Occasionally we hear folk saying things like: 'God is mad with so-and-so! He's sent cancer/meningitis on him!' From this incident, we learn from Jesus himself where sickness and disease originate: Satan. If it came from God, Jesus would not have spent so much of his ministry healing people, turning their sickness, disease and infirmity into health and wholeness.

We do not know why God allows Satan to inflict such misery; but the example of Job gives us encouragement. Satan begged God to allow him a free hand with Job, but God firmly replied: So far, and no further! 'He is in your power, only spare his life!' (Job 2:6). Job may have been so tormented that he longed to die; but with this order from God there was no way that Satan could kill him. Life and death are in God's hands. God himself knows no limits, but he has placed limits on Satan. However great we think is the evil in the world today, the Devil can only extend his power so far. And no further.

Healing ministry

'Sharing the gospel' is sometimes seen as having overtaken the ministry of healing – and yet the two should not be divided. They were never divided in the mind of Jesus: he told John's disciples, 'Go and tell John what you hear and see: the blind receive their sight, the lame walk, the lepers are cleansed, the deaf hear, the dead are raised, and the poor have good news brought to them' (Matthew 11:4–5). *That* was ministry: compound, composite, complete gospel ministry. We divide it up and pigeon-hole it into separate compartments at our own risk. It is 'holistic' ministry, divinely sanctioned – ministry to the whole person. Made healthy and strong, even a poor person became rich with the gift of the gospel.

Church Crossword

Clues Across

1. Told by the sundial. (4)
3. Usually one or two up to the altar. (4)
5. The Christian age. (3)
6. Entrance. (6, 5)
9. Ground covered by church. (4)
10. Iesus Nazarenus Rex Iudaeorum (init.) (4)
13. Where the singers sit. (5, 6)
15. Jesus is God's. (3)
16. Our immortal part? (4)
17. Commandments. (4)

Clues Down

1. To instruct. (5)
2. Curve of stone or wood. (4)
4. Walkways through churchyard. (5)
7. Used as seat. (5)
8. Top of spire. (5)
11. Five wounds of Jesus. (5)
12. Mark a cross on first day of Lent. (5)
14. '. . . had fallen, snow on snow.' (4)

The ministry jigsaw

Full gospel ministry, as Jesus practised it (and, by implication, intended us to follow his pattern), can be likened to a jigsaw or a crossword. Several parts are joined together to form a whole: the parts on their own are incomplete; they need fitting together, dovetailing in, for the whole picture to be seen, the whole puzzle to be understood. So it is with gospel ministry: our prayers for the sick, our healing services, our hospital ministries, need to be an integral part of our sharing the gospel. God and his word and his love must be paramount, because we are not struggling against enemies of flesh and blood, but against the spiritual forces of evil (Ephesians 6:12). We are battling against the damage that Satan has done to the beautiful people God made in his own likeness. It makes a difference when we know the identity of the enemy. If *God* brought sickness and disease, we should be fighting a losing battle against the Omnipotent. But Satan is a long way from being omnipotent – and we fight him in the greater power of the Holy Spirit: 'The one who is in you is greater than the one who is in the world' (1 John 4:4).

If all Christians would only dare to take on board this *full* gospel ministry, instead of acting as though they believed healing miracles went out with the first century, what a difference it could make!

Family Service input

Run off copies of the 'Church' crossword for the young people (and others, if applicable!) to solve (see p. 195).

Suggested hymns

Fill thou my life, O Lord my God; For the healing of the nations; Thine arm, O Lord, in days of old; To God be the glory.

Solution:
Across: 1. Time. 3. Step. 5. Era. 6. Church porch. 9. Area. 10. INRI. 13. Choir stalls. 15. Son. 16. Soul. 17. Laws.
Down: 1. Teach. 2. Arch. 4. Paths. 7. Chair. 8. Point. 11. Scars. 12. Ashes. 14. Snow.

Eleventh Sunday after Trinity *Second Service*

Inspiring Others Ps. 119:49–72; Isa. 30:8–21; 2 Cor. 9
or Matthew 21:28–32

'Each of you must give as you have made up your mind, not reluctantly or under compulsion, for God loves a cheerful giver. And God is able to provide you with every blessing in abundance, so that by always having enough of everything, you may share abundantly in every good work.'
2 Corinthians 9:7–8

Stirring up

'Your zeal has stirred up most of [the Macedonians],' Paul tells the Corinthians encouragingly (v. 2). We need to value rightly the capacity to influence, and to be influenced by others. Let's make sure it's always for good. The enthusiasm to support the Church among the Corinthians had spread like the bush telegraph – and Paul was all in favour of praise where praise was due. At the same time, he urged them to make good the promises they had made, or their zeal would be null and void. The fire of the gospel had been lit among them, and Paul was keen for it not to burn out.

Cheerfulness in service

Whatever form our ministry takes, may we do it cheerfully, willingly and not reluctantly – not merely as a duty but as a pleasure. And God will respond, says St Paul, by willingly giving us blessings aplenty. Can't we trust him to do that? If we have a problem with it, may we seek his will in prayer without delay. Provided we give him our willing hearts, for any service, he will not let us starve, or go without life's necessities. We have his word (e.g. Matthew 6:33).

How much joy do we find in religion? No, perhaps that's not the fairest of questions. How much joy do we give to God? If we are not showing joy to our fellows, we can't be giving much to God. The two facets must be matched together to make a jewel of our faith through which Christ's light can shine. Is our spiritual diamond sparkling brightly? Do folk smile back at us, as we pass them on the street? If not, why not? The 'cheerfulness' that Paul talks about in his letter to the Corinthians is not to be confined to a wry smile when the plate comes round during the last hymn, but to the full range of our Christian ministry.

It helps to sing!
The Russians have a saying, 'To sing is to pray twice'. Singing not only helps with prayer, but it lifts the spirits. Have you tried singing when you're 'down and out'? On the rare occasions when someone in the shopping mall has been singing, haven't you paused to think, 'Someone's happy!' Let's sing more often, for the Lord who has put 'a new song' in each one of us.

A 'lift' for Paul
What a lift the zeal of the Corinthians must have given to Paul! He'd had plenty to bother him in his ministry (2 Corinthians 11:21ff.), and his relief at being able to praise God for someone's enthusiasm is evident in our reading – made doubly joyful as he tells them what their example is meaning to others. At times we may be so taken up with our problems (or pleasures), or worries (or successes), our busyness (or boredom), that we forget the vibes that we are sending to others. There are, on the other hand, folk whose influence is simply, quietly 'good', yet who seem to be quite unconscious of doing any hard-sell evangelism. One such person was Alexander Wadham Woods, a retired admiral who took holy orders and ministered so quietly among London's East Enders that when he died few could remember much about the man himself, yet everything about the kindness he had shown and the Christian help and ministry he had given so unstintingly. May we, too, be remembered for the Christ we show, rather than ourselves.

Suggested hymns
All my hope on God is founded; Give thanks with a grateful heart; O Lord, all the world belongs to you; Through all the changing scenes of life.

Twelfth Sunday after Trinity (Proper 17)
29 August   *Principal Service*   **Sharing**   Jer. 2:4–13; Ps. 81:1, 10–16; Heb. 13:1–8, 15–16; Luke 14:1, 7–14

'Through [Jesus], then, let us continually offer a sacrifice of praise to God, that is, the fruit of lips that confess his name. Do not neglect to do good and to share what you have, for such sacrifices are pleasing to God.'
Hebrews 13:15–16

Our example
Sharing was such an integral part of the life of Jesus, it was inevitable that at least some of it rubbed off on to his disciples – though there were 'blips', such as the time when James and John sought to reserve high places for themselves in glory (Mark 10:37). Sharing became an important feature of the early Church: 'All who believed were together and had all things in common; they would sell their possessions and goods and distribute the proceeds to all, as they had need' (Acts 2:44–45). In many ways, society today does just the opposite. Even a century or so ago, before we shut ourselves in with our TV screens and computers, neighbours used to get together over the garden wall, or for a coffee, to share their ups and downs. Churches where coffee is served after worship are encouraging, even in a small way, a sharing which is as important in its way for the members of Christ's body as is worship itself.

The right balance
In the foot-and-mouth outbreak of 2001, it was borne in even upon townsfolk that acres and acres of fields shorn of animals was not only wrong and tragic, it was upsetting the balance of nature. Grassland which was not regularly overgrazed by cattle or sheep quickly grew rank and needed to be cut – and in some cases ploughed in and resown. The country as a whole woke up to the fact that the animals which had largely been taken for granted, or regarded merely as food-in-waiting, were part of Nature's balance.

So it is with Christians. A solitary Christian may go some way in prayer and meditation towards nurturing his or her own soul – but he or she is not doing much for the nurturing of anyone else's; such Christians are not playing their full part as members of the body of Christ. We need to share our lives – the ups and the downs – with others. It's often so much easier to tell a friend our woes than to share good news; but let's work on it. The Bible, after all, is the world's bestseller of good news – and we have it. Who did we share that good news with – yesterday . . . the day before . . . ? Paul (or whoever wrote the general letter to the Hebrews) tells us seriously not to neglect our continual, ongoing ministry of sharing. Why? Simply because it pleases God: who needs a better reason?

A sharing mentality
Developing a sharing mentality is so difficult we can't do it in our own strength. It needs the Holy Spirit to prompt and nudge and

whisper from inside: 'Go and see the people who've just moved in, two houses along: the husband's in a wheelchair – they'll be glad of some help . . .' ('Well, Lord, they might not; they might think I'm intruding; they might . . .'). Sure, they *might* just be needing the help you can give. If we allow Satan to butt in with all his 'they mights . . .' and 'perhaps nots . . .', God will be kept waiting before he can rejoice in our sharing.

Satan wouldn't go out of his way to help or share with anyone. Who'd want to be like him, anyway?

Even if we cannot for purely physical reasons get round next door to help, we can share through prayer and the ministry of intercession. Even, for example, as we sing 'The day thou gavest, Lord', we are sharing in spirit with untold millions of Christians around the world: and the more we practise sharing, the easier and greater it becomes – and the more we are pleasing God.

Family Service input
Share with the young people the background to the hymn, 'The day thou gavest' (see below); encourage them to (1) write an extra verse, and (2) illustrate it.

Suggested hymns
Father, I place into your hands; Help us to help each other, Lord; The day thou gavest, Lord; When I needed a neighbour.

Hymn stories

The day thou gavest, Lord
We've become used to singing this hymn at evening services, and sometimes at funerals. But Canon John Ellerton (1826–1893), one of the leading hymn-writers of Victorian times, did not target it as an evening hymn. It was published in 1870 as part of an order of service for missionary meetings. Its main theme is the worldwide provenance and growth of the Christian Church, and the constant, 24-hour offering of worship to God. As one travels (in spirit or physically) round the world, night gives way to day, and worshippers at evening services are succeeded by those rising with the dawn to give praise at the start of a new morning.

It's a hymn that gives us a sense of oneness and fellowship with Christians across the globe; and in the days when the British

Commonwealth was at its zenith, this hymn was chosen for Queen Victoria's Diamond Jubilee in 1897.

Several tunes have been written for it – but one which was scorned on all sides at its introduction has become the world's favourite: St Clement.

Twelfth Sunday after Trinity *Second Service*
Spirit-Filled Words Ps. 119:81–96; Isa. 33:13–22; John 3:22–36

'[John said], "He whom God has sent speaks the words of God, for he gives the Spirit without measure."' John 3:34

Precious words
The words of Jesus are Spirit-filled and life-giving. He has said so: 'The words that I have spoken to you are spirit and life' (John 6:63). That is Truth speaking. We can believe it. But because they are so precious, we need to handle every word with reverence and care, as well as love and Christian pride. We are Christ's ambassadors: many of those with whom we share his words will rely on our presentation of them, even our interpretation and our understanding. We need to pray for guidance and truth from the Holy Spirit, that we may be true to our calling. Centuries before Christ, the psalmist was conscious of his responsibility as a God-fearer: 'Do not let those who hope in you be put to shame because of me, O Lord God of hosts; do not let those who seek you be dishonoured because of me, O God of Israel' (Psalm 69:6). We need to make this prayer ours, too.

John's generosity
It would have been tempting for John to pander to the implied partiality of his disciples, and to have emphasized his own ministry – but he would not do it. He would never be disloyal to his Master. This is self-abnegation on a total scale. We can reverently surmise that God had schooled John well in the desert prior to his ministry: for how else could he have understood his mission so well? How else could he have found the advanced theological wisdom to teach these disciples who returned to him ostensibly

with a question of purification, but in reality querying the person and the position of Jesus?

Diversity in ministry

There are those today whose operation of ministry may seem strange to us. Do we bristle up and either ignore them or criticize simply because their way differs from ours? Jesus and John both proclaimed the true gospel – but their ministries were not carbon copies of each other: John was always at pains to stress that. We cannot expect any other Christian to say everything that we say, or to minister in exactly the same way that we minister. God deals with us as individuals. No one has precisely the same revelations, insights or expository skills; no one shares the gifts of the Spirit in exactly the same way. Wouldn't life be far less interesting, varied and stimulating if that were the case? If someone is actually breaking God's laws, then discipline is necessary; but let us pray for wisdom to discern richness and variety in ministry within the will of God. Criticism is pernicious: it grows quickly from the smallest of beginnings, into an encumbrance that spoils everything we try to do – as well as being no help to those we meet. It is the very antithesis of all the love, joy, peace, etc. that the Holy Spirit is eager for us to live out in our lives.

Red-letter words

Some of our Bible versions have the words of Jesus printed in red, and it is good to read through the Gospels majoring on these portions, and allowing nothing else to impact. They are 'spirit and life', and the more we can absorb them into our hearts, the more readily will they come to mind when we need them – in particular, when we are asked to defend the how, what or why of our faith.

> *Sing them over again to me,*
> *Wonderful words of life!*
> *Let me more of their beauty see,*
> *Wonderful words of life!*
> *Words of life and beauty,*
> *Teach me faith and duty,*
> *Beautiful words, wonderful words,*
> *Wonderful words of life!*

> *P. P. Bliss*

Father of mercies, in thy word; I heard the voice of Jesus say; Lord, thy word abideth; Tell out, my soul, the greatness of the Lord.

Thirteenth Sunday after Trinity (Proper 18)

5 September   *Principal Service*

Effective Witnessing   Jer. 18:1–11; Ps. 139:1–6, 13–18; Philemon 1–21; Luke 14:25–33

'I pray that the sharing of your faith may become effective when you perceive all the good that we may do for Christ. I have indeed received much joy and encouragement from your love, because the hearts of the saints have been refreshed through you.' Philemon 6–7

Good that we may do

Any good that we may do for Christ may come nowhere near all he has done for us – yet we must do all we can, not only for the delight it gives him, but also for the encouragement and refreshment it can give to others. The world is starved of encouragement, because it seems de rigueur in these fast-paced times to get on *despite* (not in collaboration with) everyone else. Yet if we have the will, we can be of some help to at least some one if not more, every day.

With advancing years, not to mention times of incarceration and hardship, had come an appreciation for Paul of help given to him as well as of help received by others. His little note to Philemon, for clemency and understanding in the case of Onesimus, is a model not only of diplomacy but also of consideration. Can we try to put ourselves in his position, and honestly ask ourselves if we would have written in similar vein?

As God sees

God looks at his created beings, and sees in each one the spiritual as well as the physical components that account for individuality. Do we look for these? Does their identification make each person 'special in Christ' to us? When we have accepted that no one is ever going to please us, agree with us, differ from us or even anger us, all of the time, we shall be well on the way to overcoming criticism and judgementalism. God is interested in everyone; are we, in the most positive sense, as fellow members (naturally, or in prospect) of the body of Christ? Can we see their potential to do good for Jesus, and help them to that end? Can we be known as encouragers? There are few enough of them around, unless most are hiding their 'good' so well that we don't recognize it.

William Carey was an eighteenth-century 'flop' at school; he flunked shoe-making; he was an abysmal teacher; he received loads of discouragement from many quarters, the *coup de gras* coming from a theologian to whom Carey had applied for help to take the gospel to Asia. 'Young man,' thundered the august doctor, 'when God wants to convert the heathen, he'll do it without the help of you or me!' Undeterred, Carey sailed for India and spent the rest of his long life evangelizing and translating the Bible into several languages and dialects. A flop? If William Carey had believed his criticizers, how much good would he have *not* done for Jesus? If we are tempted to put a damper on another's enthusiasm, let us remember William Carey – and St Paul, Philemon and Onesimus.

Has someone discouraged us from fulfilling an idea, a revelation, an ambition, a vision? Have we still cherished a longing for it? Then let us get serious with God, who is the Supreme Encourager, and see what, together, we can do about it. Much effective witnessing for Christ may have been stifled by even one word of discouragement.

Wearing our own footwear!

It is difficult to put oneself in another's shoes! We may be unenthusiastic about someone else's hopes and dreams – but we are not them; they have other gifts, different capabilities and talents from ourselves. They may be perfectly suited for the vision they have had: as William Carey was suited for India and mission, yet not apparently so to a learned man who himself had no desire to go to India.

And if another gives us encouragement, do we shrug it off as well intentioned but misdirected? Or do we look for the hand of God in it, and pray that encouragement into our hearts, for the Lord to nurture and expand? The more we are open to the possibility – even the likelihood – of God surprising us, the more we shall be surprised.

Encourage the young people to write or illustrate a hymn on today's theme.

Suggested hymns
Be thou my vision; God is working his purpose out; Lord, speak to me; Pray when the morn is breaking.

Thirteenth Sunday after Trinity   *Second Service*
Proof!   Ps. [120] 121; Isa. 43:14—44:5; John 5:30–47

'[Jesus said], "I have a testimony greater than John's. The works that the Father has given me to complete, the very works that I am doing, testify on my behalf that the Father has sent me."' John 5:36

Visible signs
Even Nicodemus, the 'teacher of Israel', had acknowledged that no one could do what Jesus was doing if he were not from God (John 3:2, 10), before he had understood why Jesus acted as he did. The signs had spoken for themseves. Do our lives present others with the Christian gospel, before we even begin to explain it? Can folk, looking at what we do, ascertain that we have been with Jesus?

God's agenda
Jesus was so keyed in to God's agenda that whatever God gave him to do, he was determined to complete. He did nothing of his own will, but showed an obedience to God that was awe-inspiring in its thoroughness. He could have compromised with Satan in the wilderness; he could have acceded to the crowd's request to make him a king; he could have yielded to the request for high office in heaven from James and John; he could have . . . But he stuck firm to his mission.

Each new day
There is an ongoing freshness and vitality in Jesus' words: in essence, he is saying, 'I'm giving you proof, each new day, until all my work is accomplished.' Can we translate such freshness into our life and work for God? 'New every morning' is his love.

How new and fresh do we greet every morning? As a new chance to fill the hours with new work? As a grind to be faced with stoical fortitude? As 12 or 14 hours of boredom to be struggled through? How we start each day will usually key in our attitude for the remainder of it.

We can be a blessing or a bore: the choice is ours. Whatever we decide, God will know – and there's a fair chance others will as well, unless we are pilgrimaging on a desert island. But, depending on how we have used the day, our sleep should be sound, or broken. Is there really a choice? 'If you do not take up your cross and carry it and follow me,' said Jesus seriously to his friends, 'you cannot be my disciples' (see, e.g., Mathew 16:24f.; Mark 8:34f.).

The end in sight

Jesus worked with his sights set on the accomplishment of his mission. Have we a goal we are aiming for – in the short term, or further ahead? God may have other plans for us, since we are not as cognizant of his will as was Jesus; but we shall either have time enough to complete all we want, or we shall go to glory before we've completed it, and then we shall not need time. The important thing to realize is that we shall have time enough for all that *God* has planned for us to do. We are still here, so our mission is still incomplete. It does no harm to ponder what God still has in mind for us – so long as our pondering doesn't extend into time when we should be active in doing what is nearest. The more enthusiasm we show for God's work, the more he will give us; and the more he gives us, the more will others also have cause to be blessed.

'The Devil finds work for idle hands to do' has never been more true than it is today, with increasing amounts of leisure being available to an ever-increasing number of people. We work hard to play more, to support more businesses to work hard to play more . . . It is a catherine-wheel spinning ever faster – and Satan is content to let it spin.

Breaking the mould for Christ

If we are caught up already on this spinning wheel, have we the spiritual strength to break the mould of our daily life and escape – for Christ? He will find us more work to do than probably we are doing now – and certainly less leisure; but we shall be off the wheel that demands constant attention.

There is a Russian saying that an unbeliever is like a shaving of wood, curled round and round a blank vortex of emptiness: that is something similar to the catherine-wheel of worldliness. We are made in the likeness of God – children of the King: are we not too precious to be spinning round a vortex of emptiness? Let's work for Jesus, instead!

Suggested hymns
Forth in thy name, O Lord, I go; Give me oil in my lamp; New every morning is the love; Will you come and follow me?

Fourteenth Sunday after Trinity (Proper 19)
12 September   *Principal Service*   Rejoice Together
Jer. 4:11–12, 22–28; Ps. 14; 1 Tim. 1:12–17; Luke 15:1–10

'[Jesus said], "Which one of you . . . ? Rejoice with me, for I have found my sheep that was lost . . . Or what woman . . . Rejoice with me, for I have found the coin that I had lost . . ."' Luke 15:3, 6, 8, 9

Which . . . what?
Jesus includes everyone in these two parables: the shepherd is Everyman, the woman is Everywoman. We all lose things, some more frequently than others. Often we are so pressured, we begrudge the time spent in searching, considering it wasted time. But Jesus is never pressured and never wastes time. He will spend a lifetime (if necessary) searching for a lost soul, and on finding it he does not berate it for going missing, but showers it with TLC. We can argue that he has not 'lost' it in the first place; that he therefore doesn't *need* to waste time in searching. That is true. But God does not measure his love and do only what is necessary: even though the sheep has *chosen* to go missing, God goes the extra mile to retrieve the situation.

But the coin does not choose to be lost! True again. And in the linking of these parables surely we can believe that God intends for us to see the 'randomness', the temptation of Satan at work, 'taking over' the person who goes astray, in effect reducing (even seducing) the mind of that person to the mindless capacity of an inanimate coin. What a humiliating spectacle we cut when we make compromise with Satan! Yet Jesus goes to great lengths to restore that feeble specimen to something like God intended it to be: a thinking, joying, loving child of God.

If we could only see ourselves more like God sees us, we would spend a lot less time tangling with Satan.

Lighten up!

After the struggle, the searching, the discovery and rejoicing. Lighten up! Jesus says, in effect. Take time to celebrate! Something wonderful has happened! The searching has been successful! We may spend many hours in prayer, in striving for something, in battling through a hard patch. Everything comes – to pass. But when the valley of trouble is behind us, do we lighten up and say 'Thank you, Lord', and have a time of celebration? Not as often as we should. Many a time we get busy worrying about something else. We'd do well to remember that Jesus operated a holistic ministry, for body, mind and spirit; and he knows that a lightening of the load does wonders for all these parts of us. *Would* it over-stretch us to plan a celebration now and then, before we become incorrigible Jonahs?

Getting together

The shepherd, and the woman who had found her coin, 'called together [their] friends and neighbours', to rejoice. They went to some trouble to round up quite a crowd. The more people we can share good news with, surely the better. Do we have to wait for a war to end, a monarch to be crowned, a royal wedding, before we have a party? If the Church was seen to be celebrating good news more, and worrying about empty seats less, one may go some way towards solving the other. Let us keep one serious eye on God's will and one joyful eye on delight in doing it. The two should work in tandem. In a short, three-year ministry, see from the Gospels how Jesus integrated work and joy until the two became one. Nehemiah had learned, centuries before, that the joy of the Lord is our strength (Nehemiah 8:10). And it's free! Why spend millions of perishable pounds on secular pursuits that not only save no lost souls, but don't bring lasting joy either?

> *And all through the mountains thunder-riven,*
> *And up from the rocky steep,*
> *There arose a cry to the gates of heaven:*
> *'Rejoice! I have found my sheep!'*

And the angels echoed around the throne:
'Rejoice! For the Lord brings back his own!'

Elizabeth C. Clephane

Family Service input
Encourage the young people to illustrate crosses of the Christian faith (see below), to mark Holy Cross Day (14 September).

Suggested hymns
A charge to keep I have; Happy are they, they that love God; Loving shepherd of thy sheep; Rejoice, the Lord is king.

Christian Crosses

(1) Fleurée

(2) Calvary

(3) Papal

(4) Passion

(5) Russian Orthodox

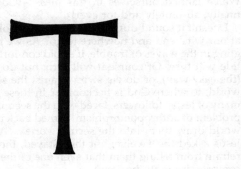

(6) St Antony's (Tau)

Fourteenth Sunday after Trinity

Second Service   **Coming to a Crossroads**

Pss. 124, 125; Isa. 60; John 6:51–69

'And [Jesus] said, "For this reason I have told you that no one can come to me unless it is granted by the Father." Because of this, many of his disciples turned back and no longer went about with him.' John 6:65–66

Time of decision?

There are times when we, too, are faced with the question of whether to go forward with Jesus, or not. God may have been singularly unresponsive to our prayers. We're in a jam, and we've prayed for guidance and help, but instead the jam has got tighter, hemming us in on every side. Where's God? Why hasn't he come through? Doesn't he care? We panic, as the disciples once panicked in the storm-tossed boat on Galilee (Mark 4:35–41). And Jesus was with them all the time!

If we're thorough about the problem, we'll get around to asking where we've gone wrong. Could we have done this – said that? We've landed ourselves in this mess – God's given up on us, finally, absolutely and for ever!

Doesn't it sound dumb! Is this how we look to God when we're at our wits' end and nowhere to go? As we're kicking and struggling in the waves of trouble, it's cold comfort to be told that every tide will turn. Of course it will turn: but do we go with the tide (the easy way), or do we swim against the set and current of the world, to where God is beckoning? In these verses from St John, many of Jesus' followers, faced with the seemingly insurmountable problem of anthropomorphism, turned back and let the tide of the world draw them into the secular vortex. 'Are you off, as well?' Jesus asked the Twelve; but they stayed, though Jesus could not refrain from telling them that even one of their number had made compromise with the Devil.

Christ's flesh and blood

'Unless you eat the flesh of the Son of Man, and drink his blood, you have no life in you,' Jesus had told them (v. 53). To a Jew (in fact, to anyone), it was a startling threat. We are so familiar with the wafer and the wine in our eucharistic services that it is probably not possible to imagine the shock that Jesus' words would have. Certainly at the Supper in the cenacle, the disciples were tense and uneasy, but not shocked.

Yet was there any other way? The Shepherd was going to give his life for the sheep. His flesh would be torn, his blood would flow – not as the flesh and blood of just 'any' crucifixion victim, but of the Lamb of God vicariously *killing death* by dying for the sins and sinners of the world. There was a sacrifice: there would be a memorial. It had to be this way. The blood of the animals on Yom Kippur – one killed on the spot and sacrificed on the altar, another sent out to die slowly of starvation in the wilderness – was commuted sacrificially into the Lamb of Calvary: God suffering for humanity, and turning the world upside down. The offering was there: the beneficiaries must enter into the divine terms of the covenant, otherwise they excluded themselves from the legacy.

'Can you take it? If not . . .' If not, the world is always waiting to absorb its own, into its whirlpool of secularism which slowly sucks lifeblood away until nothing is left. What Jesus, by contrast, took away at Calvary was sin. What he has given in return is eternal life: a magnificently unfair equation!

When God comes
Still at our crossroads? By this time, our prayers may have petered out – our pleas and cries and beseechings. When we have come to the end of them is the time to praise God for answering, believing that he has (cf. Mark 11:24), and believing that the deliverance has come, the solution has been given.

If we can get to this stage *before* we've reached the stage of panic, so much the better: Christ is in us, and we are in him; together we shall always come through.

Suggested hymns
Guide me, O thou great Redeemer; How firm a foundation; We hail thy presence glorious; Ye choirs of new Jerusalem.

Fifteenth Sunday after Trinity (Proper 20)

19 September   *Principal Service*   **No Compromise!**

Jer. 8:18–9:1; Ps. 79:1–9; 1 Tim. 2:1–7; Luke 16:1–13

'[Jesus said], "Whoever is faithful in a very little is faithful also in much; and whoever is dishonest in a very little is dishonest also in much."'
Luke 16:10

Doing business the King's way

We can do business with God or with the world, but not with both. The two do not practise in common; each operates on a policy that has been going on for thousands of years – but one policy will end with time, while the other is the stuff of which eternity is made. It is not impossible to graft God's ways on to the ways of the world but it is challenging and difficult; if we try the reverse, it certainly doesn't work. So, what are we to do? Compromise – like the dishonest manager in today's Gospel reading? Make friends with money and influence people, while trying to do good at the same time? Well, it makes for an easier ride in the short term, no doubt; but Jesus says we are playing with fire: don't do it!

Feeling the pinch?

Yet scrupulous honesty may lead us to the breadline! Is this what God wants? Couldn't we be of more use to him if, for instance, we had money to lavish on missions? Isn't it possible to make money with honour? Doesn't God give us power to become prosperous through his word (cf. Joshua 1:8)?

More awkward questions have been raised over money and the Christian way than anything else. One thing is evident from the Gospels: God does not equate poverty with sin, yet wealth is seen as a real handicap to reaching heaven. This being so, why do we spend so much time and effort in trying to gain wealth? Peer pressure? The 'good life'? Very few wealthy people have set out to realize their ambition simply for the gospel. How many millionaire preachers are there around? Usually the preacher is expected not only to be humble, but poor with it! Poverty will always be part of society; Jesus affirmed as much. Yet it's hard, when fuel, heat and food are in short supply, to rejoice – isn't it? It may be, says God, but, 'Blessed are you who are poor, for yours is the kingdom of God. Blessed are you who are hungry now, for you will be

filled. Blessed are you who weep now, for you will laugh ...
Blessed are you ...' (Luke 6:20–22). If we translate 'blessed' into
'happy' (which the Greek *makarios* also means), how come? Is God
asking the impossible?

Yes – because God always does. Otherwise, where would be
the challenge?

Turning away from the world's way

It's not going to cut much ice with God if we accept the challenge
on Sunday and return to wheeling and dealing the world's way
on Monday. Consciously, deliberately, in faith we need to pray to
God to take over our finances – small or large. Can we not trust
him to direct us in our dealings? Dare we risk the world's ridicule
– or even its envy? God out of his poverty can make many rich.
He proved he could, at Calvary – but the world still hasn't
fathomed how, or why.

One thing is certain, unless Christians make a determined and
concerted stand against the world's way, the differences not only
between rich and poor people, but nations and continents, will
worsen.

'God's in his heaven'? Yes. 'All's right with the world'? No –
but we can all, with God's grace, make a difference. Any situation
is hopeless, until we bring God in on the act. He'll probably not
cure the problem with cataclysmic force. Instead, he'll use the likes
of you and me to do it.

> *Here I am, Lord. Is it I, Lord?*
> *I have heard you calling in the night.*
> *I will go, Lord, if you'll lead me.*
> *I will hold your people in my heart.*
>
> Dan Schutte

Family Service input

Encourage the young people to design a parish jigsaw(s) – of the
church/today's theme/Christian symbols, etc. – for (1) sale for
church funds/missions; or (2) for distribution to senior citizens,
hospitals, nursing homes, etc.

Suggested hymns

Be thou my vision; Blessed are the pure in heart; I, the Lord of
sea and sky; O Lord, all the world belongs to you.

Fifteenth Sunday after Trinity   *Second Service*
A Good Resolution   Ps. [128] 129; Ezra 1;
John 7:14–36

*'[Jesus said], "Anyone who resolves to do the will of God will know
whether the teaching is from God, or whether I am speaking on my
own."' John 7:17*

The best resolve

Surely this is the best resolve anyone can make! 'Lord, I am going
to do your will.' Team up the resolve with the Holy Spirit, and
we not only have the resolution, but the power to carry it out. On
our own, in our limited strength, we can't get far; but, as the
greatest missionary of the Apostolic Church discovered, 'I can do
all things through him who strengthens me' (Philippians 4:13).
Resolving to do God's will is the first step on the road that leads
to eternal life. It means we have heard God's call on our time, our
talents, our allegiance – our selves. We are conscious that, of all
the thousands he could have chosen, he has pitched on us. It's a
greater honour by far than any wordly accolade we may be given.
On the face of it, our resolution is a small step by comparison: but
we don't know all that we are committing ourselves to: the joys,
the opportunities, the peace – with a share of struggle and sorrow
included on the way – then, after all, the glory.

Teaching from God

We have, in God's word, our itinerary, instruction manual and
guidebook rolled into one. As John the Baptist had pointed people
away from himself to Jesus, so Jesus in today's reading points his
listeners away from himself to the Father. There is no need for us
to differentiate between the two: Jesus and the Father are one
(John 10:30); though for those to whom he is talking, he is also as
one of them in human form. But the thrust of his teaching is: this
is God's word, and you can trust it.

> *Trust on, trust on, believer!*
> *Though long the conflict be,*
> *Thou yet shall prove victorious;*
> *Thy God shall fight for thee.*

Trust on! the danger presses,
Temptation strong is near;
Over life's dang'rous rapids,
He shall thy passage steer.

The Lord is strong to save us,
He is a faithful friend;
Trust on, trust on, believer!
Oh, trust him to the end!

Eliza A. Walker

By example

John the Baptist and Jesus – the first two Christian preachers – set a fine example for all who deal with the gospel: not to project themselves or polish their own image, but to point their listeners to God. After all, it is God's word – we did not write the Bible (though occasionally folk have tried to rewrite bits of it to suit themselves, with dangerous results), nor are we keeping this floating ball of earth in motion; nor are we the Master of past, present and future. We are the Master's sons and daughters, with a passport to glory through unmerited favour – but the favour is God's.

The word inviolate

What we *can* do – and what has been done since the earliest days of the Church – is to *interpret* God's word according to his guidance, our ability: his grace, our situation. The church historian, Eusebius of Caesarea, has recorded of St Matthew's Gospel: 'So, therefore, Matthew compiled the oracles in the Hebrew language, but everyone interpreted them as he was able' (Eusebius, *Historia Ecclesiastica* III. 39). The inspired word being what it is, one can read the best-known portions thousands of times, and on each reading get a new understanding, a new revelation. Yet why should this not be so? Reflect on the depth and richness of God's creativity – in the natural world and in humankind: why should his word be any less wonderful?

No matter what our situation, God's word points us to the answer. The solution-process may take much prayer and searching, but we shall find it if we persevere – in God's time, for he is the Master of time as well.

A few more years shall roll; O God, our help in ages past; Teach me, my God and king; When came in flesh the incarnate word.

Sixteenth Sunday after Trinity (Proper 21)
26 September   *Principal Service*
Reversal of Fortunes   Jer. 32:1–3a, 6–15; Ps. 91:1–6, 14–16; 1 Tim. 6:6–19; Luke 16:19–31

'But Abraham said, "Child, remember that during your lifetime you received your good things, and Lazarus in like manner evil things; but now he is comforted here, and you are in agony. Besides all this, between you and us a great chasm has been fixed, so that those who might want to pass from here to you cannot do so, and no one can cross from there to us."' Luke 16:25–26

Master of language
Jesus is a master of language. In even these two verses, he tells us more than other teachers could manage in a lifetime of lessons. Notice that Abraham calls the rich man (or, rather, the man who used to be rich) 'Child'! Doesn't this imply that the man has never grown up, never matured beyond childhood and the childish attitude: 'I want . . . I want . . . I want . . .'? His wealth had shielded him from the challenges of life, and he has brought this arrogant, petulant attitude with him through death. We are what we are, and we are what we shall be, in hell. Lazarus in heaven had kept the humility he had had; but his hardships were past, and – still humble – he was enjoying comforts that were new to him. In heaven, we shall still be what we are now, but able to take real delight in our surroundings.

The great chasm
The division between heaven and hell has not evolved, as a natural chasm evolves on earth over many years. God has 'fixed' it there: it is the Almighty's barrier between the two spiritual states, and it is uncrossable – not that anyone would want to cross over into hell (so Lazarus would be for ever safe from torment); but neither can anyone whose life has led them to hell retrieve the situation and journey over to heaven. The point of no return had been reached by the rich man.

Time for renewal

There is an old Chinese proverb which runs: 'You can change the face of nature, but you cannot change a man.' Yet while we are on earth, there is always time to change. 'If anyone is in Christ, there is a new creation' (2 Corinthians 5:17). The same can be said in answer to another saying from China: 'There are straight trees on the mountains, but no straight people in the world.' True, in a way: 'There is none righteous, no, not one; all have sinned and fall short of the glory of God' (Romans 3:23); yet there is still time to repent and ask God for forgiveness, so that eventually we can come before Jesus with heads held high and the slate wiped clean. The rich man had been so busy spending his wealth and enjoying his comforts that the well-being of his soul had passed him by.

The ransomed

Note that 'Abraham' was in heaven, though he had lived centuries before Christ. Therefore, in glory we may look forward to meeting, as well as Christians, those from previous ages who had heard God's call and had responded positively: Abraham, Isaac, Jacob, Ruth . . . These all believed by faith, and were saved by faith.

Could we make a difference?

Suppose we were asked for spiritual help by a rich unbeliever looking death in the face, how would we respond? Would we share all that Jesus has done for us, and means to us? Would we pick up the nearest Bible and read, say, Psalm 91, or John 14, or 1 Corinthians 15? Would we hold the person's hand and pray? It is a situation that could challenge any of us, at any time. We could be getting on quite calmly with life, when suddenly the words we say could make a difference for someone's whole eternity.

The call for help could come when we are physically or spiritually at a low ebb ourselves. What then? Are we too far gone to care for the state of another's soul?

> Sitting by the gateway of a palace fair,
> Once a child of God was left to die;
> By the world neglected, wealth would nothing share,
> See the change awaiting there on high!

> El Nathan

我父在天、願爾名聖、爾國臨格、爾
旨得成在地如在天焉、我儕所需
之糧、今日賜我、免我儕諸負、如我
免負我者、毋導我於誘惑、乃拯
我出於惡、蓋國也、權也、榮也、皆歸
於爾、爰及世世、誠心所願

Family Service input
Encourage the young people to write/illustrate the Lord's Prayer in Chinese (see p. 220).

Suggested hymns
Can I see another's woe; Father, I place into your hands; Light's abode, celestial Salem; There is a land of pure delight.

Sixteenth Sunday after Trinity *Second Service*
Committed to Slavery? Pss. 134, 135; Neh. 2; John 8:31–38, 48–59

'Jesus answered them, "Very truly, I tell you, everyone who commits sin is a slave to sin. The slave does not have a permanent place in the household; the son has a place there for ever. So if the Son makes you free, you will be free indeed." ' John 8:34–36

Sons of God – or slaves of Satan?
Made in the likeness of God, we are his servants; washed by faith in the blood of Christ, we become God's children – sons and daughters, heirs of his promise. Or, if we choose, we can deny Jesus and commit ourselves to a life of slavery (a death, more accurately, of slavery) to Satan: slaves to sin. What an 'occupation' for our spiritual CV! God beckons. Satan tugs. God is a Gentleman. Satan doesn't know the meaning of the word. God's forgiveness assures us a permanent place in his household: utter and complete freedom. Again, Satan doesn't know the meaning of the word.

> *I've found a Friend, oh, such a Friend!*
> *He loved me ere I knew him;*
> *He drew me with the cords of love,*
> *And thus he bound me to him.*
> *And round my heart still closely twine*
> *Those ties which nought can sever;*
> *For I am his, and he is mine,*
> *For ever and for ever.*
>
> J. G. Small

A little boy was showing his birthday presents to his schoolfriend: 'Coo! That's a grand boat!' marvelled Dick. 'My father made it!' said Chris, proudly. We can look at the beautiful things of earth and say the same; and we can look at our friends – and those we find hard to call friends – and say the same. We are not elevating ourselves as his children – but adoring, loving, respecting and worshipping him as our Father. We are making his name known. If we don't, others may not be encouraged to give him the glory which is his due.

On one condition
Our freedom is given on one condition: the giver must be Jesus. He and he alone is Advocate, Judge and Mediator; Saviour, Redeemer and Guide, all rolled into one. There is salvation in no one else, for there is no other name under heaven given among mortals by which we must be saved, says Peter (Acts 4:12). In an age when many faiths are competing for people's loyalty (as was the case in the first century when Jesus, then Peter, Paul and the others were preaching) this truth stands out above all others. No one else has died for the sins of the world. No one else has opened eternal life to all his believers. No one else has put love, joy, peace, patience, kindness, generosity, faithfulness, gentleness and self-control into the hearts of his followers, gift-wrapped in the Holy Spirit who is more powerful than anything outside of us (1 John 4:4).

Free from whom?
From whom does Jesus make us free? From Satan, the Prince of Devils. It is a tacit acceptance of Jesus' status as Saviour that Satan recognizes him. That is why the Name of Jesus (the Name that carries a power greater than anything else) is so powerful in over-coming the demons of possession, sickness, trouble and temptation. If there was nothing to fear from Jesus, Satan would not bother to know him, or to hassle his followers. And if Satan is not hassling us, that's the time to worry: 'Woe to you, when all speak well of you, for that is what their ancestors did to the false prophets,' warned Jesus (Luke 6:26). By the same token, if our names are not known to Satan, we may well ask if we are making any progress for God. The witnesses delivering depositions at any public inquiry do so on the understanding that they will subsequently run the gauntlet of cross-examination by the opposing QCs and/or barristers.

We enter Christ's army knowing that from our inception onwards Satan is also going to be taking an interest in us – from far lower motives than our Great Commander. The terms are tough, but the victory will be glorious.

Suggested hymns
And can it be; At the Name of Jesus; Jesus, the Name high over all; To God be the glory.

Seventeenth Sunday after Trinity (Proper 22)
3 October   *Principal Service*   **Trust**   Lam. 1:1–6;
Canticle: Lam. 3:19–26 or Ps. 137; 2 Tim. 1:1–14;
Luke 17:5–10

'I am not ashamed, for I know the one in whom I have put my trust, and I am sure that he is able to guard until that day what I have entrusted to him ... Guard the good treasure entrusted to you, with the help of the Holy Spirit living in us.' 2 Timothy 1:12, 14

Shared help
Paul's implication that the Holy Spirit works through *us* for the benefit of each other is vital for our understanding of this divine function. We know that the Spirit's power is greater than anything else (1 John 4:4), so his interrelationship could practically be taken for granted: it is good, therefore, to have it highlighted in today's epistle. What we may do in Christ's name is important to others; and their working-out of the Spirit is necessary to us. Our acceptance even of God's call may well involve others' prayers, assistance, example and encouragement, though the commitment is ours. Let us make sure that we give of the Spirit as much as we can to others.

Trusting Jesus
It's a two-way process, this business of trust. We trust Jesus to see us across earth's minefield to eternity. We trust him to be listening to all our prayers – the contemplative, anguished, imperative and acquiescent – and rightly to divine our intentions, even when the words don't come out right. We trust him to keep us from direst

poverty, serious illness or accident or tragedy. But he is also trusting us to fulfil the commitment we have made: to deny ourselves (even though the way may include poverty, illness, accident and tragedy), take up our cross and follow him. How often, as we're grinding our way through a long list of petitions, do we stop to reflect on the risk Jesus has taken in accepting us on board? Doesn't our 'commitment to faith' guarantee have as many holes as the average colander, with its caveats, 'if onlys', exceptions and conditions? Like Peter, we may have declared, 'Lord, I am ready to go with you to prison and to death!' (Luke 23:33) and have watered down these brave words before the night was out. Like Peter, may we redeem our condition with an in-filling of divine strength in forgiveness. We shall fall again – but may we trust our Holy Spirit to do in us yet again and again the lifting that we can't manage singlehanded.

The safe deposit

We can trust God to guard all that we have deposited with him: our love, loyalty, good intentions, eagerness, enthusiasm; our future, and all that we possess now and will leave behind for glory. But God is different from our bank manager: he will not lock anything we have given him away in a safe deposit box, in airtight suspended animation. Instead, he uses our deposits to fund our ministry and that of others. He is not in the business of letting benefits lie unused.

God's safe(?) deposit

And he expects us to do the same. He has entrusted deposits to us. How safe are they? Do we lock them away securely from ourselves, from God, from others? Or do we put them to good use? If we are *not too sure*, may we take a quick refresher course as to the content of these precious divine deposits: God has given *us* (for others, remember, as well as ourselves, in his service) as much as he knows we can use (and that's in abundance) of 'love, joy, peace, patience, kindness, generosity, faithfulness, gentleness and self-control' (Galatians 5:22–23). Are we earning a good interest on them?

Family Service input

The young people could be encouraged to model or illustrate a mountain-cave nativity scene, such as St Francis (4 October)

instituted – either to be on display at Christmas, or as a design
for a parish Christmas card.

Suggested hymns
A charge to keep I have; Gracious Spirit, Holy Ghost; Put thou
thy trust in God; Thine be the glory.

Seventeenth Sunday after Trinity
Second Service   **A Question of Identity**   Ps. 142;
Neh. 5:1–13; John 9

'[The Pharisees] said to him, "Give glory to God! We know that this
man is a sinner."' John 9:24
'Jesus heard that they had driven him out, and when he found him, he
said, "Do you believe in the Son of Man?" ... He said ... "Lord, I
believe."' John 9:35, 38

Cross purposes
It takes over forty verses for John to record this wonderful healing
of the man born blind – wonderful, in that nothing like it had
been known to happen before: a man being healed of a congenital
disease. Jesus had excelled himself, and the man, predictably, was
overjoyed. We don't know how much education he had: perhaps
it was minimal, since he was reduced to begging; but after his
cure he could hold his own in theological defence against the
Pharisees. The cure had worked a miracle not only on his sight,
but in himself. 'Give God the glory!' There was nothing amiss in
this demand of the Pharisees. God *had* performed the cure! But
beyond this they were at cross purposes, not seeing Jesus as God
but as a sinner. The irony of the situation would raise a smile
were it not so tragic: men committed to the worship of God, not
recognizing God when he stood among them and worked a great
cure.

A sound defence
The parents of the blind man were so confused, all they wanted
to do was to keep out of the limelight, so the man himself was
left to do all the talking – and he soundly defended his healer.
While still unsure of Jesus' identity (for, after all, he had not yet

seen Jesus at this point), he would not have anything said against him. Look, you criticizer, I can *see*, can't I? How can the man be no good? He was in a good frame of mind for Jesus to build thankfulness and gratitude into firm belief. Yet he went about it gently, as *Son of Man*. Even the Pharisees had followed the healed man, and so began the theological argument about sight and blindness.

What we see
Each day, whether we see with the eyes or the mind only, we are evaluating and making judgements on people and situations. Like the Pharisees, we sometimes get it wrong. Were Jesus to come among us in human form today, he would not be recognized by some – probably by some most qualified to recognize him. Why? Because, like the Pharisees, most of us have a more or less defined notion of what we would expect the Messiah to be, to look like and to do.

God is not a hypocrite!
There is no hypocrisy with God. Jesus was not pretending to be anyone else. Today (as yesterday) God does not set out to confuse any of us. When he moves in our lives, it is with the precise knowledge of what he knows we can comprehend. We may be stretched – spiritually, mentally, physically – but not beyond the limit he knows we can manage. So, why are we so often wrong-footed? Perhaps because we allow ourselves to be distracted by the world's angst or pleasures: each is as capable as the other of getting our attention away from God. The blind man could have been so taken up with the sight of people and things that he 'lost sight' of the man who had healed him – but he put gratitude first. Note, too, that Jesus sought him out; the great healer knew that here was a potential follower – a man who could, even in the relief of being cured, stand up to the Pharisees; a man of the stuff of which disciples are made!

It's good stuff. We're made of it, too, aren't we?

Suggested hymns
Amazing grace; Great is thy faithfulness; Oh, the love of my Lord is the essence; Thine arm, O Lord, in days of old.

Eighteenth Sunday after Trinity (Proper 23)
10 October   *Principal Service*   Remember Jesus
Jer. 29:1, 4–7; Ps. 66:1–12; 2 Tim. 2:8–15;
Luke 17:11–19.

*'Remember Jesus Christ, raised from the dead, a descendant of David –
that is my gospel . . . God's firm foundation stands, bearing this inscription: "The Lord knows those who are his," and, "Let everyone who calls
on the name of the Lord turn away from wickedness."* 2 Timothy 2:8,
19

How we remember
We can remember Jesus in many ways; just now, we are probably
focusing on his nativity, with the shops displaying Christmas cards
and goods, and catalogues in the mail nearly every day. We
remember him regularly in the Eucharist, as the events of Maundy
Thursday to Easter unfold at each service. But Paul tells Timothy
to remember him 'raised from the dead' – and surely that's the
best way of all: Jesus resurrected, and constantly here in spirit
with us. For, 'remembering' him is not like remembering a person
who has died: Jesus killed death, and is for ever alive. Isn't that
worth remembering, more often than anything else? We need not
join in the argument at times aired between denominations, as to
whether we should have a crucifix or an empty cross on our altars
and in our churches: both remind us of the sacrifice that gave us
eternal hope and led to Christ's resurrection. Neither should alter
the core and foundation of our faith.

My gospel
Look how proudly Paul calls it *'my* gospel' (see also Romans 2:16;
16:25). It is his: he has lived it, preached it, defended it, testified
to it, suffered for it – and he will soon die for it; then he will live
for it, in glory everlasting. It is his life. Can we say this? Do we
share 'our' gospel with others? It has been entrusted to us; Jesus
did not deprive himself in the giving, but we are immeasurably
enriched in receiving it. Anyone can read the Bible and 'get the
gospel' as book-knowledge. Some read it and accept it as 'their'
gospel, and in Jesus come to faith. Others, even before they pick
up a Bible, may be brought to faith by the likes of you and me
sharing the gospel – 'our' gospel – with them, telling them with

love in our hearts and eyes of what Jesus has done for us. That is how Paul has taught Timothy. According to tradition, Timothy became the first Bishop of Ephesus: we can reverently surmise that this was due in no small way to the early teaching of his friend and mentor, Paul.

God's foundation

Nothing is firmer than the foundation of our faith. Paul undergirds it with a promise from Nahum 1:7 (cf. John 10:14). We don't have to build from scratch, the hard core has been laid – but we don't even start from there: others have laboured on the site before us, and we take over from where they have left off. When the kingdom of God is complete, no one will be able to take the whole credit, except God who has overseen the endeavour. We shall have all contributed. We shall all share in the eventual celebrations. Shall we see our individual bricks, here and there, in the edifice? Probably not: but God will know exactly what we have done; we can safely leave the record with him. In a great cathedral, the work of many craftsmen known only to God mingles together to make the beautiful whole. So it will be, on a much grander scale, with the kingdom of God.

'Remember Jesus ... raised from the dead', yet who, in the kingdom of God, still retains the scars to show the sacrifice that made it all possible. Jesus crucified. Jesus resurrected. Jesus glorified. The same Jesus – yesterday, today and for ever.

Family Service input

Design a parish Christmas card, or series of cards, and print them for sale in the church in these weeks prior to Christmas. Write a short prayer for each card, and include the times of the Christmas services.

Suggested hymns

For ever with the Lord; How firm a foundation; Jerusalem, my happy home; Oh, what their joy and their glory must be.

Eighteenth Sunday after Trinity *Second Service*
'As I Have Loved' Ps. 144; Neh. 6:1–16; John 15:12–27

'[Jesus said], "This is my commandment, that you love one another as I have loved you. No one has greater love than this, to lay down one's life for one's friends. You are my friends if you do what I command you."' John 15:12–14

Follow my example

Jesus has set the pattern that we must follow if he is going to call us friends. *As he has loved.* How was this? It was showing friendship and loyalty (even to Judas who was to betray him), not *because* his friends were mature in their faith, but because Jesus had faith in their potential. It's no use waiting until our friends are perfect and precisely how we would like them to be: it takes all of a lifetime to reach that stage; but can we pray for discernment of what they might become, might do, or say, or go? Jesus looked at Peter and saw with physical sight a rough, impulsive, highly strung Galilean fisherman. History looks back and sees what Jesus even then saw with spiritual foresight: a dedicated missionary preacher and fearless witness for Christ, and the first Bishop of Rome.

We can see ourselves in a mirror – which, according to the light, can give a flattering, true or disparaging image. But does our spiritual self-examination give us cause to hope that it is in line with what Jesus can already see? And what about our friends, the folk we love? Do we encourage them to give of their best? Each one is so different: we perhaps don't realize it, but subconsciously we treat each friend differently, specially, according to their perceived abilities, temperament, way of life, etc.

Loving them as Jesus loved his disciples means taking a real interest in them and their development: physical, mental and spiritual – affirming, supporting, encouraging. Jesus was patient with his friends' faults, quick to praise their successes, and so often encouraging when their self-esteem took a battering. He could chide when they gave way to fear – but even this was done out of sheer love. He valued their friendship, and he made sure that they knew it. None of the Twelve is on record as being attacked by illness or disease while Jesus was with them; but he was quick to heal Peter's mother-in-law (Mark 1:30 ff.). When Peter could not pay his dues at the custom-point, Jesus found the tax for both of them, in an unusual way (Matthew 17:27). He restored Lazarus from the dead to Mary and Martha (John 11:44), and he gave his mother into the care of his beloved disciple at Calvary (John 19:27). His whole life was a model of love-in-action. Is 'love' the quality that most strongly characterizes our lives? Dare we ask our best friend to tell us?

The cost of friendship

The cost that Jesus put on friendship was the cost of Calvary. We can never love that much, because we are not 'loving away' the sins of the whole world. But how much do we value friendship? To the losing of our jobs? The love of our home? Even . . . death? Would we put someone else's life before our own? We never know when we may be torn between such choices.

The command

We are so familiar with these words of Jesus that the seriousness of them doesn't always impact. '*Love!*' It is the most imperative of commands. There is nothing in it of the mild suggestion. *Love!* Love, even if you don't particularly like the other person. Love, even though that man or woman drives you to distraction, or boredom, or anger.

It helps to remember that God loves the person. God sees in him or her something beautiful that with love can be made more beautiful. Can we learn to love through God, and subsequently on our own account? If the answer is 'No', then we need to take it to the Lord in prayer, fast.

Suggested hymns

Brother, Sister, let me serve you; Come and see the shining hope; In Christ, there is no east or west; What a Friend we have in Jesus.

Nineteenth Sunday after Trinity   17 October
Principal Service (Proper 24)
Paul's Charge to Timothy   Jer. 31:27–34;
Ps. 119:97–104; 2 Tim. 3:14—4:5; Luke 18:1–8

'In the presence of God and of Christ Jesus, who is to judge the living and the dead, and in view of his appearing and his kingdom, I solemnly urge you: proclaim the message; be persistent whether the time is favourable or unfavourable . . . do the work of an evangelist; carry out your ministry fully.' 2 Timothy 4:1–2, 5

Legal – and general!
Paul couches his charge to young Timothy in legal, and general, terms: legal, so that it may be given due weight and solemnity; general, in that it applies to every Christian worth their salt. The gospel must be on our lips, in our eyes, all the time. It needs to be our first thought on waking and our last on retiring for the night. It is our *vade mecum*, our inspiration, our answer to every situation, the foundation of our prayers. It is our reason for living and loving – and it's destined to go into eternity with us (Mark 13:31; Luke 21:33). We are all, clerical and lay alike, evangelists, in that what the world sees and hears of us as Christians must be the gospel of Christ. Chosen, called and commissioned, God recruits no part-timers into his ranks. We are all on a full-time mission – and the time-clock is on the run.

Life and death
Paul is at his most serious here. Timothy (and all Christians who were to come after him) must learn the priority of mission: getting the gospel into the hearts and lives of others. Have you ever thought of yourselves as full-time evangelists? Or have you pigeon-holed only the likes of Billy Graham, Reinhard Bonnke and Paul Yonggi Cho into that category? All three have had a high-profile evangelism – but all mission is capable of bringing many folk to Christ. When we reach glory, will the Lord ask: 'How many souls did you bring to Jesus?' Or, 'Did you share my gospel as much as you could?' If we only bring one soul to Jesus, it has made the difference for that soul – of life, rather than death.

Full proof
Go for a walk in the rain with a mac that is losing its weather-proofing, and you might as well have left it at home. The rain-weary garment is like a Christian who is not running on full power, full insurance, full proof. When the accounts are made up, the divine spiritual input from God will show a disproportionate amount compared to our returns. God, as ever, has played his part – has kept up his payment. We have defaulted on ours. Making 'full proof' of our ministry may not mean that we get better, bigger and more satisfying results than someone else; it means that we just keep on doing our best – doing all we can for God with all the means at our disposal. We can't do more, and we mustn't do less. The road to hell is full of good intentions and missed opportunities. 'Intent' needs to be converted into 'content'; for one day the contents of our ministry will count in the final analysis, when mere intention will be null and void.

There are so many ways of spreading the gospel today, the sheer variety is breathtaking. It is as though God knows that with many people the boredom threshold has become lower and lower with increased technology, wealth and leisure – and he is determined, as ever, to be in front of the new developments. The gospel of Christ continues to be the most exciting 'news of the world' – to be preached, sung, read, in hundreds, thousands, of languages, in favourable and unfavourable times. We need not ever look for a new way of evangelizing – just start sharing the good news, and God already has the best situation for it lined up.

Family Service input
Encourage the young people to make musical instruments from odds and ends, to accompany at least one or two of the hymns – today, and possibly on a more regular basis.

Suggested hymns
Come and see the shining hope; Go, tell it on the mountain; I will sing the wondrous story; Let all the world in every corner sing.

Nineteenth Sunday after Trinity

Second Service   **Joy v. Sorrow**   Ps. [146] 149;
Neh. 8:9–18; John 16:1–11

'[Jesus said], "Now I am going to him who sent me; yet none of you asks me, Where are you going? But because I have said these things to you, sorrow has filled your hearts."' John 16:5–6

Their incompatibility

Joy and sorrow are incompatible and cannot live together in the same heart. Joy will overcome sorrow, or grief will suffocate joy. It is this antithesis that is responsible for our mood swings, as we see-saw from cloud nine to the slough of despond, making life far more complicated and exhausting than God intended it to be. Nehemiah had homed in on a great truth that was to reach its climax in Jesus: God's joy is far deeper, far richer, far greater than the world's ephemeral happiness. God's joy gives an inner strength that percolates out from us in deeper, richer, greater work for him. The world's happiness comes to us from the outside and rarely penetrates to the heart, or, if it does get that far, its stay is short.

Divine joy in action

'Sorrow has filled your hearts,' said Jesus to his friends who were dismayed at his coming departure. Sorrow had taken them over. Don't we all know the helpless anguish of heart-filled sorrow? Perhaps someone we love has died, and life has changed so much we feel frozen with grief. Or perhaps a long-cherished scheme has failed, and it seems the world has collapsed around us. Or perhaps we have lost our job, our home, our independence – and suddenly the past is hurtful, the present unbearable and the future blank. Yes, we don't need much imagination to feel as those disciples felt, as Jesus calmly told them he was going to the Father. Their depression was natural, but no less anguished for that.

Yet before long a miracle (among several) had taken place. There came the Passion, the crucifixion and then the resurrection of Jesus. The disciples – very, very human – went to the depths of despair and then to the heights of joy. *And they stayed* with their joy – or, rather, it stayed with them. Jesus ascended back to glory – and those men, who by human rights should have plummeted to devastation, 'returned to Jerusalem with great joy, and . . . were continually in the temple blessing God' (Luke 24:52–53). That's what divine joy does for a person. And it was that same joyful strength, activated by the Holy Spirit, that got those men out of Jerusalem, away from their homes and families, to give the gospel to as much of the rest of the world as they could. A miracle of joy, joyful strength – and it's still having its way with Christians today, the more they open their hearts to the Lord.

Divine trust

Just suppose, for a moment, that we had been Jesus. Could we have borne to leave our hard-fought mission, our hard-won salvation, in the hands of eleven men who were very, very human, and had recently proved this by denial and desertion? 'It is to your advantage that I go away,' Jesus told them (John 16:7). God *trusted* them – just as today he has entrusted the ongoing growth of the Church to us. The only way we can cope with this great challenge is to use as much divine joyful strength – not as God will give us, but as he has already given us, as part of the make-up of his Holy Spirit.

Dismal Jonahs

We perhaps know some Christians who appear not to be using their joy: dismal Jonahs, who spread doom and gloom instead of encouragement and vitality. Hopefully, we are not of their number! They make religion a sober, straight-faced ordeal, and thus give a distorted picture of Christ to others. Can we pray our joy into their hearts? Yes, provided their own Holy Spirit engine is switched on. If not, we shall need to tell them plainly that the 'joy of the Lord is [still] strength': yesterday, today and for ever.

Suggested hymns

Glad that I live am I; Happy are they, they that love God; I will go in the strength of the Lord; O strength and stay.

Last Sunday after Trinity (Bible Sunday)
24 October   *Principal Service*
The Reason for Scripture   Isa. 45:22–25;
Ps. 119:129–136; Rom. 15:1–6; Luke 4:16–24

*'For whatever was written in former days was written for our instruction,
so that by steadfastness and by the encouragement of the scriptures we
might have hope.' Romans 15:4*

Instruction manual par excellence
To those who would argue that the Bible is not relevant in today's
world, Paul would say: 'The old scriptures [our Old Testament]
were relevant in the first century' – for those were the only scriptures written at the time he was penning his letter to the Christians
in Rome. From the earliest times described in Genesis, to Malachi
and the prophecies of Christ, the wisdom of Holy Writ was as
meaningful to Paul as it had been to the early writers. He had met
Jesus on the Damascus Road, had had personal revelations, had
talked with some of the Twelve – but all this did not persuade
him to value the old scriptures any less. We are even more blessed
than Paul: not only do we have the Old Testament (in much hand-
ier form than hundreds of scrolls), but the New also, a large part
of which is Paul's correspondence to first-century Christians from
a variety of backgrounds.

Daily medicine
Recently a missionary organization listed the following 'items'
comprising what it called 'God's Medicine Chest': Matthew 9:17;
Exodus 15:26; 23:25; Deuteronomy 7:15; Psalm 91:10; 103:2–3;
107:20; Proverbs 3:8; 4:20–23; 12:18; Isaiah 53:4–5; Malachi 4:2 and
1 Peter 2:24, and prescribed a daily dose, 'until Christ comes'.
Good spiritual doctoring! But there are many more 'medicines' to
be found in the Bible.

The will to read
When William Tyndale spent, and gave, his life to provide a first-
class English translation of the best biblical Hebrew and Greek
texts available (for the Latin Vulgate used in the Lutheran translation was full of mistakes), he knew that he was meeting a need:
the English congregations had been murmuring for some time that

a priest gabbling in Latin at the altar did not benefit the laity patiently waiting in the nave for the Mass bell to signal the critical moments of the rite. By no means everyone was roused; Tyndale knew, however, that there was sufficient dissatisfaction with the status quo for his English translation to be worth the risks involved.

How is it today? William Tyndale and his successors have done their work – so well that we have a plethora of English versions of the Bible. But can we pray for a greater longing to read these beautiful words? There are many carefully compiled plans for reading the entire Bible in a year. Can we pray for more readers to implement these plans?

When Yuri Gagarin came back to earth from space, he remarked scornfully to a priest: 'I didn't find God up there!' 'My son,' replied the priest, 'if you haven't found God on earth, you will not find him up there!' By the same token, if we have not opened our Bibles, we have denied ourselves the instruction that God has prepared for us, without which our ability to succeed in life's examination must surely be severely impaired. If Jesus had not valued the old scriptures, he would not have quoted from them so much. When he was tempted in the desert, he defeated Satan every time by this same weapon: the word of God.

We cannot overdose on this medicine; it is life-giving, not lethal; it is for all times and seasons. 'What a verse of the Bible seems to mean, it usually does mean. Treat all forced interpretations with great suspicion' (J. C. Ryle); sound advice, from one of the most respected theologians of all time.

Family Service input
Invite all members of the congregation to bring as many Bible versions and translations as possible to church. Let the young people arrange these on a table for general perusal at some time during or after the service. Share the story of William Tyndale (see 6 October), and encourage the young folk to illustrate it.

Suggested hymns
Father of mercies, in thy word; Tell me the old, old story; Lord, thy word abideth; There is a book, who runs may read.

Last Sunday after Trinity   *Second Service*
Who Believes Us?   Ps. 119:1–16; Jer. 36:9–32;
Rom. 10:5–17 or Matthew 22:34–40

'But not all have obeyed the good news, for Isaiah says, "Lord, who has believed our message?" So faith comes from what is heard, and what is heard comes through the word of Christ.' Romans 10:16–17

'What is truth?'

Pilate's question had been posed by many before the Passion: the procurator did not invent it. From the time of Eden, when Satan opened human eyes to see falsehood, the seeds of doubt had been sown. Ever since, there has only been one man whom people could trust to speak *all* truth: and even then many were so programmed into doubt, suspicion and criticism, that they could not – and many still cannot – believe 'the word of Christ'. If they will not accept his word, how will they accept someone else's (= our) giving of the gospel? They will not 'be convinced even if someone rises from the dead', prophesied Jesus sadly and so correctly (Luke 16:31).

Have Christians the monopoly of truth? No, there are many non-believers who value honesty and right-dealing. But the true *gospel*, the good news of Christ, the word of God, can only be truthfully divined by followers of Christ through the grace of God and the power of the Spirit. We have been entrusted with a truth that is able to save the world. What are we doing about it? St Paul reminds us that no one is going to hear this good news unless we tell them. Some won't believe it even then, but they will have been given their chance: if they choose instead to live on 'Death Row', that is their exercise of free will.

How far do we go?

We may have a fair distance to go in sharing the gospel, before we can be certain that we have done all we can. Mainstream churches in general don't operate a doorstep policy of evangelism – and are sometimes critical of those who do. The evangelists who cheerfully run the risk of rudeness or doors slammed in their faces predictably (and arguably with justification) respond: 'We would rather have our method of doorstep ministry than yours of not doing it.' Well, does it work? And can we truthfully say it doesn't, if we haven't tried it? Can we also run the risk of inviting a

237

doorstep evangelist in, sitting him down with a coffee, and sharing our truths with his? Are we too unsure of our beliefs to do this? What would Jesus have done – Jesus who dialogued with anyone from a leading Pharisee to a Samaritan woman of strange morality, a fisherman to a tax-collector, a puppet-king to a leper, a procurator to a betrayer? Who will know what we believe, unless we tell them? Not a lot. If we consider a particular situation or encounter is 'not for us', let us reflect that God has allowed it. Even if it seems to be of Satan, can we – with the word of truth inside us – make something beautiful of it, for God? The circumstances that Satan has twisted need to be turned convincingly upside down for God; and Christians are the ones to do the turning around. Holy boldness has not yet had its day.

Taking truth as a cure
God's prescription of daily truth is a medicine we need to avoid chronic spiritual disability: the armour that repels the advances of a Devil who is quick to move in on unprotected territory. In the words of the old hymn, let us take our arsenal with us:

> *Carry your Bible with you,*
> *Let all its blessings outflow;*
> *It will supply you each moment,*
> *Take it wherever you go!*

> *Fred P. Morris*

Suggested hymns
Christ is the world's true light; Help us, O Lord, to learn; There is a Redeemer; Thou whose Almighty Word.

Fourth Sunday before Advent   31 October
Principal Service   **Worthy of God's Call**
Isa. 1:10–18; Ps. 32:1–7; 2 Thess. 1:1–12; Luk 19:1–10

'[Jesus] entered Jericho and was passing through it. A man was there named Zacchaeus; he was a chief tax-collector, and was rich.' Luke 19:1–2
'To this end we always pray for you, asking that our God will make you

worthy of his call and will fulfil by his power every good resolve and
work of faith.' 2 Thessalonians 1:11

Misinterpretations are dangerous

'What's in it for Zacchaeus? He's rich enough already!' We can
almost hear the criticism, as Zacchaeus was greeted by Jesus and
entertained him with some of the wealth obtained under sus-
picious circumstances. 'Now he wants to buy his honour!' The
comments would flow even more freely as Zacchaeus made his
surprising confession and decision to repay.

But Jesus, having called out the good that was in Zacchaeus,
responded with acceptance and gracious encouragement, and, one
hopes, silenced the scornful. St Paul was similarly encouraging
towards the Thessalonians, praising their courage and fortitude,
and urging them ever onwards, upwards, forwards to the best
goal of all. They had been through great trials, designed to weaken
their new-found faith; but these had served to draw out what was
strong and true and good in their spiritual make-up; they were
proving themselves to be of the stuff of which saints are made.
'You're going great guns,' encourages Paul (in words to this effect),
'but there's some way to go. Don't slacken off. We're praying for
you!'

Small acorns grow to great oaks

Both Jesus and Paul recognized goodness in others and encouraged it to grow. Do we look for this in others and help them
likewise? Are we more ready to affirm than to put down, to
encourage than to criticize, to build up confidence than to humili-
ate? There was once a man who was dedicated to hounding a
group of people who in his opinion did not toe the party line. He
pursued them relentlessly, dragging them from home and family,
brutally treating them, and engineering their incarceration, torture
and even death. His name became a byword for cruelty. Yet God
saw the positive side, and by a traumatic conversion on the Damascus Road, turned Saul's abundant energy, enthusiasm and single-
mindedness into Christian drive and determination. Paul would
never forget the chance he had been given – his generosity shines
out in our reading from 2 Thessalonians. He was a living example
of what divine encouragement had done – and now he was in the
business of encouraging others in their faith.

Living up to our call

God's call puts upon us a great responsibility, which we need to see not as a pressure, but an exhilarating challenge. He has counted us worthy of the invitation to represent him on earth. Wow! (And when was the last time you said 'Wow!' to God's challenge!). A 'red-hot gospeller' has memorably declared: 'I'd rather be a nutter for God, than a sucker for Satan!' Yes, *we* may be called 'nutters', if we make enough impact for Christ. Why not? Great trees grow from little nuts. With the example of that unseen army of saintly witnesses to the fore today, can we not resolve likewise to do and dare all for God? If the sharing of the gospel was done with even as much enthusiasm as is expended, for instance, in running in the pentathlon, or climbing mountains, or sailing round the world, folk would notice. God would notice. Satan would notice, as well.

These thoughts stimulated Zacchaeus and the Thessalonians to *decide for God*. They would no doubt have a similar effect today – the more we can step out, and allow God to step in.

Family Service input

Compile a calendar of saints chosen by the young people, for parish use in the coming year.

Suggested hymns

Head of the Church triumphant; O for a closer walk with God; This is the day that the Lord has made; Will you come and follow me.

Fourth Sunday before Advent   *Second Service*
Unending Mercies   Ps. 145; Lam. 3:22–33; John 11:[1–31] 32–44

'The steadfast love of the Lord never ceases, his mercies never come to an end; they are new every morning; great is your faithfulness. "The Lord is my portion," says my soul, "therefore I will hope in him."'
Lamentations 3:22–24

An unflagging zeal

God never gets tired of his work: day after day he maintains the conditions in which he knows we can grow and mature as Christians. Morning after morning we take so much of his provision for granted. How often, for example, do we see each day as one nearer to home?

> Nearer my Father's home, where many mansions be;
> Nearer the great white throne today, nearer the crystal sea . . .
> Nearer the bound of life, where burdens are laid down;
> Nearer leaving the cross today, nearer gaining the crown.
> Nearer my home, nearer my home,
> Nearer my home today, today, than ever I've been before.
>
> Phoebe Cary

For Lazarus, the time to 'lay burdens down' had come, but only briefly, so that the power of God could impact upon the family and their friends. His raising prefigured the greater resurrection of Jesus. If it was designed to raise people's hopes on Good Friday, that death was not the end for Christ, it had limited effect; but God was giving the doubting and the fearful, the unbelievers and believers alike, the opportunity to see that he was Lord of life and death. Each night, to some extent, we 'die' in sleep and are 'resurrected' with the morning. How can we best show our gratitude for each new resurrection? How much further are we in our walk and work for God today than we were yesterday?

Steadfast hope

A steadfast hope that the best of us can do better, and the worst can make good, encourages God to keep on keeping on with his designs for humanity. What does it take to set the gospel bells ringing in heaven? Someone believing in Jesus. Think of the hundreds of tiny seeds in the packets we sow each spring. Do we sow them carefully, giving every seed room and a chance to grow and make good? Do we tear apart the packet, to get the last tiny seed out of each corner? That last little straggler may indeed make the best success of growing. So God takes a vital interest in every last one of us. No one in his eyes is unimportant, or past hope. And – let's have some encouragement – quite a lot of us are growing beautifully!

A lovely Christian

The more we grow and blossom spiritually, the more God in his faithfulness adds mercy to mercy. Grace abounding in our lives draws others to us – for simple goodness is a stronger magnet than evil, any day. Are we attracting others to Christ by how our lives portray him? Folk starved of love, compassion, joy, peace, gentleness and all the Holy Spirit can give, are drawn inevitably to those who have and show these gifts. We are under a sacred obligation not to hide the fruits of the Spirit away from others.

'The Lord is my portion'

The Lord is our *portion*, not our whole property, to keep for ourselves and our personal satisfaction. His is the world and everything and everyone in it. Jesus by his whole ministry gave us the prime example of how to share our portion of faith with others: the more we share, by divine alchemy we don't as yet understand, the more its portion grows, until – at the end of time – the wholeness of God will be enjoyed by the unity of believers in the kingdom everlasting. Staggering? Yes, maybe – so let's in the meanwhile concentrate on doing our best with each new morning that God gives us.

Suggested hymns

Great is thy faithfulness; New every morning is the love; Pray when the morn is breaking; The day thou gavest, Lord.

Third Sunday before Advent

(Remembrance Sunday)   7 November
Principal Service   **Lawless Destiny**   Job 19:23–27a; Ps. 17:1–9; 2 Thess. 2:1–5, 13–17; Luke 20:27–38

'Let no one deceive you in any way; for that day [the coming of our Lord Jesus Christ] will not come unless the rebellion comes first, and the lawless one is revealed, the one destined for destruction. He opposes and exalts himself above every so-called god or object of worship, so that he takes his seat in the temple of God, declaring himself to be God.'
2 *Thessalonians 2:3–4*

Satan's limits

Satan's days are numbered: he is 'destined for destruction'. Here it is in black and white. 'Woe to the earth and the sea, for the devil has come down to you with great wrath, because he knows that his time is short!' (Revelation 12:12). Well, we can take heart from this, even though the short term at times seems unending and the world situation pretty awful. But we don't have the advantage of knowing when Satan will be destroyed (or perhaps will self-destruct), such as is in the mind of God. On this weekend, when Remembrance is particularly in focus, the Devil seems to have had an overly long innings – and, in many parts of the world, has still got his eye in and is batting strongly.

Invading the temple

Satan has even invaded 'the temple of God', asserts St Paul. He was writing at a time when the corruption in the Jerusalem temple, which had manifested itself so convincingly at Christ's Passion, was continuing; but today the warning is no less salutary – the Church needs constantly to be on its guard, for it is not immune from Satan's attacks: the sins of betrayal, compromise and duplicity did not die out with the suicide of Judas.

A glimpse beyond

Jesus used a somewhat loaded and convoluted question about marriage to give us a glimpse of the different conditions that apply in eternity. Marriage for the procreation of children will not be necessary, for time and growing into maturity will no longer be. Nor will physical union for fellowship be necessary, since unity will be the norm. But we need not fear that recognition and appreciation will be lost: that we shall know one another as we have known on earth is evident from such experiences as the Transfiguration and Jesus' parable of Dives and Lazarus. But our status will have altered: we shall be like the angels, focused on the worship of God, united in his praise and ready to do and go as he directs.

What of our free will, which at present can be such a force for good, yet at times land us in all sorts of trouble? We can only reverently surmise that the Lord of infinite love and understanding – who is preparing us with free will for eternity – will also have provided scope for individuality in glory.

The Devil's presumption

He 'declares himself to be God', St Paul warns us, of the Devil. What presumption! Yes, he was once an angel of light, Lucifer, before he had designs on greatness. Now, even though his wings have been clipped, he aspires to more than greatness.

> *The sword may be burnished, the armour be bright,*
> *For Satan appears as an angel of light;*
> *Yet darkly the bosom may treachery hide,*
> *While lips are professing, 'I'm on the Lord's side.'*

Paulina

Judgement

Now is the time, before it's too late, to see that Satan is not batting on our crease, for judgement must begin at the house of God (1 Peter 4:17). Standing foursquare by what we confess and profess is the way in which others will see Jesus. That is our reason for living, the great truth of our calling. We are not an 'accident' trundling as best we can through time, but children of the Almighty, destined for glory. The Lord himself has witnessed our signature (in Christ's blood) on the contract.

Family Service input

Encourage young – and old – to write a hymn for Remembrance.

Suggested hymns

For the healing of the nations; I know that my Redeemer lives, what joy; O God, our help in ages past; Thy love, O God, has all mankind created.

Third Sunday before Advent *Second Service*
The Caring Christ Ps. 40; 1 Ki. 3:1–15; Rom. 8:31–39 or Matthew 22:15–22

'Who will bring any charge against God's elect? It is God who justifies. Who is to condemn? It is Christ Jesus, who died, yes, who was raised, who is at the right hand of God, who indeed intercedes for us.' Romans 8:33–34

A wonderful Friend

Is there any limit to the love of Jesus? He came to suffer for us – and, as if that were not enough, he continues to plead on our behalf at the right hand of the Almighty! And some days this great truth may not even cross our minds. Lord, forgive. Forgive us for not realizing what you have made us: the elect of God, precious, chosen, called and cared about, brothers and sisters of the Lamb who in glory still carries the scars our sin inflicted:

> *Intercessor, Friend of sinners,*
> *Earth's Redeemer, plead for me,*
> *Where the songs of all the sinless*
> *Sweep across the crystal sea.*

> W. Chatterton Dix (1837–1898)

Elect though we are, bound for glory and redeemed by the blood of Calvary though we have been, we still fall short of perfection. We can all empathize with St Paul, when he admits: 'I do not do the good I want, but the evil I do not want is what I do. Now if I do what I do not want, it is no longer I that do it, but sin that dwells within me' (Romans 7:19–20). When this happens to us, in us, there is Jesus in glory with God pleading on our behalf; pleading his blood, which is the one thing that can blot out our sins, into that gloriously deep sea of God's forgetfulness; pleading that the Holy Spirit in us will live and grow and guard us from future attacks; pleading that this Spirit will bring every word of Jesus to our remembrance, that we shall be kept from sinning; pleading, pleading, pleading, because our Lord loves us so much.

We are God's

We belong to God. We have answered the call of Christ. We have faith in him, in what he has done, in what he is doing through us – and we know that he knows what he can still accomplish through us. Satan cannot claim us while we are faithful to God. But if we let down our guard, if we do not allow the Holy Spirit to keep us loyal, if we give Satan a toe-hold on our lives – let us remember Judas Iscariot, and how his fellow disciples in the cenacle that night could not believe that one of their number could stoop so low.

There in glory the Godhead is looking out for us, willing us to keep steadfast for the truth. It is a formidable obstacle for Satan to overcome; the Devil's one hope of success lies in our being

245

taken off guard, distracted by the troubles or enjoyments of the world.

Christ the Mediator

Suppose our case comes up for divine review: there in glory the Almighty asks for the account and requires an explanation of our life. The Mediator moves him with his pleas: this is a child for whom I bear these scars, for whom I suffered and died. Can the loving Father-heart of God be deaf to such a defence? Where, then, is the accuser? But not even Satan can get past such pleading.

It's not a perfect analogy, but can we remember the woman taken in adultery (John 8:1–11)? 'Where are they?' Jesus asked her, looking round for her accusers. 'Has no one condemned you?' She said, 'No one, Sir' (vv. 10–11). In the presence of Jesus, the accusers had melted away. 'Neither do I condemn you,' said Jesus. 'Go your way, and from now on do not sin again' (v. 11). With his blood hiding our sins, he is able still to plead for us to God.

He is more than able. He is also willing.

> Dear Name! The Rock on which I build
> My shield and hiding-place;
>   My never-failing treasury filled
> With boundless stores of grace.
>
> *John Newton (1725–1807)*

Suggested hymns

Alas! and did my Saviour bleed; How sweet the Name of Jesus sounds; My God, how wonderful thou art; Once, only once, and once for all.

Second Sunday before Advent   14 November

Principal Service   **God's Open Door**   Mal. 4:1–2a; Ps. 98; 2 Thess. 3:6–13; Luke 21:5–19

'[Jesus said], "But before all this occurs, they will arrest you and per-secute you; they will hand you over to synagogues and prisons, and you will be brought before kings and governors because of my name. This will give you an opportunity to testify."' Luke 21:12–13

Don't worry!

'Don't be disheartened!' Jesus is saying. 'Even when the outlook is bleak, you've still a job to do, spreading the good news, defending your faith, making my Name known!' Our circumstances are in God's hands, whether the sea of life is smooth or rough; and as we're always on duty, ambassadors for Christ, God continues to give us opportunities to witness, even in the unlikeliest of situations. We classify our circumstances (albeit subconsciously) into the good, the bad and the indifferent. To God, they are all openings for witnessing. St Paul tried to get this point of constant awareness and preparedness across to Timothy: 'I solemnly urge you; proclaim the message; be persistent, whether the time is favourable or unfavourable' (2 Timothy 4:12). It can be hard at times not to be distracted by circumstances, but Jesus tells us to fight against being so overwhelmed that we let the pressures crowd out our willingness to share the gospel. We can focus on the troubles until our mind has shut itself down from functioning on any other wavelength – in a sort of psycho-paralysis. 'Wake up to the power of my Holy Spirit, before you allow yourself to get into such a state!' says Jesus. In the Gospels, this command often comes across very simply as: 'Do not fear!'

God's circumstances

If we have an open-heart mentality for God's guidance, we can be sure that he has brought us into circumstances of his design – opportunities that can be used to further his purpose, however we feel about the situation. While our natural tendency is to classify everything into what we like or dislike, God has a less restricted view. We're probably still a long way from looking at life with such equanimity. Human nature seems to have changed minimally on this point over thousands of years. God hasn't changed, either!

> Take me, O my Father, take me,
> Take me, save me through thy Son;
> That which thou wouldst have me, make me,
> Let thy will in me be done.
> Long from thee my footsteps straying
> Thorny proved the path I trod;
> Weary, come I now, and praying:
> Take me to thy love, my God!
>
> *Rory Palmer*

If we really want God to make us what he would have us be, we must welcome the tricky situations as well as the plain sailing. There will then be times when we can look back and say: 'Lord, when I was really up against it, only *you* could have given me the words to say that turned those circumstances around! I couldn't have said such things myself!' We may even find ourselves wondering why we don't let God direct us more often!

More than our share?
Who hasn't at some time or another complained – privately to God, or publicly to anyone who will listen – that we seem to have more than our fair share of trouble? Yet if we could look at these situations from God's standpoint, wouldn't we see, rather than 'favourable' and 'unfavourable' times, merely a variety of opportunities for continuing ministry? Given that, can we not just get on with God's work, each and every day?

Strength for our labours the Lord will provide.

Fanny J. Crosby

Family Service input
Identify the Bible Cake ingredients (see below – or find other ingredients in the Bible, for variety), and encourage the baking of these for consumption after next Sunday's service.

Suggested hymns
Christ is our cornerstone; Sometimes a light surprises; We turn to you, O God of every nation; who can cheer the heart like Jesus?

Bible Cake

1. 2 teacups 1 Samuel 30:12 (second ingredient)
2. 2 cups Nahum 3:12
3. ½ cup Numbers 17:8 (plus a few for decoration)
4. 8 oz (225 g) Psalm 55:21
5. 2 cups Jeremiah 6:20 (sugar!)
6. 4½ cups 1 Kings 4:22
7. 6 of what the bird produces Jeremiah 17:11
8. 2 tbsps 1 Samuel 14:25

9. pinch of Leviticus 2:13
10. 2 tsps Amos 4:5 (crumbs)
11. 1 cup Judges 5:25 (final clause)
12. 1/2 cup Judges 4:19 (first liquid)
13. Season with 2 Chronicles 9:9

Heat oven to 150°C (300°F, Gas mark 2)
Grease and line a 6-inch cake tin.
Separate 1.
Chop 2 and 3. Set on one side.
Blend 4 and 5.
Gradually add 6.
Beat in 7 and add 8, 9 and 10.
Stir in 1, 2 and 3.
Add 11 and 12 as necessary.
Blend in 13.
Put into prepared tin, decorate with a few flaked 3s.
Bake on a low shelf for 3½ hours.
If the top browns prematurely, reduce heat to 140°C (275°F, Gas mark 1) and cover with greaseproof paper.

Eat with prayer and thankfulness, and resolve to follow the example of 2 Timothy 1:6!

Second Sunday before Advent *Second Service*
Giving and Taking Ps. [93] 97; Dan. 6; Matthew 13:1–9, 18–23

'[Jesus said], "When anyone hears the word of the kingdom and does not understand it, the evil one comes and snatches away what is sown in the heart; this is what was sown on the path."' *Matthew 13:19*

God gives
God in his word has given sufficient seed for the whole world – past, present and future. He gives amply, good measure, pressed down, shaken together and running over ... (Luke 6:38, AV). There is plenty for all who will receive, and, since God is not willing that anyone should perish, 'all' means all. That is some seed bank, couched between the pages from Genesis to Revelation.

We may take the various editions of our Bibles for granted at times: it does no harm to reflect on how God has protected his word, from the day that Moses in anger dashed the stone tablets to pieces and the covenant had to be rewritten (Exodus 32:19; 34:1f.), through to the replacement of the heavy tablets as the years passed, by scrolls and eventually books much as we know today. Now we have the Bible on microfilm, the Internet and much else. How will God's word look in eternity? Well, it will be there, in some form, for he has promised (Mark 13:31; Luke 21:33; 1 Peter 1:25).

Satan takes

While God is a giver, Satan is a taker (cf. John 10:10). From the time in Eden when he took away human innocence and dignity, Satan has been trying his hardest to snatch, destroy, despoil and denigrate whatever is true, honourable, just, pure, pleasing and commendable (Philippians 4:8). He makes a speciality of whipping the word of God before it can take root in a person's heart. The Bible carries an invisible health warning: 'Read, mark, learn and inwardly digest', (before the Devil steals it from you – see Collect for Advent 2, BCP). The best way to defeat Satan is to operate a dual policy of 'study and share' – making the most of God's word.

The 25 per cent

When we major in the word, we are among the 25 per cent (one in four) of the seeds that grew well for the sower. Yet are we content to give the Devil a 75 per cent success rate? 'Many are called, but few are chosen' (Matthew 20:16 mg.; 22:14) – but are the 'few' really outnumbered by the 'many' at one in four? It may be so: the 'few' will be sufficient for what God has in mind. In three years, Jesus could have recruited a following large enough to have sorted out Jerusalem (even without the help of more than twelve legions of angels, Matthew 26:53), and made the crucifixion unnecessary. But where should we have been then? Struggling through this life with no prospect of anything afterwards. Perhaps, on a bad day, the disciples would look back to the time when, ascending to glory, Jesus left the evangelization of the world in only 11 pairs of hands: odds a fair way greater than one in four!

We may feel isolated in our ministry, or becalmed in a status quo that has seen no change for many years. Isn't God moving on our little cabbage patch? Surely he hasn't forgotten us? But if we earnestly believe that we are sowing seed where he intends us to be, then results will come – in our time, or later. Seed once sown has potential; seed not yet sown is inert and incapable of growing.

In Russia, there is a saying: 'When the (frog)spawn rises in the pond, it's time to sow the seeds' – and this works for non-Russian farmers and gardeners, too. But there is no set time for the sowing of God's word. We make the sowing-time – and we have 24 hours every day in which to work. At any given moment someone some-where around the world is sowing Bible seed; someone is having it stolen away by Satan; someone else is letting trouble suffocate the seed; someone else is drowning the seed in pursuit of pleasure . . .

And one person in four is making a success of growing it.

Suggested hymns
Give me oil in my lamp; I come to the garden alone; Just as I am; Sow in the morn thy seed.

Christ the King (Sunday next before Advent)
21 November   *Principal Service*
'This Is the King'   Jer. 23:1–6; Ps. 46; Col. 1:11–20; Luke 23:33–43

'The soldiers also mocked him, coming up and offering him sour wine and saying, "If you are the King of the Jews, save yourself!" There was also an inscription over him, "This is the King of the Jews."' Luke 23:36–38

'He saved others'
Meaning Lazarus and the son of the widow of Nain? Meaning those he had healed of sickness and disease? Oh, yes, but he was to save so many more! There is a sad irony in these three little words, which were to be proved truer than the scoffers intended. They are all of a piece with the earlier remark of Caiaphas, that 'it is better for you to have one man die for the people, than to have the whole nation destroyed' (John 11:50). The soldiers knew

enough about the title 'King of the Jews' to believe that, if he chose to do so, Jesus could have come down from the cross. Probably the majority of onlookers around the cross were expecting something dramatic to happen. And even the two thieves believed that Jesus had the power to save (Luke 23:39), though only one turned belief into full-blown faith (v. 42). We are usually so taken up with the King on the cross that the impact he had on the others involved in the trauma doesn't always find its mark.

King of our hearts

Giving Jesus the seat of kingship in our hearts puts us in the firing line of Satan, who hates authority because he has been stripped of any he once had. But it also means that we are 'part of the family' – the Royal Family of God – with ambassadorial status to tell others of Christ, to show Christ to the world and to get people to want what we have already accepted by faith: eternal life. It is the King's present – hardly won but freely given – to all his followers.

> King of glory, King of peace,
> I will love thee;
> And that love may never cease,
> I will move thee.
> Thou hast granted my request,
> Thou hast heard me,
> Thou didst note my working breast,
> Thou hast spared me.
>
> George Herbert

Our allegiance

If allegiance is due to an earthly monarch, how much more to the King who has conquered death for us! Witnessing for him in a largely alien culture is not easy: there are so many contenders for his throne – just as there were in the earliest days of the Church. When St Paul reached Athens, he was given a 'ready-made' sermon in the Athenians' 'Altar to an Unknown God' (Acts 17:23). I'll tell you who he is! said Paul, and witnessed for Jesus with as much eloquence as he could, to reach the sophisticated, erudite grandees on the Acropolis. They were too highly bred to show

Jesus Crossword

Clues Across

1. Where Jesus turned water into wine. (4)
3. Jesus was called the . . . of Sharon. (4)
5. . . . of Galilee. (3)
6. Jesus' ancestry. (4, 2, 5)
9. Writer of a Gospel and Acts. (4)
10. Eternity. (4)
13. Place of Jesus' baptism. (6, 5)
15. Jesus had none of this. (3)
16. 'O little . . . of Bethlehem.' (4)
17. . . . and you will find. (4)

Clues Down

1. Jesus came as this. (5)
2. The cursed fig-tree had this but no fruit. (4)
4. Pilate tried to do this by washing. (5)
7. Jesus Christ, Superstar? (5)
8. The wilderness. (5)
11. Force out, like sin. (5)
12. 'Do this, as often as you . . . it.' (5)
14. Town where Jesus restored a boy to life. (4)

anger, calmly announcing as they departed that they'd give him another hearing some time.

> *The dearest idol I have known,*
> *Whate'er that idol be,*
> *Help me to tear it from thy throne,*
> *And worship only thee.*

> *William Cowper (1731–1800)*

There is only room for one throne in our hearts: either Jesus is on it – or someone else. We owe allegiance to one monarch – either Jesus, or someone else. We obey one King's laws – either those of Jesus, or someone else. We bow the knee to one Master – either Jesus, or someone else. We shall meet one Lord in glory, and it will be Jesus – or we shall be somewhere else, with someone else. May God keep us faithful, while there is still time to decide to be loyal to no one else but Jesus.

Speaking in Jesus' Name
As ambassadors for the King, we are invested with authority to speak in his Name. Can we reflect, on this Sunday of Christ the King, exactly what this means? It's a question of speaking like Jesus, loving like Jesus, caring like Jesus: in short, walking the right Royal Way.

Family Service input
Distribute copies of the Jesus Crossword (see p. 253).

Suggested hymns
All hail the power of Jesus' name; From glory to glory advancing; King of glory, King of peace; Lord, enthroned in heavenly splendour.

Solution:
Across: 1. Cana. 3. Rose. 5. Sea. 6. Line of David. 9. Luke. 10. Ever. 13. Jordan River. 15. Sin. 16. Town. 17. Seek.
Down: 1. Child. 2. Leaf. 4. Evade. 7. Opera. 8. Drear. 11. Eject. 12. Drink. 14. Nain.

Christic the King *Second Service*
What Has Jesus Done? Ps. 72; 1 Sam. 8:4–20;
John 18:33–37

'Your own nation and the chief priests have handed you over to me. What have you done?' John 18:35

His own people

Jesus had come to his own people, and they had not given him a good reception (John 1:11); instead, they handed him over for 'trial by Rome'. Pilate's perplexity was understandable: with his army of occupation in Jerusalem, surely the Jews should have welcomed the King in their midst! But Jesus had warned his home-town neighbours that a prophet has no honour among his own people (Luke 4:24). It is the same today. A much-travelled, well-known preacher addressed a gathering of students, on his travels in Eastern Europe. His audience hung on his every word and afterwards were keen to fire questions. One of the staff asked, 'Where were you born?' and the answer came, 'Less than ten miles from this hall'. The atmosphere immediately changed from enthusiasm and respect to anti-climax and coolness. Jesus' words are as true today as two thousand years ago.

'What have you done?'

Pilate put the question in a negative way, expecting details of the crime that must surely have been committed for a prisoner to be brought thus before him. Of course, Jesus could have told the Roman of the gospel he had taught, the sick folk he had healed and the dead he had raised; he had 'done' enough to satisfy any judge worth his salt. But the judge he faced was fearful of losing his position, and open to blackmail: the threat that the chief priests would go running to Caesar with complaints (John 19:12) was enough to compromise Pilate's honour. Justice went out of the window, and Jesus was sentenced. Yet history has pilloried Pilate as the criminal of the day and the sentenced victim as Victor. The King reigned from the cross and rose to glory. The governor ended his days in obscurity in Gaul.

What have we done?

We may be asked this same question – at our entrance to glory, if not before. It will not matter what others think, or what they do; the issue on Good Friday was not the questionable probity of the chief priests or Pilate, but of what the Lord had done: the reason for his mission, and how he had fulfilled it. That was what counted with God, and what would set heaven alight with joy on Easter morning. If we are doing what we can for God, with the means he has given us, we shall be able to stand, like Jesus, and face any opposition, knowing that the one thing that matters is our God's satisfaction. Our 'royalty', as his sons and daughters, may be denied by the world – but does that matter at all? Do we do what we do for the world's recognition and plaudits, or to give delight to God? The world often makes a poor fist of understanding temporal royalty, so it's not surprising it has difficulty with the divine.

Christ is reigning
With Christ the King reigning on the throne of our hearts, we can stand against the world. If our particular part of the world rejects us, we can do what Jesus did and move on to another place – or we can stay and suffer the flak. The choice is ours. Whatever we choose, our work is to make Christ known, to get him accepted is God's part of the bargain. Why do we sometimes think he should *compel* anyone to believe?

As another church year draws to a close, we may consider what it has brought: some joy, for sure; some sadness, too; but surely some progress, some growth in grace and in our knowledge of Jesus. May it also have brought new friendships, new experiences of the love of God – in our lives and in the lives of those we love, and those around us. We probably have come to know ourselves better over the past months, and how we can serve God in ways we had not hitherto imagined. God is doing a work among us which is growing every day; let us pray that we may keep pace with our King.

Suggested hymns
Another year is dawning; Forth in thy name, O Lord, I go; Lead us, heavenly Father, lead us; Lord, for the years.

SERMONS FOR SAINTS' DAYS AND SPECIAL OCCASIONS

The readings in this section are taken from Brother Tristam SSF, *Exciting Holiness* (Canterbury Press, 1997); Robert Atwell, *Celebrating the Saints* (Canterbury Press, 1998).

St Andrew, Apostle   1 December transferred from 30 November   Will You Come?

Isa. 52:7–10; Ps. 19:1–6; Rom. 10:12–18; Matthew 4:18–22

'As [Jesus] walked by the sea of Galilee, he saw two brothers, Simon, who is called Peter, and Andrew his brother, casting a net into the lake – for they were fishermen. And he said to them, "Follow me, and I will make you fish for people."' Matthew 4:18–19

The answered call

Andrew did not hesitate. From this unlooked-for summons, he became one of the inner circle of Jesus' disciples, present at Jesus' first miracle during the Cana wedding breakfast; prominent when he introduced the young lad with the loaves and fishes to Jesus at the miraculous feeding; and at the supper in the cenacle on the night of Jesus' arrest.

According to John's Gospel, Andrew was first a disciple of John the Baptist (John 1:46). On hearing Jesus preaching, Andrew went in search of his brother Peter and brought him to Jesus. Both Matthew's and John's accounts can, of course, be correct. There is no reason why the introduction and the call to follow should not have occurred on different days.

Andrew, patron saint

As well as being the patron saint of Scotland, Andrew is also claimed by Russia, Greece, fishermen and sailors. We are dependent on extra-biblical legends for data on Andrew after Christ's ascension: one tradition says that he ministered among cannibals and converted many to Christ after freeing a number of prisoners destined for consumption at a royal banquet. Another legend has him being crucified on an 'X'-shaped cross in Patras, in Achaia, for baptizing Maximilla, the wife of the Roman Governor Egaes. Many years later, some of Andrew's relics were brought to Scotland by St Rule and St Theneva; but for centuries Amalfi, in Italy, has been his resting-place, where from time to time his bones have exuded a strange, fragrant oil. Andrew's head, stolen from Constantinople by the Crusaders, was eventually returned to the Pope by Constantine; but it did not reach Amalfi until Pope Paul VI returned it as recently as 1972.

A humble follower

To be so well known, so close to our Lord for all his earthly ministry, and yet for so little about what he actually did and said in his own ministry to be documented, is a tribute not only to Andrew's loyalty but also his humility. His was no high-profile evangelism, no hard-sell conversion hype – just a steadfast dependability that kept close to Jesus with no thought of self-advancement. Active in bringing others to Christ, Andrew had been taught in a good 'school' – for hadn't his first master, John the Baptist, declared: 'He [Jesus] must increase, but I must decrease' (John 3:30)?

Second fiddle

'Playing second fiddle' has come to be seen in a poor light, and usually from compulsion rather than choice; but unless we as Christians put Christ first and ourselves second (at least), we're merely on an ego-trip that will end in disaster. Andrew, who sought no recognition for himself, would surely never have imagined that one day he would be world-famous.

But if he had, it would probably not have changed his life at all. When we get our priorities in line with God's, unimportant matters like fame and prestige don't enter into the equation.

Suggested hymns

I danced in the morning; Jesus calls us! o'er the tumult; Take up thy cross, the Saviour said; Will you come and follow me?

St Nicholas, Bishop of Myra *c.* 326
6 December   Godly Contentment
Isa. 61:1–3; Ps. 68; 1 Tim. 6:6–11; Mark 10:13–16

'Of course, there is great gain in godliness combined with contentment, for we brought nothing into the world, so that we can take nothing out of it; but if we have food and clothing, we will be content with these.'
1 Timothy 6:6–7

A good man
Nicholas appears to have been born in the third century at Patara, in Lycia (a province of Asia Minor). Priested early in life, he was soon consecrated bishop of his home see of Myra, and not only well known but dearly loved for his concern for the poor. He heard of a citizen of Patara who had fallen on hard times, and whose three daughters faced the prospect of being sold into prostitution because their father had no dowry for them. At night, Nicholas threw a bag of gold through the family's open window, which paid for the eldest daughter's marriage. Later, the kindly bishop did the same for the second daughter. His third act of generosity was discovered by the girls' father, who embraced Nicholas, quite overcome by the bishop's kindness.

Brave opponent
Nicholas is said to have attended the great Council of Nicaea in AD 325, where he stoutly defended orthodoxy against the Arian heresy. Legend has it that he was tortured and suffered martyrdom in the terrible persecution instigated by Diocletian. Some say he actually died in the reign of that emperor, which would mean that Nicholas could not have attended Nicaea. His relics were rescued from a besieged Myra in 1087, and taken to Bari, in Italy, where they now repose in the Basilica of St Nicholas. Many churches in Britain in the Middle Ages were dedicated to this saint; and in Europe – particularly in the Netherlands (where he is called 'Sinter Claes', from where our 'Santa Claus' derives), Germany and Switzerland, it became the custom to give presents on St Nicholas' Day; later this custom coalesced with the Christmas celebrations.

The saint is, *inter alia*, the patron of pawnbrokers, and the sign of three golden balls is said to represent the three bags of gold which Nicholas gave to the brides' father.

Sinter Claes

While St Nicholas may not have approved of the secularism that tends to suffocate the origins of 'Santa Claus', he would surely take delight in the giving at this season which brings so much joy to so many people. That his own festival has been all but subsumed in the Nativity of Christ would probably please him even more. He may have done many great things as a bishop; he may indeed have done much to quell the Arian heresy at Nicaea; but to be known primarily for his kindness and generosity is surely an even better memorial. 'Godliness with contentment is great gain' is how the AV renders our text, and it takes some beating. Even from the little we know of Nicholas, he appears to have been a man at peace with his God and his flock: *not* a pacifist, for he was quick to fight for the right – but content in the knowledge that he was on the right lines, putting into constant practice the two greatest commandments: love God and your neighbour.

We may all subscribe to this in theory, and that's a wonderful beginning; but the real test comes when we translate theory into practice.

Suggested hymns

Happy are they, they that love God; Praise, my soul, the King of heaven; The Kingdom of God is justice and joy; When I needed a neighbour.

Conception of the Blessed Virgin Mary
8 December   Immaculata, Stella Maris
Gen. 3:9–15a; Ps. 97; Eph. 1:3–6, 11–12; Luke 1:26–38

'But the Lord God called to the man, and said to him, "Where are you?" . . . *Then the Lord God said to the woman, "What is this that you have done?" The woman said, "The serpent tricked me, and I ate."'* Genesis 3:9, 13

'Where are you?'

History's first question! Ever afterwards, God was asking human-kind the same question, as humanity struggled with the problems that the Fall in Eden had brought into the world – until, many centuries later, the Lord fulfilled his plan to redeem the world. A

Saviour – his only Son – would come. Because, in his wisdom, God had planned for Jesus to be born of a woman, the right woman must be found. Catholics believe that Mary was conceived in St Anne's womb without sin; many Protestants still have a problem with this, and often use the Gospel account of the conception of *Jesus* (Luke 1:26–38) for this day, as well as on 25 March.

Immaculata

The question surely is not whether Mary was immaculate, without sin from conception, but rather, that she was considered worthy of bearing Jesus. 'Mary Immaculate, Star of the Sea' is only one (or two) of her many titles; for whatever our feelings about her status before Christ's conception, we may surely believe she was purely special from that day forward. Pope Pius IX declared her Immaculate, as the patron of America, in 1847; and the Immaculate Conception as Catholic dogma was infallibly affirmed on this day in 1854, since when it has been observed across the Catholic world, and now increasingly in Protestant circles.

Mary's place

At the time of the Reformation, when many Protestants considered that the Catholic Church had pushed Mariology (the recognition of Mary) into Mariolatry (the worship and veneration of Mary), the tendency was to avoid the subject altogether – which surely did the beloved mother of Jesus a disservice. Can we not love the woman who obviously meant so much to our Lord? Can we not revere her, without diminishing the worship and honour which is Christ's due? Mary was chosen, highly favoured of God, for a position and a privilege no other woman had ever known. That is wonderful.

As Mary

Even more wonderful, even harder to comprehend, is Jesus' own teaching that those who follow him and do his will, deny themselves and take up the cross can be as close to him as his mother (Matthew 12:50; Mark 3:35)! Can we fathom a heart of love as big as this? No – but in faith we can believe in it . . . just as we cannot know precisely *why* God chose Mary to be the mother of his Son. Elizabeth had been chosen to bear John the Baptist in her old age – which was a miracle in itself. Mary was chosen for a different reason. Even in our lives, God does inexplicable, often impossible, things, One day we may know why, but until then we can surely trust him to carry on filling our lives with surprises, challenges and excitement.

Perhaps Mary never knew the reason for her choice – but with her 'fiat', she put herself in God's hands, and quietly met each new challenge the Lord provided.

> *Mary Immaculate, Star of the morning,*
> *Chosen before the creation began;*
> *Chosen to bring, for thy bridal adorning,*
> *Woe to the serpent, and rescue to man.*

> *F. W. Weatherell*

Suggested hymns
For Mary, Mother of our Lord; Hail, thou Star of ocean; Maiden, yet a Mother; O purest of creatures! Sweet Mother, sweet Maid.

St Stephen, Deacon, First Martyr
26 December   **First of Many**   2 Chr. 24:20–24; Ps. 119:161–68; Acts 7:51–60; Matthew 10:17–22
'"Look," [Stephen] said, "I see the heavens opened and the Son of Man standing at the right hand of God!"' Acts 7:56

Heaven on earth?
This proto-martyr – to be the first of many, one of the original 72 missionaries, and appointed deacon in the early Church – this table-waiter, had Jesus on his feet! Heaven beamed down to earth to welcome Stephen into glory. Did he even feel the stones and brickbats? With his last breath, he asked for forgiveness for his murderers – and then his spirit flew to Jesus.

Although coming as something of a shock, as we are celebrating Christmas, the martyrdom of Stephen reminds us that earthly joy, for whatever estimable reason, is not the greatest thing on earth. Top of our list of priorities must be our preparation for glory. If that includes celebration, fair and good; but the vision of Stephen shows us (if we needed showing) that by far the best is in store.

A loyal servant

He was a table-waiter, taking every opportunity that the work afforded to preach and share the gospel (Acts 6:8, 10). He could have aimed for a high-profile ministry, but instead gained honour by doing what was nearest faithfully and well. When the crunch came, he could defend his beliefs with verve, thoroughness and integrity. Not a bad showing for a waiter of tables! It's not what we do that makes the difference between mediocrity and greatness; it's how it's done. Remember the oft-quoted stonemason, who spent as much care on carving the back of the statue that was to adorn a high niche on the cathedral front as he did on the side that everyone would see: 'The Lord sees the back, as well as the front,' he told the scornful onlookers. We can be sure that the Lord had been observing how loyally the table-waiter had worked at his ministering.

The earliest martyrs

There had been the Holy Innocents and John the Baptist; but Stephen is the first known martyr of the early Church – and pretty soon after its inception when the Holy Spirit came down at Pentecost. The ranks of martyrs grew after this, particularly in the Neronic and Diocletian persecutions. And they continue to grow today, in places where Christians are still tortured for their faith. Although Satan knows his days are numbered (Revelation 12:12), he seems unable to stop himself from attacking the Church for as long as he can. He apparently has not realized that the more the martyrs' blood flows, the more seeds of growth are sown: *Semen est sanguis christianorum* – 'the blood of the martyrs is the seed of the church'; Tertullian's famous remark of the second century is still as relevant today.

Our lesser Calvaries

We shall probably not be called upon to die a martyr's death; but every day Christ calls us to carry our cross to lesser Calvaries. Every day is an opportunity for us to 'die' a little more to self: to see Jesus before our own ambitions, comforts and troubles; and to put his will before our own so consistently that eventually it becomes such a habit that we don't think about it.

Who knows? Perhaps our first vision of Jesus in glory will be of him standing to greet us!

Suggested hymns
Fill thou my life, O Lord my God; Meekness and majesty; Put
thou thy trust in God; Teach me, my God and King.

St John, Apostle and Evangelist
27 December   **The True Light**   Ex. 33:7–11a;
Ps. 117; 1 John 1; John 21:19b–25
*'This is the message we have heard from him and proclaim to you, that
God is light and in him there is no darkness at all.' 1 John 1:5*

This is the message
It does not really matter whether there are one, two or three
authors behind the Gospel of John, the Letters of John and the
Book of Revelation: it is the message in these writings that counts.
The light of God shines out of them, and this light is so pure
because it comes from the God who is *all* light. For that reason, it
can light up the whole world. 'The light shines in the darkness,
and the darkness did not overcome it' (John 1:5).

Part of a document, known as the *Muratorian Fragment*, dealing
with scriptures acknowledged *c.* AD 190 by the Roman Church,
runs:

The fourth of the Gospels was written by John, one of the disciples. When exhorted by his fellow-disciples and bishops, he
said, 'Fast with me this day for three days; and what may be
revealed to any of us, let us relate it to one another.' The same
night it was revealed to Andrew, one of the apostles, that John
was to write all things in his own name, and they were all to
certify. And, therefore, though various ideas are taught in the
several books of the Gospels, yet it makes no difference to the
faith of believers, since by one sovereign Spirit all things are
declared in all of them concerning the Nativity, the Passion, the
Resurrection, the conversations with his disciples and his two
comings, the first in lowliness and contempt, which has come
to pass, the second glorious with royal power, which is to come.
What marvel therefore if John so firmly sets forth each statement
in his Epistles too, saying of himself, 'What we have seen with
our eyes and heard with our ears and our hands have handled,

264

these things we have written to you' (1 John 1:1, 3, 4). For so he declares himself not an eyewitness and a hearer only, but a writer of all the marvels of the Lord in order . . .
The Apocalypse also of John . . . we receive, which some of our friends will not have read in the Church.

Writing in exile

John was exiled to Patmos, towards the end of the first century, presumably during the Domitian persecution, for refusing to deny his Christian beliefs. There, on 'the Lord's Day' (Revelation 1:10), he received news and visions to be shared with seven of the churches of Asia: Ephesus, Smyrna, Pergamum, Thyatira, Sardis, Philadelphia and Laodicea. Together, they constitute arguably the most exciting book of the Bible, for it opens for us so many windows not only into heaven, but into the past, present and future workings of God on the earth:

> From Jesus the Saviour, the Lord of the nations,
> Come blessings and letters and what is to be;
> There are horsemen and angels, St Michael and victory,
> A heavenly city, and life full and free.

God's ordering

Perhaps the bleak island of Patmos, 35 miles off the coast of Asia Minor, seems an unlikely place to hear from God. But John, despite the rigours of his exile, was open to receive what God wanted to give him. May we, too, be ready, wherever we are, whether the time seems to be favourable, or not (2 Timothy 4:2).

Suggested hymns

Be thou my vision; Lead, kindly light; Light's abode, celestial Salem; Lord, the light of your love is shining.

Holy Innocents (28 December or transferred to 29th). Death in Vain? Jer. 31:15–17; Ps. 124; 1 Cor. 1:26–29; Matthew 2:13–18

'But God chose what is foolish in the world to shame the wise; God chose what is weak in the world to shame the strong.' 1 Corinthians 1:27

Childermas

Until the seventeenth century in England, this day was known as 'Childermas', when the plight of these innocent Bethlehem children was commemorated. Was their tragedy in vain? No, for God allowed it, and we still interrupt our Christmas celebrations to remember the youngsters who died so that Another may live. Every parent will empathize with those who mourned: we don't know the numbers involved, but even one would have been one too many. Nor do we know if, thirty or so years later, news of a young preacher in Galilee and Jerusalem would fan the flames of memory among these parents, as having been the Child for whom their children died. They were little ones, ushered into eternity before they had committed sin, for ever precious in their Maker's eyes. We may reverently wonder what these innocent souls had in store for them in eternity.

Every one matters

The fragility of these children is emphasized by their important role in the salvation of the world. What a contrast! But it shows us that even the weakest among us can be called to great service in the will of God. We should not bemoan our weakness (or that of others), nor should we use it as an excuse for slackness in ministry. If helpless babies could prove so crucial in the preservation of Jesus, there is much to be expected from every Christian. 'Excess baggage' gets rerouted away from the road to glory, and on to another route we would not wish to take.

The fate of the Innocents is an illustration of the truth that we are not privy to all the workings of God. There seems to be an inbuilt desire with most people to seek a 'happy-ever-after' state, not only 'ever after' but throughout the journey there. Anything that upsets the tidy scheme of things comes as an unpleasant shock. Had we been writing history, would we have included this 'unnecessary' carnage? Probably not – so who can blame God for not allowing us to run the world on our own?

Good – and evil

There is plenty of evil in the world, for much of which we can find no reason. That is Satan's *modus operandi*: randomness. He relies on our inbuilt desire for order to be thrown out of kilter, and he knows no other way of working. But God is not like that: look at the physical laws of the natural world, which observe fixed parameters. Therefore, when God allows Satan to wreak havoc, he again fixes parameters; but because we are unfamiliar with this spiritual dimension, often we cannot understand them. God's limits on Satan are set far enough apart for us to translate as 'random' what is really within order. The carnage at Bethlehem appears dreadful – but not a single child would be killed for whom God had plans on earth to be fulfilled first.

Next time Satan attacks us, let us look also for the restraining influence of God, but for whose overall control we should all go down in Satan's first salvo.

Suggested hymns
Children of the heavenly King; In vain the cruel Herod's fear; Let saints on earth in concert sing; Unto us a boy is born.

Naming and Circumcision of Jesus 1 January
The Identity of Christ Num. 6:22–27; Ps. 8;
Gal. 4:4–7; Luke 2:15–21

'After eight days had passed, it was time to circumcise the child; and he was called Jesus, the name given by the angel before he was conceived in the womb.' Luke 2:21

Saviour
Even the angels 'know not Christ as Saviour, but worship him as King' (A. Midlane). We are specially privileged: every time we call on the name of Jesus, we are acknowledging (1) him as the Saviour who came and died for our sins; (2) the Saviour who rose from the dead to precede us to glory; and (3) his ongoing power to keep us safe all the day, every day. Often we say 'Jesus' so easily, we forget all this. Today is a good time to reflect on all that the Saviour means to us.

> *Save us, O Lord, waking;*
> *Guard us, sleeping;*
> *That awake we may watch with Christ,*
> *And asleep we may rest in peace.*
>
> *Office of Compline*

If we careen through even one day oblivious of the power and presence of Jesus – operating a DIY policy and trying to make it on our own – we are in effect negating the sacrifice of Calvary and turning away from all the help that Jesus presently has to offer. 'Oh, I can manage this!', we are telling him – and he is a gentleman, and will not intervene when he is not wanted. We are quick to appeal for his help when we're in a sticky situation; can we not involve him in our happier times? Jesus has always something to give – and we never have as much as we need.

Jesus, stand among us at the meeting of our lives.
Graham Kendrick

If our Lord had considered his work done when he ascended back to the Father, he would not have told his friends he would always be with them (Matthew 28:20). We need him, constantly, to work in us through his Spirit; we need his power against Satan; we need his word for each and every situation – and we need his precious joy to keep us spiritually healthy and balanced, because left on our own we make a poor showing of having and spreading joy. Christians today seem largely to have forgotten what real, deep-down, heart-throbbing exhilaration-for-God means. And if we've lost it, however can we share it with others?

Jesus!

Jesus! How many times a day is his name in our hearts and on our lips? Sometimes we hear it used profanely, and that should bring us up short: if the Devil can drag the best name in the world through the mire, can we not respond by using it as Jesus taught: 'Whoever welcomes one . . . child in my name, welcomes me' (Mark 9:37); 'Where two or three are gathered in my name, I am there among them' (Matthew 18:20); 'No one who does a deed of power in my name will be able soon afterwards to speak evil of me' (Mark 9:39); 'Whoever gives you a cup of water to drink because you bear the name of Christ will by no means lose his reward' (Mark 9:41); 'These signs will accompany those who believe by using my name: they will cast out demons . . . speak in new tongues . . . pick up snakes in their hands . . . lay hands on the sick . . .' (Mark 16:17–18); 'I will do whatever you ask in my name, so that the Father may be glorified in the Son' (John 14:13).

Lord, thank you for all that your name stands for; as one you have saved, I claim all the privilege you have given me – and I delight in using your name. May I never use it unworthily. Amen.

Suggested hymns
At the name of Jesus; How sweet the name of Jesus sounds; Jesus, the name high over all; There is a Redeemer.

Epiphany 6 January A Positive Attitude
Isa. 60:1–6; Ps. 72:[1–9]10–15; Eph. 3:1–12;
Matthew 2:1–12
'When King Herod heard this, he was frightened, and all Jerusalem with him.' Matthew 2:3

Meeting our Lord
The command of Jesus that outweighs in sheer frequency even his 'Love your neighbour' in the Gospels is 'Do not fear'. God has been to some lengths to give us everything we need – and Jesus came and suffered and triumphed to give us eternal life as the best top-up ever on our earthly package; yet still Satan moves in the hearts of those whose faith is questionable or non-existent, to give fear instead of trust. Herod was a long way from the joy that should have been his, that a Saviour had come into the world.

The Magi came in trust, hope, expectation – and, above all, joy. But God also gave them discernment, and so Herod was thwarted of his purpose.

How great is our joy?
How great is our joy, this Epiphanytide? Are we offering to Jesus the best of our gifts, or is fear in some way diluting our joy and minimizing our offering to God? If we have admitted fear of any kind into our lives, our joy is less than perfect. The command not to fear has become so watered down in many people's minds that we break our Lord's commandment without even a thought of doing wrong. Had the Magi given way to fear, they quite possibly would never have met up with the newborn King – or they would have been so afraid of displeasing Herod that they would have told him how to find the Child.

While not descending to morbid or introspective navel-gazing, can we run a check on our spirituality, to see the percentage of joy there? Focusing on the coming of the Saviour into our lives and into the lives of those we meet, those who are precious to us, those who come to us seeking God, will leave less room in our lives for fear to gain a toe-hold.

The God of the breakthrough
God broke through convincingly into the lives of the Magi, and each Epiphany their challenge is in some way our own. God, given the chance, surprises us every day, many times a day; but fear of one sort or another provides a block between the Lord's surprises and our awareness of them.

Can you think of a day when you lived without fear? Probably none of us can. 'I'm afraid I can't', we're probably thinking, even now. We overwork that word 'afraid', until it has lost its danger for us. As we focus today on the bravery and determination, the meekness and wisdom of the Magi, can we get serious with our Lord, and ask him to work in our lives for joy? That's a very courageous prayer to make. Dare we make it?

Dare we not make it?

Suggested hymns
As with gladness men of old; Brightest and best; Songs of thankfulness and praise; O worship the Lord in the beauty of holiness.

St Antony of Egypt, Hermit, Abbot 356
17 January   'With Long Life Will I Satisfy'
1 Ki. 17:2–6; Ps. 91; Phil. 3:7–14; Matthew 19:16–26

'Yet whatever gains I had, these I have come to regard as loss because of Christ. More than that, I regard everything as loss because of the surpassing value of knowing Christ Jesus my Lord.' Philippians 3:7–8

Born to riches
Born in Egypt *c.* 257, for the first twenty or so years of his life Antony was sheltered from the normal rigours of life by wealth and virtual seclusion, being tutored at home and seeing little of the world outside his immediate family. On the death of his

parents, he inherited land and a fortune, but was persuaded by the command of Jesus to 'go and sell all'. He deposited his sister in a 'house of maidens' – possibly the first nunnery to be mentioned in church history – and began a solitary life in the desert, following the example of a local hermit, Paul the Holy.

A frugal existence

He busied himself making brushes and weaving mats, eating only bread and a little salt which was brought to him occasionally by a friend. For over twenty years he lived in a cave high on a mountain, but eventually was persuaded to move nearer to civilization, where he established the first of several monasteries, consisting of a collection of individual cells. The rest of his long life was to be spent in founding others and in visiting each monastery in turn. When persecution broke out, Antony went to encourage those imprisoned and condemned to death; but he forebore to clash with the authorities or to provoke them in any way.

A written record

We are indebted to Archbishop Athanasius of Alexandria for a written record of the life of Antony. The two were great friends, with a mutual regard for their respective gifts. When Antony died, at the grand age of 105, he left one of his two sheepskins to Athanasius.

Antony is often portrayed with a pig and a bell, and to this day the smallest bell – and the runt of the litter – is called 'Tantony'.

Peace in solitude?

One may have thought that Antony's long life was the result of an untroubled solitude: but at times Antony's life was anything but peaceful. In the desert stillness he was attacked by demons and strange vision of horrible beasts and naked women. On one occasion a demon beat him so violently that Antony was discovered by a friend stretched out on the ground, almost at death's door.

One way to try to avoid the demons of solitude is to cram as much busyness into one's schedule as possible – but Satan also knows how to invade our preoccupations; and the struggle of a hard-pressed city-slicker can be ever as tough as that of a shepherd on the remote northern hills.

With long life will I satisfy him,
and show him my salvation.

Psalm 91:16, BCP

Antony was spared to be a blessing to many, and he would no doubt have been the first to believe that the fierce struggles were more than worth the effort. While we may marvel at the rigours he faced, we can surely on his festival reflect on how our own struggles are fitting us for service. If we are unsure about the effect they are having, may we gain some encouragement from the thought that if we were not doing some good for God, Satan probably would leave us alone.

Suggested hymns
Be thou my guardian and my guide; Fight the good fight; Lead, kindly light; Oft in danger, oft in woe.

Conversion of St Paul   25 January
(or transferred to 26th)   Three Days in the Dark
Jer. 1:4–10; Ps. 67; Acts 9:1–22; Matthew 19:27–30

'Saul got up from the ground, and though his eyes were open, he could see nothing; so they led him by the hand and brought him into Damascus. For three days he was without sight, and neither ate nor drank.' Acts 9:8–9

A promising start
Born a Jew, in Tarsus, thereby gaining the Roman citizenship which was to stand him in such good stead later in life, Saul was sent to Jerusalem to study under the learned Rabban Gamaliel, who trained him into the first-century equivalent of an orthodox churchman. But from that promising start, Saul deteriorated into an implacable opponent of what he saw as unorthodox – i.e., the 'new' movement, not yet called 'Christianity' but to which the followers of one Jesus Christ adhered. Saul hounded these men and women, getting them arrested, imprisoned, tortured and even killed. It was Saul who minded the clothes that had been ripped from Stephen; and Saul who watched in approval the stoning of

272

the young table-waiter who became the first Christian martyr (Acts 7:58; 8:1).

Post-haste to Damascus

His blood up, Saul heard of Christians in Damascus, and, armed with warrants for their arrest, set off post-haste to serve them. But God had allowed the misdirecting of Saul's fiery zeal for long enough. On the road to Damascus came high drama: a bright light, a vision of Jesus, then blindness – absolute, Stygian darkness for three days. Having needed to be led by others to a house in the city, Saul had 72 hours in which to reflect. Was he afraid? Who wouldn't be? Was he angry? Probably. Suicidal? Possibly.

When he had run through the gamut of emotions, Ananias (against his will, but in deference to God's will) came and restored Saul's sight. Came the moment of decision: would he return to the old life of persecution, or take a round-about turn and become one with the folk he had been hounding?

Resurrection – of a kind!

Jesus had spent three days or so in the tomb, and come out a new man. And people didn't believe what they were seeing and hearing. Saul, after his three days of darkness, emerged from the house in Damascus a new man. And again, folk were going to find it hard to believe what they would see and hear. Still today we are so programmed by our comparatively settled lives, our expectations (or lack of them), our fairly ordered timetables and itineraries, that anything out of the ordinary can likewise take us by surprise.

It was to take faith-filled encouragers like Barnabas (Acts 9:2f.), to persuade the doubters that Saul's (Paul's) conversion was 'for real'.

This, then, was the man earmarked by God to be the greatest missionary of the first-century Church. Everything about Paul was dramatic: his early persecuting; his conversion; his tangles with the Jews; his missionary travels, preaching and vicissisitudes. He was *alive*, he was *earnest*, he was God's man for the mission. You can never use words such as 'boring', 'lukewarm', 'ordinary' or 'conventional' when you think of Paul. He was on fire for God, and he got things done.

May the Christian fire that burned in Paul burn also in us.

Suggested hymns
All for Jesus, all for Jesus; Christian, seek not yet repose; Give me oil in my lamp; Take my life and let it be.

Presentation of Christ in the Temple
(Candlemas)   2 February (or transferred to 1st)
To be a Sign   Mal. 3:1–5; Ps. 24:[1–6] 7–10;
Heb. 2:14–18; Luke 2:22–40

'And the child's father and mother were amazed at what was being said about him. Then Simeon blessed them and said to his mother Mary, "This Child is destined for the falling and rising of many in Israel, and to be a sign that will be opposed, so that the inner thoughts of many will be revealed – and a sword will pierce your own soul too."'
Luke 2:33–35

Opposition ahead
Mary and Joseph would wonder what Simeon meant when the old man spoke of coming opposition to the child nestling in his arms. Through his years of childhood they would remember – until Mary stood at Calvary, and did not need to wonder any more.

Candlemas has been observed at least since the fifth century. Many churches maintain the custom of blessing two bundles of candles – long, thick candles for use in the church during the coming year, and a bundle of smaller candles for worshippers to carry in procession today, and then take home to light again in remembrance of this festival.

Candlemas marks the end of the Christmas season, when the crib and other evidences of the Nativity are taken out of the church, and the start of the time leading up to Easter.

A Candlemas Hymn

> 1. *The light of the world, in our hearts as we pray,*
>   *Is shown in our candles of Candlemas Day.*
>
> *(Refrain) O loving Lord, of heaven and earth,*
>   *From whom in faith we all have birth.*

2. *Blessed Mary and Joseph, fulfilling the law,*
   Took two doves as offering, for they were so poor.
   (Refrain)

3. *The service completed, an old man drew near,*
   And cradled the Christ-child with tenderness dear.
   (Refrain)

4. *'Let me now depart, for the Child I have seen,*
   The Saviour, far greater than all that has been.'
   (Refrain)

5. *A King to rule nations – but where is his crown?*
   A Lord in the highest, from glory come down.
   (Refrain)

6. *We pray, little Child, bring us light for our way,*
   And courage to live in your service each day.
   (Refrain)

Tune: Lourdes

St Bernard tells of people at Candlemas walking two by two, holding in their hands 'candles lighted, not from common fire, but from that which had first been blessed in their church by the priests, and singing in the way of the Lord, because great is his glory' (*Sermons*).

Final Responsory of Candlemas
Father, here we bring to an end our celebration of the Saviour's birth.
Help us, in whom he has been born, to live his life that has no end.

Here we have offered the Church's sacrifice of praise.
Help us, who have received the Christ-child into our hearts, to be thankful for your gift.

Here we have rejoiced with faithful Simeon and Anna.
Help us who have found the Lord in his temple, to trust in your eternal promises.

Here we have greeted the Light of the world.
Help us, though we extinguish these candles, never to forsake the light of Christ.

Here we meet in this place of Baptism.
Help us who are marked with the cross, to share the Lord's death and resurrection.

Here we turn from Christ's birth to his Passion.
Help us, for whom Lent is near, to enter deeply into the Easter mystery.

Here we bless one another in your Name.
Help us, who now go in peace, to shine with your light in the world.

Suggested hymns
A Man there lived in Galilee; Christ is the world's true Light; For Mary, mother of our Lord; Jesus, good above all other.

St Polycarp, Bishop of Smyrna, Martyr *c.* 155
23 February   **Be Faithful**   Wis. 5:15–20; Ps. 34; Rev. 2:8–11; John 15:1–8

'And to the angel of the church in Smyrna write, "These are the words of the First and the Last, who was dead and came to life . . . Be faithful until death, and I will give you the crown of life!"' Revelation 2:8, 11

Close to Christ
Polycarp was close to Christ, not only in spirit, but in time, being among those known to the 'Apostolic Fathers' who received instruction from the very apostles who had known Jesus when he was on earth. St John the Evangelist had tutored Polycarp, who in turn taught many who later became prominent in the Church, including Bishop Papias of Hierapolis and Bishop Irenaeus of Lyons.

Irenaeus has left us an account of Polycarp:

Polycarp also was not only instructed by apostles, and conversed with many who had seen Christ, but was also, by apostles in

Asia, appointed bishop of the church in Smyrna, whom I also saw in my early youth, for he tarried on earth a very long time; and, when a very old man, gloriously and most nobly suffering martyrdom, departed this life, having always taught the things which he had learned from the apostles, and which the church hands down, which also are true. To these things all the Asian churches testify, as do also those men who have succeeded Polycarp down to the present time – a man who was far more reliable and more steadfast a witness of truth, than Valentinus and Marcion, and the rest of the evil-minded ... Polycarp himself replied to Marcion, who met him on one occasion and said, 'Do you recognize me?' 'I do recognize you, the first-born of Satan.' Such was the caution which the apostles and their disciples used against holding even a verbal communication with any corruptors of the truth.' (*Argument from Tradition*)

The martyrdom of Polycarp, to which Irenaeus referred, took place in the wave of persecutions under Marcus Aurelius. Polycarp would not leave Smyrna for safety, but opened his door to the squad sent to arrest him, gave them a meal and after a time of prayer accompanied them to prison. He was given the chance to recant, but declared: 'Eighty and six years have I served my King, and he has never deserted me. Will I deny him now?' He was ordered to be burned to death, but the flames refused to touch him, and eventually a soldier despatched him with a spear, after which Polycarp's blood flowed so freely as to quench what was left of the fire.

John's letter to Smyrna

In or around AD 95, in a vision on Patmos John had been given a letter by God to Smyrna's little church. The Smyrnians were a consumer-conscious society, but the Christians had managed to get their priorities right. This was enough to get Satan really roused (Revelation 2:10). Materially, the little church is poor, but they have their sights set on treasure in heaven, and receive praise for standing firm. Spiritually, they are rich. The Jews in Smyrna are causing trouble for the church; and only 60 years after John wrote, Polycarp was martyred here, the record stating that when wood was being collected for the bishop's pyre 'the Jews were extremely zealous, as is their custom, in assisting at this', even though the execution took place on 'a great sabbath day' (*Martyrdom of Polycarp*).

Our own Calvary is almost certainly taking place on a less physically tortuous plane – but it requires ever as much spiritual stamina to oppose Satan today as in the early days of the Church. We may surely take courage that the power that sustained Polycarp is the same as that inside ourselves – the very same: yesterday, today and for ever.

Suggested hymns

For the might of thine arm, we bless thee; Led by the Spirit's power; Onward, Christian soldiers; Spirit of the living God, fall afresh on me.

George Herbert, Priest, Poet 1633
27 February   Write This!   Mal. 2:5–7; Ps. 1; Rev. 19:5–9; Matthew 11:25–30

'And the angel said to me, "Write this; Blessed are those who are invited to the marriage supper of the Lamb". And he said to me, "These are the true words of God."' Revelation 19:9

'My tongue is the pen . . .'

'My tongue is the pen of a ready writer,' sang the psalmist (Psalm 45:2, BCP) – and, in a short life of 40 years, of which only the last three were spent in full-time ministry, George Herbert put his tongue and his pen to good use. A brilliant scholar, he came down from Trinity, Cambridge, fluent in five languages and an accomplished musician. A high-flier, he was welcomed at Court and seemed destined for a dazzling public career; but the deaths of his two patrons, the Duke of Richmond and the Marquess of Hamilton, as well as that of King James I, put paid to this, and Herbert left the Court for the Church, becoming in 1630 Rector of Bemerton, a little rural parish not far from Salisbury. There, he proved an exemplary parish priest, but also found the time to write religious prose and poetry, some of his hymns continuing to be firm favourites today.

His lines on Christmas are among his most beautiful:

The shepherds sing, and shall I silent be?
My God, no hymn for thee?
My soul's a shepherd, too; a flock it feeds,
Of thoughts, and words, and deeds.
The pasture is thy word; the streams, thy grace
Enriching all the place.

Shepherd and flock shall sing, and all my powers
Out-sing the daylight hours.
Then will we chide the sun for letting night
Take up his place and right;
We sing one common Lord, wherefore he should
Himself the candle hold.
I will go searching, till I find a sun
Shall stay, till we have done;
A willing shiner, that shall shine as gladly
As frost-nipped suns look sadly.
Then we will sing, and shine all our own day,
And one another pay;
His beams shall cheer my breast, and both so twine,
Till even his beams sing, and my music shine.

In us, as well

There is a hymn, a poem, a new song in each of us: a song that
God heard when he composed it for us and implanted it. We may
reach glory with it still inside us – but will it go all the way to
eternity, or shall we perhaps leave it behind? Had we not better
consider airing it, sharing it now? Herbert could have allowed the
first three years of ministry for 'settling-in' at Bemerton; had such
been the case, we should have been the poorer. Nothing of any
value has yet been accomplished 'tomorrow'.

'Write!'

'Write!' was the command to the aged John on Patmos. He could
have asked: 'Why, Lord? Here I am in exile on a bleak and barren
island, 35 miles from the mainland of Asia Minor. Whoever is
going to read anything I write? Who is going to get these letters
to the Seven Churches of Asia?'

God simply said: 'Write this!' and began his dictation. And the
Lord safeguarded the subsequent passage of his revelations.

The God of love my Shepherd is; Teach me, my God and King; King of glory, King of peace; Let all the world in every corner sing.

St David, Bishop of Menevia, Patron of Wales
c. 601   1 March   **Approved by God**
Ecclus. 15:1–6; Ps. 16; 1 Thess. 2:2–12;
Matthew 16:24–27

'Just as we have been approved by God to be entrusted with the message of the Gospel, even so we speak, not to please mortals, but to please God who tests our hearts.' 1 Thessalonians 2:5

Entrusted with the gospel
David (Dewi) was born around AD 520, the son of the Celtic chieftain Sant and the religious St Non. He was priested, and studied under St Paulinus, whose blindness (said to have been caused by excessive weeping) David cured.

At that time, Pelagianism – an unhealthily liberal brand of heresy – was growing in Britain, and David was stout in his fight against it. A strict ascetic, his diet consisted of bread, salt and leeks – the latter was to become his symbol. He was active in founding monasteries, but the turning-point in his ministry came when, with St Deiniol and St Dubricius, he attended a Synod at Brefi, in Cardigan, and spoke out publicly against heresies in general and Pelagianism in particular. His opinion carried so much weight that Dubricius resigned as Primate of the Cambrian Church, in favour of David.

An episcopal move
David immediately moved his episcopal seat from Caerleon to Mynyw (now St David's), where in the monastery he was to die *c.* 601, his relics later being transferred to the cathedral.

'From one to whom much has been given, much will be required,' Jesus told his friends. 'And from one to whom much has been entrusted, even more will be demanded' (Luke 12:48). As Christians we could not have been entrusted with anything more precious than the word of God: how we study it, learn it, cherish it, put it to work in our lives and share it with others is an indication of how much we value this trust. Each week on average over the past sixty or so years, someone is asked: 'What would you take to a desert island, assuming you had the Bible and Shakespeare already?' It seems rather an unusual question: surely we could exist quite well without Shakespeare – and surely if we have the Bible we need nothing else.

David, like many other saints whose lives we study as the year advances, had a prominent position in the Church; and he used it to full advantage – not for his own aggrandisement or luxury, but for the spiritual and material benefit of others: as St Paul says, 'to please God, who tests our hearts'. Whether God's testing is traumatic, painful, exhilarating or joyful, it is designed for one purpose: to further our spiritual growth and, through our growing, the growth of others. We may seem to be stretched in several ways at the same time – just as David was, in parochial, local matters; in the founding of monasteries over much of his country; and in arguing in high synodical theological debates, where decisions were being made which could affect thousands of people in many churches for years, even centuries, to come. If, at such times as these, we are tempted to take our eyes off the power of Christ, and to focus instead on the weakness and inadequacy of ourselves, like St Peter when he floundered on the water, we shall sink at the thought of our own unworthiness (Matthew 14:30). May God give us strength to fix our attention on him.

Suggested hymns
Fierce raged the tempest; Fierce was the wild billow; Guide me, O thou great Redeemer; O Jesus, I have promised.

St Chad, Bishop of Lichfield, Missionary 672
2 March The Missionary Bishop Ecclus. 3:17–24; Ps. 84; 1 Tim. 6:11b–16; Luke 14:7–11
'Fight the good fight of faith; take hold of the eternal life to which you were called and for which you made the good confession in the presence of many witnesses.' 1 Timothy 6:12

Called to high office

St Chad is a man from whom we have a lot to learn. The British churches of the seventh century were facing in many ways a situation similar to the one we are facing today. Small, scattered communities were threatened by successive waves of Anglo-Saxons bent on trouble. Some fled to the Welsh mountains, to escape the flak: others stayed to combat it. Chad was born into an exciting time for the Church in Britain.

He was a pupil of St Aidan, on Lindisfarne (Holy Island), and showed a remarkable aptitude for religious studies. When Cedd, Abbot of Lastingham and Chad's eldest brother, died, Chad succeeded him as abbot. Soon after this, he was made Bishop of York. But then loomed another problem: a combative, forceful character named Wilfrid had been consecrated Bishop of York in France. Wilfrid returned to England – and the Church here was faced with two bishops of York! Theodore, who had recently arrived as Archbishop of Canterbury, solved the problem by declaring Chad's appointment 'irregular'. With dignity and humility, Chad accepted the decision and retired back to Lastingham.

A bishop for Mercia

He was not allowed to rusticate in the peace of Lastingham for long. The King of Mercia, Wulfhere, applied to Theodore to find a bishop for his area, and Theodore consecrated Chad the new Bishop of Mercia and Lindisfarne. In a pretty little town called Lyciddfelth (Lichfield) Chad established his see: it extended over a wide area – and still does, though other dioceses have since been carved out of it.

A humble prelate

Chad saw himself not as an administrator, hedged about in an office with reams of paper, but as a missionary bishop, walking miles to visit his various congregations. Theodore strongly objected to this, holding that it befitted a bishop's office to ride on horseback. In Chad's cathedral at Lichfield today can be seen a roundel illustrating Theodore setting Chad off on a mission – on horseback!

One day, Chad was praying beside a pool in a forest clearing close by the cathedral. A startled deer ran out of the trees, drank at the pool and sped off into another part of the forest. A little time later, a huntsman burst out of the forest and demanded of

Chad where the deer had gone. It was Wulfhade, the non-believing son of Wulfhere. 'The deer came, only so that I could speak to you of Christ,' Chad replied, gently. 'I'd rather have the deer than religion,' Wulfhade snapped. Chad immediately began to pray – and from the trees across the water, the deer reappeared. Wulfhade was so overcome by this answer to the saint's prayer that he knelt before Chad and asked for baptism.

When plague swept through Mercia in 672, Chad was among hundreds who died. He had been at Lichfield for only two-and-a-half years.

A good teacher
Chad had been privileged to have a wonderful teacher in St Aidan. Thanks to the Venerable Bede, we too can share some of his wisdom:

> Teach them to fill their lives with deep, meaningful affirmations about God and his world. Let the words be loud on their lips, the very vibrations give them strength. Teach 'Marana tha' – 'Come, Lord Jesus'. Encourage them to say it morning and evening – not to bring him down, but to lift themselves up.
>
> *Bede*, A History of the English Church and People

Chad knew what it was to accept a challenge, but who would deny that the missionary bishop from Lindisfarne made good?

Suggested hymns
A charge to keep I have; Fill thou my life, O Lord my God; In full and glad surrender; To the God of our salvation.

St Patrick, Bishop, Missionary, Patron of Ireland *c.* 460   17 March
Going Back – and Forward   Isa. 51:1–11; Ps. 96; Rev. 22:1–5; Matthew 10:16–23

'When they persecute you in one town, flee to the next; for truly I tell you, you will not have gone through all the towns of Israel before the Son of Man comes.' Matthew 10:23

Born an Englishman

Patrick was born in England: some say in Cumberland, others in the Welsh Marches; one tradition even goes north of the border, to the Clyde. But he was not Irish. Born around 389, he was kidnapped by raiders in 406 and taken to Ireland, where he was kept as a cattle-hand. He escaped in a ship taking dogs to France, where he trained for the priesthood. He then felt called to return to the land of his slavery, and began evangelizing the Irish. Life did not go smoothly. He was constantly under pressure, even animosity, from the English clergy; and he struggled in vain to adopt the parochial system which he had seen work so well in France. Ireland was a different country, largely rural; and the Irish did not want what they saw as the rigidity of the French system.

So Patrick toiled hard, often for little to show for his efforts. He travelled almost constantly from town to town, like the disciples whom Jesus sent out (Luke 10). In or around the year 460, he is thought to have died at Saul, on Strangford Lough, where he had built the first of his churches.

St Patrick's Purgatory

On Saints' Island, Lough Derg, in County Donegal, are the ruins of what is believed to be a church founded by St Beoc, who lived at roughly the same time as Patrick. His church was known as St Patrick's Purgatory, and became an important centre for prayer; today pilgrims still come to the site.

It is possible to feel a great sadness as one walks through the ruins of what were once towering monasteries and churches: a feeling even of desperation can set in. Where is the Church of today going? Has the craftsmanship and beauty of centuries past gone for nothing? Many abbeys fell at the Dissolution: was the despoliation, the rapacious seizing of assets, the stripping of the altars, worth it? Should we rebuild the great monastic houses, and use them (if not exactly as before) as Christian colleges, mission houses, even Christian conference centres? (In fact, all these uses were often incorporated in their former days of glory.) Is the Devil mocking us, as we gaze up at the glassless rose windows, the rooms open to the sky, the fallen masonry?

Such questions have been exercising the Church for years, yet what has been done about the messages that these once-glorious buildings give to people, in 2004?

The churches that Patrick and his successors founded are also mainly in ruins; yet the gospel he took to Ireland lives on – in new churches where people worship, and in the hearts of so many that Patrick would surely feel today that all his labours were worthwhile.

> *Father of all those far-scattered sheep of Christ.*
> *Wherein sad Erin hath the mother's claim,*
> *Lo! fourteen centuries*
> *And shores of all the seas*
> *Music make to God in thy mighty name.*
>
> *Thy God is theirs, O Patrick, the living God,*
> *Comfort and crown of thine unfriended youth,*
> *Bringing thy prison-land*
> *Thrall to thy croziered hand*
> *In the bright allegiance of holy truth.*
>
> *Love for the souls of Erin's benighted sons*
> *Broke thy great heart and killed thy cloistered peace,*
> *Till every sobbing gale*
> *Sung thee the Irish wail,*
> *Pleading with the night for the day's release.*

J. O'Connor

Suggested hymns
For all the saints who from their labours rest; Hail, glorious Saint Patrick, dear saint of our isle; Jerusalem the golden; O Patrick, hail, who once the wandering race.

St Joseph of Nazareth 19 March
The Silent Carpenter 2 Sam. 7:4–16; Ps. 89:27–36; Rom. 4:13–18; Matthew 1:18–25

'An angel of the Lord appeared to [Joseph] in a dream, and said, "Joseph, son of David, do not be afraid to take Mary as your wife, for the child conceived in her is from the Holy Spirit."' Matthew 1:20

Not a word

We hear not a single word from him, the silent carpenter of Nazareth who is, to all intents and purposes, to be the father of Mary's child. He will play his part, looking after Mary and the little one, until, at some point before Jesus is 30, Joseph's passing will leave Mary to carry on alone.

Joseph must have been the type of person it is good to know: mindful of God's instructions, he stands by Mary, though he could not have understood why or how she was pregnant. He must have struggled to find her a suitable place at Bethlehem for the birth – and at least they had a roof over their heads. Obedient once more, Joseph took his family away from Herod's paranoia, and 250 miles into Egypt – and back. Did he wonder what was happening? Of course he must have wondered – but he obeyed that still, small voice.

Of David's line

The evangelists Matthew and Luke have traced the genealogy of Joseph up and down the line of David. This, and Mary's simple acceptance of him as Jesus' 'father' (Luke 2:48), are indications that in God's eyes Joseph was fulfilling a special role, if not quite as special as that of Mary. Other than this, we know nothing more about this enigmatic carpenter – though, perhaps predictably, there are many unsubstantiated legends.

In Joseph's shoes

Had we been in Joseph's shoes, would we have kept such a low profile? Do we in fact resist any temptation to inflate our image, or are we more eager to affirm and encourage others? Joseph had quietly nurtured Mary and Jesus, until, his work completed, God took him home. We believe that St Luke derived material for his Gospel from Mary (who else would have such an intimate knowledge of the birth stories?); we don't know whether she was also instrumental in the account of Joseph's vision of Matthew 1, and the visit of the Magi in Matthew 2 – but is it not strange that she apparently recalled no word there from Joseph? We may reverently – if with a little smile – wonder if Mary was the talkative one and Joseph the strong, silent type! We may remember, also, that until the birth of John the Baptist, Zechariah was silent.

Faithfulness
But it is the undeniable faithfulness of Joseph that we commemorate today; faithfulness in believing what he could not understand; faithfulness in calmly going on even when Simeon prophesied that tragedy would overtake Mary (Luke 2:35). Could Joseph sense the storm clouds gathering, even as Simeon cradled the child Jesus in his arms? We may reverently wonder, also, why God intervened and took Joseph to glory, before the ministry of Jesus began. Was it so that Jesus could refer to his 'proper' Father, without causing confusion among his listeners? His home-town neighbours caused their own confusion when they reminded Jesus of who (they thought) he was, and where (they thought) he came from (Luke 4:22): 'Is not this Joseph's son?'

Perhaps, in glory, Joseph heard, and felt a father's pride.

Suggested hymns
Come, sing with holy gladness; Hail, holy Joseph, hail!; Joseph, pure spouse of that immortal Bride; Joseph, the scriptures love to trace.

Annunciation of our Lord to the Blessed Virgin Mary 25 March God of the Impossible
Isa. 7:10–14; Ps. 40:5–10; Heb. 10:4–10; Luke 1:26–38

'"For nothing will be impossible with God." Then Mary said, "Here am I, the servant of the Lord; let it be with me according to your word." Then the angel departed from her.' Luke 1:37–38

The 'fiat'
Fiat voluntas tua, sicut in caelo et in terra, we pray in the Paternoster every day; and Mary's own fiat set in motion the divine conception of the Saviour of the world. Did she know to what she was committing herself? Almost certainly, no; but she was prepared to let God have his will with her. He is asking for the same from us: not to conceive the Saviour – that has already been done – but to be willing to let him work out his purposes in and through us, whatever that may entail. We are used to the ways of the world, where elaborate contracts are drawn up, ostensibly with every eventuality covered. We sign them and then (not in all cases, but

in sufficient to make it a lucrative business) certain professionals go to work searching for loopholes and get-out clauses; and sometimes we discover that the paper on which all the printing has been done could more profitably and honourably have been used for something else. God doesn't work like that: his contract has been signed with the personal, uncontrovertible, absolutely honest blood of Jesus. It doesn't deal in innumerable finite benefits, but in the dual blessings of short-term constant guidance, and long-term eternity – and one cannot have a longer-term provision than that.

A humble virgin

Suppose the Saviour had not come; suppose God had given notice of his coming in 2004 and had handed the arrangements over to humanity. Just imagine the committees, councils and synods we should convene to plan the operation! Think of the legal, economic and social problems we should invent as being terribly, terribly necessary! God simply sent an angel to a humble virgin and announced the news in the most low-key manner possible. And Mary, taking her cue from Gabriel, didn't rush out to tell all and sundry, but quickly set out over the hills to spend three months in helping her cousin Elizabeth as the latter neared her delivery of John the Baptist.

And so today

God is working in the same way today – quietly, without a fuss, his purposes are carrying on. We may wonder why wonderful healings and resurrections are not making world headlines – yet they certainly make an impact among their local communities. A Christian conference has a healing session in which a girl is healed of deafness in one ear. Remarkable? Yes, because the physical structures for hearing in that ear had been absent from birth. She is examined by doctors after the miracle, and the X-rays prove that she still has no equipment with which to hear in that ear! Does the miracle make national news? No! War in the Holy Land is dominating the headlines.

Around 25 March, in the year of Gabriel's visit, we should doubtless have scanned the 'Nazareth Telegraph' in vain for news of Mary's annunciation.

But it happened, that's for sure.

For Mary, mother of our Lord; I'll sing a hymn to Mary; Jesus, good above all other; O purest of creatures, Sweet Mother, sweet Maid.

St George, Martyr, Patron of England *c.* 304
23 April **The Dragon-Killer** 1 Macc. 2:59–64 or Rev. 12:7–12; Ps. 126; 2 Tim. 2:3–13; John 15:18–21

'Therefore I endure everything for the sake of the elect, so that they may also obtain the salvation that is in Christ Jesus, with eternal glory. The saying is sure: If we have died with him, we will also live with him; if we endure, we will also reign with him; if we deny him, he will also deny us; if we are faithless, he remains faithful – for he cannot deny himself.' 2 Timothy 2:10–13

Lost in legend
'St George of England' has a prominence today that suggests a well-documented history, but we actually know next to nothing for certain of our patron saint. It seems likely that he suffered martyrdom in the persecution prior to Constantine's conversion. According to legend, he was a Cappadocian knight, riding one day through Sylene, he found a community in crisis – a dragon had terrorized the neighbourhood, eating its way through a couple of sheep each day when it couldn't feed on human flesh. Attempts had been made to kill it, but the breath of the beast was so dreadful that no one could get close enough. When George arrived on the scene, the supply of sheep had dried up, and the king's own daughter had been prepared for sacrifice. George told the king that he would slay the dragon, on condition that the population of Sylene converted to Christianity. The king agreed, and George speared the beast with his lance, saved the princess – and thousands of Sylenians were baptized.

Some believe that the Crusaders brought the cult of St George back to England, but his fame was brought here before the Norman conquest. 'St George's Day' was included in the list of lesser holidays at a synod in Oxford in 1222. It was elevated to a 'chief feast' in 1415, on Archbishop Chichele's authority; and by the seventeenth and eighteenth centuries it was a 'feast of obligation' for English Catholics, George being recognized by Benedict XIV as 'Protector of the Kingdom'.

Test of endurance
'I endure everything for the sake of the elect,' Paul had told Timothy (with justification): a good text on which to reflect as we commemorate the brave St George. Not that the Christian life is one of unadulterated endurance – God wants us to 'delight' in doing his will, and certainly he gives us many blessings as cause for joy; but without the stamina and stickability of endurance, we should not get very far along the way to God.

Endurance is required of us in many situations. We're unlikely to be faced with a man-eating dragon – but danger to the soul is no less real today than in the time of St Paul or St George. Let us pray for grace to trust the God who, when our faith falters, remains faithful because he cannot deny himself.

Suggested hymns
And did those feet in ancient times; I vow to thee, my country; O faith of England, taught of old; O God, our help in ages past.

St Mark the Evangelist 26 April (transferred from 25th) **It's Up To Us!** Prov. 15:28–33 or Acts 15:35–41; Ps. 119:9–16; Eph. 4:7–16; Mark 13: 5–13

'[Jesus said], "And you will be hated by all because of my name. But the one who endures to the end will be saved."' Mark 13:13

Personal stamina
The 'endurance' that Jesus is talking about here is sheer, gutsy spiritual stamina. No one can endure for us: it's a personal matter between ourselves and God – but in this combination lies our hope (the only hope we've got), that God's Holy Spirit will supply the extra 'oomph!' we need to make it to eternity. St Mark knew this sort of stamina: as a young lad he had been in Gethsemane on the night of the arrest (Mark 14:51–52); and after the resurrection and ascension, his mother's house was one of the places where Christians met for worship, prayer and fellowship in Jerusalem (Acts 12:12). Mark was a Levite and a Cypriot, related to Barnabas

– so it was inevitable that Paul would meet up with him sooner or later. When he and Barnabas went on a mission to Cyrpus, Mark joined them, but after the two senior apostles had journeyed to Perga in Pamphylia, for some reason Mark left them and returned to Jerusalem. Paul saw this as desertion, but Barnabas disagreed with him, and on a later journey parted company with Paul and took Mark again to Cyprus. By the time that Paul was in prison (Colossians 4:10), Mark is reunited with him – and again, from his final house imprisonment in Rome, Paul writes to Timothy at Ephesus, asking for both Timothy and Mark to come to him.

Peter's secretary
This Mark is generally regarded as being the author of the second Gospel, and his association with St Peter is borne out by Irenaeus, Papias and Clement of Alexandria, according to the church historian Eusebius of Caesarea:

> This also the elder used to say, Mark, indeed, having been the interpreter of Peter, wrote accurately, howbeit not in order, all that he recalled of what was either said or done by the Lord. For he neither heard the Lord, nor was he a follower of his, but, at a later date (as I said), of Peter; who used to adapt his instructions to the needs [of the moment], but not with a view to putting together the Dominical oracles in orderly fashion; so that Mark did no wrong in this, writing some things as he recalled them. For he kept a single aim in view: not to omit anything of what he heard, nor to state anything therein falsely.
> *Eusebius*, Historia Ecclesiastica III.39.15

It is surprising that neither Clement of Alexandria nor Origen mentions Mark in connection with Alexandria, yet tradition holds that Mark became bishop there after several years of ministry. And it appears that early in the ninth century the relics of Mark were brought from Alexandria to Venice. Whether those in St Mark's Cathedral are St Mark's is unproven; but he has been honoured as Venice's patron saint for at least twelve centuries.

The second Gospel
Second in position in the New Testament canon, Mark's Gospel is actually the earliest of the four. It is written in unpolished Greek,

moves quickly, and has the hallmarks of eye-witness testimony – which would support the claim that Mark was instrumental in getting Peter's reminiscences into writing. It is also quite short enough to be read at a sitting – and many Christians have done just this, on St Mark's Day.

Suggested hymns
A Man there lived in Galilee; Hills of the north, rejoice; Lord, thy word abideth; Tell out, my soul, the greatness of the Lord.

SS Philip and James, Apostles   1 May
The Gospel of Your Salvation   Isa. 30:15–21;
Ps. 119:1–8; Eph. 1:3–14 (extended); John 14:1–14

'In [Christ] you also, when you had heard the word of truth, the gospel of your salvation, and had believed in him, were marked with the seal of the promised Holy Spirit; this is the pledge of our inheritance towards redemption as God's own people, to the praise of his glory.' Ephesians 1:13–14

Dedication
Who were these two apostles (known to Londoners as 'Pip 'n' Jay', from the famous church that bears their name)? They were in the elect Twelve, constantly with Jesus – and yet we know so little about them. Theirs was a dedication to Christ's gospel of salvation, which put their Lord first and themselves nowhere. Perhaps they had also been disciples of John the Baptist, who inculcated in his followers the policy: 'He [Jesus] must increase, but I must decrease' (John 3:30).

Philip
The Gospels give us snippets of information about Philip: he brought the rather cynical Nathanael to Jesus (John 1:43f.). He himself came from Bethsaida, and presumably already knew Andrew and Peter. He introduced the lad with his loaves and fishes to Jesus, at the feeding of the five thousand; and it was Philip's request to be shown the Father that encouraged Jesus' teaching on the oneness of the Father and the Son (John 14:8ff.).

Tradition has it that Philip was a fisherman and the father of three daughters. After the ascension, he is thought to have taken the gospel to Phrygia, where he suffered martyrdom by being crucified upside down.

Eusebius of Caesarea, writing on the Easter (Quartodeciman) Controversy, records:

> As for us then, we keep the day without tampering with it, neither adding nor subtracting. For indeed in Asia great luminaries have fallen asleep, such as shall rise again on the day of the Lord's appearing, when he comes with glory from heaven to seek out all his saints: to wit, Philip, one of the twelve apostles, who has fallen asleep in Hierapolis, [as have] also his two daughters who grew old in virginity, and his other daughter who lived in the Holy Spirit and rests at Ephesus.
>
> *Eusebius*, Historia Ecclesiastica *V.24.2*

James

Known as 'James the Less', to distinguish him from James the brother of John, this James was the son of Alphaeus. He could also have been 'James the Younger', whose mother Mary witnessed the crucifixion (Mark 15:40).

While the Lord's second coming was believed to be imminent, there was little or no interest in recording lesser names with pride. Today we are much closer to his coming, yet the world's emphasis on CVs and profiles and 'information technology', its preoccupation with finding out as much as possible about seemingly everyone, has apparently rubbed off in some places into the Church, and few are permitted (or want) to do, say or write anything without identity being acknowledged, often with trumpets. While there is still some polish left, can we take a leaf out of 'Pip 'n' Jay's' book, and set about shining up the Name of Christ instead?

Suggested hymns

Great is thy faithfulness; Just as I am; Thy way, not mine, O Lord; To God be the glory.

St Julian of Norwich, Spiritual Writer
c. 1417   8 May   **Saying 'Yes' to God**
1 Ki. 19:9–13a; Ps. 27; 1 Cor. 13:8–13; John 20:11–18

'Jesus said to [Mary], "Do not hold on to me, because I have not yet ascended to the Father. But go to my brothers and say to them, I am ascending to my Father and your Father, to my God and your God." Mary Magdalene went and announced to the disciples, "I have seen the Lord", and she told them that he had said these things to her.' John 20:17–18

The one thing

'The one thing that matters is that we always say Yes to God whenever we experience him,' Julian said (*Revelations of the Divine Love*). Diagnosed with terminal illness at the age of 30, in 1373, Julian of Norwich (we don't know her real name) received a series of 16 visions dealing with God's love. Her health having been restored, she committed these experiences to writing, in her *Revelations*, which was probably the first book to be written by a woman in English.

> Our Lord showed me a little thing, the quantity of a hazel nut, in the palm of my hand, and it was as round as a ball. I looked thereupon with the eye of my understanding, and thought, 'What may this be?' And it was answered generally thus: 'It is all that is made.' I marvelled how it might last, for methought it might suddenly have fallen to nought for littleness. And I was answered in my understanding, 'It lasteth and ever shall last for that God loveth it. And so All-thing hath Being by the love of God.' In this little thing I saw three properties. The first is that God made it, the second that God loveth it, the third that God keepeth it.
>
> *Julian of Norwich*, Revelations, V

At some point in her life, we are not sure whether it was before or after writing her *Revelations*, Julian took up residence in a cell attached to the Church of St Julian at Norwich, arranging for the door to be sealed. Until her death, in or around the year 1417, she accepted food and the bare necessities of life through the cell's one small window – to which also many would come to receive help and advice.

It was a way of saying 'Yes' to God, which would not have appealed to many others: certainly not to Mary Magdalene, who in early days had sought a freedom of morality; and after conversion – as her flight from the tomb to find the disciples showed – valued her physical agility and freedom.

There are many ways of following Jesus, and if the way for Mother Julian was self-imposed incarceration in a small cell, who are we to criticize? In fact, we shall stand in danger of inconsistency if, when we feel God's warm sun on our heads, and the resilience of his grass under our feet, we take our physical freedom for granted. Julian found much to do, many people to see, much to discuss with God, from her tiny cell. Are we sure that we are making the most of our freedom in saying 'Yes' to God?

Suggested hymns
All my hope on God is founded; It is well with my soul (When peace like a river); I've got peace like a river; Jesus calls us, o'er the tumult.

St Matthias the Apostle   14 May
The Lot Fell on Matthias   Isa. 22:15–25; Ps. 15;
Acts 1:15–26; John 15:9–17

'[Jesus said], "You did not choose me, but I chose you. And I appointed you to go and bear fruit, fruit that will last, so that the Father will give you whatever you ask him in my name. I am giving you these commands so that you may love one another."' John 15:16–17

A humble novitiate
Judas' defection left a gap in the Twelve, which after Jesus' ascension the disciples sought to fill. The criteria for selection were that each candidate must have served a 'novitiate' of having been in the wider mission team of Jesus since its inception, and had seen him since his resurrection. Matthias and Joseph Barsabbas were eligible – and the lot fell on Matthias (Acts 1:26). This is practically all we know of Matthias, apart from a tradition that he suffered martyrdom by an axe on the shores of the Caspian Sea, and a reference to him by Clement of Alexandria:

He, then, who has first moderated his passions and trained himself for impossibility, and developed to the beneficence of gnostic perfection, is here equal to the angels. Luminous already, and like the sun shining in the exercise of beneficence, he speeds by righteous knowledge through the love of God to the sacred abode, like as the apostles. Not that they became apostles through being chosen for some distinguished peculiarity of nature, since also Judas was chosen along with them. But they were capable of becoming apostles on being chosen by him who foresees even ultimate issues. Matthias, accordingly, who was not chosen along with them, on showing himself worthy of becoming an apostle, is substituted for Judas.

Clement, Stromateis, *VI.105.1*

Still God's choice

Why, one may ask, was it so important to bring the number of apostles back up to twelve? Presumably so that they could in glory sit on twelve thrones judging the twelve tribes of Israel (Matthew 19:28; Luke 22:30). And, mindful of Jesus' caution: 'You did not choose me, but I chose you', the matter was decided by lot, so that it could be said that God still made the choice.

God is still exercising his right to choose: not only on the question of who will follow him, but of how he will guide us on to glory; the individual talents he gives us; the unique opportunities he brings knocking on our door; our friends and colleagues; our joys, and our times of testing. All these are not of our choosing, however at times we may try to persuade ourselves (and others) that we are the masters of our destiny.

In the casting of those lots, one man would be chosen, and one would not. We may reverently pray today for Joseph Barsabbas, as well as for Matthias – Joseph, who equally faithfully had been a part of Jesus' ministry and had seen the resurrected Christ. His mission would continue, please God, even though the lot had not fallen his way.

Suggested hymns

Breathe on me, breath of God; Come and see the shining hope; Strengthen for service, Lord, the hands; Thy way, not mine, O Lord.

John and Charles Wesley, Evangelists, Hymn-Writers 1791 and 1788   24 May
Making the Most of the Time   Ezek. 2:1–3; Ps. 33; Eph. 5:15–20; Mark 6:30–34

'Be careful then how you live, not as unwise people but as wise, making the most of the time, because the days are evil.' Ephesians 5:15

Two businessmen of God
Born at Epworth Rectory, John and Charles grew up in a large family. Their father was an Anglican clergyman, their mother a Puritan. Susannah was a loving but strict disciplinarian, and had many quaint ways. One which the children quickly got to know was that whenever she wanted to pray, she would sit in a certain chair, and calmly and deliberately draw her voluminous apron over her head: Mother was then communing with God, and everyone else in the house must be quiet.

John Wesley: Anglican cleric
After university, John was ordained in the Anglican Church, but the parochial system in which his father had served was not to his son's liking: John saw the whole country as his parish, travelling many miles by coach, on horseback and on foot, preaching in the open air wherever he could find people ready to listen. His was a message of salvation by grace, fellowship in the Eucharist and a steady, ordered growth in holiness. At no time did he urge people to leave the Anglican Church – though after his death hundreds of Methodist chapels were built.

Both brothers sailed to Georgia, but the trip did not turn out as they had expected. As they returned to England, John became friendly with Peter Böhler, one of the group of Moravians on board. He was most impressed with the quiet dedication of these believers. Soon afterwards, he went through a very dark time of self-doubt and spiritual darkness, recorded with touching honesty in his *Journal*. He came to the conclusion that many in his congregations had considerably more faith than he had himself. Whatever was he to do? Providentially, he met up again with Böhler, and asked the Moravian's advice. Böhler did not hesitate: 'On no account neglect the gift that God appears to have given you,' he told Wesley. 'Preach until you have faith – and then preach because you have it!' This counsel, and Wesley's so-called 'second conversion', when he was 'strangely warmed' at Aldersgate, set him back firmly on course, with renewed energy and zeal.

Charles Wesley
Charles' ministry was based at first in Bristol and afterwards in London. He was more of a hymn-writer than a preacher, composing over six thousand hymns, many of which we still enjoy today. When he was dying, John came to see him and asked how Charles felt about the prospect. 'It will be all activity,' smiled Charles, and soon afterwards reached the Great Crossroads. His words have given hope and resolution to many nearing that same point.

We celebrate both men today: busy businessmen for God, who knew how to use time to the full for their Lord. Would they have approved of the breach which many people subsequently made with the Anglican Church? Probably not – but they would surely take delight in the current trend of the two churches coming more closely together for worship and fellowship.

Suggested hymns (all Charles Wesley's)
And can it be; Jesus, the Name high over all; Love Divine, all loves excelling; Rejoice, the Lord is king.

The Venerable Bede, Monk at Jarrow, Scholar, Historian 735   25 May   Recorder of History
Ecclus. 39:1–10; Ps. 78; 1 Cor. 1:18–25; John 21:20–25

'[The scribe] seeks out the wisdom of all the ancients, and is concerned with prophecies; he preserves the sayings of the famous, and penetrates the subtleties of parables . . . Many will praise his understanding: it will never be blotted out. His memory will not disappear, and his name will live through all generations.' Ecclesiasticus 39:1–2, 9

Ecclesiastical historian
From the ninth century, Bede has been known as the 'Venerable', in tribute to his holiness. His was no itinerant ministry; instead, he spent practically the whole of his life in the monasteries at Wearmouth and Jarrow. Nor was it a long life, for he died, on

Ascension Day, 735, at the age of 63. Yet his monumental *History* is a classic of Christian literature. A grammarian and scientist, Bede resisted the trend of his day to 'miraculize' the honest truth; and his *Lives* of English churchmen are models of down-to-earth reportage. Bede remarked:

> If history records good things of good men, the thoughtful hearer is encouraged to imitate what is good: or if it records evil of wicked men, the good, religious listener or reader is encouraged to avoid all that is sinful and perverse, and to follow what he knows to be good and pleasing to God.

Bede surely bids fair to be the most prolific of English church writers. He divided his time between commentaries on the Bible, church history, biography, science and poetry, and his books total over sixty. He writes:

> I was born on the lands of this monastery (i.e. Jarrow), and on reaching seven years of age, I was entrusted by my family first to the most reverend Abbot Benedict and later to Abbot Ceolfrith for my education. I have spent all the remainder of my life in this monastery and devoted myself entirely to the study of the scriptures. And while I have observed the regular discipline and sung the choir offices daily in church, my chief delight has always been in study, teaching and writing. I was ordained deacon in my nineteenth year, and priest in my thirtieth, receiving both these orders at the hand of the most reverend Bishop John at the direction of Abbot Ceolfrith. From the time of my receiving the priesthood until my fifty-ninth year, I have worked, both for my own benefit and that of my brethren, to compile short extracts from the works of the venerable Fathers on Holy Scripture and to comment on their meaning and interpretation.
>
> *Bede*, A History of the English Church and People

'Father of the Middle Ages'

Known in Germany as 'Father of the Middle Ages', Bede had an influence that was remarkable for a man who it is thought probably travelled no further north than Holy Island (Lindisfarne) and no further south than York. Our own road of life may be long or short: the distance is immaterial. What matters, is how we spend the time God gives us.

Suggested hymns
Amazing grace; Like a mighty river flowing; O Lord my God, when I in awesome wonder; Oh, the love of my Lord is the essence.

St Augustine, First Archbishop of Canterbury
605   26 May   Canterbury's First Archbishop
Isa. 49: 22–25; Ps. 98; 1 Thess. 2:2b–8;
Matthew 13:31–33

'We had courage in our God to declare to you the gospel of God in spite of great opposition ... just as we have been approved by God to be entrusted with the message of the gospel, even so we speak not to please mortals, but to please God who tests our hearts.' 1 Thessalonians 2:2, 4

Sent on a mission
In 596, Pope Gregory sent Augustine, with 40 monks from the monastery of St Andrew in Rome, to England. The company got as far as Provence when, discouraged by rumours of the wild Anglo-Saxons, the monks persuaded Augustine to return to Rome with a request to Gregory to abort the mission. But Gregory had been told that the harvest-ground of England was ready for the gospel, and sent Augustine back to his monks with words of encouragement that gave them fresh heart. They arrived in Kent around Eastertide, 597, to be met by King Ethelbert who had married the Catholic Frankish princess, Bertha. Before long, Ethelbert converted to Christianity and was baptized.

The see of Canterbury
Augustine sailed back to France, where St Vergilius, the Metropolitan of Arles, consecrated him bishop. He set up his see at Canterbury – Gregory would have preferred London, but on this Augustine stood firm. He began evangelizing the Anglo-Saxons, being well briefed from Rome on the details: don't sack the pagan temples; consecrate them and use them as Christian churches,

ordered Gregory. And don't play around with the calendar: convert the pagan festivals into Christian ones.

Augustine became so busy that he sent a couple of monks, Peter and Lawrence, back to Rome for reinforcements. Gregory sent them back with the saints Mellitus, Justus and Paulinus; with more and more instructions on mission – and with the pallium: Augustine was to be the first Archbishop of Canterbury!

Episcopal conservatism

But it was not all plain sailing for the new archbishop. The English bishops had evolved their own methods – due mainly to England being separated by the Channel from the rest of Europe. Augustine called them to a synod in an attempt to persuade them to come fully into line with European church practice. The bishops deliberated, but at a second synod, where Augustine angered them by not rising to greet them, they refused point blank to recognize his authority. Undeterred, Augustine and his monks continued evangelizing, and established sees at London and Rochester.

On 26 May 605, eight years after arriving in England, Augustine died – with the stubborn English bishops still refusing to help him in his mission to convert the Anglo-Saxons; still refusing to adopt the Roman tradition of baptism; and still refusing to go along with the Roman method of determining the date of Easter.

But this 'good and faithful servant' had made his mark: the Church in England was far stronger than when he had landed in Kent in 597.

We may not be the Primate of All England, but can we say that we are making a difference for God, in the place where he has put us?

Suggested hymns

For ever with the Lord; I will go in the strength of the Lord; Lord of all hopefulness; Lord, the light of your love is shining.

Visit of the Blessed Virgin Mary to Elizabeth

Magnificat   31 May   Zeph. 3:14–18; Ps. 113; Rom. 12:9–16; Luke 1:39–49[50–56]

'And Mary said, "My soul magnifies the Lord, and my spirit rejoices in God my Saviour, for he has looked with favour on the lowliness of his servant. Surely, from now on all generations will call me blessed, for the Mighty One has done great things for me, and holy is his name."'
Luke 1:46–49

How great is God!

The Magnificat is a very personal hymn, yet Mary manages to make it unselfishly a paean of praise, magnifying the greatness and goodness of God. Her own news, brought by Gabriel, had sent her hurrying over to see Elizabeth – and the sharing of the women's happiness brought the first rejoicing of John, while still in his mother's womb. In ecstasy, Mary sings, little thinking, perhaps, that her song would go round the world.

While choirs of angels sang in heaven, just two women celebrated on earth. It was how the great and good God had planned. Slowly, so slowly, the salvation of the world was beginning.

The visit that meant so much

Mary could have stayed at home, hugging her good news to herself. She could have gone to Joseph – but what would she have said? But Gabriel had mentioned Elizabeth's own good news – and, thus prompted, Mary set out on the visit that would mean so much for them both. In these times of telephone, fax and Internet, we tend not to visit in person as often as we used to – and something precious is thereby lacking in our lives. We miss the shared smiles, and sometimes tears; the chats over coffee, the children running in and out, the sunshine in someone else's garden ... Visits are not reproducible on the Net or the telephone.

There are hospitals and nursing homes, where some of the patients receive no visits from one year to the next; the housebound, the new neighbours, the families who never seem to integrate in the community ... there are even the friends to whom we are quick to say: 'I'll pop round one evening this week!' – and then too often forget. God deals with each of us personally; but have *we* lost 'the personal touch'? Do we 'visit' the TV screen or the computer more than anyone else? Is our door open to callers, or have they other things to do as well?

Staying to help
Mary's was not a five-minute chat. She stayed to help Elizabeth through the older woman's last three months of pregnancy. What a wonderful cousin to have! Our visits to others will probably be nowhere near as long – but perhaps we could offer help with someone's need, someone's emergency? Whether it's doing the ironing or weeding the rose bed, 'helping out' is as valuable and valued as it ever was: it's that simple 'cup of cold water', given in the Name of Jesus (Matthew 10:42; Mark 9:41).

Our knowledge of Mary is little enough: are there not many questions we're ready to ask when we meet her in glory? But today we can give special thanks to God for this precious account of her visit to Elizabeth; it tells us, above everything else, that God chose a beautiful woman to be his Son's mother.

Suggested hymns
Hail, Queen of heaven; I'll sing a hymn to Mary; Mary Immaculate, Star of the morning; O purest of creatures, Sweet Mother, sweet Maid.

Boniface (Wynfrith) of Crediton, Bishop, Apostle of Germany, Martyr 754   5 June
The 'Flying' Bishop   Isa. 49:5–10; Ps. 115;
Acts 20:24–28; Luke 10:1–11

'I do not count my life of any value to myself, if only I may finish my course and the ministry that I received from the Lord Jesus, to testify to the good news of God's grace.' Acts 20:24.

Wynfrith of Crediton
Born Wynfrith (Winfrid) of Crediton, in Devon, in about the year 680, Boniface entered a monastic school near Exeter at the age of seven, and later the Abbey of Nursling, in Winchester diocese, where eventually he became director. He was a brilliant scholar and compiled what is thought to have been the first Latin

Grammar for English students. But his sights were set on Europe: a mission to Friesland in 716 terminated early, and Boniface and his companions returned to Nursling, where, on the death of Abbot Winbert, attempts were made to persuade Boniface to succeed him. He declined the position, and in 718 obtained an audience with Pope Gregory II in Rome, who commissioned him to be virtually a 'flying' bishop, with general authority in mission for Europe; if Gregory didn't cross all the Ts and dot every I, Boniface interpreted the commission as 'general' in the widest sense of the word.

Into Germany
Armed with papal authority, Boniface went to the powerful Charles Martel and obtained a sealed pledge of protection which gave him access as bishop to all the dioceses in Germany. At Geismar, he famously attacked the pride of the pagans – a venerable oak tree. Hardly had Boniface begun chopping, when the great tree crashed to the ground and smashed into four pieces. From the wood, Boniface supervised the construction of a Christian church.

Help from England
As the mission expanded, Boniface sent for reinforcements from England, of both monks and nuns – including St Lull (who eventually succeeded Boniface as Metropolitan at Mainz), St Eoban (who suffered martyrdom with Boniface) and St Wigbert. Among the sisters who came were the saint's learned cousin, St Lioba, and Thecba and Walburga.

One of the monasteries founded by Boniface was at Fulda, where his young protegé St Sturmi stayed for many years. On Gregory II's death in 731, Gregory III was elected to Peter's Chair, and sent Boniface the pallium: our saint was now 'Metropolitan of Germany beyond the Rhine'. As monasteries were founded or extended, Boniface continued to call English monks to take up the abbacies.

Synodical prelate
Charles Martel died in 741, and was succeeded by his sons Pepin and Carloman, under whom Boniface convened several synods, presiding over each and managing to carry through all the reforms that were closest to his heart. The Church in Germany took on a new lease of life.

His end came tragically. While waiting for the arrival of Whitsuntide confirmands at Dokkum, on the River Borne, Boniface's camp was attacked by a band of marauders. The saint's companions wanted to protect him, but he would not allow them. He and Eoban were among those who were killed. His body was taken to his beloved monastery of Fulda, where it remains today. Every time we sing the hymn, 'We have a gospel to proclaim', to the tune called 'Fulda', we can reflect on the bravery of Boniface, who left country and kin for Christ.

Suggested hymns
Fill thou my life, O Lord my God; Lord of all hopefulness; We have a gospel to proclaim, Ye choirs of new Jerusalem.

St Columba, Abbot of Iona, Missionary 597
9 June The Iron Dove Isa. 61:1–3; Ps. 34;
1 Thess. 2:2–12; Luke 12:32–37

'As you know, we dealt with each one of you like a father with his children, urging and encouraging and pleading that you should lead a life worthy of God, who calls you into his own kingdom and glory.'
1 Thessalonians 2:11–12

Of noble birth
Columba ('Dove') was born of noble parents of the royal clan O'Neill, in Donegal. He studied under St Finbar at Moville and St Finnian at Clonard, and was ordained early. He divided his time between preaching and founding monasteries – and in writing poetry and sacred books. Trouble appears to have flared up when the O'Neills objected to Columba's copying of another's work; a lawsuit – probably the first public infringement of copyright – was brought, and Columba so enraged feelings on both sides between King Diarmid and the O'Neills that virtual civil war broke out.

To Scotland
It seemed appropriate to leave for Scotland, where he and 12 companions landed on Iona. The monastery they established on the island was to serve as the base for much of Columba's ministry

among the Scots. The years brought a mellowing of his temper, and he became known as the 'Gentle Dove'. But to the end he was an implacable opponent of the Druids and their pagan beliefs. A breakthrough came when the pagan king of the Picts, Brude, converted to Christianity. Many baptisms followed, and Columba at last began to see some fruits of his labours. A dedicated scholar and able rhetorician, he moved in high as well as lower circles, to the end of his life still finding time to copy books of the Gospels for his monks to use on their preaching missions.

The worth of the monastery
Columba firmly believed in building up the monastic system, seeing in each monastery the ideal base for worship and outreach, ministry and mission. It was a plan that the people of Scotland appeared to accept with great profit. Columba's effort did much to bolster Christianity in Western Europe following the collapse of the Roman empire.

Fire and brimstone
Columba, though he could be so gentle, was no bread-and-butter saint. Forceful, dogmatic, even arrogant, he was of the stuff that was needed to confront the deep-seated paganism of the druidical North. The sheer volume of his work must have meant that Columba spent very little time in sleep. He could be impatient with his monks, yet he maintained a loyal following throughout his ministry. He was *alive* – very human, very fallible, yet totally committed to the work to which he believed God had called him.

Can we really live?
Can we, like Columba, really *live* for God? Can we, like him, unshackle ourselves from the plethora of suffocating caveats and worries about whether we *dare*, or not? One can be so afraid of ruffling anyone's feathers, or rocking the boat – we can use innumerable clichés to mean the same thing. If we 'go for God', as Columba did, we shall make mistakes – yes, and probably make some ripples on the smooth waters of mediocrity – but there's a good chance that we shall do a better job of making God known.

Suggested hymns
Inspired by love and anger; Let me have my way among you; O Jesus, I have promised; Will you come and follow me?

Corpus Christi (Day of Thanksgiving for the Institution of the Holy Eucharist)   10 June
The Body and the Blood   Gen. 14:18–20;
Ps. 116:12–19; 1 Cor. 11:23–26; John 6:51–58

'[Jesus said], "Those who eat my flesh and drink my blood abide in me, and I in them. Just as the living Father sent me, and I live because of the Father, so whoever eats me will live because of me."' John 6:56–57

A comparatively late feast

Corpus Christi has a relatively short history, being adopted in 1247 at Liège, and in Rome not until 1264, when Pope Urban IV promulgated it for the whole Church. Its acceptance was patchy; by 1314 most of the Italian churches had still not taken it on board, though churches further north were observing it. Nowadays, many Anglican churches mark it by special services, though few treat it as the holiday ('holy day') it enjoyed in the later Middle Ages.

Focus on the Eucharist

Sometimes known as the 'Institution of the Eucharist', Corpus Christi focuses our minds on the Last Supper: why Jesus turned the meal in the cenacle, on the night of his arrest, into such a special occasion; why he used such unique terms; and the particular importance that the observance has had ever since in the Church – to the extent that it now forms in many Anglican churches the main service each Sunday, as of course it has for centuries in the Roman Catholic Church.

Why was the meal made special?

It would be the last meal that Jesus would share with the Twelve before his Passion. Even Judas was not excluded. Jesus knew what lay ahead – for himself and for his disciples. They would be tested to the limit: he had to give them something positive to remember for *after* the Pasch. He needed to emphasize not only the memorial, but the sacrifice – knowing that they would not understand at the time, but that his resurrection would make some of it plain, and that his Holy Spirit would supply a deeper understanding in due course.

'My body – my blood'

To Jewish ears, this was sheer anthropomorphism, and shocking in the extreme; yet it was the simple truth. Jesus was not going to float away – immanent, impassive, impersonal, non-human. He was going to give his back to the smiters, his blood to the floggers, for the sins of Everyman. As Everyman's sins had made the sacrifice necessary, Everyman needed to be totally committed to entering into the contract of salvation as intimately as only God could devise. The sin was ours – the terms of redemption, God's. We can take them – or leave them.

The Church's Eucharist

That the Eucharist made an immediate impact on the early Church was hardly surprising. On the actual day of his resurrection, Jesus re-enacted it in part at Emmaus, and then in the upper room. The message: 'Do this in remembrance of me', that had left the disciples on Maundy Thursday perplexed and fearful, suddenly took on its full meaning. The sacrifice had now been made. The memory of it may still hurt, but the 'thanksgiving' ('eucharist') element had now real significance.

Whether we subscribe fully, partially or not at all to the doctrine of transubstantiation, we can surely mingle our understandings of 'sacrifice' and 'memorial' as we accept the bread and wine. Where we go from there is between ourselves and our Lord.

Suggested hymns

And now, O Father, mindful of the love; Author of life divine; Once, only once, and once for all; We hail thy Presence glorious.

St Barnabas the Apostle   11 June
Full of Spirit and Faith   Job 29:11–16; Ps. 112;
Acts 11:19–30; John 15:12–17

'They sent Barnabas to Antioch. When he came and saw the grace of God, he rejoiced, and he exhorted them all to remain faithful to the Lord with steadfast devotion; for he was a good man, full of the Holy Spirit, and of faith.' Acts 11:22–24

The encourager

St Paul, for all his missionary zeal, could not have been the easiest of men with whom to travel. Barnabas and Paul had their differences. But it was Barnabas who first convincingly believed in Paul's conversion, and stood by him when others were doubtful that the arch-persecutor of the Church could change his spots. It was Barnabas who later accompanied Paul to Jerusalem, with donations for the Church; Barnabas who supported Paul in his altercation with Peter over the Gentiles; Barnabas who defended Mark's apparent desertion at Perga, and who took the young Mark with him on his next mission to Cyprus, leaving Paul to recruit Silas and go off in the opposite direction. Paul subsequently seems to have forgiven Mark, but his invitation for Mark to join him at Rome during his last imprisonment presupposes that by AD 60/61 Barnabas has died. According to tradition, he suffered martyrdom by stoning at Salamis, on his native Cyprus.

Patron saint of haymakers

Barnabas is revered as the patron saint of Cyprus, haymakers and harvests, his festival occurring at the peak of the haymaking season. In the old calendar, this day was the longest, warmest and sunniest of the year: it is still known as 'Barnaby Bright' in some areas. Particularly in parts of Cheshire, 'Barnaby Fairs' are still held.

Although not one of the Twelve, Barnabas has quite a high profile in Acts. He began his ministry by selling his entire estate and presenting the money to the Church; from that time forwards, he was a dedicated and disciplined evangelist, allowing Paul the 'pole position' on their joint missions, but also able to take the lead – as, for example, when he took the younger Mark to evangelize on his native island of Cyprus. He was a good man to know, and a dependable companion, encourager and friend. As we celebrate his festival, may we, too, ponder whether God is calling us to lead a mission of any kind – or whether he is asking us to support and encourage someone else. The encouragers of this world are not so numerous that their ranks cannot be enlarged. It is an important ministry, and should never be viewed as being 'low-profile' or 'second fiddle'. If Jesus had intended mission to be a one-man band, he would have operated it himself. The fact that he valued the mutual support of the Twelve, the seventy, friends like Lazarus and his sisters at Bethany, and his mother and her team of women who ministered to his team, suggests the very highest value he placed on supportive, encouraging co-ministers.

It's easy to be a criticizer: much harder to be a Barnabas.

Suggested hymns
Father of heaven, whose love profound; God be in my head; Help us to help each other, Lord; When all thy mercies, O my God.

St Alban, First Martyr of Britain *c.* 250.
22 June   A Soldier-Saint   Wis. 3:1–3; Ps. 63; 2 Tim. 2:3–13; John 12:24–26

'Share in suffering like a good soldier of Christ Jesus. No one serving in the army gets entangled in everyday affairs; the soldier's aim is to please the enlisting officer.' 2 Timothy 2:3–4

A brave man
St Alban was a soldier in the Roman army based at Verulamium (later St Albans), in Hertfordshire. One day, a Christian priest fleeing from persecution asked him for shelter. Alban gave him food and hid him in his house for several days, during which time the priest shared with him the gospel to such effect that Alban was converted and accepted baptism from the fugitive. When the soldiers eventually came to the house searching for the priest, Alban exchanged clothes with him and allowed himself to be arrested and tortured, leaving the priest to escape to safety. Repeatedly, the officers demanded that Alban recant, but he refused and suffered martyrdom by being beheaded. His shrine at St Albans' Cathedral still attracts many pilgrims, and he is seen as the first British martyr.

A fine example
It's a fine example of selfless devotion and commitment. And while Alban was not the first nor the last to save another at the expense of his own life, his sacrifice is no less inspiring for that. One inevitably recalls the similar sacrifice of Maximilian Kolbe, in the Auschwitz concentration camp, in May 1941, when he – the priest – offered himself for death in lieu of a fellow prisoner. On Kolbe's

canonization, in November 1982, Kenneth Woodward called him a new kind of saint – 'a martyr of charity'.

A little every day
Most of us are not called to make such a dramatic sacrifice: instead, as Christians, we die a little every day – to self, to sin, to everything that is anathema to God and which we try to excise from our lives. But, like St Paul, too often we end up doing what we know we shouldn't – and which sincerely we don't want to do – and leaving such a lot of good undone (see Romans 7:19). We rise – to fall – to rise again, and so see-saw our way through life, marvelling that saints like Alban could find such courage to do and dare all. They are surely worthy of our commemoration, for theirs was 'Christ in action'; but we should not get disheartened if our own efforts seem minuscule by comparison. God calls us to die – just a little every day. Until he demands anything more, can we concentrate on doing our best as each new *little* challenge comes? Who knows, one day he may ask for something that really hurts. Remember the plane that did *not* reach New York or Washington on that fateful day of 11 September 2001. Remember the passenger on it who rang home to his wife on his mobile and told her that, as a Christian, he had to do something – and he went forward to the cockpit . . . and the plane crashed in open country. Did he think, at breakfast that morning, that he would give his life for others, maybe thousands of others, before the day was done? He was no less courageous, when the call came, than the long line of saints he joined that day. We can never thank God enough for giving men and women – just like us – such courage.

Suggested hymns
Brother, sister, let me serve you; Captains of the saintly band; Fight the good fight; True-hearted, whole-hearted, faithful and loyal.

Birth of John the Baptist   24 June
'He Is to Be Called John'   Isa. 40:1–11; Ps. 85:7–13;
Acts 13:14b–26 or Gal. 3:23–29; Luke 1:57–66, 80

'On the eighth day they came to circumcise the child, and they were going to name him Zechariah after his father. But his mother said, "No, he is to be called John."' Luke 1:59–60

As the angel had said
Elizabeth was sticking faithfully to what the angel had told Zechariah at John's annunciation: 'Your wife Elizabeth will bear you a son, and you will name him John' (Luke 1:13). The first part of the prophecy had come to pass. God had kept his part of the bargain, and Elizabeth was determined that she and her husband were going to keep theirs.

There are often people lining up to deflect us, if possible, from our Christian duty. We can listen to them – or, like Elizabeth, we can keep our minds on God and what he has said. Did it matter whether her son was called John, or James, or Peter? Yes, simply because the angel had been unequivocal: 'You will name him John.' It wasn't Elizabeth's place to wonder or to ask why. It had to be.

Largely because the birth of John was heralded and marked so definitively, the Church has traditionally made more of his earthly birthday than his *Natalitia* (birthday in heaven). It replaced in Britain the plethora of pagan midsummer rites, and marked the long, six-month shortening of daylight and lowering of temperatures until the Birth of Christ (which replaced the midwinter traditions of pagan belief) marked the shortest day and the beginning of Nature's re-emergence into spring. This is mainly why so many of our native flowers have names relating to St John, for they previously formed part of the midsummer celebrations.

Dedicated to the Lord
From conception through birth and childhood into adolescence, John was dedicated to the Lord. Zechariah and Elizabeth may not have lived for many years after his birth. At any rate, we don't hear of them again; and the childhood years of John himself are a closed book. It is as a young man of thirtyish, that we next meet him, coming from the wilderness as an ascetic, preaching the kingdom of God and preparing people for Someone greater

than John himself, who would not (only) baptize them with water (as John was doing), but with the Holy Spirit and with fire. Consistently humbling himself and exalting Jesus, John retires from the limelight, though continuing to teach and baptize, when Jesus begins his own ministry.

John's is an example of selfless dedication: a short life, but a fruitful one; a life that did not show any wasted time, but much sowing of seed; a life that prepared a harvest for reapers to come; a life that, to the world, was a shocking waste – but to God, a jewel most precious.

> *O sylvan prophet, whose eternal fame*
> *Resounds from Jewry's hills and Jordan's stream,*
> *The music of our number raise*
> *And tune our voice to sing thy praise.*
>
> *Heaven's messenger from high Olympus came*
> *To bear the tidings of thy life and name,*
> *And told thy sire each prodigy*
> *That heaven designed to work in thee.*
>
> *He heard the news, and dubious with surprise,*
> *His faltering speech in fettered accents dies;*
> *But providence with happy choice*
> *In thee restored thy father's voice.*
>
> Ut queant laxis, ascribed to
> J. Dryden (1631–1701)

Suggested hymns

Lo, from the desert homes; On Jordan's bank the Baptist's cry; Sing we the praises of the great forerunner; The great forerunner of the morn.

St Irenaeus, Bishop of Lyons, Teacher of the Faith c. 200   28 June   Zealous for the Truth

Wis. 7:7–10, 15–16; Ps. 34; 2 Pet. 1:16–21;
Luke 11:33–36

'[Jesus said], "Your eye is the lamp of your body. If your eye is healthy, your whole body is full of light, but if it is not healthy, your body is full of darkness."' Luke 11:34

In apostolic line

Born in or around the year 130, probably at Smyrna, Irenaeus had been a pupil of Bishop Polycarp, who in turn had known the apostle John. He received holy orders and travelled to Gaul to minister under Pothinus, Bishop of Lyons. His eastern background fitted him later for a delicate mission to Rome, to present the case of certain members of the Phrygian church. It was providential that Irenaeus was thus absent from Gaul when persecution broke out resulting in several martyrdoms including that of Bishop Pothinus.

A generation of peace

On his return to Lyons, Irenaeus was consecrated bishop, and enjoyed a 20-year period of relative peace. He found time to write, and much of his work has been preserved, including his 'Doctrine of Recapitulation':

Whence then is the substance of the first-formed man?
From the Will and the Wisdom of God, and from the Virgin earth. 'For God had not sent rain,' the Scripture says, 'upon the earth', before man was made; 'and there was no man to till the earth.' From this, then, while it was still virgin, God took dust of the earth and formed the man, the beginning of mankind. So then the Lord, summing up afresh this man, took the same dispensations of entry into flesh, being born from the Virgin by the Will and the Wisdom of God; that he also should show forth the likeness of Adam's entry into flesh, and there should be that which was written in the beginning, 'man, after the image and likeness of God'. And just as through a disobedient virgin man was stricken down and fell into death, so through the Virgin who was obedient to the Word of God man was re-animated

and received life. For the Lord came again to seek the sheep that was lost, and man it was that was lost; and for this cause there was not made some other formation, but in that same which had its desert from Adam he preserved the likeness of the first formation. For it was necessary that Adam should be summed up in Christ, and that mortality might be swallowed up and overwhelmed by immortality; and Eve summed up in Mary, that a virgin should be a virgin's intercessor, and by a virgin's obedience undo and put away the disobedience of a virgin.

> *Irenaeus*, Demonstration of the Apostolic Preaching, 32–33

It is thought that Irenaeus suffered martyrdom in or around the year 200. By his diplomacy in putting the case of the Quartodecimans before the Pope, peace of a kind had been restored, which laid the foundations for the Council of Nicaea (AD 325), when the Quartodecimans accepted the Roman usage regarding Easter without further pressure from the pope.

A man who could save situations before they developed into major disagreements, Irenaeus has much to teach us in the world of 2004.

Suggested hymns
Be thou my guardian and my guide; Lead, kindly light; O, for a heart to praise my God; Peace, perfect peace, in this dark world of sin.

SS Peter and Paul, Apostles   29 June
Martyrs at Rome   Ezek. 3:22–27; Ps. 125;
Acts 12:1–11; Matthew 16:13–19

'After they had passed the first and the second guard, they came before the iron gate leading into the city. It opened for them of its own accord, and they went outside and walked along a lane, when suddenly the angel left him. Then Peter came to himself, and said, "Now I am sure that the Lord has sent his angel and rescued me from the hands of Herod and from all that the Jewish people were expecting."' Acts 12:10–11

Two sons of Christ

These two apostles had had very different journeys to God, but according to tradition their lives at the end came together in Rome, in or around the year 64, during the Neronic persecutions. Peter was the Galilean fisherman, called by Christ, accompanying the Lord through his three-year ministry, denying, deserting and finally convincingly accepting his resurrection, and subsequently taking the gospel to Gentiles as well as Jews.

Paul, trained by Gamaliel, was active in persecuting the early Christians, then dramatically converted on the Damascus Road, and ever afterwards the most active and dedicated of missionaries.

The church historian Eusebius has this to say of the martyrdom of this great duo:

> Thus, then, was Nero the first to be heralded as above all an antagonist of God and stirred up to murder the apostles. It is related that in his day Paul was beheaded at Rome itself, and that Peter likewise was crucified, and this story is accredited by the attachment, which prevails to this day, of the names of Peter and Paul to the cemeteries there; and in no less degree also by a churchman, named Gaius, who lived in the time of Zephyrinus, bishop of the Romans. Gaius, in a written discussion with Proclus, a champion of the heresy of the Phrygians, speaks thus of the places where the sacred tabernacles of the said apostles have been laid:
>
> But I can point out the trophies of the apostles. For if you would go to the Vatican, or to the Ostian Way, you will find the trophies of those who founded this church; and that they were martyred both on the same occasion, Dionysius, bishop of the Corinthians, writing to the Romans, affirms as follows:
>
> 'In these ways you also, by such an admonition, have united the planting that came from Peter and Paul, of both the Romans and the Corinthians. For indeed both planted also in our Corinth, and likewise taught us; and likewise they taught together also in Italy, and were martyred on the same occasion.'
>
> *Eusebius*, Historia Ecclesiastica *II.25.5–8*

In the final analysis, it is not a question of whether Peter baptized more converts than Paul, or how many more miles Paul travelled than Peter; but that each apostle did what he could. The same question applies to every Christian today: are we doing all we can? Perhaps, if we were to take away, or even reduce, the distractions of modern times that did not impact on Peter and Paul, we should find some time that we didn't know we had.

Suggested hymns
Firmly I believe and truly; For ever with the Lord; How firm a foundation; Look, ye saints, the sight is glorious.

St Thomas the Apostle   3 July
Apostle of India   Hab. 2:1–4, Ps. 31:1–6;
Eph. 2:19–22; John 20:24–29
'So then you are no longer strangers and aliens, but you are citizens with the saints and also members of the household of God, built upon the foundation of the apostles and prophets, with Christ Jesus himself as the cornerstone.' Ephesians 2:20–21

Citizens with the saints
Generally the thought that springs first to mind with Thomas, is that he refused to believe the other disciples when they told him that Jesus had risen: refused, unless he could see and touch the wounds of Jesus for himself. One short week later, Jesus gave him every opportunity, and Thomas believed immediately (John 20:28).

Tradition has it that Thomas later went to India and operated such a profitable ministry that some Indians still today call themselves 'the Christians of St Thomas' – citizens with the saints of every land.

The Thomasine writings
There are several apocryphal works bearing Thomas' name: the *Acts*, the *Gospel*, and the *Apocalypse of Thomas*. A portion from the latter runs:

Hearken, Thomas, for I am the Son of God the Father and I am the father of all spirits. Hear from me the signs which will be at the end of the world, when the end of the world will be fulfilled before my elect come forth from the world. I tell you openly what is now about to happen to me. When these are to

317

take place the princes of the angels do not know, for they are now hidden from them. Then the kings will divide the world among themselves; there will be great hunger, great pestilences and much distress upon the earth. The sons of men will be enslaved in every nation and will perish with the sword. There will be great disorder on earth. Thereafter when the hour of the end draws near there will be great signs in the sky for seven days and the powers of the heavens will be set in motion. Then at the beginning of the third hour of the first day there will be a mighty and strong voice in the firmament of the heaven; a cloud of blood will go up from the north and there will follow it great rolls of thunder and powerful flashes of lightning and it will cover the whole heaven. Then it will rain blood on all the earth. These are the signs of the first day. And on the second day a great voice will resound in the firmament of heaven and the earth will be moved from its place. The gates of heaven will be opened in the firmament of heaven from the east. The smoke of a great fire will burst forth through the gates of heaven and will cover the whole heaven as far as the west. In that day there will be fears and great terrors in the world.

Thomas' resting-place

Several traditions hold that Thomas was buried at Mylapore, now a suburb of Madras. A tomb purporting to be his, and several small relics, are in St Thomas' Cathedral at Mylapore. Other traditions would have us believe that the major part of his relics were taken from India to Edessa and from there to Ortona, in the Abruzzi, where they still attract pilgrims today.

Suggested hymns

From Greenland's icy mountains; Hills of the north, rejoice; In Christ there is no east or west; Tell out, my soul, the greatness of the Lord.

St Swithun, Bishop of Winchester *c.* 862
15 July   **Adviser to a King**   Prov. 3:1–8; Ps. 20;
Jas. 5:7–18; Matthew 5:43–48

'[Jesus said], "And if you greet only your brothers and sisters, what more are you doing than others? Do not even the Gentiles do the same? Be perfect, therefore, as your heavenly Father is perfect."' Matthew *5:47–48*

The saint who liked rain

Swithun (sometimes spelled 'Swithin') was not only a very holy man, but also had a good grasp of mathematics. He became adviser to Egbert, King of Wessex, as well as leading a busy life as Bishop of Winchester.

Apparently Swithun loved rain, and would walk miles to visit the sick or those in trouble, cheerfully getting soaked en route. Before he died, he asked not to be interred in the cathedral with pomp and circumstance, but in a simple grave in the churchyard, so that the rain may fall on him. His wishes were granted, but in the year 971, on the day of his canonization, his relics were exhumed and interred in the cathedral. Although several miracles occurred at the inhumation, the heavens are believed to have opened in a torrential downpour, which lasted – on and off – for the next forty days. And so the jingle was born:

> *If St Swithun's day be fair,*
> *For forty days 'twill rain nae mair;*
> *But if St Swithun's day be wet,*
> *For forty days all rain we'll get.*

There are many regional variations – and in the usual British summer, the rain can come and go for many more than forty days from 15 July.

A strange remembrance?

It seems to be a strange remembrance. Swithun perhaps looks down from glory and smiles somewhat wryly that the rain has proved the most memorable facet of his ministry! Presumably the divine record is a more balanced account of the good that he said and did.

What would we like to be remembered for, more than anything

else? Dr Billy Graham was once asked that question, and he replied, after a little thought: 'I'd like for them to say, "He had integrity."' Who could ask for more? 'Be perfect,' says Jesus, in today's Gospel reading. Having integrity in our dealings with God and our neighbours is surely aiming in that direction.

But Swithun's association with rain – whether indeed induced by his liking for it, or a subsequent imposition on a life that had been inadequately chronicled – shows us that it is possible to be remembered for the wrong reasons, or for reasons that don't really matter and are peripheral to our actual living out of God's will.

Under a bushel
We can keep our doings so secret that no one but God knows; and we can argue that no one but God needs to know. But Jesus did not operate in secret, and his commission to evangelize the world is impossible to carry out in secret. Who has not attended a funeral where the person giving the address has been hard pressed to describe the life of the departed? Just imagine, if Jesus had not involved others in his mission we might never have known his gospel.

Suggested hymns
Fill thou my life, O Lord my God; I cannot tell, why he whom angels worship; O Lord, all the world belongs to you; O Lord my God, when I in awesome wonder.

St Mary Magdalene   22 July
Healed for Ministry   S. of Sol. 3:1–4; Ps. 42:17;
2 Cor. 5:14–17; John 20:1–2, 11–18

'For the love of Christ urges us on, because we are convinced that one has died for all, so that those who live might live no longer for themselves, but for him who died and was raised for them.' 2 Corinthians 5:14–15

Right-about turn
It is thought that Mary had been healed from sexual immorality by Jesus, but her trouble could have been recurrent physical sickness. In any case, the healing proved a turning-point in her life,

and she devoted herself, with Mary the mother of Jesus and other women, to caring for our Lord and his mission team.

It is possible that this Mary was the sister of Lazarus and Martha – the woman who anointed Jesus' feet with oil and wiped them with her hair. Mary was at Calvary, and a witness to the burial of Jesus. She was, even more importantly, the first at the tomb on Easter morning – the first to see the resurrected Christ.

Healing brings wholeness

Mary's healing by Jesus had wiped out every sin she had previously committed. Other people could have long memories, and could continue to hold her past sins against her; but God had wiped them off his record. It does not redound to the credit of humanity that we can be so unforgiving in our dealings with others – less compassionate than God. The Dutch evangelist Corrie ten Boom recounted how, after the Second World War and her atrocious treatment in Ravensbruck concentration camp, she felt (against her will) the Lord directing her to go back to Germany with the gospel. After some delaying and prevaricating, she went. At one of her talks she recognized a former guard from the camp, one who had been particularly brutal and sadistic. She had a real struggle with her natural feelings of revulsion; but then God's love seemed to surge through her, and she found herself doing the impossible – shaking the hand of the man who had been instrumental in her sister's death.

Mary Magdalene needed to overcome the obstacle of gossip and of people's criticism as she tried to lead a reformed life helping Jesus and his team. Perhaps we know someone like Mary, someone who is also trying to bury the past and to work now for God. Can we affirm them in their Christian ministry? Or perhaps they have not yet come to Jesus; can we help them along their way? Or perhaps we ourselves are still hung up over something in the past. Have we repented of the sin? Have we come to God for forgiveness? And then have we taken the sin back and brooded over it? Once we have asked God for forgiveness, that sin is no longer ours to take back: God is prepared to drop it into the sea of his merciful forgetfulness.

Yet sometimes we're so attached to it, we hoick it out again before it has sunk out of sight. If Mary Magdalene had done that with her forgiven sin, it's unlikely that she would have been at the tomb on Easter morning.

Hark! the sound of holy voices; How bright these glorious spirits shine; Lo, round the throne a glorious band; Magdalene, thy grief and gladness.

St James the Apostle 25 July (or transferred to 26th) **The First Apostolic Martyr** Jer. 45:1–5; Ps. 126; Acts 11:27—12:2; Matthew 20:20–28

'About that time King Herod laid violent hands upon some who belonged to the church. He had James, the brother of John, killed with the sword.' Acts 12:1–2

A vain attempt
James' martyrdom, in or around the year 44, was a vain attempt by Herod Agrippa to halt the rise and spread of Christianity. If he could liquidate the leadership, the new movement may lose heart. So he had James killed, and then tried to take Peter also – but Peter was not to be taken.

Known as 'James the Great', to distinguish him from James the son of Alphaeus (James the Less), the James we honour today was the brother of John, the son of Zebedee, one of the Galilean fishermen called by Jesus early in his ministry.

Close to our Lord
One of the inner circle of four (Andrew, Peter and John being the others), James was present at the healing of Peter's mother-in-law and at the raising of Jairus' daughter. At the time of their call, James and John were fiery characters, and Jesus nicknamed them 'Boanerges', 'Sons of Thunder'. On one occasion, they (or their mother) asked for high places in the kingdom of God; on another day, they were so incensed on Jesus' behalf, when some Samaritans spurned the gospel, that they asked Jesus to call down fire from heaven to consume the recalcitrants. James was also one of the three disciples permitted to share Jesus' transfiguration experience; on a more tragic occasion, James was also with our Lord during the agony in Gethsemane on the night of his arrest.

The body of James was interred at Jerusalem, but a Spanish tradition says that his relics were later taken by a somewhat circuitous route, to Compostela in the late ninth century, where today thousands of pilgrims continue to travel to pay their respects.

Staying on duty
That James was immensely brave is not in dispute. He stayed in the seething religious cauldron that was Jerusalem; and as head of the Church there, he was a prime target for any persecution. As Jesus, in the days leading up to his arrest and crucifixion, rode openly into Jerusalem, cleared the temple of money-changers, and taught daily in the temple precinct, so James operated an open ministry: the Jewish authorities could have apprehended him at any time. Are we as open in our ministry? Or do we spend so much time in calculating the risks that we never take any risks? The great commission of Jesus was: 'Go into all the world and proclaim the good news to the whole creation' (Mark 16:15). The world will be none the wiser, if we whisper it to the corner-cupboard, or sing it to the cat. James, like Jesus, was virtually saying to the Jews: 'I'm here: come and get me, if you wish. I shall not go into hiding.'

There may be times when the pressures become so great that all we want to do is creep like a dormouse into our home and hibernate for six months; or we consider resigning from this council or that committee. May we not jump the fence, or step down, before we have remembered James, and have asked God whether he's really in favour of such drastic action.

Suggested hymns
Be thou my guardian and my guide; Dear Lord and Father of mankind; Oft in danger, oft in woe; Spirit of the living God, fall afresh on me.

Transfiguration of our Lord   6 August
Shekinah-Glory   Dan. 7:9–10, 13–14; Ps. 97;
2 Pet. 1:16–19; Luke 9:28b–36

'Then from the cloud came a voice that said, "This is my Son, my Chosen; listen to him!" When the voice had spoken, Jesus was found alone. And they kept silent and in those days told no one any of the things they had seen.' Luke 9:35–36

'A lovely, lovely holiday'

Asked what she thought 'Paradise' was like, a five-year-old replied, 'A lovely, lovely holiday!' For Peter, James and John the Transfiguration experience was surely not far removed from this. God was treating them to a glimpse of *Shekinah* (glory). Jesus could have had the experience on his own, with Moses and Elijah; and, for all we know, he may have had other similar experiences. But on this occasion, three of his closest friends were permitted to share in the glory. To give them courage? Hope? To confirm, if they needed it, that Jesus was indeed who he said he was? Perhaps a bit of all three.

'Listen to him!'

Jesus' words were precious: every one of them. Heaven and earth one day will pass away, but his words are eternal. Therefore, the disciples must mark, learn and inwardly digest every word. If they failed to listen, they would be wrong-footed. They did falter, at Calvary, but Easter brought a recovery. How well do we listen to Jesus? How seriously do we study the Gospels, pray and take time to listen to what God is saying? We like to think that he is interested in everything we do: why do we sometimes assume that he has nothing to say to all that we get up to? *Listen*! When was the last time we really listened out to Jesus?

Putting Jesus first

Peter, James and John had put being with Jesus before ministry that day. The other disciples were ministering to a 'great crowd' (Luke 9:37) – and getting in a tangle over a difficult case of epilepsy. But the three closest friends of Jesus had taken a 'lovely, lovely holiday' – and they must have been so thankful they had. Those who had stayed with the crowd found that either through mental, physical or spiritual weariness (perhaps a combination of all three) they couldn't heal. There are times when we need to take a break, a holiday; when to soldier on, at half-strength, means an impaired ministry that does not benefit us, the people we are trying to help, or Jesus.

Spiritual shyness?

The three disciples kept quiet about their experience. Was this due to spiritual shyness, a fear of being laughed at or misunderstood? No. Mark gives us the reason: Jesus 'ordered them to tell no one about what they had seen, until after the Son of Man had risen from the dead' (Mark 9:9). Some would not believe them, even then. But for those who could believe, the Transfiguration would be a window into glory.

Suggested hymns
For ever with the Lord; In days of old on Sinai; Jesus, the Name high over all; 'Tis good, Lord, to be here.

St Clare of Assisi, Founder of the Minoresses (Poor Clares) 1253   11 August
Hearing God's Voice   Hos. 2:14–15, 19–20; Ps. 62; 2 Cor. 4:6–10; John 15:4–10

'For it is the God who said, "Let light shine out of darkness", who has shone in our hearts to give the light of the knowledge of the glory of God in the face of Jesus Christ. But we have this treasure in clay jars, so that it may be made clear that this extraordinary power belongs to God and does not come from us.' 2 Corinthians 4:6–7

The call to poverty
Clare Offreduccio was born into a wealthy family of Assisi but from an early age appeared to realize that there was more to life than money. She was in her late teens when St Francis' preaching of the series of Lenten services at her local church made her decide to follow him into the religious life. On Palm Sunday, 1212, with the bishop presiding at the cathedral service in Assisi, Clare was too overcome to leave her seat and go up to receive a branch of olive. In an unprecedented move, the bishop came down from the sanctuary and presented her with the branch. Later, Clare went to La Portiuncula, where Francis cut off her hair, gave her a simple habit of sackcloth tied with a cord, and – having no nunnery of his own – placed her in the Benedictine convent of St Paul, near Bastia. Clare exchanged her beautiful gown and jewellery for a life of extreme poverty, eventually founding her own order, still known today as the Poor Clares. The sisters were totally dependent on alms, wore no shoes, kept to an austere vegetarian diet and slept on the ground. Papa Offreduccio became very angry when

Clare's sister Agnes followed her into the religious life, and sent a party of young men to bring her home; but miraculously Agnes became so heavy the men could not move her, and they went away in frustration.

Appointed abbess of the convent by Francis, Clare held the position for 40 years, dying after a long illness at the age of 60, in the forty-second year of her profession.

The early vision

Francis died some years before Clare, but for the rest of her life she supported those brothers in the order who stayed loyal to the early vision that Francis had tried to keep alive even after he had relinquished the leadership of the Friars Minor. Modifications and relaxations of his austerities had been introduced, and this grieved both Francis and Clare who saw it as a compromise, a watering-down of the original aspirations to a life of simplicity, poverty and obedience.

In today's world

The Franciscan austerities may seem far removed from the world of 2004 where so many luxuries are regarded as essential, and deprivation is associated with denigration, where the bank balance governs status, and Sunday has become virtually another day of business. Can we learn from Clare the values of the simple life? Can any of these be superimposed on modern times? Can we, in some way if not as thoroughly as Clare, 'live simply, so that others may simply live'?

Well, we can try.

Suggested hymns

All for Jesus, all for Jesus; Firmly I believe and truly; In full and glad surrender; Said Judas to Mary.

Assumption of the Blessed Virgin Mary

15 August   **Mary's 'Birthday'**   Isa. 61:10–11 or
Rev. 11:19—12:6, 10; Ps. 45:10–17; Gal. 4:4–7;
Luke 1:46–55

'But when the fulness of time had come, God sent his Son, born of a woman, born under the law, in order to redeem those who were under the law, so that we might receive adoption as children.' Galatians 4:4–5

Dormition or assumption?

Mary's 'birthday' – her *natalitia*, or birthday in heaven (her death) – has been celebrated in the middle of August from at least as early as the seventh century, according to St Aldhelm (*c.* 690). The question of whether it is seen as her Dormition (Falling Asleep), as is current in the Eastern Church, or her Assumption, as in the Catholic West, is still unclear. Did she die, and was she buried, while her *soul* was assumed into heaven? Or was she bodily assumed, without experiencing physical death? One legend has it that she died on the anniversary of her Son's birth, and that veneration of Mary had thus to be moved to a day other than Christmas.

It was not until 1950 that the Roman Catholic Church produced some definitive doctrine, when Pius XII declared:

> The remarkable unanimity of the Catholic episcopacy and faithful in the matter of the definability of our Lady's bodily assumption into heaven as a dogma of faith showed us that the ordinary teaching authority of the Church and the belief of the faithful which it sustains and directs were in accord, and thereby proved with infallible certainty that that privilege is a truth revealed by God and is contained in the divine deposit which Christ entrusted to his bride the Church, to be guarded faithfully and declared with infallible certainty.

Munificentissimus Deus

Pius followed this up with a public pronouncement in St Peter's Square, Rome, on All Saints' Day, 1 November 1950:

> Having repeatedly raised prayers of urgent supplication to God and having called upon the light of the Spirit of Truth – to the glory of Almighty God, who has bestowed his signal favour on Mary; in honour of his Son, deathless King of all the ages and

conqueror of sin and death; to the increase of the glory of the same exalted Mother; and to the joy and exultation of the whole Church: By the authority of our Lord Jesus Christ, by that of the blessed apostles Peter and Paul, and by our own authority, We pronounce, declare and define to be divinely revealed the dogma that the immaculate Mother of God, the Ever-Virgin Mary, was on the completion of her earthly life assumed body and soul into the glory of Heaven.

The question of infallibility apart, we may surely honour Mary today for her life of dedication to the work chosen for her by God. She was the Mother of God, *Theotokos* – 'Maiden, yet a mother, daughter of her Son', as David Alighieri phrases it so beautifully in his hymn. Her fiat placed her humbly yet firmly in God's will, whatever that will would require. Our Lord loved his mother so much in life, even in his agony providing for her (John 19:25f.); surely he would see that her assumption to glory – whether bodily or spiritually – was special.

Suggested hymns
For Mary, mother of our Lord; I'll sing a hymn to Mary; Maiden, yet a mother; O Mother blest, whom God bestows.

St Bernard, Abbot of Clairvaux, Teacher of the Faith 1153 20 August Dr Mellifluous
Prov. 4:5–9; Ps. 19; Rev. 19:5–9; John 15:7–11
'[Jesus said], "If you abide in me, and my words abide in you, ask for whatever you wish, and it will be done for you. My Father is glorified by this, that you bear much fruit and become my disciples."' John 15:7–8

A gatherer of kindred spirits
Born into a noble family at Fontaines near Dijon in 1090, Bernard was one of seven brothers, four of whom he encouraged to take up with him the religious life; in all, he gathered 31 kindred spirits, who arrived at the monastery of Citeaux in the year 1112. An Englishman, St Stephen, was then abbot, and he received the peaceful invasion with enthusiasm, having had no additions to

the novitiate for several years. After three years, Bernard and 12 brothers were dispatched to the diocese of Langres, to build a new monastery. Bernard became known for his strict asceticism, which at first discouraged some of the monks. Seeing this, Bernard took a prolonged vow of silence and mitigated his strictures somewhat. The monastery grew steadily, and soon the number of monks had risen to 130. The site chosen for Bernard's monastery had been known as the Valley of Wormwood, but now it was changed to Clairvaux. The order, known as 'Cistercian', from the mother-house at Citeaux, grew rapidly and spread to England where great houses such as Fountains and Rievaulx were founded.

Honey-tongued

This expansion meant that Bernard could spend little time in seclusion, but he managed to write a quantity of letters and sermons, as well as to preach. He had a wonderful way with words: though a strict ascetic, he was so gentle in teaching others that he came to be known as 'Dr Mellifluous'; his emblem is a beehive and he came to be known also as the patron saint of bee-keepers.

In 1130 there was some controversy about the papal election, and Bernard was strong in his support of Innocent III. At one of the general councils in Rome, he met St Malachy of Ireland, who was later to appoint Bernard over the first intake of monks at the newly built Mellifont Abbey, the first Cistercian house in Ireland.

Called back to the Continent to deal with various problems including the Albigensian heresy, in 1145 Bernard preached throughout Languedoc, and the heresy subsided. Weak and ill, he returned to Clairvaux. He was to die before Albigensianism flared up more strongly than before, some 25 years later.

The ageing crusader

When the Seljuk Turks took Edessa on Christmas Day 1144, Pope Eugenius III commissioned Bernard to preach a crusade, which eventually began on Palm Sunday at Vézelay in 1146, and roused many to the cause in France, Germany and much of Western Europe. But by early 1153 Bernard was a sick man. Nevertheless, he rallied to quell a disturbance in Metz, where the Duke of Lorraine had attacked the city. That done, in his sixty-fourth year (thirty-eighth as abbot) with 68 monasteries having been founded from Clairvaux, Bernard died, on 20 August 1153. Canonized in

1174, he was formally declared a Doctor of the Church (*Doctor Mellifluous*), in 1830.

We remember the 'Honey-sweet Doctor' today, as we pray that our own witness for Christ will be as bracing as salt, and yet sweetened with honey.

Suggested hymns
O love, that wilt not let me go; Sweet is the work, my God and King; Sweet sacrament divine; There's a wideness in God's mercy.

St Bartholomew the Apostle   24 August
Nathanael the Questioner   Isa. 43:8–13; Ps. 145:1–7; Acts 5:12–16; Luke 22:24–30

'[Jesus said], "You are those who have stood by me in my trials, and I confer on you, just as my Father has conferred on me, a kingdom, so that you may eat and drink at my table in my kingdom, and you will sit on thrones judging the twelve tribes of Israel."' Luke 22:28–30

A hesitant beginning
Thought to have been the 'Nathanael' whom Philip brought to Jesus (John 1:45ff.), Bartholomew's rather cynical question, 'Can anything good come out of Nazareth?' was not the most promising of beginnings; however, Jesus soon disarmed him of his doubt, and Bartholomew became a loyal, if largely unknown, disciple. Eusebius mentions him, in his *History*:

> For there were . . . many evangelists of the word, desirous to contribute an inspired zeal, after the manner of the apostles, for the increase and building up of the divine word. Pantaenus also was one of these, and is mentioned as having gone to India; and the story goes, that there he found in the hands of some persons who had come to know Christ in that land, the Gospel according to Matthew, which had anticipated his arrival; for that Bartholomew, one of the apostles, had preached to them and left behind the writing of Matthew in the actual Hebrew characters, and that it was preserved up to the said time.
>
> *Eusebius*, Historia Ecclesiastica *V.10.2–3*

According to tradition, Bartholomew also journeyed into Armenia, where he suffered martyrdom by being flayed alive.

The Gospel of Bartholomew

There are several ancient texts carrying the authorship of Bartholomew including Coptic fragments of a 'Gospel' dating from the fifth to the seventh centuries, and a series of 'Questions' (*Quaestiones sancti Bartholomaei apostoli*):

In the time before the Passion of our Lord Christ all the apostles were gathered together. And they asked and besought him: Lord, show us the secrets of the heaven. But Jesus answered: I can reveal nothing to you before I have put off this body of flesh. But when he had suffered and risen again, all the apostles at the sight of him did not dare to ask him, because his appearance was not as it was before, but revealed the fulness of his godhead. But Bartholomew went up to him and said, Lord, I wish to speak to you. Jesus answered him, Beloved Bartholomew, I know what you wish to say. Ask then, and I will tell you all you wish to know. And I myself will make known to you what you do not say. Bartholomew said to him, Lord, when you went to be hanged on the cross, I followed you at a distance and saw how you were hanged on the cross and how the angels descended from heaven and worshipped you. And when darkness came, I looked and saw that you had vanished from the cross; only I heard your voice in the underworld, and suddenly there a wailing and a great gnashing of teeth arose. Tell me, Lord, where you went from the cross. And Jesus answered, Blessed are you, Bartholomew, my beloved, because you saw this mystery. And now I will tell you everything you ask me. When I vanished rom the cross, I went to the underworld to bring up Adam and all the patriarchs, Abraham, Isaac and Jacob. The archangel Michael had asked me to do this.

Gospel of Bartholomew *I.1–9*

St Paul, we remember, phrased it thus: 'He [Jesus] disarmed the rulers and authorities and made a public example of them, triumphing over them' (Colossians 2:15). Until we meet our Lord (and Bartholomew, Paul and so many more), and hear from him exactly what happened between Good Friday and Easter morning, we may simply, reverently believe that Jesus spent that time very profitably – for us.

Suggested hymns
Blest are the pure in heart; For ever here my rest shall be; Meekness and majesty; To the Name of our salvation.

St Augustine, Bishop of Hippo, Teacher of the Faith 430 28 August Wildness Tamed
Ecclus. 39:1–10; Ps. 84; Rom. 13:11–14;
Matthew 23:8–12

'Let us live honourably as in the day, not in revelling and drunkenness, not in debauchery and licentiousness, not in quarrelling and jealousy. Instead, put on the Lord Jesus Christ, and make no provision for the flesh, to gratify its desires.' Romans 13:13–14

Sowing his oats
Augustine led a fast lifestyle in his youth and early manhood. Born in North Africa in 354, his studies took him to Carthage, Rome and Milan. He lived well, and loved better. His father Patricius converted to Christianity after Monica his wife had prayed for him for 16 years. For a marathon of 22 years, Monica continued to pray for her son – and eventually Augustine saw the light. He was resting in the garden one day, when from over the wall he heard a child singing, 'Take and read, *tolle lege*.' He opened the Bible, to the page where he read our text for today. Augustine sought out the saintly Bishop Ambrose of Milan and began to study the scriptures, not merely as a tool for rhetoric (as he had been doing), but as the *Vade mecum* for life. In seeming recognition of her devotion to prayer, God allowed Monica to live long enough to see Ambrose baptize Augustine at the Easter Vigil in 387.

A great writer
Augustine became Bishop of Hippo and was a prolific writer of books which to this day form essential reading for many theological students. This comes from his treatise *Nature and Grace*:

Truly the nature of man was originally created blameless and without any vice; but that nature of man, with which each is born of Adam, now needs a physician because it is not healthy. Every good thing indeed which it possesses in its constitution, life, senses, intellect, it has from the most high God, its Creator and Maker. But the vice which darkens and weakens those good gifts of nature, so that it needs illumination and healing, was not derived from its blameless Maker, but from original sin which was committed through free choice; and on this account a penal nature is a part of a most righteous punishment. For if we are now 'in Christ a new creature, still we were by nature children of wrath, even as the rest also; but God, who is rich in mercy, for his great love wherewith he loved us, even when we were dead in sins, quickened us together with Christ, by whose grace we have been made whole' [Ephesians 2:3–5].

But this grace of Christ, without which neither infants nor aged can be made whole, is not paid for merits, but is given gratis; and for this reason is termed 'grace'. As the Apostle says, 'Being justified freely (gratis) through his blood' [Romans 3:24], wherefore those who are not by this means set free (either because they have not yet been able to hear, or because they refused to obey, or even because, when by reason of age they could not hear, they received not the washing of regeneration which they might have received and been saved), are certainly righteously condemned, since they are not without sin, either that which they derived from their birth, or that which they added by their evil lives. 'For all have sinned [either in Adam or in themselves], and need the glory of God' [Romans 3:23].

Augustine, De Natura et Gratia II.3–4

May we reflect on this grace – the undeserved favour of God – as we give thanks today for the life of a saint whose learning and theology has helped so many in their walk with God.

Suggested hymns
Firmly I believe and truly; In full and glad surrender; To the Name of our salvation; Ye holy angels bright.

St Aidan, Bishop of Lindisfarne, Missionary
651 31 August A Humble Guest of Royalty
Isa. 45:22–25; Ps. 47; 1 Cor. 9:16–19; John 13:16–20

'If I proclaim the gospel, this gives me no ground for boasting, for an obligation is laid on me, and woe betide me if I do not proclaim the gospel!' 1 Corinthians 9:16

Disciple on Scattery Island
Little is known of Aidan's early life, but he is believed to have been a disciple of St Senan on Scattery Island. His move to Iona from Ireland signalled a very different stage in his life, for he quickly became Bishop of Lindisfarne and greatly respected and loved by King Oswald. Invitations to dine at the king's table were showered upon Aidan, but the bishop invariably took one or two of his clergy with him, and after the meal made his escape as soon as was conveniently possible.

The English Iona
Under the Rule of Columcille, Aidan established a monastery on Lindisfarne (Holy Island), and a ministry of outreach which proved so fruitful that the island became known as 'The English Iona'. He opened a school for boys to train for the priesthood, and from here went such scholars as Cedd, who became Abbot of Lastingham, and his brother Chad who succeeded Cedd at Lastingham and later became Bishop of Lichfield (see 2 March). King Oswald remained a staunch friend, as also his successor, Oswin. The latter's murder at Gilling in 651 was such a blow to Aidan that the bishop only survived the king by 11 days. Aidan's body was taken from Bamburgh Castle, where he died in the mission tent pitched against the church wall, back to Lindisfarne. The monks buried him in the cemetery, but later he was interred in the newly built Church of St Peter on the island.

A saint to all
Neither ashamed of poverty nor flattered by opulence, Aidan treated paupers and royalty alike, and is a fine example of how the practice of Christian values impressed the dour, northern pagans. He was also blessed with the trust and respect of two successive kings, and enjoyed a relatively peaceful period in history, when missionary work was allowed to proceed largely

untroubled by war or persecution. The time was ripe for Christianity to grow in the North, and Aidan was the man to whom God gave the work.

If we are where God has put us, he will already have prepared work for us to do. We may not yet have recognized it – but in his time he will make it clear if we operate an open-heart mentality. There have been many who have dreamed of wonderful missions in far-off, exotic places, only to realize sooner or later that God has been helping them achieve an even more beautiful mission right on their home front. 'An obligation is laid on me', Paul told the Corinthians – to preach in Spain? No; it is believed Paul never got to Spain, though he had wanted to. To preach before Caesar? Again, it's thought that Paul's case never came before Caesar. No – Paul had the obligation to preach in the places and to the people where God directed him.

And we, likewise, are not to be so focused on people and places half a world or more away that we fail to see the needs of those we meet in the supermarket, on the train, or coming out of the next-door apartment. Their needs are so much greater, because they are brought to us where we *are*.

Even the most-travelled Christian can only be in one place at a time: and that's the place that God has chosen.

Suggested hymns
A charge to keep I have; Guide me, O thou great Redeemer; Hills of the north, rejoice; Thy way, not mine, O Lord.

Birth of the Blessed Virgin Mary
8 September   **A Special Vocation**   Mic. 5:1–4;
Judith 16:13–16; Rom. 8:18–30; Matthew 1:1–16, 18–23

'We know that all things work together for good for those who love God, who are called according to his purpose.' Romans 8:28

In Mary's honour
The Church in both Eastern and Western Christendom has long observed this day as that of Mary's birth, following nine months from the festival of her conception. Whether or not we subscribe to the belief of the sinlessness of Mary from her birth, this is a

day to honour her who was called by God to a special vocation. Not knowing all that was in store, she trusted that the Lord who had called for her all would give her everything that she needed to do his will.

According to tradition, Mary's parents were called Joachim and Anne (Anna), who are mentioned in the second-century *Protoevangelium* of James:

And [Anna's] time was fulfilled, as the angel had said: in the ninth month she brought forth. And she said to the midwife: 'What have I brought forth?' And she said, 'A female.' And Anna said: 'My soul is magnified this day.' And she lay down. And when the days were fulfilled, Anna purified herself from her childbed and gave suck to the child, and called her Mary. Day by day the child grew strong; when she was six months old her mother stood her on the ground to try if she could stand. And she walked seven steps and came to her bosom. And she took her up, saying: 'As the Lord my God lives, you shall walk no more upon this ground until I take you into the temple of the Lord.' And she made a sanctuary in her bed-chamber, and did not permit anything common or unclean to pass through it. And she summoned the undefiled daughters of the Hebrews, and they cared for her amusement.

On the child's first birthday, Joachim made a great feast, and invited the chief priests and the scribes and the elders and the whole people of Israel. And Joachim brought the child to the priests, and they blessed her, saying, 'O God of our fathers, bless this child and give her a name renowned for ever among all generations.' And all the people said, 'Amen, so be it.' And they brought her to the chief priests, and they blessed her, saying, 'O God of the heavenly heights, look upon this child and bless her with a supreme and unsurpassable blessing.' And her mother carried her into the sanctuary of her bed-chamber and gave her suck. And Anna sang this song to the Lord God:

'I will sing praises to the Lord my God, for he has visited me and taken away from me the reproach of my enemies.
And the Lord gave me the fruit of righteousness, unique and manifold before him.
Who will proclaim to the sons of Reuben that Anna gives suck?'

And she laid the child down to rest in the bed-chamber with
its sanctuary, and went out and served them. When the feast
was ended, they went down rejoicing and glorifying the God
of Israel.

Mary's visit today

As we greet Mary today, honouring her as her Son so obviously
honoured her, even in his agony at Calvary caring for her (John
19:25f.), let us humbly echo the greeting of Elizabeth, when Mary,
as an ecstatic young woman, went to share Gabriel's news with
her cousin: 'Why has this happened to me, that the mother of my
Lord comes to me?'

Suggested hymns

Daily, daily, sing to Mary; Hail, Queen of heaven; O Mother blest,
whom God bestows; O purest of creatures, Sweet Mother, sweet
Maid.

St John Chrysostom, Bishop of Constantinople
Teacher of the Faith 407   13 September   The
Golden Orator   Jer. 1:4–10; Ps. 101; Eph. 3:8–12;
Matthew 5:13–19

*'Although I am the very least of all the saints, this grace was given to
me to bring to the Gentiles the news of the boundless riches of Christ,
and to make everyone see what is the plan of the mystery hidden for ages
in God who created all things, so that through the church the wisdom
of God in its rich variety might now be made known to the rulers and
authorities in the heavenly places.' Ephesians 3:8–10*

Student of law

Born of a Roman father and a Greek mother, at Syrian Antioch in
about the year 347, John studied law and rhetoric, switching to
theology after baptism at the age of 21. In 374 he joined a community of hermit monks in the mountains near Antioch for seven
years until the damp conditions drove him for the good of his
health back into Antioch, where he was ordained deacon by
St Meletius. Priested in 386 by Bishop Flavian, John was consecrated Bishop of Constantinople in 398, when he had already

established himself as one of the most eloquent preachers the Church had ever heard.

Too close to the Court

It is fruitless to speculate how different life may have been had John stayed in Antioch. In Constantinople, he was too close to the Court for a man of his outspokenness: he inveighed against the lax morals of Court and city: in particular, against the flamboyant, arrogant Empress Eudoxia. John was fearless. Whether Eudoxia was in the congregation or not, the bishop said what he felt compelled to say from his pulpit. The empress took umbrage, and planned revenge.

Exiled!

Eudoxia prevailed on her husband Arcadius – against his will – to have John sent into exile; but when Constantinople was shaken by an earthquake, Eudoxia superstitiously ordered Arcadius to recall John to pray for the people. He returned, but the calm did not last for long. Eudoxia had a silver statue of herself erected in front of John's cathedral, and the attendant public games and entertainment at its unveiling spilled over on to Good Friday. John was vehement in his condemnation. 'Once more Herodias raves!' he thundered. 'Once more she demands John's head on a charger!' Eudoxia again retaliated, manipulating another order for exile from Arcadius. John was conducted to Nicaea, and from there to Cucusus, where he received great kindness and consideration. However, when news of this percolated back to Constantinople, Arcadius (smarting from the sudden death in childbirth of Eudoxia) ordered that John be taken further away, to Pityus on the Black Sea. John, by this time old and infirm, died on the way due to heat exhaustion in Cappadocia.

The character of John has been described by Socrates, a church historian of the fifth century, in his *History*:

A man, as I have before observed, who on account of zeal for temperance was inclined rather to anger than forbearance: and his temperance led him to indulge in too great latitude of speech. Indeed, it is most inexplicable to me, how with a zeal so ardent for the practice of temperance he should in his sermons appear to despise temperance. For whereas by the synod of bishops repentance was accepted but once from those who had sinned after baptism, he did not scruple to say, 'Approach, although you may have repented a thousand times.' For this doctrine, many even of his friends censured him, but especially Sisinnius bishop of the Novatianists, who wrote a book condemnatory of the above-quoted expression of Chrysostom's, and severely rebuked him for it.

Socrates, Historia Ecclesiastica VI.21.2–6

Had John Chrysostom been able to read Socrates' analysis of his character, might the golden-tongued bishop not have asked: 'How is it that God's friends seem to suffer more than his enemies?'

Suggested hymns
Be not afraid; Give me the wings of faith to rise; Let saints on earth in concert sing; Tell out, my soul, the greatness of the Lord.

Holy Cross Day   14 September
So Must He Be Lifted Up   Num. 21:4–9; Ps. 22:23–28; Phil. 2:6–11; John 3:13–17
'[Jesus said], "Just as Moses lifted up the serpent in the wilderness, so must the Son of Man be lifted up, that whoever believes in him may have eternal life."' John 3:14–15

A cross in the heavens
Bishop Cyril of Jerusalem's *Letter to the Emperor Constantius* dates from the year 351, from which the following extract is taken:

In the days of Constantine your father, most dear to God and of blessed memory, there was discovered the wood of the cross fraught with salvation, because the divine grace that gave piety to the pious seeker vouchsafed the finding of the buried holy places. But in your time, your Majesty, most religious of Emperors, victorious through a piety towards God greater even than that which you inherited, are seen wonderful works, not from the earth any more, but from the heavens. The trophy of the victory over death of our Lord and Saviour Jesus Christ, the only-begotten Son of God, I mean the blessed cross, has been seen at Jerusalem blazing with refulgent light!

For in these very days of the holy feast of Pentecost, on the seventh of May, about the third hour a gigantic cross formed of light appeared in the sky above holy Golgotha stretching out as far as the holy Mount of Olives. It was not seen by just one or two, but was most clearly displayed before the whole population of the city. Nor did it, as one might have supposed, pass away quickly like something imagined, but was visible to sight above the earth for some hours, while it sparkled with a light above the sun's rays. Of a surety, it would have been overcome and hidden by them had it not exhibited to those who saw it a brilliance more powerful than the sun, so that the whole population of the city made a concerted rush into the Martyry, seized by a fear that mingled with joy at the heavenly vision. They poured in, young and old, men and women of every age, even to maidens hitherto kept in the seclusion of their homes, local folk and strangers together, not only Christians but pagans from elsewhere sojourning in Jerusalem. All of them as with one mouth raised a hymn of praise to Christ Jesus our Lord, the only-begotten Son of God, the worker of wonders. For they recognized in fact and by experience that the most religious creed of Christians is, 'not with enticing words of wisdom, but in demonstration of the Spirit and of power' (1 Corinthians 2:4), not merely preached by men, but having witness borne to it by God from the heavens.

Helena's discovery

Helena, the mother of Constantine, during her overseeing of excavations in Jerusalem, claimed in the fourth century to have discovered the true cross of Christ. A church was built on this site, still known today as the Church of the Holy Sepulchre. It was consecrated in the year 335, on 14 September.

The Calvary cross

For Christians, the Calvary cross of life presents us with a lesser Calvary than our Lord suffered: it is here in our hearts, at the meeting of ourselves and Christ. As the two parts of the cross come together, the Holy Spirit within us goes to work with the same power that gave Jesus the victory two thousand years ago.

We may reflect on Cyril's description of the vision of the cross, and on the wood discovered by Helena; but it is the cross within us that demands our greater attention, every day in every way.

Suggested hymns
Beneath the cross of Jesus; In the cross of Christ I glory; On a hill far away, stood an old rugged cross; Take up thy cross, the Saviour said.

St Cyprian, Bishop of Carthage, Martyr 258
15 September   Being True to Oneself
Ezek. 34:11–16; Ps. 75; 1 Cor. 12:4–13, 27; Luke 9:23–26

'[Jesus said], "Those who want to save their life will lose it, and those who lose their life for my sake will save it. What does it profit them if they gain the whole world, but lose or forfeit themselves?"'
Luke 9:24–25

The judgement of others
We all at times do and say things which we believe to be right, but which others misunderstand with seemingly little effort. One of the judgements made on Cyprian was that he 'did right in a wrong cause'. We may agree or disagree, that history has been in his case too harsh a judge.

Trained as a rhetorician and lawyer, Cyprian did not come to the faith until he was around forty-five. In the year 248, after an initial hesitation, he accepted the bishopric of Carthage. Within a few months, renewed persecution broke out under the Emperor Decius. To avoid arrest and torture, a certificate of paganism was necessary, and people queued up in the magistrates' courts to obtain these. Meanwhile, Cyprian quietly left the city, and the cry went up: 'Coward!'

An aggravating couple set out to cause trouble in the bishop's absence: Novatus, a priest, headed a schismatic sect, and went to Rome where Novatian had proclaimed himself anti-pope. Cyprian returned to Carthage to fight the Novatian schism and to support Cornelius as the duly elected pope.

Retribution – or forgiveness?

The persecution over, people began trickling back into the Church. Bishop Cyprian welcomed them (with certain reservations), while the pope declared that 'once an apostate, always an apostate'. Hardly had this furore died down, than Cyprian became involved in the question of baptism and the standing of those priests who administered it. He had strongly supported Cornelius when pope, but disagreed over baptism with the new pope, Stephen I. Stephen maintained that 'the invalidity of a minister does not invalidate the sacrament', and allowed heretics and schismatics to baptize. Cyprian, in a famous reply, said: 'There is no baptism outside the Church.' Stephen won the day on this question, but Cyprian won the respect of the majority of those concerned.

When persecution again erupted, this time under Emperor Valerian, Cyprian again left Carthage, but was recalled to stand trial. He refused to deny his Lord, and was sentenced to death on 14 September 258:

> When the executioner arrived Cyprian charged his friends that they should give to the executioner 25 golden pieces. Napkins and handkerchifs were strewn before him by the brethren. Thereafter blessed Cyprian bound his eyes with his own hand, but as he could not fasten the ends of the handkerchief for himself, the presbyter Julian and Julian the sub-deacon fastened them for him.
>
> So the blessed Cyprian suffered, and his body was laid out hard by to content the curiosity of the heathen. Thence it was removed by night, and accompanied by tapers and torches, was conducted with prayers in great triumph to the burial-ground of Macrobius Candidianus the procurator, which lies on the Mappalian Way near the fishponds. A few days later Galerius Maximus the pro-consul died.
>
> The most blessed martyr Cyprian suffered on the 14th. day of September under the Emperors Valerian and Gallienus, but in the reign of our Lord Jesus Christ, to whom be honour and glory for ever and ever. Amen.
>
> Acta Proconsularia of St Cyprian, Corpus Scriptorum
Ecclesiasticorum Latinorum III.3.5–6

Ecclesiastical controversies and questions today may not end (at least in Britain) with the beheading of a bishop; but their debates still account for a good deal of time, in synods, councils and committees. It will probably be so until the end of time for the Church is still growing, still developing, still learning. There are still the Cyprians of our day, whom many find hard to understand.

Suggested hymns
And can it be; Breathe on me, Breath of God; Prayer is the soul's sincere desire; Thy kingdom come, O God.

St Matthew, Apostle and Evangelist
21 September   **Compiler of Oracles**   Prov. 3:13–18; Ps. 119:65–72; 2 Cor. 4:1–6; Matthew 9:9–13

'Therefore, since it is by God's mercy that we are engaged in this ministry, we do not lose heart. We have renounced the shameful things that one hides; we refuse to practise cunning or to falsify God's word; but by the open statement of the truth we commend ourselves to the conscience of everyone in the sight of God.' 2 Corinthians 4:1–2

Early testimony
Eusebius of Caesarea, the church historian, gives us a record of early comments on the evangelists, from Papias, Bishop of Hierapolis, *c.* AD 130: 'So, then, Matthew compiled the oracles in the Hebrew language, but everyone interpreted them as he was able' (*Historia Ecclesiastica* III.39.16).

A Jew, yet a virtual exile among his own people because of his office; a tax-collector suspected of profiteering (whether guilty or not), hated also by the Gentiles, Matthew was in a no-win situation until Jesus challenged convention by his command, 'Follow me'. And Matthew did not hesitate.

A well-balanced Gospel
The Gospel of Matthew gives us a nice balance of Jesus' birth stories, ministry and passion. From Matthew, we get the annunciation to Joseph; the visit of the Magi; the massacre of the Innocents, and the flight into Egypt – none of which we find in the other three Gospels. A Jew writing primarily for Jews, Matthew nevertheless is the evangelist who tells us of the first Gentile visitors to the young Jesus – and of Christ's parting injunction to the disciples, to baptize

343

people of all nations. It is also Matthew who gives us the most orderly setting-out of Jesus' teaching, in the Sermon on the Mount; much of this material is also in St Luke's Gospel, but in smaller, scattered portions.

According to tradition, Matthew suffered martyrdom in Ethiopia, but we do not know exactly when, how or where.

By God's mercy

'It is by God's mercy that we are engaged in this ministry,' Paul told the Corinthians. It was by this same mercy that Matthew was called to leave the customs house and follow Jesus. Today, wouldn't we want to see his CV, to establish his credentials, to decide whether he was suitable material for training, and so on? Does he have a real vocation? Jesus simply said, 'Follow me'. By God's same mercy, and through no merit of our own, we are where we are today. This should make us very humble, and very compassionate towards others who are perhaps struggling or straggling: there, but for God's gracious mercy, we could very well be.

On this festival of a man who was called in mercy from sin to sainthood, perhaps we can make this prayer to Christ, written a thousand years ago, our own:

> Lord Jesus Christ, my merciful Redeemer,
> and my compassionate Saviour,
> I praise thee and I give thee thanks.
> I know my thanks are quite inadequate
> for all the kindness thou hast shown to me;
> I know they lack the fervour that they ought to have,
> and are a poor return
> for the abundance of thy tender love,
> that I so much desired.
> And yet my soul
> must pay its debt somehow.
> I cannot praise and thank thee as I ought,
> but I at least will do the best I can.

St Anselm (1033–1109)

Suggested hymns

For all thy saints, a noble throng; He sat to watch o'er customs paid; Let saints on earth in concert sing; Tell me the old, old story.

344

St Michael and All Angels   29 September

All-out War   Gen. 28:10–17; Ps. 103:19–22;
Rev. 12:7–12; John 1:47–51

*'And war broke out in heaven; Michael and his angels fought against
the dragon. The dragon and his angels fought back, but they were defeated,
and there was no longer any place for them in heaven.' Revelation
12:7–9*

'Who is like God?'

Michael's name means 'Who is like God?' He is one of the three
archangels named in the Bible, the others being Gabriel and Rafael.
He is the protector of Israel and – by extension – of Christians,
and the leader of the angels in the heavenly war against the Devil.
An apocryphal work, *The Apocalypse of Paul*, dating at least from
the third century when it was quoted in part by Origen, runs:

> And after that I saw heaven opened and the archangel Michael
> coming down from heaven, and with him the whole host of
> angels, and they came to those who were placed in the punish-
> ments. And seeing him they cried out again with tears, and said,
> Have mercy on us, Archangel Michael, have mercy on us and
> on the human race, for because of your prayers the earth con-
> tinues. We have now seen the judgement and known the Son
> of God. It was impossible for us to pray for this previously
> before we came to this place. For we did hear that there was a
> judgement before we came forth from the world, but tribulations
> and a worldly-minded life did not allow us to repent. And
> Michael answered, and said, Listen when Michael speaks. It is
> I who stands in the presence of God every hour. As the Lord
> lives, in whose presence I stand, for one day or one night I do
> not cease from praying continually for the human race, and I
> pray for those who are on earth. They, however, do not stop
> committing iniquity and fornication, and they do not help me
> in what is good while they are placed on the earth. And the
> time during which you ought to have repented you used up in
> vanity. But I have always thus prayed and now I beseech that
> God may send dew and that rain may be appointed over the
> earth, and I continue to pray until the earth bring forth its fruit;
> and I say that if anyone has done only even a little good I will
> strive for him and protect him until he escapes the judgement

of punishments. Where are your prayers? Where is your repentance? You have squandered time contemptibly. But now weep, and I will weep with you, and the angels who are with me together with the dearly beloved Paul, if perchance the merciful God will show mercy and give you ease. And when they heard these words, they cried out and wept much and said all together, Lord God, have mercy on what thou hast fashioned, have mercy on the children of men, have mercy on thine own image!

Apocalypse of Paul, 43

Angelic assistance

We cannot imagine the number of God's angel force. Jesus had more than twelve legions of angels waiting to come to his aid at any time (Matthew 26:23). The power that Michael wields is phenomenally great, but it also gives us a clue as to the extent of Satan's power. Yes, Satan lost the war in the heavenly realms, but a defeated opponent is a very dangerous character, and the Devil is, literally, hell-bent on causing as much trouble and heartache as he can, in the time that remains to him on earth.

Let us thank God today that Michael and his army are on our side!

Suggested hymns

Angel-voices, ever singing; Around the throne of God a band; Ye choirs of new Jerusalem; Ye holy angels bright.

St Francis of Assisi, Friar, Deacon, Founder of the Friars Minor 1226 4 October

The Poor Rich Man Mic. 6:6–8; Ps. 100; Gal. 6:14–18; Luke 12:22–34

'May I never boast of anything except the cross of our Lord Jesus Christ, by which the world has been crucified to me, and I to the world . . . From now on, let no one make trouble for me, for I carry the marks of Jesus branded on my body.' Galatians 6:14, 17

The rich young man
Born around 1182 in the Umbrian town of Assisi, Francis had a
fairly pampered childhood. His father Pietro Bernadone was a rich
cloth merchant, and Francis enjoyed being in the fast set. In his
teens, he played an enthusiastic role in the inter-town skirmishes
that were an integral part of Umbrian life; though after a fraças
with Perugia, he ended up in jail. While thus confined it dawned
on the careless young man that there must be more to life than
parties and skirmishes. Returning home, he was praying one day
in the neglected chapel of San Damiano, when the crucifix above
the altar seemed to say: 'Francis, repair my church!' He ran home,
selected a bale of prime scarlet cloth from his father's shop, sold
it and gave the money to San Damiano's priest for the church
repairs. Pietro Bernadone flew into a rage and haled his son to
court, where the presiding bishop ordered Francis to make repar-
ation. In a dramatic gesture, the young man stripped naked, flung
his clothes at Pietro and declared that from that day he had no
father but God. The bishop gently draped his own cloak around
Francis, but ordered him to return the money to Pietro.

The poor young man
Francis left home, and the life of poverty began – but first he
repaired San Damiano with his bare hands. Gradually others of
like mind joined him, and the Rule which was to become so well
known began to evolve. Francis would not allow the brothers to
have any possessions. They lived in natural or homemade shelters
and could not even own books, for, as Francis told them, books
needed shelves and shelves needed a house. And they begged
their food. It proved too hard a life for some – yet still the numbers
grew. With growth came a gradual modification of Francis' original austerities; and in the end he resigned the leadership of the
order. For the rest of his life, he was deeply grieved at what he
thought was a compromising of his early simplicity and rigorous
asceticism. The Franciscans were to continue long after his death,
but he never became reconciled to the watering-down (as he saw
it) of his original vision.

The crib in the mountains
One Christmas, Francis determined to have his own version of
the Nativity; and folk trekked for miles up to a mountain cave
where he had assembled animals and a crib in a scene which is

still today as beautiful a feature of our churches and homes at Christmas.

Mission to the Muslims
In 1219 Francis felt called to take the gospel to the Muslims, and he journeyed with 12 friars to Damietta on the Nile delta, where he charmed all whom he met, including the Sultan, but with limited success in converting them. Back home in Umbria, the order continued to grow. In 1224, in a cell on Mount Alvernia where Francis lived with Brother Leo, he received the stigmata, but kept the wounds a secret for the two remaining years of his life. After he died, Brother Bruno, preparing his body for burial, discovered the stigmata, and remarked, 'It is as though Francis has just been crucified!'

Perhaps the original vision had been watered down; to have adhered to it may have meant that fewer would join the Order of Friars Minor. Who knows? Let us give thanks today that Francis himself stood firm to that vision.

Suggested hymns
All creatures of our God and King; Blest are the pure in heart; In full and glad surrender; Make me a channel of your peace.

William Tyndale, Translator of the Scriptures, Reformation Martyr 1536   6 October
For England, Home and Duty   Prov. 8:4–11;
Ps. 119:89–96; 2 Tim. 3:12–17; John 17:6–8, 14–18

'Indeed, all who want to lead a godly life in Christ Jesus will be persecuted ... Continue in what you have learned and firmly believed, knowing from whom you learned it ... All scripture is inspired by God and is useful for teaching, for reproof, for correction, and for training in righteousness, so that everyone who belongs to God may be proficient, equipped for every good work.' 2 Timothy 3:12, 14, 16

Thwarted by a bishop
Born in Gloucester around 1494, Tyndale proved an apt scholar, first at Oxford and then at Cambridge. He came down determined

to translate – from the best Greek versions available – the New Testament into English. Meanwhile, he took a job tutoring the children of a wealthy family, and sounded out the religious hierarchy. He must have known there would be opposition – and he was not disappointed. The Bishop of London was frankly antagonistic. For centuries the services in England had been in Latin, understood by perhaps only 1 per cent of the congregation. The priest celebrated looking east with his back to the congregation, who could therefore often not even hear the words much less understand them. Latin was largely confined to the clerics, and the hierarchy seemed more concerned about possible Lutheran influence than in opening up the Bible in English to the Christian in the pew. In the end, Tyndale lost patience: 'By God's grace, I'll see that the boy who follows the plough knows more of God's word than you!' he told the bishops – and sailed for the Continent. He was never to return to his homeland.

The work goes on
There in Hamburg in 1524 he set to work with dedication, and with an inner compulsion to get it done as fast as possible, as though God was telling him that he was a wanted man. The first of his New Testaments were despatched to England in 1526, and caused a furore among the clergy. Many copies were burned. Undeterred, Tyndale revised the work and then began translating the Old Testament from the Hebrew texts. In 1535, an informer shopped him to the authorities, and he was strangled and then burned at the stake, on 6 October 1536. 'Lord, open the king of England's eyes!' he is reported to have prayed just before he died.

Within a few years of his execution, Tyndale's New Testament was sanctioned for use in England. Others completed his Old Testament, and today, among our many English versions, we still have cause to thank God for this dedicated man. Over 90 per cent of the Authorized Version New Testament is Tyndale. And when Dom Henry Wansbrough produced his beautiful New Jerusalem Bible version, he was generous in his appreciation of the scholarship of Tyndale.

May we never take the privilege of being able to read and study the Bible in our mother tongue for granted; and today may we also remember the many William Tyndales of 2004, who even now are dedicating their lives to producing new translations of God's word – for there are still hundreds of minority languages and dialects without a Bible translation.

Suggested hymns
Father of mercies, in thy word; Lord, thy word abideth; Oft in danger, oft in woe; Through all the changing scenes of life.

St Teresa of Avila, Teacher of the Faith 1582
15 October Woman of Hope Wis. 7:7–10, 15–16; Ps. 138; Rom. 8:22–27; John 14:1–7

'For in hope we were saved. Now hope that is seen is not hope. For who hopes for what is seen? But if we hope for what we do not see, we wait for it with patience.' Romans 8:24–25

A sickly child

Born near Avila, in Castile, in 1515, Teresa suffered recurrent illness from an early age. Against her father's wishes, she joined a convent of Carmelite nuns at the age of 20, and for the next 25 years her life was a spiritual see-saw of conversing freely with the convent's many visitors (for at that time and place the laws of the religious allowed more freedom than in Italy), and in solitary communion with God. Then came the founding of a new monastery of St Joseph, where rigid asceticism was practised; Teresa and four sisters were sent to the house. The nuns were enclosed, in almost total silence and strict poverty. They were discalced, wearing sandals instead of shoes, and bound by absolute chastity. Teresa, instituted as head of the sisters, would at first allow no more than 13 sisters to join her, but later revised this up to 21.

The movement advances

From St Joseph's, she moved to Medina del Campo in 1567 and founded a second convent. Before her death, she was to found 15 more. Mixing practicality with mysticism, she would meet aspiring novices with instructions to roll up their sleeves and learn how to scrub the convent floors before moving towards contemplation. One day while driving with some sisters in a pony-trap between convents, one of the wheels hit a stone and the cart ended up in a ditch – with the sisters. As she tried to wring the mud from her habit, Teresa looked heavenwards and upbraided the Almighty: 'Lord, if this is how you treat your friends, I'm surprised you have so many!'

Misunderstandings

Teresa's brand of Spanish Catholicity was often at variance with Rome's, and her life was made more difficult by some of the Italian clergy. She was sent to oversee a convent where the nuns had been used to a far less rigorous life, and they did not take kindly to her reforms. When several High Churchmen took the nuns' side, Teresa appealed to one of her many influential friends, King Philip II, who pitched in enthusiastically on her behalf. But in general, Teresa's sincere love for others, and her acute psychological awareness, could often turn a confrontational situation into one of harmony.

She never regained the health she had lost early in life, and her last two years saw a further serious deterioration. The last of her foundations, at Burgos, was completed with great effort, and she then asked to return to Avila. Instead, she was persuaded to attempt the journey to Alba de Tormes, where Duchess Maria Henriquez was waiting to see her. Within three days of arriving, Teresa died. It was 4 October 1582, but the next morning saw the start of the Gregorian reformed calendar, and her festival has therefore always been observed on 15 October.

Even in her busy life, Teresa found time for writing; her two works which are most widely read today are *The Way of Perfection* and *The Interior Castle*.

> *I have confidence, O Lord,*
> *in these servants of yours gathered here,*
> *who seek and desire to do*
> *only what is pleasing to you.*
> *For your sake*
> *they have left what little they had;*
> *they would not have asked for more*
> *unless it was to give up more,*
> *the better to serve you.*
> *You, my Creator, are not ungrateful,*
> *and I am sure you will not fail*
> *to answer their prayers;*

351

for when you were on this earth, O Lord,
you did not despise women:
you helped them
and treated them always with great compassion.
Do not hear us if we ask for honour,
money, riches, or anything else
that is of this world;
but if we pray for the honour of your Son,
why, eternal Father,
should you not hear those who
would sacrifice all honour,
and would lose their lives many times over
for your sake?
Not for ourselves, Lord,
for we do not deserve it,
but through the blood and merits of your Son.

The Way of Perfection, 3

Suggested hymns
At the Name of Jesus; Make me a channel of your peace; Rejoice,
the Lord is King; Teach me, my God and King.

St Luke the Evangelist   18 October
A Good Friend   Isa. 35:3–6 or Acts 16:6–12a;
Ps. 147:1–7; 2 Tim. 4:5–17; Luke 10:1–9

'Do your best to come to me soon, for Demas, in love with this present
world, has deserted me and gone to Thessalonica, Crescens has gone to
Galatia, Titus to Dalmatia. Only Luke is with me. Get Mark and bring
him with you, for he is useful in my ministry.' 2 Timothy 4:9–11

Man of letters
Luke was a Greek, qualified in medicine and handy with his pen;
St Luke's Gospel and the Book of Acts, both addressed to a certain
Theophilus (or, by a pun on his name, to humankind whom
God loves), are written as a factual record of people, places and
events in history. Well grounded against a background of verifi-
able public figures, Luke is so certain of his material that it needs

no embellishment. Where he is describing the annunciation of Gabriel to Mary, or the ascension of Christ, or the shipwreck of St Paul, he confines himself to straightforward reportage – in essence, believing in what he is writing and expecting his readers to do the same.

Loyalty to a friend

Paul's second letter to Timothy ends on a poignant note: the friends who have ministered alongside him have gone their separate ways – Crescens to Galatia, Titus to Dalmatia – probably both continuing the Lord's work; but to the aged Paul in prison and nearing death their departure has been hard to take; harder still, the defection of Demas, who has exchanged the rigours of prison-visiting for the luxuries of Thessalonica; that Demas may combine ministry there with pleasure, is a possibility – but Paul does not sound hopeful. 'Only Luke is with me' says a lot for the staunch-ness and loyalty of the Greek doctor, who by this time is himself getting on in years. Luke was no fairweather friend, but obviously the sort that sticks closer than a brother: such friends are real gifts from God. We are blessed if we have such a friend: we give a blessing if we are a friend like this.

In nothing the scriptures acknowledged by the Roman Church, *c.* AD 190, the *Muratorian Fragment* reads:

> The third book of the gospel, that according to Luke, was com-piled in his own name on Paul's authority by Luke the physician, when after Christ's ascension Paul had taken him to be with him like a legal expert. Yet neither did he see the Lord in the flesh; and he too, as he was able to ascertain events, begins his story from the birth of John.

In good old age

According to tradition, Luke never married. His Gospel is thought to have been written in Greece, and he himself to have died at the good old age of 84 in Boeotia; though one legend has him being crucified together with Andrew at Patras. Luke's relics mysteri-ously came to light at Padua's San Antonio basilica in 1998, and were reunited the following year with his skull which had been kept in St Vitus' Cathedral, Prague, since 1354. Richard Owen, writing in *The Times* (13 February 1999) after rigorous tests had been carried out on the relics, reported: 'St Luke was a stocky man

353

with a bad back, who was arthritic and short of breath ... [he] died in his eighties, and suffered from back trouble, arthritis and emphysema.' Owen quotes Vito Wiel Martin, Professor of Anatomy and Histology at Padua University, who said the bones were of a male who died in old age between 80 and 85. He was about 5 ft 3 ins tall, of powerful, stocky build, with a dolicocephalic cranium typical of the population of Antioch at the time.

Whether or not this is an accurate description of the physical Luke, today it is surely his spiritual stamina in keeping Paul company through difficult times that makes its impact.

Suggested hymns
Brother, sister, let me serve you; Happy are they, they that love God; Thine arm, O Lord, in days of old; When I needed a neighbour.

SS Simon and Jude, Apostles   28 October
Beaten to Glory   Isa. 28:14–16; Ps. 119:89–96;
Eph. 2:19–22; John 15:17–27

'So then you are no longer strangers and aliens, but you are citizens with the saints and also members of the household of God, built upon the foundations of the apostles and prophets, with Christ Jesus himself as the cornerstone.' Ephesians 2:19–20

Simon the Zealot
Simon is called 'the Zealot' in the Gospels, presumably because he belonged to a patriotic party opposed (sometimes forcefully) to the Roman occupying army. It may have been that he left the Zealots to follow Jesus, or that he joined them after Christ's ascension as a means of extending his ministry. We hear so little of Simon the Zealot, yet he with Jude (Judas) was among the Twelve, intimately associated with Jesus and his ministry for three years.

Jude
It was Jude's misfortune to have the same name as the betrayer, and for this reason he was often overlooked in the early centuries of Christian history – until he became known as the patron saint

of hopeless cases, being invoked by many who were not believers. He is also known as Thaddaeus, and in his letter describes himself as 'the brother of James' (Jude 1), while Luke – who could also be right – calls him 'son of James' (Luke 6:16).

Martyred together

According to a sixth-century tradition (*Passio Simonis et Judas*), both apostles took the gospel to Persia, where they suffered martyrdom by being beaten to death with clubs. Jude has left us an encouraging little letter, written for all who have to contend with those who try to pervert the cause of Christ. Jude goes back to the days of Cain, Balaam and Korah, tracing the patterns of sin through history. It is from this brief letter that we also learn of the intriguing contention between Archangel Michael and the Devil for the body of Moses, giving us a glimpse of the very active, exciting and dramatic world of the spirits (of which one day we shall be a part).

Our divine guide

There is only one 'who is able to keep us from falling, and ... make [us] stand without blemish in the presence of his glory,' says Jude – and it is 'the only God our Saviour through Jesus Christ'. He will meet all trouble in his strength working through us. Satan's battle is not with us, it is with Christ in us. This means, in practice, that if we try to meet Satan on our own, we haven't – literally – a chance in hell. But if we face up to him in the strength of Jesus, the Devil has not only met his match, but his Victor.

The following hymn, a translation of words by St Ambrose (340–397), is sometimes sung on the festival of these two apostles.

> *Aeterna Christi munera*
> *The eternal gifts of Christ the King,*
> *The apostles' glorious deeds, we sing;*
> *And while due hymns of praise we pray,*
> *Our thankful hearts cast grief away.*
>
> *The Church in these her princes boasts,*
> *These victor chiefs of warrior hosts;*
> *The soldiers of the heavenly hall,*
> *The Lights that rose on earth for all.*

'Twas thus the yearning faith of saints,
The unconquered hope that never faints,
The love of Christ, that knows no shame,
The prince of this world overcame.

In these the Father's glory shone;
In these the will of God the Son;
In these exults the Holy Ghost;
Through these rejoice the heavenly host.

Redeemer, hear us of thy love,
That with this glorious band above,
Hereafter, of thy endless grace,
Thy servants also may have place.

tr. J. M. Neale (1818–1866)

Suggested hymns
Captains of the saintly band; Disposer Supreme, and Judge of the earth; O Christ, thou Lord of worlds; The eternal gifts of Christ the King.

All Saints' Day 1 November (or transferred to 31 October) Festival of Martyrs Dan. 7:1–3, 15–18; Ps. 149; Eph. 1:11–23; Luke 6:20–31

'I pray that the God of our Lord Jesus Christ, the Father of glory, may give you a spirit of wisdom and revelation as you come to know him, so that, with the eyes of your heart enlightened, you may know what is the hope to which he has called you, what are the riches of his glorious inheritance among the saints.' Ephesians 1:17–18

A moveable feast
The fourth century saw the collective commemoration of martyrs (martyrdom was early thought to confer sainthood) earlier in the year, on the Sunday after Pentecost (Whit Sunday); and 1 November was not recorded as the observance until the time of Alcuin of York, AD 800, since when it has grown in importance – 'All Saints', including many who did not die a martyr's death. Three

days of fasting used to be prescribed prior to the feast; and it was seen as particularly appropriate to hold it at this time, to counteract the pagan practices that had grown up around 31 October.

The cloud of witnesses

They are watching, these giants of the faith for whom the Church Militant has become the Church Triumphant. Their interest should give us courage and fortitude to 'go and do likewise', though not so that we can book our place in the history books of the future – the saints whom we honour today had no thought of personal profiles: they preached Christ, and Christ crucified; 'self' was way down the list of their priorities, if indeed it was there at all.

Called to be saints

We may think that we are so far below the likes of Peter and Paul in spiritual stature, that even in glory we may never come near them; but there is no biblical justification for this. God in Christ calls us all to be saints, to lay our lives down for him, to die a little more to self every day, to put Jesus first all the time. We shall not necessarily be stoned to death – or hung, drawn and quartered for our faith – but if we have crucified the 'I' and 'me' and 'mine' and 'my' of what the world calls ordinary life, we shall be living extraordinary lives for God. There was something extraordinary about every saint whom we acknowledge today: they did ordinary things extraordinarily well; in the strength of Jesus they showed extraordinary courage for God; they endured extraordinary trials and tribulations, because Satan took an extraordinary interest in them. But because God gave them extraordinary grace, they won through in the end.

'Lord, make me an extraordinary Christian!' was the prayer of one man whom his friends thought eccentric – but wasn't he on the right lines? God told the lukewarm, boring, indifferent, mediocre Christians in Laodicea to wake up and get excited about their faith – or even earnest about something else, anything else: 'I wish that you were either cold or hot' (Revelation 3:15). At least this should tell us that heaven will be anything but boring!

A year of saints

Can we get excited about today's commemoration of all the saints? Then let us carry this enthusiasm into all the days ahead. It is a good beginning if each day we can give a few minutes to thank

357

God for the day's particular saint (and many days share several saints). The Reformation had the effect of quashing to some extent the veneration of the saints, but gradually the pendulum is swinging back. We can surely help it on its way.

Suggested hymns
For all the saints; Let saints on earth in concert sing; Look, ye saints, the sight is glorious; Ye holy angels bright.

All Souls' Day (Commemoration of the Faithful Departed)   2 November   **Living Hope**

Lam. 3:17–26, 31–33, or Wis. 3:1–9; Ps. 23 or
Ps. 27:1–6, 16–17; Rom. 5:5–11 or 1 Pet. 1:3–9;
John 5:19–25 or John 6:37–40

'Blessed be the God and Father of our Lord Jesus Christ! By his great mercy he has given us a new birth into a living hope through the resurrection of Jesus Christ from the dead, and into an inheritance that is imperishable, undefiled, and unfading, kept in heaven for you.' 1 Peter 1:3–4

The faithful departed
They have gone on ahead, across the field of snow which remains untrodden, for the departed leave no footprints except for the precious memories that, like them, are undying. And, try as we might, we cannot explain how they can be 'there' and 'here' at one and the same time: how we can be so sure of them one minute, and light-years away the next. We do not move (for, as yet, we cannot) – but they seem to be able to move – through time and space. However inadequately, it is good to meditate on this, not only on All Souls' Day, but at other times; had God not intended us to wonder and to ponder, he would not have given us the longing to do so by the many glimpses of glory in Holy Writ.

Abbot of Cluny
The festival of All Souls was instituted in 998 by Abbot Odo of Cluny, and on this day the Roman Catholic Church continues to pray for the souls they traditionally believe are neither in heaven nor hell, but are suffering in purgatory for the sins committed in

this life. Protestants, on the other hand, pray today for those souls whom they believe (in pursuance of Jesus' words from the cross to the penitent thief) are in Paradise with their Lord. Whichever side of the denominational divide one is on, it is still appropriate to reflect on the souls whom we have known, and of their continuing life hereafter – a life where we, in time (or, more accurately, beyond time), hope to pick up again the threads that have been temporarily severed by death.

Heavenly places in Christ Jesus

What is heaven? Oswald Chambers once defined it thus:

> That is where God raises us. We do not get there by climbing, by aspiring, by struggling, by consecration, or by vows. God lifts us right straight up out of sin, inability and weakness, lust and disobedience, wrath and self-seeking – lifts us right up out of all this, up, up to the whiter than snow shine, to the heavenly places where Jesus Christ lived when he was on earth, and where he lives to this hour in the plenitude of his power. May God never relieve us from the wonder of it.
>
> *Oswald Chambers*, Our Brilliant Heritage

The 'departure' of Jesus at his ascension was different from most departures. First, it infused the disciples left behind not with sorrow but with great joy; second, it was beautifully dramatic, attended by angels; and third, as he went he promised that he would always be with us until the world's end. This last point has been focused on in one of our modern hymns:

> *His believers, when they've met,*
> *Know he's there with them, and yet*
> *He's with God (what makes us think that's somewhere else?).*
> *Who is this who, when they've met,*
> *Is right there with them, and yet*
> *He's with God (what makes us think that's somewhere else?).*
>
> *Hubert Richards*

The less we think of our loved ones as being 'somewhere else', the nearer they will be to us.

Brief life is here our portion; Day of wrath! O day of mourning;
Now the labourer's task is o'er; O Lord, to whom the spirits live.

A Sermon for Harvest Thanksgiving

'But how are they to call on one in whom they have not believed? And how are they to believe in one whom they have not heard? And how are they to hear without someone to proclaim him?' Romans 10:14

A trio of missionaries discussing their respective problems, found the subject of 'harvest' crop up. 'We had so little sunshine this year, the crops in village after village failed to grow,' one remarked. 'Our problem was lack of rain,' another commented. 'The earth just baked harder and harder.' The third missionary smiled wryly: 'At least you had some earth!' he said. 'We had storms that washed all our soil away!'

Does God deprive certain areas of the world, so that those more fortunate can share their abundant harvests? Or, is he testing some people harder, to bring out a latent potential for innovation, adaptation and sheer trust that they didn't know they had?

'You will always have the poor with you,' Jesus said, 'and you must do good to them while you can.'

How can we help the poor? So often we equate helping the poor with giving them aid – material and financial. But that was not the way Jesus worked: he's not on record as having changed the financial status of any poor person. Instead, he took the gospel to them. We may – and indeed should – thank God for the richness of our material harvest; but what counts for eternity is the spiritual harvest we bring in.

James Evans went to live among the Cree Indians, on the shores of Lake Winnipeg. He had a burden on his heart – to give the Crees the gospel of Jesus. But he found that while they had a simple spoken language, there was no alphabet, no written language for the Indians. So James began prayerfully to devise an alphabet for them. He used simple signs – mostly triangles and pot-hooks, carving these from the wood of the birch trees that grew in the forests around the lake. The letters could be arranged on the sandy shore, to form words – but James needed paper for more permanent use. Seeing how the Indians used the various layers of birch bark for their canoes, he chose the inner layers of bark which reminded him of the pulp he had seen in the paper-mills back home. Having been beaten out and laid in the sun to dry, James found he had very presentable sheets of 'paper'.

He now had paper and an alphabet. The next step was the type. He made moulds of the letters from the hardest wood he could find – watched at every stage by the fascinated, wondering Indians. 'We need lead,' he told them: but for all their comprehension he might as well have talked to himself. Then he remembered the lead that lined the tea-chests. Carefully he prised it out, melted it down, poured it into his tiny moulds – and he had his type! Into the press used by the Cree Indians for treating the skins of the various animals they caught, James fitted his little leaden letters.

Almost there! But what could he use for ink? He'd have settled for a good supply of cuttlefish, but Lake Winnipeg didn't host cuttlefish. So James pressed oil from the fish that were to hand, and mixed it with soot from the fires. He could now begin printing! The first book to roll off his press was St John's Gospel. Carefully James sewed the bark pages together with thin strips of leather, and the Indians sat round him at the fire, to hear and marvel, as – slowly, and pointing to each letter as he read – James shared the word of God with them, from their own Bible in their own tongue.

'The birch bark talks!' they cried, in awe. And James Evans gave thanks that his missionfield was coming closer to its harvest.

For us today, with a plethora of Bible versions, in thousands of languages, God's word is surely much more accessible than it was for James Evans. And our energy in sharing it is a measure of our enthusiasm to give God a harvest-return on his investment of this precious seed.

'The seed is the word of God,' said Jesus, simply and unequivo-cally, at the centre of his parable of the sower. Yet in how many homes today does that seed lie unused, inert, carefully packaged between its covers, on a bookshelf, in a loft – or, even worse, given away to a jumble sale?

Ever since the fall of Adam, we have had to work hard to wrest a living from the land. Seed costs money – or time, if we have to build up stock over several years before a respectable harvest is possible. But with the word of God, the seed-price has already been paid – at Calvary – so we start out on the work of our spiritual harvest at a great advantage.

But having got the seed, the work of the physical harvest has only begun. There are many factors that need taking into account – some of them clearly destructive, others with a potential for growth if handled rightly. Similarly with the spiritual harvest, Satan will try his best to frustrate our efforts, even to the stealing of our seed; but there are factors which can be used to further our harvest, such as the apparent lack and deprivation that James Evans turned to good account for the first Bible of the Cree Indians. While Satan will see that we are presented with the black side of a situation, God gives us the potential for a reversal of fortune, to further the good work of his precious seed.

We like to see the results of our physical labours – in barns full of grain, freezers packed with summer fruit and veg, pantry shelves stacked with preserves . . . And indeed we shall probably enjoy some of the fruits of our spiritual work – but if not, the record will be in the almighty memory of God . . .
. . . which is all that matters.

Remembrance Day 11 November (observed on 7 November in 2004) **Listen!** Ezek. 37:1–14; Ps. 22; 1 Cor. 15:42–58; Mark 13:3–8

'Listen, I will tell you a mystery! We will not all die, but we will all be changed, in a moment, in the twinkling of an eye, at the last trumpet. For the trumpet will sound, and the dead will be raised imperishable, and we will be changed.' 1 Corinthians 15:51–52

Constant change

Of course, in many ways we are constantly changing, concurrently, on all three fronts: spiritual, mental and physical. One would imagine we should become used to change, but we don't. Generally, we kick against change, seeking sometimes to great lengths to maintain the status quo.

War brings violent changes, and Remembrancetide is an opportunity not only to remember, but to learn from the changes. In 1918 the 'war to end all wars' drew to a close after four years of unprecedented carnage – yet the carnage goes on; it is almost as though the world has become programmed for war. We are all changed by it – not always for the better.

There was once war in heaven, when Archangel Michael led the fight against the Devil and his forces. Michael convincingly won the engagement, and Satan was toppled to earth. That is why, at the end of the wars that the Devil instigates on earth, we can look forward to a changed life where war really is no more. Until then, are we obliged to endure continuing warfare? Yes, says Jesus: 'Nation will rise against nation, and kingdom against kingdom; there will be earthquakes in various places; there will be famines. This is but the beginning of the birth-pangs' (Mark 13:8).

Remembrance

Each November, there are more souls to remember – more white crosses in serried rows on acres of well-trimmed cemeteries: more memorials, more poppies and wreaths, more congregations and cenotaph crowds singing the hymns that have become such an integral part of Remembrance Day.

Are we really, inevitably, inescapably on a Satanic roller-coaster of war upon war upon war? Can we do nothing to alter it? Was it part of the aftermath of Michael's victory over Satan, that the Devil would plague us with war until the end of time? Yes, he will plague us; but, as St Paul says, with every temptation God gives us a way of escape (1 Corinthians 10:13).

The way of escape

Both Matthew (Matthew 24:14) and Mark (Mark 13:10) record this way of escape: the gospel must be published in all nations; *then* the end will come. In other words, we need to get this world evangelized first. Jesus does not say, Get everyone on the planet converted – many will hear, but few will choose to follow. But since it is not God's will that any should perish, everyone must be given the chance of being saved. Millions have already died from lack of knowledge: perhaps millions more will die before the gospel has reached them. Do we care about giving as many people a chance as we can? If we really care, we can do a lot. We are thereby not only fulfilling the command of Jesus, but also hastening the time when war will be no more. We can become overwhelmed by the tremendous truth that God has given us this opportunity to change the world: how much better than merely working ourselves up to a state of overwhelming wonder would it be for us simply to get out and get on with the evangelizing.

Gospel warfare
Taking the gospel into war against Satan is the best and surest weapon that God has given us. It is also the most convincing and potentially longest-lasting tribute we can make to the courage and dedication of all those whom we are remembering today.

Suggested hymns
All people that on earth do dwell; I vow to thee, my country; O God, our help in ages past; O valiant hearts, who to your glory came.

St Martin, Bishop of Tours *c.* 397
11 November   The Soldier Saint   Deut. 15:7–8, 10–11; Ps. 112; 1 Thess. 5:1–11; Matthew 25:34–40

'For you yourselves know very well that the day of the Lord will come like a thief in the night. When they say, "There is peace and security", then sudden destruction will come upon them, as labour pains come upon a pregnant woman, and there will be no escape! But you, beloved, are not in darkness, for that day to surprise you like a thief.'
1 Thessalonians 5:2–4

A reluctant soldier
Born around the year 316 in Hungary, Martin's father was an officer in the army. The family soon afterwards moved to Pavia in Italy. His schooling done, Martin was automatically drafted into the army; but soldiering was not his bent, and an incident when he was stationed at Amiens proved a critical turning-point in his life. He passed a beggar, shivering with cold. Turning back, Martin cut his cloak in half with his sword, gave the beggar one piece and wrapped himself in the other. That night he had a vision of Christ wearing the half of the cloak he had given away. He was immediately baptized, and some months later, when an armistice with Gaul was signed, Martin gladly left the army, went to Poitiers, where Hilary was bishop, and enrolled as one of the saint's disciples.

Another vision
While at Poitiers, Martin had a dream in which he was bidden to return home. Back in Hungary, he converted (among others) his mother, though his father remained adamant. On his return to

Poitiers, Hilary, busy with problems of heresy, commissioned Martin to found a monastery at Ligugé, thought to be the first of its kind in Gaul. The year was 360. Twelve years later, Martin was elected Bishop of Tours, despite opposition from some neighbouring bishops who objected to his unkempt appearance. He proved, nevertheless, to be a good bishop, though his latter years were dogged by ill-health. He died on 8 November 397, in a remote part of his diocese, and was buried three days later in his beloved Tours.

Martin's days in the monastery have been chronicled by Sulpicius Severus:

It is beyond my powers to set forth adequately how Martin distinguished himself in the discharge of his duties as Bishop of Tours. He remained just the same as he had been before his ordination. There was the same humility in his heart, and the same unpretentious clothing. He always maintained his role as bishop with true dignity and courtesy, without ever setting aside the life and virtues of a monk.

For a long time he made use of a cell connected to the church, but increasingly this became impracticable with the vast numbers of people visiting him. So he established a monastery two miles outside the city. This exact spot he kept secret and away from people, so that he could enjoy the solitude of a hermit . . .

Many of the other monks also built for themselves hermitages, but most of these were hollowed out caves on the mountainside. Altogether there were eighty disciples who followed the discipline of their saintly master. No one kept anything as his own; everything was held in common. No one bought or sold anything for himself, as is monastic custom. No craft was practised there except that of transcribing texts, and this task was allocated to the younger brothers, leaving the seniors free to devote themselves to prayer. Rarely did one of the brothers go beyond his cell, unless it was to assemble for corporate prayer. They ate communally, once their daily fast was completed; no one drank wine, except in illness; and most of the brothers wore simple, rough garments. Softer material was frowned upon . . . A number of the monks were subsequently made bishops. For what city or church would not covet as its priests those trained in the monastery of Martin?

Vita Martini 10:1–9

On this day, when many are remembering those who fell in war, let us also give thanks for one soldier who was spared to continue the fight on the spiritual front.

Suggested hymns
Christian, dost thou see them; Fight the good fight; Prayer is the soul's sincere desire; Through all the changing scenes of life.

St Margaret, Queen of Scotland, Philanthropist, Reformer of the Church 1093
16 November   Lover of the Gospels
Prov. 31:10–12, 20, 26–31; Ps. 128; 2 Tim. 1:1–7; Matthew 13:34–46

'I am reminded of your sincere faith . . . For this reason I remind you to rekindle the gift of God that is within you through the laying on of my hands; for God did not give us a spirit of cowardice, but rather a spirit of power and of love and of self-discipline.' 2 Timothy 1:5–7

Sent from exile
Coming from exile in Hungary to Scotland, Margaret married King Malcolm Canmore and influenced for good both the Church and nation. She brought the Benedictines to Scotland and founded Dunfermline Abbey, where she is buried. Margaret was the daughter of Prince Edward, the exiled son of King Edmund Ironside of England, but educated in Hungary, where her family lived during the reign of Danish kings in England. In 1057, at the age of 12, she came to the court of the English king, Edward the Confessor. In 1066, after the Norman William (the Conqueror) defeated Harold at the Battle of Hastings, Margaret was seen as a threat to the new monarchy. She and her mother fled to Scotland, where she was welcomed at the royal court of Malcolm III; soon afterwards she married him. The couple had six sons and two daughters.

Church reformer
Margaret instituted a number of church reforms and founded many monasteries, churches and pilgrim hostels. Much given to

prayer and good works, she brought the English Benedictine monks north of the border. They settled in the Benedictine priory at Dunfermline, Fife, where in 1072 Margaret had built a beautiful new church. One of her closest friends was Prior Turgot, builder and prior of the great Norman cathedral at Durham; later, as Bishop of St Andrews, he became Margaret's biographer.

An avid reader

Margaret was an avid reader and usually carried a copy of the Gospels with her when out on journeys. One day when travelling, the cleric who was carrying the book accidentally dropped it into a river. Miraculously, it was retrieved undamaged apart from some slight marking on two pages at the end. Turgot remarked: 'Whatever others may think, I for my part believe that this wonder was worked by our Lord out of his love for the venerable Queen.' Today the book can be seen in the Bodleian Library, Oxford (MS Lat. Liturg. f.5.fols. 3v–4r).

In 1993, the 900th anniversary of her death, more than fifteen thousand pilgrims visited St Margaret's Cave, Dunfermline Abbey, St Margaret's Shrine and the relic of the saint in the Church of St Margaret.

High or low estate

One does not need to live in kings' courts to influence people – though it certainly helped in Margaret's case. Jesus operated a largely rural and small-town ministry for three years. St Paul sought out the urban centres of paganism, sophistication and immorality. Each of us has our mission where we are, not where someone else may be. Margaret quietly and diligently made the most of her opportunities. God will open different doors for us – but they will lead to opportunities that he knows we can use.

Suggested hymns

My faith it is an oaken staff; New every morning is the love; O happy band of pilgrims; Thou didst leave thy throne and thy kingly crown.

Sources and Acknowledgements

Sources of quoted material

pp. 217, 296, 314–5, 316, 330, 342, 353 J. Stevenson (ed.), *A New Eusebius* (SPCK, 1959).

pp. 283, 299 Bede, *A History of the English Church and People*, tr. Leo Sherley-Price (Penguin Classics, 1955, rev. edn. 1968).

p. 294 Julian of Norwich, *Revelations of the Divine Love*, tr. Clifton Wolters (Penguin Classics, 1966).

pp. 317–8, 345–6 E. Hennecke, *New Testament Apocrypha*, Vol. II, ed. W. Schneemelcher (SCM Press, 1965, 1975).

pp. 331, 336–7 E. Hennecke, *New Testament Apocrypha*, Vol. I, ed. W. Schneemelcher (SCM Press, 1965, 1975).

pp. 333, 338–9, 339–40 J. Stevenson (ed.), *Creeds, Councils and Controversies* (SPCK, 1966, 1973).

pp. 363 R. Atwell (ed.), *Celebrating the Saints* (Canterbury Press, 1998).

Scripture Index

Subject Index

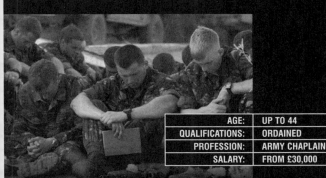

Selected Index of Authors and Hymn Writers

Notes

....
....
....
....
....
....
....
....
....
....
....
....
....
....
....
....
....
....
....
....
....
....
....
....
....
....
....
....
....
....
....

Notes